# AQA GCSE french

## Students' Book

Danièle Bourdais
Sue Finnie
Marian Jones
Sarah Provan
Elizabeth Fotheringham
Kate Scappaticci

OXFORD
UNIVERSITY PRESS

**OXFORD**
UNIVERSITY PRESS

Great Clarendon Street, Oxford OX2 6DP

Oxford University Press is a department of the University of Oxford.

It furthers the University's objective of excellence in research, scholarship, and education by publishing worldwide in

Oxford New York
Auckland Cape Town Dar es Salaam Hong Kong Karachi
Kuala Lumpur Madrid Melbourne Mexico City Nairobi
New Delhi Shanghai Taipei Toronto

With offices in

Argentina Austria Brazil Chile Czech Republic France
Greece Guatemala Hungary Italy Japan South Korea
Poland Portugal Singapore Switzerland Thailand
Turkey Ukraine Vietnam



First published 2010



British Library Cataloguing in Publication Data

Data available

ISBN 978 019 913898 2

10 9 8 7 6 5 4 3 2 1

Printed in Spain by Cayfosa-Impresia Ibérica

Paper used in the production of this book is a natural, recyclable product made from wood grown in sustainable forests. The manufacturing process conforms to the environmental regulations of the country of origin.

**Acknowledgements**
The publishers would like to thank the following for permission to reproduce photographs:

p6: OUP; p9tl: Dean Mitchell/Shutterstock; p9tr: Monkey Business Images/Shutterstock; p9ml: Yuri Arcurs/Shutterstock; p9m: Monkey Business Images/Shutterstock; p9mr: Felix Mizioznikov/Shutterstock; p9b: Galina Barskaya/Shutterstock; p12tl: Bigstock; p12tr: BLOOMimage/Getty Images; p12(1): Andi Duff/Alamy; p12(2): OUP/Image100; p12(3): Bigstock; p12(4): Gerard Vandystadt/Tips Images; p14a: Fabio Cardoso/Corbis; p14b: Picture Partners/Alamy; p14c: Helene Rogers/Alamy; p14d: Imagebroker/Alamy; p14e: Michael A. Keller/Corbis; p14f: LWA-Stephen Welstead/Corbis; p14b: Mark Seelen/www.photolibrary.com; p16b: Bon Appetit/Alamy; p18: Peter Widmann/Alamy; p19: ICP/Alamy; p20t: Adrian Britton/Shutterstock; p20m: Radu Razvan/Shutterstock; p20mb: Illych/Dreamstime.com; p20b: Elena Elisseeva / Shutterstock; p24tl: Paul Turner/Shutterstock; p24tr: Monkey Business Images/Shutterstock; p24bl: Jenny Horne/Shutterstock; p24br: Robyn Mackenzie/Shutterstock; p26: Afaizal/Shutterstock; p32tl: Zatac/Tips Images; p32tr: Bigstock; p32bl: Stephen Oliver/Alamy; p32br: John Birdsall/Press Association Images; p33r: Hans Neleman/Corbis; p33l: Clare Marie Barboza/Corbis; p34t: lozas/shutterstock; p34tb: OUP; p34tm: Michele Burgess / Alamy; p34m: Sielemann/shutterstock; p34b: Bigstock; p36: Sascha Burkard/shutterstock; p38&p44: Kuzma/shutterstock; p47: OUP; p48a: OUP/Corbis; p48b: Peter Cade/Getty Images; p48c: Tim Platt/Getty Images; p48d: Julia Grossi/Corbis; p48e: Wideangle Photography/Alamy; p50t: David Lefranc/Kipa/Corbis; p50c: Bigstock; p50d: Tracy Kahn/Corbis; p50e: Stephen Oliver/Alamy; p52t: Orkhan Aslanov/Shutterstock; p52m: Ustyujanin/Shutterstock; p52b: Kristof Degreef/Shutterstock; p54l: Roy Morsch/Corbis; p54r: Alex Segre/Alamy; p55: Junker/Shutterstock; p56t: Stephen Bisgrove/Alamy; p56mr: OUP/Digital Vision; p56bl: OUP; p56br: John Birdsall/Press Association Images; p59: Matthew Ashton/AMA/Corbis; p60: Monkey Business Images/Shutterstock; p62t: Julia Pivovarova/Shutterstock; p62b: Monkey Business Images/Shutterstock; p68a: Bigstock; p68b,e, f: Chris Hellier/Corbis; p68c: Photononstop/Tips Images; p68d: Bo Zaunders/Corbis; Edward Bock/Corbis; p70t: EPF commercial/Alamy; p70(1): Pack-Shot/Shutterstock; p70(2): Edward Bock/Corbis; p70(3): Christian Liewig/Corbis; p70(4): Alessandra Benedetti/Corbis; p70(5): Nada Surf; p70(6): OUP/ Media Minds; p74l: Bigstock; p74m: Gary Cook/Alamy; p74r: Jose Fuste Raga/www.photolibrary.com; p76: Galyna Andrushko/Shutterstock; p77: Bigstock; p78: Bill Brooks/Alamy; p80: Chrstian Wheatley/Shutterstock; p84t: Tracy Kahn/Corbis; p84m: Paul Barton/Corbis; p84(1): Jane Post/Hardwick Studios; p86(2): ImagesEurope/Alamy; p86(3): Lonely Planet Images/Ariadne Van Zandbergen; p86(4): Kheng Guan Toh/Shutterstock; p87: Martin Sookias/OUP; p88(1): Tom Joslyn/Alamy; p88(2): Ian Dagnall/Alamy; p88(3): Les. Ladbury/Alamy; p88(4): Roger Mechan/Photographers Direct; p88(5): Camille Moirenc/Hemis/Corbis; p88(6): Holmes Garden Photos/Alamy; p88(7): Tom Joslyn/Alamy; p88(8): Roger Stowell/Alamy; p88(9): Bigstock; p88(10), p88(11): ImagesEurope/Alamy; p88(12): Patrice Latron/Corbis; p88b: Mike Briner/Alamy; p90l: Robin Weaver/Alamy; p90r: STOCKFOLIO®/Alamy; p92t: Bigstock; p92b: Lonely Planet Images/Jean Robert; p96: Radius Images/www.photolibrary.com; p98: Dubassy/Shutterstock; p102l: Rainford/www.photolibrary.com; p102m: Deco/Alamy; p102r: Mark Horn/Getty Images; p10tl: Stephen Horsted/Alamy; p10tm: Ian Shaw/Alamy; p104tr: Jaume Gual/www.photolibrary.com; p104m: Index Stock/www.photolibrary.com; p106: Clive Tully/Alamy; p107t: Bigstock; p107b: Rob Cole Photography/Alamy; p108(1): Hemis/Alamy; p108(2): STOCKFOLIO/Alamy; p108(3): Bob Gibbons/Alamy; p109t: Index Stock/www.photolibrary.com; p109tm: Jaume Gual/www.photolibrary.com; p109bm: Ian Shaw/Alamy; p109b: Stephen Horsted/Alamy; p110t: Images of Africa Photobank/Alamy; p110m: Zheng Zheng/Xinhua Press/Corbis; p110b: The Photolibrary Wales/Alamy; p112: Richard List/Corbis; p113: Edward Parker/Alamy; p114: Maxstockphoto/Shutterstock; p116: Eric Thierry Berluteau; p120: STOCK4B/Getty Images; p122l: Bigstock; p122m; p122r: Dan Forer/Beateworks/Corbis; p122b: Christina Kennedy/Getty Images; p124l: Hemis/Alamy; p124r: Peter Treanor/Alamy; p126l: Picture Partners/Alamy; p126r: David Woolfall/Alamy; p126b: Bigstock; p128t: 81A Productions/Corbis; p128m: Sasha Radosavljevich/Shutterstock; p128b: Elena Elisseeva/Shutterstock; p132: OUP; p134: VIEW Pictures Ltd/Alamy; p139: Robert Fried/Alamy; p140r: John Norman/ Alamy; p140l: Bigstock; p144l: Jeff Greenberg/Alamy; p144lm: Paul Paris/Alamy; p144rm: WoodyStock/Alamy; p144r: Bigstock; p146a: Yuri Arcurs/Shutterstock; p146b: Alan Oddie/Photoedit; p146c: OUP; p146d: Picture Contact/Alamy; p150: Mark Dyball/Alamy; p156: Alessandra Benedetti/Corbis; p157tr: Reflekta/Shutterstock; p157tl: Michael Jung/Shutterstock; p157bl: Aliaksei Sabelnikau/Shutterstock; p157br: Rob Marmion/Shutterstock; p157b: Daisuke Kobayashi/Anyone/amanaimages/Corbis; p158: Roy Morsch/zefa/Corbis; p159 & P160: Antonio Mo/Getty Images; p161t: Jason Stitt/Shutterstock; p161b: Suzanne Tucker/Shutterstock; p162t: Bigstock; p162l: Photononstop/Tips Images; p162r: Walter Geiersperger/Corbis; p162b: Arco Digital Images/Tips Images; p163tl: Roy Morsch/Corbis; p163ml: Angela Hampton Picture Library/Alamy; p163mr: Michelle Pedone/Corbis; p163tr: Rick Gomez/Corbis; p163bl: Creasource/Corbis; p163br: Reuters/Corbis; p164t: Fox Photos/Getty Images; p164tm: Dan Atkin/Alamy; p164m: Photononstop/Tips Images; p164b: PeerPoint/Alamy; p166: Vice-chancellorship of Martinique; p167t: OUP; p167b & p168: Yuri Arcurs/Shutterstock; p169: Real gap/Africa; p170t: Antonio Mo/Getty Images; p170b: Real Gap, Africa.

Illustrations by: Stefan Chabluk, Olivier Prime, Mark Turner, Moreno Chiacchiera, Nigel Dobbyn, Lee Nicholls/Hardwick Studios, Mark Draisey, Gemma Hastilow.

Cover image: Don Hammond/design pics/Corbis

The authors and publishers would like to thank the following people for their help and advice:

Editor: Kathryn Tate; Language consultant: Geneviève Talon; Audio recordings: Colette Thomson and Andrew Garrett (Footstep Productions); Course advisor: Stuart Glover

# AQA GCSE French

Danièle Bourdais
Sue Finnie
Marian Jones
Sarah Provan
Elizabeth Fotheringham
Kate Scappaticci

## Welcome to *AQA GCSE French*!

The following symbols will help you to get the most out of this book:

- listen to the audio CD with this activity
- work with a partner
- work in a group

**B↔A** swap roles with your partner

**GRAMMAIRE** an explanation of an important aspect of grammar

**STRATÉGIES** a skill or strategy that will help you maximise your marks

**VOCABULAIRE** key expressions for a particular topic

**À vous!** a round-up activity that helps you to put the skills and grammar you have learnt into practice. Additional support for these activities is provided on the *Resources & Planning OxBox CD-ROM*.

**Grammaire active** Grammar explanations and practice

**Controlled Assessment** Extended tasks which will help you to prepare for your speaking and writing controlled assessments. Additional support for these activities is provided in the *Exam Skills Workbooks*.

**Vocabulaire** Unit vocabulary list

**Écouter et lire** Additional exam-style listening and reading material to accompany each unit

# Contents

# Welcome to *AQA GCSE French*!

## What will you be studying?

You will be studying topics from the following four areas:

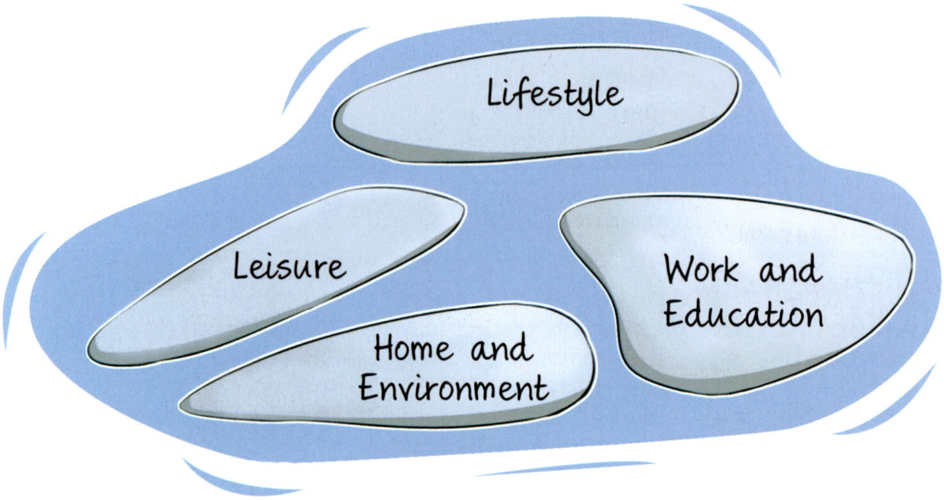

## What are the aims of *AQA GCSE French*?

*AQA GCSE French* is all about making French work for you, and making it fun and relevant at the same time. You will be given all the tools you need to develop your French (grammar, skills and vocabulary) and plenty of interesting topics so that you can talk about the things that really matter to you.

Not only that, but we give you lots of support to help you succeed in the AQA GCSE exam, for both the Listening and Reading papers and the Speaking and Writing Controlled Assessments.

By the end of this course you will be able to feel confident about your GCSE exam and able to communicate in French in lots of different situations.

## What is in the exam?

For the AQA GCSE exam, you will be tested in four skills. Speaking and Writing count for 60% of your total mark (see pie-chart), so for 60% of the exam, what you will end up with in the assessment is up to you!

**Listening and Reading** are assessed in exams. The examiners are not trying to trick you or confuse you:
- all instructions will be in English
- questions are designed to find out how much you understand.

**Speaking and Writing** are tested by Controlled Assessment. That's designed to let you show off what you can do.

**Overall GCSE grade: 100%**

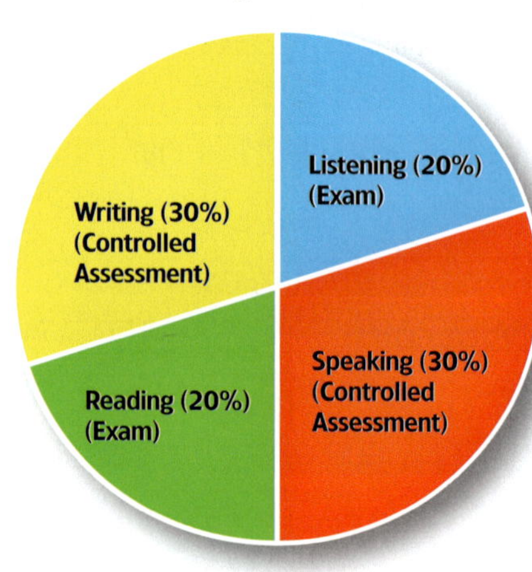

## What is Controlled Assessment?

There are two types of Controlled Assessment that you will need to do for your AQA French GCSE: one for Speaking and one for Writing.

For the Speaking Controlled Assessment you will have to complete two speaking assessment tasks: one task will be in the style of an interview and the other will be a conversation, and both tasks have to be on different themes. The great news is that you can choose what topics you want to talk on, so you can pick something that interests you!

For the Written Controlled Assessment you will have to complete two assessment tasks. Again, you can choose to write on topics that really appeal to you.

The Speaking and Writing Controlled Assessment sections at the end of each unit give you lots of helpful advice and practice, so that by the time you come to do your Controlled Assessments you will be more than ready!

## How does *AQA GCSE French* equip me for the exam?

- It develops your Listening, Speaking, Reading and Writing skills, step by step, building your confidence in tackling material in French.
- It focuses on strategies for success in the exam so you can do your best on the day. There are skills boxes in each unit to set out the best way to learn, and a skills page which encourages you to focus on applying and evaluating these strategies yourself. Also, there are loads of useful tips and practice questions in the *Exam Practice* section, starting on page 171. You will find lots of targeted exam strategies that really work!
- It tells you exactly what you need to approach the Speaking and Writing Controlled Assessments with confidence. At the end of each unit there is a Speaking and a Writing Controlled Assessment: these are similar to the AQA GCSE Controlled Assessment tasks and so you have the opportunity to get lots of practice. All the French and all the grammar and skills you have learnt so far will come into play, so you can use the task as a chance to show off and express yourself.
- You will also find lots of extra reading and listening practice in the *Écouter et Lire* section on page 155. This section has two pages of further reading and listening activities for every unit in the style of the exam so that you can get lots of exam practice in those areas.
- The *Exam Practice* section on page 171 provides useful exam tips and sample exam papers for you to develop your exam skills.

## What else will help me succeed?

- The *Exam Skills Workbooks* (Foundation and Higher) which bring together lots of useful advice and strategies, and provide you with activities to put them into practice.
- The *Resources and Planning OxBox CD-ROM*, which provides overviews of French grammar and pronunciation, plus flashcards to help you to master the AQA prescribed vocabulary list. Use the Record & Playback activities to record practice Speaking Controlled Assessment tasks and perfect your pronunciation and delivery.
- The *Assessment OxBox CD-ROM* is there to give you lots of interactive assessment practice, so that you are well prepared for your GCSE exam.

## How to learn new words and use them

There are many strategies for learning French vocabulary. The most important thing is to try them, evaluate them, and stick to what works for you. Spending time learning words thoroughly is a simple thing that will make a big difference to your grade. It is something no one else can do for you!

## Top Five Strategies for Learning Vocabulary

**Crack the spelling/ pronunciation link**

Learn the French spelling rules

Pronounce any French word correctly

Spell any French word correctly

Notice links between related words

Spend more time on learning the meaning of words

**Fun techniques**

Word association pictures

Flashcards/Memory games

Stories

Text your friends in French

**Focus on important words**

Core vocabulary

Vocabulary that transfers to all topics

"Tricky" words

Words that make you stand out from the crowd

Word families

**Use your own system**

Organise your vocabulary your way: alphabetically, by topic, or in some other way that is meaningful to you

Keep using the vocabulary you learned in previous units

Test yourself frequently to see if you can remember everything

Have your own Top Five Strategies

**Eat, drink, read, write, speak, listen**

When you are swimming, count your lengths in French

When you are jogging, listen to your words on your MP3 player

On the bus, have a look at your French verb list

Set the menus on your phone and games console to French

Label everything around your house in French

## What works for you?

I record myself speaking and then listen to the recording.

I read words over and over again and then repeat them in my head or out loud.

I write new words on a small card with the English translation on the back and use them to test myself.

I write each new word out ten times and then I write a sentence using it.

I spell new French words out for myself, silently or out loud.

I ask a friend or relative to test me.

**Which of these ideas would work best for you? Try some and see!**

# Getting to grips with grammar

You will have already come across lots of useful grammar but remember that you need to pay special attention to the following for your GCSE studies:

- Tenses (present, past and future)
- Opinions and reasons
- Linking words
- Descriptions

## Where will you find your grammar tools in *AQA GCSE French*?

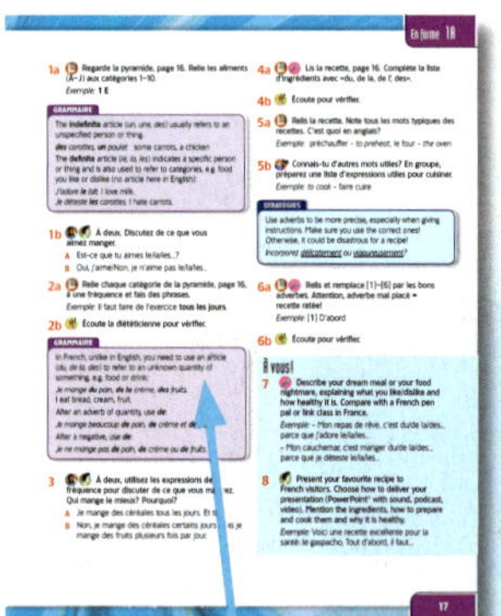

*Grammaire active* pages towards the end of each unit of the *Students' Book*, with more in-depth explanation and practice activities.

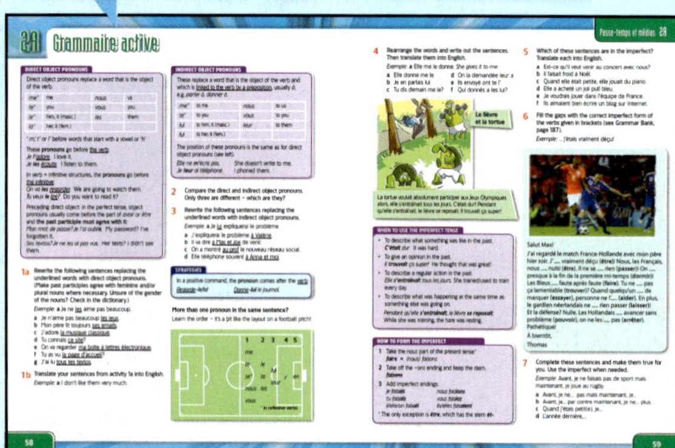


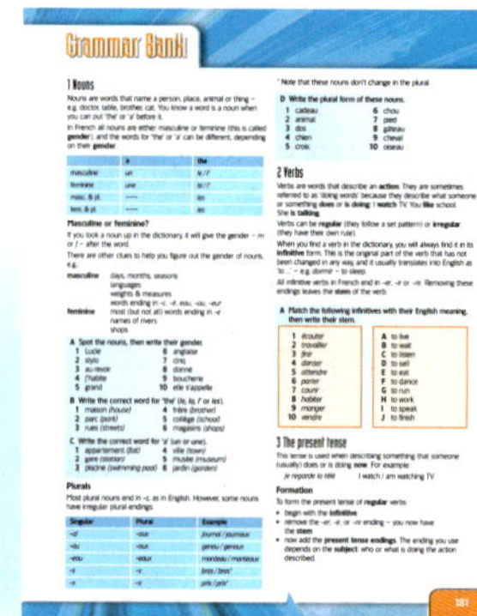


Purple grammar panels on most pages of the *Students' Book*.

A GCSE *Grammar Bank* at the end of the book, for reference and extra practice.

One page of grammar activities for each unit in the *Exam Skills Workbooks*.

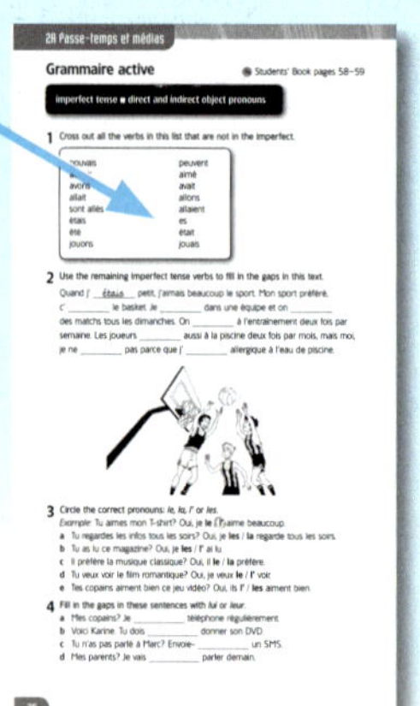


Extensive practice of all of the grammar points covered at GCSE level.

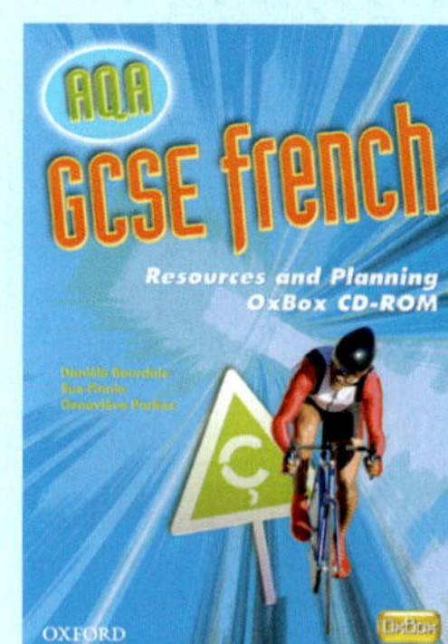


ICT presentations of the core grammar points you need for GCSE

# 1A En forme

## Sais-tu comment...

- ❑ choisir le sport idéal?
- ❑ se muscler sans danger?
- ❑ bien manger?
- ❑ éviter les mauvaises habitudes?
- ❑ retrouver la forme?

## Controlled assessment

- **Have a conversation about healthy lifestyles**
- **Present your candidate for a sports personality award**

**Comment garder la forme?**

## Stratégies

### À l'oral

When speaking, how do you...

- make liaisons between words correctly?
- speak expressively and convincingly?
- add examples to illustrate what you say?

### À l'écrit

In French, how do you...

- use determiners correctly?
- make your sentences longer and more detailed?

## Grammaire active

As part of your French language 'toolkit' can you...

- form regular and irregular verbs correctly in the present tense?
- use modal verbs?
- use reflexive verbs?
- use the perfect tense?

# 1A Comment choisir le sport idéal

G Les verbes au présent; les verbes modaux V Les activités sportives
S Bien prononcer les groupes de mots P Les liaisons

## Quel genre de sportif/sportive êtes-vous? Allergique ou fanatique?

Je déteste le sport parce que je suis nul. Je n'ai pas envie de faire des activités physiques, ça ne m'intéresse pas. Je ne joue pas au foot, je ne soutiens pas d'équipe et je ne regarde pas le sport à la télé. Même les Jeux Olympiques ne m'intéressent pas. Mes parents me disent de faire plus de sport. Je sais que l'activité physique est nécessaire pour la santé et je n'en fais pas assez, mais je ne sais pas quoi faire!

Noé

Max

Moi, j'aime le sport, tous les sports. Je fais de la musculation et je joue au foot dans un club. Je fais partie d'une équipe de handball depuis trois ans. Je participe à des championnats et des compétitions. Je veux faire des sports qui offrent des sensations plus fortes, comme les sports extrêmes! Mes parents disent que c'est dangereux mais je dois essayer des choses nouvelles et dépasser mes limites!

## Sports extrêmes

1 la chute libre

2 la plongée sous-marine

3 le kitesurf

4 le speed riding

**A** Pour qui rêve de découvrir un autre monde! On fait ce sport seulement si on ... nager et on ... être en bonne forme physique. On ... si on ... se familiariser avec l'équipement en piscine. On ne ... jamais faire ce sport seul.

**B** Le sport pour toi si tu ... glisser et voler! C'est un sport à envisager seulement si tu ... très bien skier, hors-piste et dans n'importe quelle* neige. Comme tu ... aller très vite et très haut quand il y a du vent, tu ne ... pas avoir le vertige!

**C** Pour ceux qui ... voler comme un oiseau! Les candidats à ce sport extrême ... le faire sans être des athlètes mais ils ... passer une visite médicale. Quand ils ... un minimum de choses sur les techniques de vol, ils ... sauter seuls.

* any

**1a** Lis les textes de Max et Noé, page 12. Qui est allergique au sport? Qui est fanatique? Pourquoi?

**1b** Lis à haute voix les mots qui s'appliquent à toi.

*Exemple:* Je déteste le sport parce que...

**GRAMMAIRE**

**Verbs in the present tense**
See pages 181–182 of the Grammar Bank to revise what you know about the three types of verb endings *(-er, -re, -ir)* and typical verb endings in the present tense.

**1c** Relis les textes et trouve l'infinitif de tous les verbes.

*Exemple:* déteste = détester

**2a** Écoute Sophie. Complète les phrases en anglais.

- **a** *the sport she does occasionally*
- **b** *the sport she does in a club*
- **c** *where she trains twice a week*
- **d** *the team she supports in the Olympics*

**2b** Réécoute Sophie. Prends des notes et complète ses phrases.

J'aime... J'ai envie de... Je joue...
...ça m'intéresse Je fais... Je participe à...
Je regarde... Je soutiens...

**STRATÉGIES**

Remember that determiners are used differently in English and French.

I love _ football = *j'aime le football*
to play _ football = *jouer au foot*
at _ school = *à l'école* on _ TV = *à la télé*

**3** Parle de ton attitude par rapport au sport. Utilise les expressions de l'activité 2b. Attention aux verbes et aux déterminants!

**4a** Lis «Sports extrêmes», page 12. A, B, C: c'est quels sports?

**GRAMMAIRE**

**Modal verbs: *pouvoir, devoir, savoir, vouloir***
These indicate whether you can, must, know how or want to do something. They are followed by an infinitive: e.g. *je sais nager*. See page 22.

**4b** Lis l'encadré Grammaire et complète les textes A, B et C avec les bons verbes.

*Exemple:* On fait ce sport seulement si on sait nager...

**4c** Écoute (A–D) pour vérifier. Prends des notes sur le quatrième sport.

*Exemple:* Un sport pour vous si vous savez...

**5** Parle des sports pour toi (un point par verbe modal utilisé!)

*Exemple:* Je veux faire du speed riding mais je ne peux pas parce que je ne sais pas skier, alors je dois apprendre. = 4 points.

**STRATÉGIES**

Be aware of *liaisons* – when a normally silent consonant at the end of a word is pronounced at the beginning of the word that follows it. Certain liaisons are compulsory. Knowing when and how to make them helps you speak more fluently as well as understand better when you listen.

**6a** Relis les textes A, B et C, page 12. Prononce les liaisons obligatoires ■. Attention aux liaisons interdites! ■

**6b** Lis ces phrases à haute voix. Écoute pour vérifier.

- **a** Le ski de fond est un sport passionnant.
- **b** Les heures d'EPS? Je les aime de moins en moins.
- **c** J'apprends à skier et à nager.

## À VOUS!

**7** 'Call my bluff'. Write ten things about the sports and hobbies you do (some false). Read them out. The class decides which ones are lies.

*Exemple:* Je suis très sportif/ive: je fais du jogging tous les matins. Je joue au tennis...

**8** In groups, choose a sport from around the world and present it to the class (using PowerPoint® or video, or by giving a demonstration, etc.). Use modal verbs and be aware of liaisons!

*Exemple:* La capoeira vient du Brésil. C'est un sport entre l'art martial et la danse. Le joueur doit combattre un adversaire mais il ne peut pas le toucher. etc.

# 1A Comment se muscler sans danger!

G Les verbes pronominaux; les adverbes V Sport et santé S L'intonation pour convaincre

A

Hugo

J'adore le sport et surtout le football. Je joue dans une équipe mais je me blesse souvent aux muscles des jambes. C'est frustrant parce que je ne peux pas aller à tous les entraînements ni jouer dans tous les matchs.

B

Morgane

Des fois, j'ai trop envie d'aller au fast-food avec les copains! Et puis j'adore le chocolat et les bonbons et je ne peux pas m'empêcher d'en manger même si je sais que ce n'est pas bon pour la santé!

C

Malika

On me dit de me coucher tôt pour être en forme, mais moi, je ne m'endors pas avant 11h 30 ou minuit. Par contre, le matin, je ne me réveille pas, c'est dur de me lever et on se dispute avec mes parents!

D

Julien

Je joue au handball dans un club et j'adore ça mais comme je me fatigue assez vite, je ne joue pas toujours dans les matchs. C'est frustrant! Je ne sais pas quoi faire pour m'améliorer.

E

Marianne

Je n'aime pas le sport et je n'ai pas vraiment envie d'en faire. Je n'arrive pas à me motiver. Je veux quand même faire une activité physique parce que je sais que c'est important. Mais quoi faire?

F

Yohann

J'aime bien le sport mais j'ai aussi envie de me distraire, de jouer sur ma console, de m'amuser avec les copains, de sortir, d'aller aux fêtes. Ce n'est pas facile quand il y a aussi les devoirs et les entraînements sportifs!

## Partagez les secrets des champions

**Six règles d'or pour être en forme**

**1) Bien se bouger**
Ne rate [1] une occasion de faire de l'exercice! Tu peux brûler des calories sans faire de sport. Par exemple, prends les escaliers et non l'ascenseur; sors [2] le chien (marcher, c'est 80 Kcal/h)! D'autres idées: danser (450 Kcal/h) ou faire du jardinage ou le ménage (200 Kcal/h)!

**2) Bien s'échauffer**
Les étirements sont l'activité physique la plus négligée pendant les activités sportives. Pourtant, c'est [3] vital pour la souplesse et pour se protéger contre les accidents musculaires. Étire-toi [4] avant et après chaque activité sportive.

**3) Bien s'entraîner**
Travaille différents aspects: la force (par exemple, musculation avec haltères) pour avoir plus de puissance, la vitesse (sprint) pour réagir plus [5], l'endurance (jogging, saut à la corde) pour te fatiguer moins [5].

**4) Bien s'alimenter**
Il est vital de prendre un bon petit déjeuner et de manger des fruits et légumes (oui, écoute ta mère!). Bien sûr, tu peux manger des hamburgers-frites et des sucreries, en petites quantités.

**5) Bien se relaxer**
Faire un sport ne veut pas dire se priver de tous les plaisirs. Au contraire, c'est important de se donner du bon temps, mais il faut savoir s'organiser pour pouvoir tout faire.

**6) Bien se reposer**
Il est essentiel pour un sportif de [6] dormir car c'est pendant le sommeil que le corps se répare et qu'on recharge ses batteries. Évite les excitants au moins une heure avant de te coucher: pas de thé, café, ou sodas, et éteins TV, Internet, MSN et téléphone.

**1** Lis A–F, page 14. C'est qui?

- **a** *Who can't get motivated to do exercise?*
- **b** *Who can't help eating junk food?*
- **c** *Who finds it hard to fit in leisure with schoolwork and sport training?*
- **d** *Who gets tired very quickly?*
- **e** *Who often gets injured?*
- **f** *Who goes to sleep late and finds it hard to get up?*

**2** Lis tous les textes, page 14. Relie chaque personne à une règle qui peut l'aider.

*Exemple*: **A 2**)

**3a** Relis les six règles d'or, page 14. Remplace les numéros par les bons adverbes.

*Exemple:* **1 = b)** jamais

| | | |
|---|---|---|
| **1** | **a)** souvent | **b)** jamais |
| **2** | **a)** rarement | **b)** régulièrement |
| **3** | **a)** absolument | **b)** un peu |
| **4** | **a)** bien | **b)** mal |
| **5** | **a)** lentement | **b)** vite |
| **6** | **a)** bien | **b)** trop |

**3b** Écoute pour vérifier.

**GRAMMAIRE**

**Adverbs** (see page 188 of the Grammar Bank)

An adverb can indicate when and how something is done (time, manner and intensity) e.g. *souvent, lentement, très,* etc. It can be a single word or a phrase, e.g. *souvent, un peu.*

**GRAMMAIRE**

**Reflexive verbs**

In French, many verbs referring to actions are reflexive, for example *se lever* (to get up) or *se laver* (to have a wash).

**The reflexive pronouns are: *me/te/se/nous/vous/se***

*Je me réveille. On s'améliore.*

**The pronouns go before the conjugated verb:**

*Je <u>me</u> lève, je <u>me</u> suis levé(e), je vais <u>me</u> lever!*

**4a** Relis les textes, page 14, et note tous les verbes pronominaux (= *reflexive verbs*).

*Exemple*: je me blesse

**4b** À qui (A-F) ressembles-tu? Explique pourquoi. Utilise des verbes pronominaux.

*Exemple*: Je ressemble à Malika parce que je me couche tard, etc.

**5** Écoute les jeunes (1-4). Note ce qu'ils disent sur leur problème et la solution.

*Exemple*: **1** Avant, je me blessais; maintenant, je m'étire doucement...

**6** Relis la page 14. Résume la situation des six jeunes en français.

*Exemple*: **A** Hugo - Avant, il se blessait souvent aux muscles des jambes quand il jouait au football. Maintenant, il s'échauffe bien, il s'étire avant et après chaque activité sportive.

**7** Écoute le problème de Léa et les suggestions de deux coachs. Lequel est le plus convaincant? Pourquoi?

**STRATÉGIES**

To sound convincing you need to speak clearly and expressively: be lively and enthusiastic, stress certain words to make them stand out. Use adverbs too!

**8** Jeu de rôle. **A** mentionne un problème et **B** est l'expert qui propose une solution (avec le ton!). (**B⟷A**)

*Exemple*: **A** Je ne cours pas assez vite.

**B** Il faut t'entraîner à la vitesse. Fais souvent un sprint!

## À VOUS!

**9** Your favourite French celebrity is looking for a fitness buddy! Present your health profile at the interview, saying why you are the best person for the job (you need to be convincing!).

*Exemple*: Je suis très en forme et très sportif/ive. Je mange toujours ce qui est bon pour la santé, etc.

**10** Which generation is the healthiest? In groups, prepare a questionnaire, interview at least two people: one from your parents' and one from your grandparents' generation and compare their answers with your own. Write a report and present it to other groups in the class. Discuss your conclusions, giving your opinion on them.

*Exemple*: Dans la génération des grands-parents, on ne mange pas beaucoup de fruits et légumes mais on fait de l'exercice...

# 1A Comment bien manger

G Les articles: du, de la, des  V Les aliments et les recettes  S Utiliser des adverbes pour être précis

## Bien manger tous les jours...

A le poisson, le poulet, les œufs
B les légumes
C le riz et le pain blancs; les pâtes; les bonbons
D le riz et le pain complets; les céréales
E la viande rouge; le beurre
F les fruits secs; les légumes secs
G les huiles végétales
H le lait, le fromage
I les fruits
J l'exercice

**STRATÉGIES**

**Adverbs of frequency**

tous les jours
à chaque repas
plusieurs fois par jour
une ou deux fois par jour
beaucoup (cinq portions par jour)
régulièrement
certains jours, avec modération

## Et comme dessert?
## dessert léger = dessert santé

*Le soufflé aux fraises*

*Ingrédients pour 4 personnes*
Un moule à soufflé
.... margarine (1 cuillerée à café)
.... fraises (200 g.)
.... œufs (2 jaunes et 4 blancs)
.... sucre en poudre (10 g.)
.... aspartame (10 g.)

1 **[1]**, préchauffez le four à 210 °C (th.7) et beurrez le moule avec la margarine.
2 **[2]** cassez les œufs et séparez les jaunes des blancs.
3 Mixez les fraises et filtrez le jus: gardez 4 cuillerées à soupe. Versez **[3]** le jus des fraises sur les jaunes d'œufs et le sucre.
4 Fouettez **[4]** les 4 blancs d'œufs en neige ferme avec l'aspartame.
5 Incorporez **[5]** ce mélange aux jaunes d'œufs. Versez le tout dans le moule et mettez au four pendant 10 minutes.
6 Servez **[6]** pour que le soufflé ne tombe pas.

puis  D'abord  délicatement
immédiatement  progressivement
vigoureusement

**1a** Regarde la pyramide, page 16. Relie les aliments (A–J) aux catégories 1–10.

*Exemple:* **1 E**

**GRAMMAIRE**

The **indefinite** article (*un, une, des*) usually refers to an unspecified person or thing.

***des** carottes, **un** poulet* some carrots, a chicken

The **definite** article (*le, la, les*) indicates a specific person or thing and is also used to refer to categories, e.g. food you like or dislike (no article here in English):

*J'adore **le** lait.* I love milk.
*Je déteste **les** carottes.* I hate carrots.

**1b** À deux. Discutez de ce que vous aimez manger.

**A** Est-ce que tu aimes le/la/les...?

**B** Oui, j'aime/Non, je n'aime pas le/la/les...

**2a** Relie chaque catégorie de la pyramide, page 16, à une fréquence et fais des phrases.

*Exemple:* Il faut faire de l'exercice **tous les jours**.

**2b** Écoute la diététicienne pour vérifier.

**GRAMMAIRE**

In French, unlike in English, you need to use an article (*du, de la, des*) to refer to an unknown quantity of something, e.g. food or drink:

*Je mange **du** pain, **de la** crème, **des** fruits.*
I eat bread, cream, fruit.

After an adverb of quantity, use ***de***:

*Je mange beaucoup **de** pain, **de** crème et **de** fruits.*

After a negative, use ***de***:

*Je ne mange pas **de** pain, **de** crème ou **de** fruits.*

**3** À deux, utilisez les expressions de fréquence pour discuter de ce que vous mangez. Qui mange le mieux? Pourquoi?

**A** Je mange des céréales tous les jours. Et toi?

**B** Non, je mange des céréales certains jours mais je mange des fruits plusieurs fois par jour.

**4a** Lis la recette, page 16. Complète la liste d'ingrédients avec «du, de la, de l', des».

**4b** Écoute pour vérifier.

**5a** Relis la recette. Note tous les mots typiques des recettes. C'est quoi en anglais?

*Exemple:* préchauffer - *to preheat*, le four - *the oven*

**5b** Connais-tu d'autres mots utiles? En groupe, préparez une liste d'expressions utiles pour cuisiner.

*Exemple: to cook* - faire cuire

**STRATÉGIES**

Use adverbs to be more precise, especially when giving instructions. Make sure you use the correct ones! Otherwise, it could be disastrous for a recipe!

*Incorporez délicatement ou vigoureusement?*

**6a** Relis et remplace [1]–[6] par les bons adverbes. Attention, adverbe mal placé = recette ratée!

*Exemple:* [**1**] D'abord

**6b** Écoute pour vérifier.

## À VOUS!

**7** Describe your dream meal or your food nightmare, explaining what you like/dislike and how healthy it is. Compare with a French pen pal or link class in France.

*Exemple:* - Mon repas de rêve, c'est du/de la/des... parce que j'adore le/la/les...

- Mon cauchemar, c'est manger du/de la/des... parce que je déteste le/la/les...

**8** Present your favourite recipe to French visitors. Choose how to deliver your presentation (PowerPoint® with sound, podcast, video). Mention the ingredients, how to prepare and cook them and why it is healthy.

*Exemple:* Voici une recette excellente pour la santé: le gaspacho. Tout d'abord, il faut...

# 1A Comment éviter les mauvaises habitudes

(G) Le futur proche (V) Les bonnes et les mauvaises habitudes

(S) Illustrer ce qu'on dit par des exemples

## Forum-santé: Questions-réponses

**A** On doit bien manger au petit déjeuner mais moi, je ne peux pas parce que je n'ai vraiment pas faim. Par contre, pendant la matinée, je me sens faible et je n'arrive plus à me concentrer en classe. Qu'est-ce que je dois faire? — **Simon**

**B** Je n'ai pas le temps de manger à midi à l'école parce que je fais beaucoup de sport. Je sais qu'il existe des suppléments de vitamines et minéraux. Est-ce que je peux en prendre à la place? — **Katie**

**C** Je dois perdre quelques kilos mais j'aime trop le chocolat! Je ne peux pas m'empêcher de manger plusieurs barres chocolatées par jour. Qu'est-ce que je peux faire pour en manger moins? — **Edgar**

**D** Je sais que le fast-food, c'est nul pour la santé! Je veux être en bonne santé, alors est-ce que je dois ne pas en manger du tout ou bien est-ce que je peux en manger de temps en temps? — **Alex**

**1** Lis les questions du forum-santé. C'est qui?

*Exemple:* **a A** Simon

- **a** *Who can't eat at breakfast but then feels weak and lacks concentration?*
- **b** *Who is thinking of taking vitamin supplements at lunchtime due to lack of time?*
- **c** *Who wonders whether eating junk food occasionally is ok?*
- **d** *Who can't help eating chocolate every day despite needing to lose weight?*

**2** Relis les textes A–D et retrouve ces verbes conjugués.

*Exemple:* devoir **A** doit/dois

avoir devoir être faire savoir sentir pouvoir vouloir

**3a** Lis ces conseils et résume en anglais. C'est pour qui?

**Tu vas essayer de moins manger; par exemple, tu vas couper une barre en petits bouts et tu vas en manger un petit bout au lieu de la barre entière. Tu vas prendre du chocolat noir, comme le chocolat à 60% de cacao, parce qu'il est moins gras et moins sucré. Tu vas remplacer le chocolat par des fruits secs, entre autres des abricots, des pommes ou des mangues.**

**3b** Relis les conseils et trouve ces expressions utiles pour donner des exemples.

*like* *for instance* *among others*

**4a** Écoute les conseils de l'expert. Réponds en anglais (a–c).

*Exemple:* **a** *To try and drink something in the morning...*

- **a** *What three suggestions does the expert make to help Simon?*
- **b** *What two things mustn't Katie do and what must she do for 20 minutes?*
- **c** *Name three ways that Alex can enjoy fast food safely.*

**GRAMMAIRE**

***aller* + infinitive**

Use the present tense of ***aller*** + a verb in the infinitive to say what your resolutions are and to speak about the future.

*Je vais manger moins de frites.* I am going to eat fewer chips.

*Je vais perdre du poids.* I am going to lose weight.

**4b** Réécoute et note les exemples précis dans chaque réponse.

*Exemple:* **Simon – *Il va boire*** *un jus de fruit frais.*

## ALCOOL = DANGER

**A** **À petite ou moyenne dose**, l'alcool va donner l'impression de relaxer, mais en fait, on va perdre le contrôle de soi-même et on va avoir une «gueule de bois*».

**B** **À très forte dose**, l'alcool va causer des troubles graves (hallucinations, pertes de mémoire), des maladies du foie*, des cancers et parfois des comas mortels.

**C** **Les mélanges** (alcool-soda) ne vont pas diminuer les effets de l'alcool, au contraire: on va moins sentir l'alcool et on va en boire plus.

**D** **L'alcool est une drogue** et on peut devenir dépendant. Plus on boit jeune, plus on risque de devenir dépendant.

* une gueule de bois – *hangover*
le foie – *liver*

**Constance:** «Quand je sors, je bois quelques verres. Je ne suis pas ivre* mais je ne suis pas toujours en forme le dimanche pour faire mes devoirs!»

**Clément:** «J'ai commencé à boire à 12 ans: cidre, bière et maintenant vodka. Ma copine dit que je suis alcoolique et que je ne vais plus pouvoir arrêter de boire.»

**Adam:** «L'an dernier, j'ai trop bu pendant une soirée. Je ne me souviens de rien, sauf de voir mes parents pleurer à l'hôpital. Ils pensaient que j'allais mourir!»

**Étienne:** «Je mélange toujours l'alcool avec du coca ou des jus de fruits et je bois des premix, c'est mieux je pense: j'en bois beaucoup mais c'est moins fort.»

* ivre – *drunk*

**5** Lis et résume ce que disent les jeunes en anglais.

*Exemple: Constance only drinks a few glasses when she goes out...*

**6a** Relie les effets de l'alcool (A–D) à un jeune.

*Exemple:* **A** = Constance

**6b** Écoute pour vérifier.

**STRATÉGIES**

Speak in a more interesting and convincing way by adding examples.

*Si on prend l'exemple de X, on voit que...*

*Le cas/L'exemple de X montre/prouve que...*

**6c** Réécoute. Note les phrases de la conseillère avec les expressions ci-dessus.

*Exemple:* Si on prend l'exemple de Constance, on voit que l'alcool a des effets négatifs.

**7** Quelles mauvaises habitudes ne vas-tu pas prendre? Explique oralement avec un exemple.

*Exemple:* Je ne vais plus boire de premix. L'exemple d'Étienne montre que c'est dangereux...

## À VOUS!

**8** Organise a health forum to exchange ideas with a link class in France. Students each write a query. In small groups, come up with replies (using ***aller*** + infinitive and examples). Discuss in class.

*Exemple:* **Q** Je dé-tes-te manger des légumes!

**R** Tu vas ajouter des petits bouts de légumes à des plats que tu aimes, comme des pâtes ou du riz.

**9** In groups, prepare a campaign to warn young French children of the dangers of alcohol. Choose a medium (poster, video, quiz, etc.) and use lots of examples.

*Exemple*: L'alcool est mauvais pour la santé. L'exemple des premix montre qu'il faut faire très attention!

# 1A Comment retrouver la forme

(G) Le passé composé (V) La vie saine (S) Faire des phrases détaillées

## Comment éviter le pire: témoignages d'ados

**A** Bonjour,

Je m'appelle Sabine. J'ai 17 ans. Je suis allée voir le docteur l'année dernière parce que j'étais toujours extrêmement fatiguée. J'ai eu très peur quand il m'a dit qu'il était urgent de maigrir pour éviter les problèmes graves comme le diabète* ou l'hypertension*!

**B** J'ai toujours détesté le sport et je n'en ai jamais fait assez; par contre, j'ai toujours adoré les sucreries, les frites, la charcuterie, etc. et j'en ai trop mangé!

J'ai eu de la chance: mon docteur, ma famille et mes amis m'ont beaucoup aidée. Avec leur aide, j'ai radicalement changé mon style de vie et mon alimentation.

**C** Je suis allée en salle de gym deux fois par semaine: j'ai fait du tapis de course et du vélo d'entraînement. Je suis sortie plus souvent me promener à pied et je suis restée moins longtemps devant la télé ou l'ordi.
J'ai remplacé les sucreries par des fruits, les frites par des légumes-vapeur, et la charcuterie, je n'en mange presque plus!

Ça n'a pas été facile tous les jours mais cette année, j'ai perdu 15 kilos. J'ai réussi à éviter le diabète et je suis en pleine forme!! Maintenant, je vais tout faire pour garder mon nouveau style de vie!

* diabetes
* high blood pressure

**1** Lis le texte de Sabine. Décide si les phrases 1–8 sont vraies (V) ou fausses (F). Justifie ta réponse par une phrase du texte.

*Exemple:* **1 F** – Je suis allée voir le docteur... j'étais toujours extrêmement fatiguée.

**A**
- **1** *Last year, Sabine saw the doctor because she wanted to lose weight.*
- **2** *She had a shock when the doctor told her she had diabetes and high blood pressure.*

**B**
- **3** *She has always hated sport and has never really done any. Furthermore, she ate too much junk food.*
- **4** *Her doctor, family and friends did nothing to help her change her lifestyle: she was left to struggle on her own.*

**C**
- **5** *She exercised in the gym, went for walks and spent less time sitting in front of a screen.*
- **6** *She found it easy to eat healthily and to lose weight.*
- **7** *She lost the weight she needed in order to avoid getting ill.*
- **8** *She is not sure she can keep up her healthy habits.*

**GRAMMAIRE**

***En***
This pronoun means 'of it' or 'of them', 'some' or 'any'. Find examples of it in Sabine's text and explain what ***en*** refers to.

Je m'appelle Louis **[1]** j'ai 17 ans. Mon problème, c'était l'alcool… **[2]**, j'ai bu un peu de cidre dans les fêtes avec des copains, juste pour essayer **[3]** je n'ai pas aimé, **[4]** j'ai commencé à boire de la bière. **[5]**, j'ai voulu faire comme les autres et j'ai bu de la vodka. Pendant longtemps, j'en ai bu beaucoup trop: ça a eu un effet sur ma santé et sur mon travail au lycée **[6]** je n'étais pas vraiment en forme. Un soir, pendant une fête,…

**GRAMMAIRE**

**The perfect tense**

The perfect tense is formed by taking the correct part of *avoir* or *être* in the present and adding the **past participle**.

Most verbs take *avoir*. With *avoir*, the past participle never agrees with the subject.

Some verbs take *être*. With *être*, the past participle **always agrees** with the subject.

| | | |
|---|---|---|
| *adorer* | *J'ai **adoré*** | I loved/have loved |
| *aller* | *Je suis **allé(e) à...*** | I went to... /have been to... |

The perfect is used to refer to an event which took place and ended at a specific moment in the past.

***J'ai changé de style de vie.*** I have changed my lifestyle = I no longer do what I used to do before.

See the Grammar Bank, page 186.

**2** **À deux. Relisez le texte de Sabine. Trouvez tous les exemples de passé composé *(perfect)* et notez l'infinitif.**

*Exemple:* je suis allée = aller; j'ai eu = avoir, etc.

**3** **Mets ces phrases au passé composé.**

*Exemple:* **a** J'ai arrêté de fumer.

- **a** Je vais arrêter de fumer.
- **b** Je vais manger plus de poisson.
- **c** Je vais faire du sport.
- **d** Je vais boire de l'eau plus souvent.
- **e** Je vais aller à la piscine.
- **f** Je vais sortir plus souvent au parc.

**4** **Écoute trois jeunes parler de ce qu'ils ont fait pour être en forme. Note la bonne lettre pour chacun.**

**1** *This week Alina...*

| | |
|---|---|
| **A** | *did a two-hour gym training in a club* |
| **B** | *only did PE at school* |
| **C** | *went to the gym on Wednesday morning* |

**2** *This week Thibault...*

| | |
|---|---|
| **A** | *went on a diet* |
| **B** | *did something he doesn't normally do* |
| **C** | *followed his sugar-free diet* |

**3** *This week Christelle...*

| | |
|---|---|
| **A** | *smoked fewer cigarettes* |
| **B** | *smoked 10 cigarettes a day* |
| **C** | *stopped smoking* |

**STRATÉGIES**

When writing a text, make your sentences longer and more sophisticated by using:

- linking words: *et, mais, quand, parce que, par contre,* etc.
- adjectives and adverbs to add colour: *radicalement* = radically.

Find examples of these two strategies in Sabine's text.

**5a** **Lis le texte de Louis. Complète avec les mots ci-dessous.**

*Exemple:* **[1]** et

parce que  mais  D'abord  alors  et  Puis

**5b** **Écoute la première partie de son témoignage pour vérifier.**

**6a** **À deux. Qu'est-ce qui est arrivé à Louis? Faites des suggestions.**

*Exemple:* Un soir, pendant une fête,... il a trop bu/il a été malade, etc.

**6b** **Écoute pour vérifier.**

**6c** **Réécoute et réponds aux questions.**

- **a** *Why did Louis start drinking? (2 reasons)*
- **b** *What did his drinking affect? (2 things)*
- **c** *Why did he go to A&E?*
- **d** *What did he understand when he was in hospital?*
- **e** *How different are things now? (2 things)*

## À VOUS!

**7** **You have been asked to record a story for an advert being made to deter young children from smoking. Invent a testimony, like Sabine's and Louis's. Use the perfect tense to explain what happened.**

*Exemple:* Je m'appelle Paul. J'ai commencé à fumer à 10 ans...

**8** **Write a health questionnaire for your partner. Write 10 questions using the perfect tense. Then swap questionnaires and write your answers.**

*Exemple:* **1** As-tu déjà bu de l'alcool?
**2** As-tu mangé au fast-food cette semaine? etc.

# 1A Grammaire active

## WHEN TO USE THE PRESENT TENSE

| Use the present tense to say: | |
|---|---|
| – what is happening now. | *Je prends mon petit déjeuner.* |
| – what happens regularly. | *Tu promènes le chien tous les jours?* |
| – what will happen (in the near future). | *Demain, je fais un régime.* |

**1** Write one sentence illustrating each use of the present tense.

## VERB ENDINGS

When you use a verb in the present tense, the ending will change depending on who is doing the action of the verb.

Most verbs have regular patterns. Check the Grammar Bank, pages 181–182 for *–er* verbs, *-ir* verbs and *–re* verbs.

**2** Are these verbs *–er*, *-ir* or *–re* verbs? Write down the infinitive for each one.

*Exemple:* **a** adorer

**a** nous adorons
**b** on parle
**c** ils perdent
**d** elle remplit
**e** nous écoutons
**f** elles finissent
**g** je descends
**h** tu préfères
**i** nous mangeons
**j** vous commencez

## IRREGULAR VERBS

Some common verbs are irregular and you will need to learn them by heart. Consult the Verb tables, pages 195–196 to see how to form them. These include:

*aller, avoir, boire, écrire, être, faire, lire, partir, prendre, sortir, venir.*

**3** Translate the irregular verbs listed above.

*Exemple: aller* – to go, *avoir* – to ...

## MODAL VERBS

Modal verbs indicate the ability, possibility, capacity or desire to do something. They are followed by an infinitive, e.g. *je sais nager*.

| | *je* | *tu* | *il/elle/ on* | *nous* | *vous* | *ils/elles* |
|---|---|---|---|---|---|---|
| *pouvoir* | *peux* | *peux* | *peut* | *pouvons* | *pouvez* | *peuvent* |
| *vouloir* | *veux* | *veux* | *veut* | *voulons* | *voulez* | *veulent* |
| *devoir* | *dois* | *dois* | *doit* | *devons* | *devez* | *doivent* |
| *savoir* | *sais* | *sais* | *sait* | *savons* | *savez* | *savent* |

**4** Complete the sentences with the correct form of the verb.

*Exemple:* **a** veux

**a** Je (vouloir) faire plus de sport.
**b** On (sortir) le chien?
**c** Ils (partir) en vacances la semaine prochaine.
**d** Elle (aller) à la piscine chaque week-end.
**e** Vous (devoir) manger plus sainement.
**f** Nous (être) très en forme.
**g** Tu (avoir) peur de grossir?

## REFLEXIVE VERBS

Reflexive verbs (*se lever*, *s'habiller*, etc.) have an extra pronoun between the subject and the verb:

*je* ***me*** *lève*
*tu* ***te*** *lèves*
*il/elle* ***se*** *lève*
*nous* ***nous*** *levons*
*vous* ***vous*** *levez*
*ils* ***se*** *lèvent*

**5** It's chaos in the Legrand household at 7.30 am! Complete Louise's description by writing in the missing reflexive pronouns.

*Exemple:* **a** me

Alors, moi je **a** lève tard, vers sept heures vingt. Maman **b** douche déjà et mes frères **c** habillent dans leur chambre. Papa **d** lave vite dans la salle de bains, puis il **e** occupe de nos deux chiens. Après un petit déjeuner rapide, nous **f** brossons les dents et nous partons. Moi, j'ai déjà envie de **g** recoucher!

### WHEN TO USE THE PERFECT TENSE

You use the **perfect tense** (*passé composé*) to say what happened at a particular time in the past. It is used to translate two different tenses in English:

| | |
|---|---|
| I **have eaten** a piece of fruit. | ***J'ai mangé** un fruit.* |
| I **ate** a piece of fruit this morning. | ***J'ai mangé** un fruit ce matin.* |
| He **has gone** out. | ***Il est sorti.*** |
| He **went** out last night. | ***Il est sorti** hier soir.* |

### TIME EXPRESSIONS

Use **time expressions** to say when the action you want to describe took place:

*en 1999, l'année dernière, le mois dernier, la semaine dernière, hier,* etc.

### HOW TO FORM THE PERFECT TENSE

You need two parts:

1) *avoir* or *être* in the present tense +

2) a special form of the verb called **the past participle**

*manger: j'ai **mangé*** *sortir: je suis **sorti(e)***

To make a past participle, take off the infinitive verb ending of regular verbs and add a new ending:

- verbs ending in **-er**: *visit**er** = visit- + é = visit**é***
- verbs ending in **-ir**: *sort**ir** = sort- + i = sort**i***
- verbs ending in **-re**: *vend**re** = vend- + u = vend**u***

Some common irregular past participles:

*avoir = eu; être = été; boire = bu; dire = dit; écrire = écrit faire = fait; lire = lu; mettre = mis; prendre = pris; venir = venu; voir = vu*

**6** **Copy out the sentences with the correct past participle.**

**a** J'ai (décider) de retrouver la forme.
**b** J'ai (acheter) des fruits et des légumes.
**c** J'ai (prendre) mon vélo, pas la voiture.
**d** J'ai (boire) beaucoup d'eau.
**e** J'ai (faire) de l'exercice tous les jours.
**f** J'ai (perdre) des kilos!

### WHEN TO USE *AVOIR* OR *ÊTRE*

- Most verbs use *avoir* in the perfect tense.
- Some common verbs, mostly verbs associated with movement, use *être*.

Learn them by heart (pair them up or create a mnemonic from the first letter of each verb, such as *Ms van der Tramp*).

*aller/venir; entrer/sortir; arriver/partir; monter/descendre; rester/retourner; naître/mourir; tomber.*

**7** **Copy out and complete these sentences with either *être* or *avoir*.**

*Père:* Qu'est-ce que tu ** fait, hier soir? Où **-tu allée?
*Fille:* Euh... je ** sortie avec Luc et Léo et j'** mangé au Macdo.
*Père:* Et après le Macdo, où **-vous allés? Qu' **-vous fait?
*Fille:* Euh. On ** joué au flipper dans un bar.
*Père:* Menteuse! Hier soir, Luc et Léo ** venus ici! Ils ** demandé où tu étais. Nous ** discuté longtemps. Alors? La vérité?
*Fille:* Je ** allée chez ma copine Zoé et on ** fait nos devoirs ensemble...
*Père:* Quoi! Quelle horreur!

### AGREEMENT OF PAST PARTICIPLES

The past participle agrees like an adjective when it is used...

- after *être*: it agrees with the subject of the verb

| | |
|---|---|
| *Je suis/Tu es parti(**e**)* | *Nous sommes parti(**e**)**s*** |
| *Il est parti/Elle est parti**e*** | *Vous êtes parti(**e**)(**s**)* |
| *On est parti(**e**)(**s**)* | *Ils sont parti**s**/Elles sont parti**es*** |

- after *avoir*: it agrees with the object of the verb when the object is placed before the verb

*J'aime la recette (fem.) que tu m'as donné**e**.*
*Le problème, c'est les sucreries (fem. pl.) que j'ai mangé**es**.*
*J'ai aimé les légumes (masc. pl.) que j'ai mangé**s**.*

**8** **Copy and fill in the past participle endings.**

**a** Toute la classe a passé __ la journée au stade.
**b** Les filles sont all__ nager à la piscine.
**c** Ma copine Léa est resté__ dans les vestiaires.
**d** Elle n'a pas voulu__ nager.
**e** Les garçons ont fait__ de l'athlétisme.
**f** La natation est l'activité que j'ai préféré__.

# 1A Controlled Assessment: Speaking

## TASK: Healthy lifestyle

You are going to have a conversation with your teacher about healthy lifestyles. Your teacher will ask you the following:

- What is your usual diet at home and when you are out?
- How sporty are you?
- What do you do that is particularly good or bad for your health?
- What have you done recently to keep fit and healthy?
- What are your resolutions for keeping fit and healthy?
- !

*(! Remember: at this point, you will have to respond to something you have not prepared.)*

The dialogue will last between 4 and 6 minutes.

## 1 THINK!

**Read the phrases below. Write down any others that you might find useful for the speaking task.**

- ☐ **My diet:** Je mange... tous les jours, de temps en temps, je suis allergique à...
- ☐ **Sports I do:** Je fais du/de la..., je joue au/à la... je suis membre de...
- ☐ **Healthy or unhealthy habits:** Je me couche tôt/tard, je fume, je bois..., je mange équilibré/des sucreries...
- ☐ **What I have done to keep fit:** je suis allé(e)..., j'ai fait... je n'ai pas bu/mangé/fumé...
- ☐ **Healthy resolutions:** Je vais... (faire plus d'exercice), je ne vais plus... (boire/fumer)...
- ☐ **Giving reasons and examples:** pour, parce que, par exemple, comme

***! Can you predict what the unexpected question might be?***

Why is it important to keep fit and healthy when you are a teenager?

What sports facilities or activities are there in your area?

**Add to your list any language you would need to answer these questions too.**

## 2 PLAN!

- **Listen to the model conversation. Your teacher has the script.**
- **Listen again and note down any phrases you could use or adapt. Add these to your list from Step 1.**

## 3 ACTION !

**Now prepare your answers. Use the bullet points below to help you and your list of useful words and phrases from Steps 1 and 2.**

**1** What is your usual diet at home and when you are out?

- Use the present tense to say what you usually do, e.g. ***je mange, je bois...***
- Mention different food types and places: ***fruits, légumes, viande, poisson,*** etc; ***à la maison, à la cantine,*** etc.
- Add a little extra detail to make it more interesting, e.g. ***Je ne bois pas de lait parce que je suis allergique.***

**2** How sporty are you?

- Mention the sports you do and when you do them, e.g. ***je fais de la natation tous les samedis.***
- If you are not sporty, say why and mention the exercise you do, e.g. ***je n'aime pas le sport parce que ça ne m'intéresse pas mais par contre, je marche beaucoup.***
- Try explaining in different ways, e.g. ***parce que je n'aime pas ça, car c'est trop difficile.***

**3** What do you do that is particularly good or bad for your health?

- Give examples of what you do that you think is good for your health, e.g. ***j'ai une bonne alimentation; par exemple, j'évite les aliments gras comme les frites.***
- You can use ***par contre*** to oppose this to what you do which may not be so healthy, e.g. ***Par contre, je mange trop de chocolat et de gâteaux.***
- Show off your use of reflexive verbs: ***je me lève tôt, je me couche, je m'entraîne.***

**4** What have you done recently to keep fit and healthy?

- This is your chance to show off your use of the perfect tense. If you haven't done anything, invent something!
- Mention several things you did, using perfect tense verbs, e.g. ***j'ai fait du vélo, je suis allé(e) en ville à pied.*** You could add an opinion using the imperfect, e.g. ***c'était génial/j'étais content(e).***
- Use words to link your ideas together, e.g. ***Comme j'avais le temps, j'ai fait...; Quand je suis allé(e)..., j'ai fait...***

**5** What are your resolutions for keeping fit and healthy?

- This is your chance to show off your use of the future with ***aller*** + infinitive, which is the typical tense used for speaking about resolutions, e.g. ***Je vais faire plus d'exercice.***
- You could use the conditional to mention your goals, e.g. ***Je voudrais me muscler/perdre du poids.***
- Remember to use a variety of expressions of time and frequency, e.g. ***tous les jours, régulièrement, souvent.***

### GRADE TARGET

**To reach Grade C, you need to:**

- speak clearly (try to remember the liaisons!).
- use the main tenses correctly (e.g. present tense for what you usually do, perfect tense for what you did in the past, future tense with ***aller*** + infinitive for what you are intending to do).
- use ***parce que*** to give reasons.

**To aim higher than a C, you could:**

- use a greater variety of tenses, e.g. use the imperfect or a future tense to give an opinion about something (***c'était/ce sera super!***) or a conditional to say what you would like (***j'aimerais/je voudrais arrêter de fumer***).
- use link words to create longer sentences, e.g. ***parce que, mais***.
- use a range of expressions of time or frequency (***hier, demain, souvent, régulièrement***).

**To aim for an A or A*, you could:**

- use a '***quand***' clause, e.g. ***quand il fait beau, je vais me promener***.
- use the pronouns ***en*** and ***y***, e.g. ***j'aime les fruits et les légumes et j'en mange tous les jours; j'y vais à pied***.
- use adverbs to add detail and colour to what you are saying, e.g. ***Je vais probablement/radicalement changer mes habitudes***.

# 1A Controlled Assessment: Writing

## TASK: An article about your favourite sportsperson

A French magazine is asking young people to present their favourite sports personality for the 'Top Ten Sports Personality Award'. Choose yours and write a text explaining why you think he/she should be included in the Top 10.

You could include the following:

- Their personal details.
- Their sport (what they do, when they started, etc.).
- Their career (when, where).
- Their main achievements (what, where, when).
- What you think they will achieve in the future.
- Why you chose this person.

## 1 THINK!

**Start by researching and noting down a few key facts and phrases:**

1. Personal details: name, age, where he/she is from, etc.
2. Sport: *sport individuel? sport d'équipe?*
3. Career: research the landmarks (year he/she first started, first tournament/victory) etc. *championnat, victoire, vainqueur,* etc.
4. Achievements: list the highlights of his/her career, his/her successes and victories: *en 2009, il/elle a participé; il/elle a gagné...*
5. Achievements: what you think he/she will go on to achieve in the future.
6. Why him/her: explain why you chose him/her, give your opinion. Try to be convincing!

## 2 PLAN!

- **Read the model text.**

Mon sportif préféré s'appelle Lewis Hamilton. Il est né en 1985 et il vient de Stevenage, en Angleterre. C'est un pilote de Formule 1. Il a toujours aimé les automobiles: il a commencé par le karting à 8 ans. Il a gagné son premier championnat national de karting à 9 ans! Il a commencé le sport automobile en 2002; il avait juste 17 ans. Il a participé au championnat deux ans après et il a gagné. Il est devenu champion de formule 3 en 2005, champion de formule 2 en 2006. En 2007, il est devenu professionnel et a commencé en Formule 1 dans l'équipe McLaren. C'était génial!

Il est allé à plusieurs grands prix et il est devenu vice-champion du monde. En 2008, il a remporté les Grands Prix d'Australie, de Monaco, de Grande-Bretagne et d'Allemagne. Il est devenu champion du monde!

J'ai choisi Lewis Hamilton car il est jeune, passionné par son sport et il a un excellent palmarès. Comme il doit s'entraîner comme les grands sportifs, ce n'est pas une vie facile: il fait de la course à pied, du vélo et de la natation environ quatre heures par jour. En plus, il doit suivre un régime strict pour contrôler son poids. Selon moi, c'est admirable chez un jeune! Je pense très sincèrement que Lewis Hamilton va encore gagner beaucoup de courses et qu'il sera le plus grand pilote automobile de Formule 1 du monde!

- **Read the text again and note down any words or phrases that you could use. Add these to your list from Step 1.**
- **Look carefully at the tenses used and make a note of any you could reuse:**
  present tense for descriptions – ***il s'appelle/il vient de/il a... ans***
  perfect tense for completed actions – ***il a commencé...***
  future tense for what will happen in the future – ***il va devenir...***

## 3 ACTION!

**Now prepare what you will write. Use the bullet points below to help you and use your list of useful words and phrases from Steps 1 and 2. Aim to write about 200 words.**

**1** Personal details
- ***Il/Elle s'appelle...; Il/Elle est né(e) en..., à... Il/Elle a... ans.***
- Concentrate on details that are relevant to describe him or her.

**2** Sport
- ***Il est footballeur; il/elle fait du ski/joue au tennis.***
- Remember to use ***faire du/de l'/de la*** for a sport practised individually and ***jouer au/à l'/à la...*** for a sport played in a team.

**3** Career
- ***Il/Elle a commencé... en [date], à l'âge de... il/elle a fait son premier match/tournoi...***
- Use the perfect tense for actions that took place in the past and are now over.
- Use the imperfect to describe what it was like at the time or to give an opinion, e.g. ***il avait 17 ans. C'était génial!***

**4** Achievements
- ***Il/Elle a participé à...; il/elle a gagné...; il/elle est devenu(e) champion(ne).***
- Use the perfect tense. Remember, some verbs make the perfect tense with ***être***, e.g. ***il/elle est allé(e), il/elle est devenu(e)...***

**5** Future achievements
- ***Il/Elle va participer..., Il/Elle participera..., Il/Elle va devenir/deviendra...***
- Use ***aller*** + infinitive or a future tense to say what you think will happen to your sports personality.

**6** Why him/her
- ***Il/Elle est génial(e); c'est un/une sportif/ive extraordinaire; c'est le meilleur/la meilleure... il/elle va devenir...***
- Express your opinion strongly to be convincing, e.g. ***Je pense sincèrement que.../Je pense que vous êtes d'accord avec moi pour dire que X est le sportif idéal...***

### GRADE TARGET

**To reach Grade C, you need to:**
- include explanations and opinions, using e.g. ***parce que*** and ***Je pense que...***
- use the perfect tense correctly.
- check all spellings.

**To aim higher than a C, you could:**
- use a greater variety of tenses, e.g. use the present to describe the sportsperson's routine, the perfect to describe his/her achievements, the future to say what else he/she is likely to achieve.
- use French determiners correctly, e.g. ***il aime le sport automobile; il joue au tennis***.
- create longer, more complex sentences by using link words (***et, mais,*** etc.).

**To aim for an A or A*, you could:**
- try to use a variety of verbs: modal verbs (***devoir, pouvoir,*** etc.) and reflexive verbs, e.g. ***s'entraîner, s'améliorer***.
- use adverbs to give more weight to your argument, e.g. ***vraiment, sincèrement***.
- use description and more sophisticated link words, e.g. ***comme..., alors,*** etc. to avoid short sentences.

# 1A Vocabulaire

### Comment choisir le sport idéal

| | |
|---|---|
| allergique | *allergic* |
| fanatique | *fanatical, enthusiastic* |
| nul(le) | *no good at* |
| sportif/sportive | *sporty* |
| avoir envie de | *to feel like...* |
| ça m'intéresse | *I'm interested in* |
| détester | *to hate* |
| devoir | *to have to, must* |
| faire partie d'une équipe | *to play in a team* |
| se familiariser | *to familiarise oneself* |
| participer | *to take part* |
| pouvoir | *to be able to* |
| savoir | *to know how to* |
| soutenir une équipe | *to support a team* |
| voler | *to fly* |
| vouloir faire | *to want to do* |

### Comment se muscler sans danger!

| | |
|---|---|
| souvent | *often* |
| jamais | *never* |
| rarement | *rarely* |
| régulièrement | *regularly* |
| absolument | *absolutely* |
| s'alimenter | *to eat* |
| s'améliorer | *to improve* |
| se blesser | *to get injured* |
| bouger | *to move* |
| se disputer | *to argue* |
| se distraire | *to have fun* |
| s'endormir | *to go to sleep* |
| s'échauffer | *to warm up* |
| s'empêcher | *to stop oneself* |
| s'étirer | *to stretch* |
| se fatiguer | *to get tired* |
| se lever | *to get up* |
| se motiver | *to motivate oneself* |
| s'organiser | *to get organised* |
| se priver | *to deprive oneself* |
| se protéger | *to protect oneself* |
| se réparer | *to mend itself* |
| se reposer | *to rest* |
| se réveiller | *to wake up* |

### Comment bien manger

| | |
|---|---|
| ajouter | *to add* |
| beurrer | *to butter* |
| fouetter | *to beat* |
| garder | *to keep* |
| incorporer | *to fold* |
| préchauffer | *to preheat* |
| remuer | *to stir* |
| verser | *to pour* |
| certain/certaine | *some, certain* |
| chaque | *each* |
| plusieurs | *several* |
| tout/toute/tous/toutes | *all* |

### Comment éviter les mauvaises habitudes

| | |
|---|---|
| C'est dangereux pour la santé | *It's dangerous for your health* |
| Il va boire | *He's going to drink* |
| Je dois perdre | *I must lose* |
| Je ne peux pas m'empêcher de manger... | *I can't stop myself eating...* |
| Je ne vais plus boire... | *I'm not going to drink... any more* |
| Je veux être en bonne santé | *I want to be healthy* |
| Le cas/L'exemple de X montre/prouve que... | *The case/example of... shows/ proves that...* |
| On doit manger | *You must eat* |
| Qu'est-ce que je dois faire? | *What should I do?* |
| Si on prend le cas/l'exemple de X, on voit que... | *If we take the case/example of..., we see that...* |
| comme | *like* |
| entre autres | *among others* |
| par exemple | *for example* |

### Comment retrouver la forme

| | |
|---|---|
| la charcuterie | *cooked meats* |
| un effet sur ma santé | *an effect on my health* |
| les sucreries (*fpl*) | *sweet things* |
| déjà | *already* |
| par contre | *on the other hand* |
| radicalement | *radically* |
| Ça n'a pas été facile | *It hasn't been easy* |
| changer son style de vie | *to change one's lifestyle* |
| maigrir | *to lose weight* |
| j'ai commencé à fumer | *I started to smoke* |
| j'ai eu de la chance | *I was lucky* |
| j'ai remplacé | *I replaced* |
| j'ai toujours détesté | *I've always hated* |
| je suis allé(e) | *I went* |
| juste pour essayer | *just to try* |
| pendant longtemps | *for a long time* |

# 1B Vivre ensemble

## Sais-tu comment…

- ❑ trouver ton copain idéal?
- ❑ discuter de ta vie de famille?
- ❑ dire si le mariage est pour toi?
- ❑ en savoir plus sur un ado en prison?
- ❑ parler du problème de la pauvreté?

## Controlled assessment

- **Talk about your virtual family on *Second Life***
- **Write a letter to the president of France about a social issue that concerns you**

**C'est comment, ta vie de famille?**

## Stratégies

### À l'oral

When speaking, how do you…
- pronounce vowel sounds and endings correctly?
- learn vocabulary to ensure you have the right word at your fingertips?
- keep a conversation going when you don't understand?

### Lecture

When reading, can you…
- correctly interpret conjunctions which connect opposing ideas?
- identify key words that indicate opinions?
- scan for the important points in a reading passage?

## Grammaire active

As part of your French language 'toolkit' can you…
- position adjectives correctly and make them agree?
- use the immediate future and simple future?
- use 'if' clauses?
- use different negatives correctly?

# 1B Comment trouver ton copain idéal

(G) Les adjectifs (V) Personnalité (S) Stratégies pour apprendre; le français parlé
(P) Les adjectifs masculins et féminins

## Son signe = son caractère?

Tu connais le signe de ton copain/ta copine? Alors, on te révèle les secrets de son caractère! (Mais ne prends pas ça trop au sérieux.)

### Bélier

**21 mars – 20 avril**

Il/Elle est charismatique et il/elle adore être le centre d'attention. Il/Elle aime s'amuser mais il/elle peut être* un peu têtu(e).

### Taureau

**21 avril – 21 mai**

Il/Elle est indépendant(e) et romantique. Pour lui/elle, la famille et les amis sont très importants. Il/Elle travaille bien en groupe.

### Gémeaux

**22 mai – 21 juin**

Il/Elle a très bonne mémoire. Il/Elle a besoin de* sécurité dans la vie. Il/Elle est assez romantique.

### Cancer

**22 juin - 22 juillet**

Il/Elle est loyal(e) et passionné(e). Il/Elle est aussi têtu(e). Il/Elle adore les petits luxes de la vie. Il/Elle a l'air* sympa.

### Lion

**23 juillet – 22 août**

Il/Elle a beaucoup de copains/copines et de centres d'intérêt. Il/Elle aime parler et discuter. Il/Elle est assez actif/active.

### Vierge

**23 août – 22 septembre**

Il/Elle est enthousiaste et aventureux/aventureuse. Il/Elle adore apprendre des choses nouvelles mais il/elle n'est pas très organisé(e).

### Balance

**23 septembre – 22 octobre**

Il/Elle est responsable et très organisé(e). Il/Elle peut être un peu timide. Il/Elle est intelligent(e) et déterminé(e).

### Scorpion

**23 octobre – 22 novembre**

Il/Elle est créatif/créative et romantique. Il/Elle est très actif/active et il/elle aime le sport et l'art dramatique.

### Sagittaire

**23 novembre – 21 décembre**

Normalement il/elle fait beaucoup de choses en même temps et il/elle peut être un peu anxieux/anxieuse. Il/Elle est gentil/gentille et il/elle a un très bon sens de l'humour.

### Capricorne

**22 décembre - 20 janvier**

Il/Elle est très drôle, mais il/elle est aussi sensible et déterminé(e). Il/Elle peut être un peu égoïste.

### Verseau

**21 janvier – 19 février**

Il/Elle a beaucoup d'énergie et il/elle est très généreux/généreuse. Il/Elle adore voyager et il/elle est aventureux/aventureuse mais aussi responsable.

### Poissons
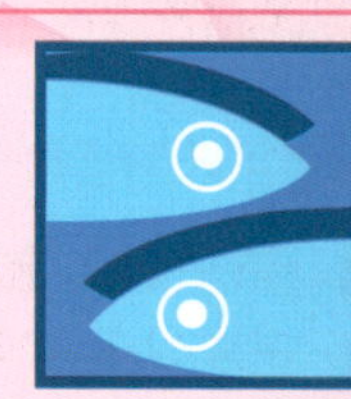

**20 février – 20 mars**

Il/Elle est indépendant(e) et fidèle. Il/Elle est travailleur/travailleuse et il/elle aime étudier. Il/Elle peut être un peu excentrique!

* il/elle peut être – *he/she can be...*
il/elle a l'air – *he/she seems...*

* il/elle a besoin de – *he/she needs...*

**1** Lis l'article. C'est a ou b?

- **a** *Horoscope predictions based on your sign of the zodiac*
- **b** *Personality description based on your star sign.*

**2** Ton anniversaire, c'est quand? Quel est le nom de ton signe en français?

**3** Relis les descriptifs. Relie les mots soulignés avec l'équivalent anglais.

*Exemple:* **a** *kind* – gentil(le)

- **a** *kind*
- **b** *independent*
- **c** *organised*
- **d** *funny*
- **e** *selfish*
- **f** *active*
- **g** *stubborn*
- **h** *hard-working*
- **i** *shy*
- **j** *generous*

## GRAMMAIRE

**Adjectives**

When you use an adjective, make sure it agrees with the noun it is describing, i.e. masculine or feminine, singular or plural. Most adjectives follow this regular pattern:

| | masculine | feminine |
|---|---|---|
| Singular | Il est intelligent. | Elle est intelligent**e**. |
| Plural | Ils sont intelligent**s**. | Elles sont intelligent**es**. |

However, some have a different pattern, e.g.: *sensible/sensible, travailleur/travailleuse, gentil/gentille, actif/active.*

Also, some adjectives never change, e.g. *sympa, cool.*

**4** Quelles sont les formes féminines des adjectifs dans la liste (activité 3)?

**5** Écoute Samuel et Sarah. Note les différences entre les adjectifs masculins et féminins.

**6** Dans les descriptifs, trouve d'autres adjectifs pour décrire quelqu'un et traduis-les en anglais.

*Exemple:* charismatique – *charismatic*

## STRATÉGIES

There are different ways to learn new words. The best method for you depends on what type of learner you are.

**If you remember by seeing...** make a wall poster.

**If you learn better by hearing...** record them and play them back to yourself.

**If you prefer to learn by doing...** cut up small cards with the words and their meanings and play matching games.

**7** Choisis et apprends huit mots de la page 30 en utilisant une des stratégies ci-dessus.

**8a** À deux. A dit le nom d'une célébrité. B dit un adjectif pour la décrire. Attention – utilisez la bonne forme de l'adjectif! (B↔A)

*Exemple:* Alan Carr – drôle; Serena Williams – active

## STRATÉGIES

Improve your spoken French by making sure that when you use adjectives you leave silent endings and only pronounce final syllables when necessary, e.g. *un garçon indépendant/une fille indépendante*. Also make your pronunciation clear so that the listener can differentiate between, e.g., *actif/active*.

**8b** Faites des phrases plus longues pour exprimer votre opinion. Attention à la prononciation!

*Exemple:*

**A** À mon avis, Alan Carr est extrêmement drôle.

**B** Je trouve que Serena Williams est très active.

**9** Traduis les phrases en français.

- **a** *My parents are very active and hard-working too.*
- **b** *My sister is independent and very organised.*
- **c** *My brothers are a bit selfish.*
- **d** *My stepmother is quite stubborn but very funny.*
- **e** *My grandparents are very generous and kind.*

**10** Écoute (1–5). Choisis a ou b.

1. *Carine's ideal friend is*
   - **a** *intelligent and sensitive*
   - **b** *hard-working.*
2. *For Hugo the most important quality is*
   - **a** *loyalty*
   - **b** *a sense of humour.*
3. *Sara's ideal friend is*
   - **a** *not selfish*
   - **b** *not shy.*
4. *Ali's ideal friend would be*
   - **a** *adventurous and active.*
   - **b** *sporty and independent.*
5. *Juliette values*
   - **a** *kindness and enthusiasm*
   - **b** *creativity and loyalty.*

**11** Lis et écoute tous les descriptifs. Ton descriptif te va bien? À ton avis, quel descriptif te correspond le mieux? Donne tes raisons.

*Exemple:* Le descriptif Poissons me correspond le mieux parce que je suis travailleuse... etc.

## À VOUS!

**12** Write the profile of your ideal friend (boy or girl) for a French website. Which star sign do you think they should be? Write about 50 words.

**13** You are applying to go on the reality TV show, *Koh Lanta*, which is the French equivalent of *Shipwrecked*. Write a few lines about your personality (strong and weak points) and explain why you are the ideal candidate. Then work in groups. Each person does an audition. Choose the best candidate.

# 1B Comment discuter de ta vie de famille

(G) Position des adjectifs (S) Éviter les silences (P) Les voyelles (V) La vie de famille

## La vie de famille – un lieu de bonheur?

À votre avis, est-ce que la famille est le premier lieu de bonheur?

Théo, 17 ans

La vie de famille est très importante pour moi. J'habite avec mes parents et mon frère aîné. Je m'entends très bien avec mon père. Il m'écoute et me conseille. Je suis adopté et j'apprécie beaucoup la stabilité et le soutien de ma famille. Nous faisons beaucoup de choses ensemble et je crois que c'est important.

Noémie, 15 ans

Mes parents sont divorcés et j'habite avec mon père, ma belle-mère et mes deux demi-frères. On s'entend assez bien, mais il y a des disputes familiales de temps en temps bien sûr. Moi, je préfère éviter les conflits. J'ai un bon rapport avec ma belle-mère. Elle est très sympa et je peux lui parler de tout.

Pour moi, la vie de famille est un peu difficile. Je ne m'entends pas du tout avec ma mère. On se dispute souvent et j'ai l'impression qu'elle ne m'écoute pas. Mes parents sont divorcés et je ne vois plus mon père. Il y a souvent une ambiance tendue chez moi. Par conséquent, je parle de mes problèmes avec mes copains. Non, la vie familiale n'est pas heureuse pour moi.

Aurélie, 16 ans

Mes parents peuvent être assez exigeants mais on s'entend bien quand même. Je me dispute un peu avec ma sœur mais la plupart du temps, ça va. J'ai de très bonnes relations avec mes grands-parents et je passe beaucoup de temps chez eux. Je trouve que la vie de famille n'est pas parfaite tout le temps, il faut faire un effort pour vivre heureux ensemble.

Laurent, 16 ans

**1** Lis les textes. Qui...

*Exemple:* **a** Aurélie

- **a** est membre d'une famille monoparentale?
- **b** évite les disputes si possible?
- **c** s'entend très bien avec sa famille?
- **d** pense qu'il faut faire un effort pour avoir de bonnes relations?

**2** Note les phrases qui correspondent aux suivantes:

*Exemple:* **a** Je m'entends très bien avec mon père

- **a** *I get on really well with my dad*
- **b** *I don't get on at all with my mum*
- **c** *We argue a lot*
- **d** *I talk about my problems with my friends*
- **e** *there are family arguments from time to time*
- **f** *my parents can be quite demanding*
- **g** *I argue a bit with my sister*
- **h** *I have a really good relationship with*
- **i** *to make an effort to live happily together*

**3** Écoute Sandrine qui parle de sa vie de famille. Puis écris trois phrases de son journal intime.

*Exemple:* je m'entends assez bien avec mes parents...

**VOCABULAIRE**

Je m'entends bien avec... On s'entend bien.
J'ai un bon rapport avec...
Je me dispute avec... Il/Elle (ne) me comprend (pas).
Nous (ne) faisons (pas) beaucoup de choses ensemble.
J'ai de bonnes relations avec...

**STRATÉGIES**

If you don't understand what someone is asking you or aren't sure, avoid uncomfortable silences by asking for clarification, e.g.

*Pouvez-vous répéter, s'il vous plaît?*

*Comment?*

*Qu'est-ce que ça veut dire,...?*

*Je ne sais pas. Je ne suis pas sûr(e).*

**4** Jeu de rôle: **A** choisit une personne de ta page 32 et **B** pose des questions sur sa famille. Tu peux utiliser le «vocabulaire», page 32. (**A**↔**B**)

*Exemples:* Dans ta famille, tu t'entends bien avec qui?

Et tu te disputes avec qui? Pourquoi?

Ta vie de famille est heureuse? Pourquoi?

## Des changements dans la vie familiale

Actuellement on peut dire qu'il n'existe pas de famille typique. La famille est toujours en train de changer et maintenant la famille existe sous plusieurs formes différentes. Familles monoparentales, familles traditionnelles, séparations et divorces...

Il y a des changements aussi quant au travail. Dans les années cinquante, la plupart des mères de famille ne travaillaient pas. Aujourd'hui, on voit une variété de situations. Beaucoup de mères travaillent, plus de personnes travaillent chez elles, les pères s'occupent de la maison et des enfants, tout est possible.

Mais est-ce que les relations familiales aussi ont changé? Il y a toujours des difficultés relationnelles dans les familles et des disputes entre parents et ados. L'image de la famille a changé mais la vie de famille est peut-être toujours la même.

**5** Recopie et complète le résumé de l'article.

*Exemple:* **a** familles

Aujourd'hui, il y a plusieurs types de **a**.

De la même façon, le monde du **b** a évolué. Plus de femmes travaillent et les **c** peuvent choisir de rester à la maison et garder les **d**.

Les relations **e** ne sont pas très différentes, il y a toujours des **f** et des difficultés.

Même si **g** de la famille n'est plus la même, la vie de famille n'a pas trop **h**.

familiales pères changé familles enfants disputes l'image travail

**6** Écoute pour vérifier.

**GRAMMAIRE**

**Adjectives**

Most adjectives go after the noun:

*une famille* ***sympa****, des relations* ***difficiles****, les parents* ***exigeants***

Some adjectives come before the noun:

*une* ***grande*** *famille, ma* ***petite*** *sœur, de* ***bonnes*** *relations*

Other common adjectives which come before the noun are:

*jeune, vieux, mauvais, nouveau, beau, gros, joli.*

(See page 183 for more information.)

**7** Trouve d'autres exemples d'adjectifs dans cette unité. Recopie et remplis la grille.

| Adjectifs avant le nom | Adjectifs après le nom |
|---|---|
| un énorme verre | les cheveux bruns |

**STRATÉGIES**

When speaking, pay attention to the sounds *u*/*ou*, *en*/*on*/*an*, accented letters and nasal sounds (m or n after a vowel).

**8** Écoute les phrases suivantes et répète.

- **a** mon frère aîné
- **b** je m'entends
- **c** il m'écoute
- **d** on se dispute souvent
- **e** mes parents sont divorcés
- **f** j'ai un bon rapport

## À VOUS!

**9** Prepare a mini-presentation of about one to two minutes on your family life.

- Décris ta famille.
- Comment est ta vie familiale?
- Quels sont les ingrédients d'une vie de famille heureuse à ton avis?

**10** Write a message on your real or imaginary blog. Describe your relationships with the members of your family.

# 1B Comment dire si le mariage est pour toi

(G) Adjectifs possessifs; parler du futur (V) Mariage, rapports avec les autres

(S) Reconnaître les oppositions

**C'est vrai!**

- En France, l'âge moyen du mariage: 31 ans pour les hommes, 29 ans pour les femmes.
- Le mois le plus populaire pour les mariages, c'est juillet.
- Un bébé sur deux naît hors mariage.
- À Paris, un couple sur deux divorce.

## Forum-Internet

Fichier Actions Outils ?

**Mes parents pensent que se marier et avoir des enfants est le mode de vie idéal. Pourtant, les divorces sont nombreux. Qu'en penses-tu?**

**1 Tu es pour ou contre le mariage?**
**2 Est-ce que tu vas te marier plus tard?**
**3 Crois-tu qu'il est possible de trouver ton/ta partenaire idéal(e) sur le web?**

Fatiah

Je suis pour le mariage. Je ne suis pas solitaire. En France, un adulte sur trois vit seul et c'est triste. Pourtant, de plus en plus de couples ne sont pas mariés. Plus tard, je ne veux pas vivre seul mais je ne me marierai pas trop jeune. Je vais peut-être me marier à 30 ans. Mon copain a trouvé sa petite amie sur Internet, mais je ne vais pas chercher des relations amoureuses sur le web. À mon avis, sur Internet, les gens vont cacher leurs défauts.

Martin

Beaucoup de gens vivent seuls: célibataires, divorcés, veufs. Nos parents pensent que le mariage est important tandis que les jeunes préfèrent leur liberté. Je n'ai pas l'intention de me marier. Je ne vais pas avoir d'enfants non plus. Par contre, si je tombe amoureuse, on pourra toujours vivre ensemble. Le coup de foudre* sur le web? Pourquoi pas? Les sites de rencontre en ligne sont une bonne idée. Je vais les essayer!

Valentine

* falling in love

**1** À deux. Regardez les photos et le texte «C'est vrai!», page 34. Vous avez cinq minutes pour faire une liste de mots associés au mariage. Qui a la liste la plus longue? (Utilisez un dictionnaire pour vous aider.)

**2** Lis et écoute Fatiah et Martin. Réponds en anglais.

- **a** *What do Fatiah's parents think is the ideal way of life?*
- **b** *Why does Fatiah think they may be wrong?*
- **c** *Is Martin in favour of getting married? Why?*
- **d** *What will he do when he is thirty?*
- **e** *Does he think you can find love on the internet?*

**3** Lis la réponse de Valentine. Comment dit-elle...?

- **a** *lots of people live alone*
- **b** *single people*
- **c** *I don't intend to get married*
- **d** *I am not going to have children*
- **e** *we'll always be able to live together*
- **f** *I'll try them*

**GRAMMAIRE**

**Possessive adjectives**

Possessive adjectives indicate who something belongs to (**my** idea, **your** DVD, **his** car). The adjective changes to match the noun which follows: masculine or feminine, singular or plural, e.g.

| | |
|---|---|
| ***Sa*** *cousine déteste* ***ton*** *frère.* | His cousin hates your brother. |
| *Où sont* ***mes*** *baskets?* | Where are my trainers? |

See also page 184.

**4** Recopie et complète la grille avec les adjectifs possessifs que tu trouveras, page 34.

| | Singular | | Plural |
|---|---|---|---|
| | masculine | feminine | masculine/feminine |
| my | ? | ma | ? |
| your | ton | ta | tes |
| his/her | son | ? | ses |
| our | notre | notre | ? |
| your | votre | votre | vos |
| their | leur | ? | ? |

**5** À deux. **A** pose les questions de Fatiah. **B** joue le rôle de Martin ou de Valentine et répond. (**A↔B**)

**6** Écoute (1–5). De quoi parlent-ils? Choisis la bonne lettre.

- **A** *having children*
- **B** *getting married*
- **C** *divorce*
- **D** *online dating sites*
- **E** *staying single*

**STRATÉGIES**

Be alert when reading or listening. The following expressions indicate opposing ideas:

| | |
|---|---|
| ***mais*** | but |
| ***pourtant*** | however |
| ***tandis que*** | whereas |
| ***par contre*** | on the other hand |

Find an example of each on the internet forum, page 34, and translate the sentences into English.

**GRAMMAIRE**

**Talking about the future**

There are two ways to talk about the future:

- *Aller* + infinitive: *Tu vas te marier?* Are you going to get married?
- Future tense verb: *Je ne me marierai pas.* I won't get married.

**7** Imagine ton avenir. Écris huit phrases qui commencent par: ***Un jour, je vais...***

*Exemple:* Un jour, je vais avoir une belle moto.

**8a** Écoute (1–5). Ils sont pour ou contre le mariage?

**8b** Réécoute deux ou trois fois. Note le plus possible de détails. Compare avec un(e) partenaire.

## À VOUS!

**9** Write your own message in answer to Fatiah's questions (page 34) to post on the internet forum.

**10** Interview your partner about the pros and cons of getting married. Prepare a list of between six and eight questions, but be prepared to respond to his/her answers rather than just sticking to the questions on your list. Record your interview for the class to listen to.

# 1B Comment en savoir plus sur un ado en prison

(G) Les pronoms sujets; si + verbe au présent (V) Les jeunes en prison
(S) Repérage d'infos dans un texte

## «JE M'APPELLE RÉMI, J'AI 15 ANS ET JE SUIS EN PRISON.»

Rémi est dans le quartier des mineurs d'une prison dans le nord de la France. Il parle de sa vie quotidienne.

«Ça fait six mois que je suis en prison. J'ai fait des bêtises… je suis condamné pour vol avec violence. Dans le quartier des mineurs (appelé section C), on est 15 adolescents de 13 à 18 ans.

Je dors dans une cellule individuelle. Le matin, je me réveille à sept heures. Pas question de rester au lit! Si je n'ai pas le droit de prendre une douche (douches collectives!), je me lave dans ma cellule mais je n'aime pas ça parce que l'eau est froide. Après, il faut nettoyer la cellule. Ensuite, c'est la promenade… on se promène dans une grande cour. J'aime ça. On peut aussi jouer au foot. Après la promenade, on rentre en cellule et on reste enfermés jusqu'à midi.

À midi, il faut manger seul dans la cellule. Les repas ne sont pas bons: ils ressemblent à ceux de la cantine quand j'étais au collège! Trois après-midi par semaine, j'ai cours. Il y a des profs qui viennent dans la prison.

Si je n'ai pas un entretien avec la psychiatre, il y a un film ou une autre activité, mais c'est rare. Nous passons la plus grande partie du temps dans nos cellules.

**Qui sont les mineurs en prison? En France, il y a environ 700 mineurs (moins de 18 ans) en prison. Leurs délits sont graves: vol, violence, usage de drogue, etc.**

On s'ennuie en prison. La dépression est un grand problème pour les jeunes ici. Moi, je dors beaucoup et je pense à ma mère et à mon chien. Ma mère vient me voir trois fois par semaine. Les visites (dans une petite cabine vitrée) durent une demi-heure. Ce n'est jamais assez long. Si je me comporte bien, dans trois mois je pourrai sortir. Je compte les jours!»

**1** Lis l'article, page 36, en entier. Rémi a quelle attitude?

**a** Être en prison, ça lui est égal.
**b** Il n'attend qu'une chose: sortir!
**c** Il pense que la prison, c'est une bonne chose pour lui.

**2** Relis l'article et note les mots français qui veulent dire:

**a** *to do something stupid*
**b** *theft*
**c** *a cell*
**d** *an interview*
**e** *a glass booth*
**f** *if I behave well*

**STRATÉGIES**

When scanning a text for specific information, don't waste time working out unnecessary detail. For example, in activity 3a question a, you will be on the lookout for an age, in question b for a time, etc.

**3a** Réponds aux questions.

**a** Les ados dans le quartier des mineurs ont quel âge?
**b** À quelle heure est-ce que Rémi se lève?
**c** Qu'est-ce qu'il fait comme exercice physique?
**d** Que pense-t-il des repas?
**e** Quand est-ce qu'il étudie?
**f** Qu'est-ce qu'il a comme activités?
**g** Comment est-ce qu'il trouve la vie en prison?

**3b** À deux. **A** pose les questions a–g. **B** joue le rôle de Rémi et répond. Si possible, ajoute des détails.

*Exemple:* Ils ont entre 13 et 18 ans et ils sont là parce qu'ils ont commis des délits graves.

**GRAMMAIRE**

***Si* = if**

*Si* + present tense can be followed by a present or future tense verb, e.g.

*Si je m'ennuie, je dors.* If I'm bored, I sleep.
*Si on attend, ce sera trop tard.* If we wait, it will be too late.

**4** Trouve dans l'article, page 36 des exemples de «si» et traduis-les en anglais.

**5** Écoute (1–10). Les phrases sont vraies ou fausses? Corrige les phrases fausses.

**GRAMMAIRE**

**Subject pronouns**

**Definite pronouns**

These are the little words that stand in for the names of specific people or things:

| | | | |
|---|---|---|---|
| Singular | *je* | *tu/vous* | *il/elle* |
| Plural | *nous* | *vous* | *ils/elles* |

In French, ***on*** often replaces ***nous*** to mean 'we':
*on se promène (= moi et les autres)*

**Indefinite pronouns**

Indefinite pronouns refer to people or things without mentioning who or what they are precisely.

***Il*** is used in set expressions, e.g. *il faut...*
***On*** is used to refer to 'one' or to people in general:
*On s'ennuie.* People get bored.

**6** Choisis un mot de l'encadré pour compléter chaque phrase.

**a** Les *** ont moins de dix-huit ans.
**b** Le *** est un délit grave.
**c** Les prisonniers dorment dans une ***.
**d** La *** est un grand problème dans les prisons.

dépression cellule vol mineurs

## À VOUS!

**7** Work with a partner. Imagine an interview with Rémi's mother. **A** asks the question and **B** replies using the information in the article, page 36. (**A**↔**B**)

*Exemple:* **A** Rémi est où en prison?
**B** Il est en prison dans le nord de la France. etc.

**8** Post a message (80–100 words) on a French internet forum saying what you think about putting young people in prison. You could say:

- how you think it will help (control, lessons, exercise, psychiatrist, etc.)
- the negative aspects (making bad friends, boredom, depression, can't see family, etc.)
- how you think the system for dealing with young offenders could be improved.

*Exemple:* À mon avis, il ne faut pas mettre les mineurs en prison, sauf quand ils ont commis... etc.
Pour améliorer le système, on pourrait...

# 1B Comment parler du problème de la pauvreté

Ⓖ La négation Ⓥ Opinions sur les inégalités dans la société
Ⓢ Identifier les mots clés qui indiquent un point de vue

**Noé:**
La France est un pays riche, alors pourquoi y a-t-il des gens pauvres? Trois millions de Français sont mal logés ou n'ont pas de logement. À mon avis, financer la construction d'appartements, c'est plus important que dépenser de l'argent pour l'armée ou les armes nucléaires.

**Cyrielle:**
La pauvreté, c'est quoi? Si on est pauvre, on n'a jamais assez d'argent, de nourriture, de chauffage. Dans mon quartier, il y a des SDF* qui n'ont rien. Toutes leurs possessions sont dans des sacs en plastique. Je pense qu'il faut les aider avec leurs problèmes.

* homeless people

**Ali:**
La pauvreté est partout: en Europe, en France, autour de nous. Le gouvernement promet des allocations aux chômeurs, aux retraités et aux familles monoparentales, mais ce n'est pas assez. Ce sont des actions qu'il faut, pas des promesses.

**Kévin:**
Il existe des organisations comme l'Armée du Salut et les Restos du Cœur qui aident les pauvres. À mon avis, en France, le problème n'est pas trop grave. Dans le reste du monde, les gens sont plus pauvres qu'en France. Dans le monde, une personne sur cinq vit avec seulement un euro par jour.

**Julie:**
On peut être exclu parce qu'on n'a pas beaucoup d'argent, parce qu'on n'est pas de la même nationalité ou parce qu'on n'est pas 'cool'. Mais dans notre société, la misère et l'exclusion sociale ne sont plus acceptables.

**Laura:**
Je dis 'non' à la pauvreté. C'est une question de dignité. La pauvreté est souvent causée par le chômage. La vie est moins difficile si on travaille. Mais je crois que même certains travailleurs vivent dans la misère parce qu'ils ne gagnent pas assez d'argent.

**1** Lis et écoute. Qui pense que la pauvreté n'est pas un grand problème en France?

**2** À deux. Relisez les bulles, page 38, et cherchez les mots nouveaux.

**3** Relis encore une fois les bulles. Qui l'a dit?

- **a** *France is a rich country.*
- **b** *Poverty is all around us, even in Europe.*
- **c** *Poverty and social exclusion are no longer acceptable.*
- **d** *There are organisations to help the poor.*
- **e** *Life is easier for those who work.*
- **f** *Homeless people keep their belongings in plastic bags.*
- **g** *Build homes rather than spend money on nuclear weapons.*
- **h** *Across the world, one in five people live on one euro a day.*

**4** Termine les phrases en anglais.

*Exemple:* **a** *who are badly housed or have no home.*

- **a** *Noé says there are three million people in France...*
- **b** *Cyrielle says homeless people...*
- **c** *Ali says promises...*
- **d** *Laura says even people who work...*
- **e** *Kévin says that the French are not...*
- **f** *Julie says people can be excluded because...*

**GRAMMAIRE**

**Negatives**

To make a sentence negative, put ***ne**... *pas*** around the verb:

| | |
|---|---|
| *Je suis riche.* | I am rich. |
| *Je **ne** suis **pas** riche.* | I am not rich. |

* *ne* becomes *n'* before a vowel:

| | |
|---|---|
| *il **n'a pas** de logement* | he doesn't have anywhere to live |

There are other negatives that work in the same way as ***ne... pas***:

| | |
|---|---|
| ***ne... jamais*** | never |
| ***ne... rien*** | nothing |
| ***ne... personne*** | no one |
| ***ne... plus*** | no longer |

See also *Grammaire active*, page 41.

**5** À deux. **A** joue le rôle d'un(e) des ados, page 38, et lit leur commentaire à haute voix. Sans regarder le livre, **B** lève la main quand il/elle entend une phrase négative. Ensemble, traduisez la phrase négative en anglais. (**B↔A**)

**GRAMMAIRE**

**Making comparisons**

| | |
|---|---|
| ***plus*** + adjective + ***que*** | = more... than... |
| ***moins*** + adjective + ***que*** | = less... than... |
| *La France est plus riche que le Mali.* | France is richer than Mali. |
| *J'ai moins d'argent que mon frère.* | I have less money than my brother. |

See also the Grammar Bank, page 184.

Find examples of comparisons on page 38 and give the English equivalents.

**STRATÉGIES**

Learn the key words to help you spot that someone is **giving an opinion** – useful when reading or listening! Find two more phrases on page 38 to add to this list.

| | |
|---|---|
| ***À mon avis*** | In my opinion |
| ***Je crois que*** | I believe that |

**6** Donne ton opinion sur les thèmes ci-dessous. Commence chaque phrase de façon différente.

la pauvreté, le chômage, les armes nucléaires, les organisations comme les Restos du Cœur.

## À VOUS!

**7** Write your own speech bubble to add to the *Non à la pauvreté!* article. Include:

- more than one phrase to introduce your opinions
- more than one negative phrase
- a comparison using *plus* or *moins*.

**8** Write five questions for a survey on social injustice. Then interview your partner. Record your interview if possible.

*Exemple:* Quelle est ta définition de la misère?

Est-ce qu'il y a des SDF dans ta ville?

À ton avis, est-ce que le chômage est un gros problème?

# 1B Grammaire active

## À l'agence matrimoniale

### ADJECTIVES

Most adjectives follow this regular pattern:

| | Masculine | Feminine |
|---|---|---|
| Singular | *Il est grand.* | *Elle est grand**e**.* |
| Plural | *Ils sont grand**s**.* | *Elles sont grand**es**.* |

| Masculine | Feminine |
|---|---|
| Adjectives ending in *-e*: *sensible* | remain the same: *sensible* |
| Adjectives ending in *-eur/-eux*: *travaill**eur**/aventur**eux*** | usually change to *-euse*: *travaill**euse**/aventur**euse*** |
| Adjectives ending in *-el/-il/-en*: *genti**l*** | double the final consonant: *genti**lle*** |
| Adjectives ending in *-if*: *acti**f*** | usually change to *-ive*: *acti**ve*** |
| Some adjectives stay the same: *sympa, super, marron, cool.* | |

Some adjectives are completely irregular. See page 184 for more information.

**1** **Read the cartoon. List the masculine and feminine forms of all the adjectives.**

*Exemple:*

| m. | f. |
|---|---|
| idéal | idéale |

**2** **Sébastien describes his pets. Copy and put the adjectives in brackets into French.**

*Exemple:* **a** têtu

Mon chien est **a** (stubborn), mais aussi très **b** (adventurous). Mes poissons sont **c** (beautiful) mais un peu **d** (shy). Ma souris est très **e** (active) et **f** (determined) et mes oiseaux sont un peu **g** (anxious). Et mon chat? Je crois que tous les chats sont **h** (independent) et **i** (selfish).

**3** **Copy and complete each sentence with at least three adjectives.**

**a** Les filles sont…
**b** Les garçons sont…
**c** Mes parents sont…
**d** Mon/Ma prof est…

### POSITION OF ADJECTIVES

Most adjectives go after the word they describe, e.g.:

*un ami* ***loyal***, *une idée* ***excentrique***, *des enfants* ***gentils***.

But some common adjectives go in front of the word they describe:

***grand, petit, gros, bon, beau, joli, nouveau, jeune, vieux.***

E.g. *une grande surprise, un vieux copain, de petits appartements.*

### NEGATIVES

In French, negatives usually have two parts: ***ne ... pas*** is the first negative you learn, but there are others which work in the same way:

***Ne ... jamais*** – never

| | |
|---|---|
| *Nous ne sortons jamais.* | We never go out. |

***Ne ... personne*** – no one (not anyone)

| | |
|---|---|
| *Je ne connais personne.* | I don't know anyone. |

***Ne ... plus*** – not any more (no longer)

| | |
|---|---|
| *Il ne va plus au club.* | He doesn't go to the club any more. |

***Ne ... rien*** – nothing (not anything)

| | |
|---|---|
| *Je ne vais rien acheter.* | I'm not going to buy anything. |

You might also meet ***ne ... guère*** (hardly, scarcely) and ***ne ... nulle part*** (nowhere).

***ne*** before a vowel or silent h = ***n'***: *Tu n'aimes pas le sport?*

Remember to look out for the second half of the negative when you are reading a text to make sure you understand the meaning fully.

**To make a sentence or question negative**

Put ***ne*** in front of the conjugated verb and ***pas*** after it:

***ne*** + verb + ***pas*** (or ***rien/jamais,*** etc.)

*Je ne vais pas à la fête.*

- in the perfect (or pluperfect) tense:
  *Asif* ***n'a pas*** *invité son cousin.*
  *Je* ***n'avais pas*** *répondu.*
- with verb + infinitive: *Tu* ***ne*** *peux* ***pas*** *venir?*
- with reflexive verbs: *On* ***ne*** *s'amuse* ***pas!*** (***ne*** before the pronoun, ***pas*** after the verb)
- reflexive verbs in the perfect: *Vous* ***ne*** *vous êtes* ***pas*** *ennuyés?*
- with imperatives: ***N'****invite* ***pas*** *Marie!* ***Ne*** *mangez* ***pas*** *mes chips!*

In informal spoken French, ***ne*** is often dropped:
*Je ne sais pas* → *Je sais pas* – I don't know.

**4** Translate into French. Think about the position of each adjective – before or after the noun?

- **a** the little girls
- **b** a generous old lady
- **c** an interesting family
- **d** a big fat dog
- **e** an anxious mother
- **f** a pretty garden

**5** Jim always does the opposite of Jules. Adapt sentences a–g for him.

*Exemple*: **a** Je n'aime plus aller à la plage.

- **a** J'aime aller à la plage. (*no longer*)
- **b** Je regarde la télé. (*no longer*)
- **c** J'ai lu le journal. (*not*)
- **d** Je veux manger au restaurant. (*never*)
- **e** Je mange le matin. (*nothing*)
- **f** Je vais jouer au foot. (*not any more*)
- **g** J'avais invité tous mes copains. (*not*)

**6** Translate into English.

- **a** Tu n'as rien fait d'intéressant?
- **b** Je ne suis jamais allé à l'étranger.
- **c** Loïc ne s'est pas amusé à la fête.
- **d** N'achète pas les baskets jaunes, Mathieu!
- **e** Vous n'allez pas inviter vos parents au concert?
- **f** Elle ne peut plus sortir le soir.

### NEGATIVE + *DE*

After a negative, *un/une/des* + noun changes to *de* (or *d'* in front of a vowel):

| | |
|---|---|
| *Il n'y a pas* ***de*** *pizza.* | There isn't any pizza. |
| *Il n'y a plus* ***de*** *chips.* | There aren't any more crisps. |
| *Je n'ai jamais* ***d'****argent.* | I never have any money. |

**7** Translate into French.

- **a** I don't go out with Laura any more.
- **b** She never spoke to her parents.
- **c** We can't do anything this evening.
- **d** There are no shops in this street.
- **e** I never buy any presents at Christmas.
- **f** Don't you have any questions?

**8** Write ten instructions: what NOT to do at a party. Compare with a partner.

Use *il ne faut pas* and imperatives (see page 69, Unit 2B).

*Exemple:* **Il ne faut pas** arriver en retard. **Ne buvez jamais** trop d'alcool. etc.

# Controlled Assessment: Speaking

## TASK: Invent a virtual family

You are going to invent a new personality and family for yourself for the virtual world of Second Life and then have a conversation with your teacher about it. Your teacher will ask you the following:

- Who is in your family?
- Describe the personality of two or three of the family members.
- How do you get on with each family member and why?
- What will your family situation be in 20 years' time?
- Is your Second Life family typical? How has family life changed in recent years?
- !

*(! Remember: at this point, you will have to respond to something you have not prepared.)*

The dialogue will last between 4 and 6 minutes.

## 1 THINK!

**Read the phrases below. Write down any others that you might find useful for the speaking task.**

- ☐ **Family members:** mes grands-parents, mon père,...
- ☐ **Personality adjectives:** sympa, têtu(e), travailleur/travailleuse,...
- ☐ **Getting on together:** j'ai un bon rapport avec..., on ne s'entend pas bien...
- ☐ **Giving reasons:** comme on a les mêmes goûts, parce qu'il est très gentil...
- ☐ **Future family:** je n'ai pas l'intention de me marier, je vais avoir beaucoup d'enfants...
- ☐ **How families have changed:** dans le passé, on se mariait plus jeune, aujourd'hui, il y a moins de familles nombreuses, les couples ne divorçaient pas...

***! Can you predict what the unexpected question might be?***

Is family life important to you? What sort of parent would you be if you had children?

**Add to your list any language you would need to answer these questions too.**

## 2 PLAN!

- **Listen to the model conversation. Your teacher has the script.**
- **Listen again and note down any phrases you could use or adapt. Add these to your list from Step 1.**

## 3 ACTION !

**Now prepare your answers. Use the bullet points below to help you and your list of useful words and phrases from Steps 1 and 2.**

**1** Who is in your family?

- Make sure you have revised the vocabulary for family members and the possessive adjectives that go with them, e.g. ***mes grands-parents, mon père, ma demi-sœur***
- You could start by saying how many there are in the family and then listing them, e.g. ***Dans ma famille, nous sommes trois. Il y a ma mère...***
- Add a little extra detail to make it more interesting, e.g. ***J'ai choisi un grand frère parce que..., J'ai décidé d'avoir six sœurs pour...***

**2** Describe the personality of two or three of the family members.

- Use a range of adjectives to describe personality (look back at pages 30–31).
- Remember to make adjectives masculine or feminine to go with the person they are describing, e.g. ***mon frère est gentil, ma sœur est gentille.***
- Try different ways to express your ideas, e.g. ***il a tendance à être un peu impatient, elle peut être sensible, il a l'air très organisé.***

**3** How do you get on with each family member and why?

- You could start in a different way each time, e.g. ***Je m'entends très bien avec ma mère, J'ai un bon rapport avec mes grands-parents, Mon frère et moi, on s'entend assez bien...***
- Don't forget to give your reasons, e.g. ***comme on a les mêmes goûts, on sort souvent ensemble; je peux lui parler de tout, parce qu'il est toujours sympa,...***

**4** What will your family situation be in 20 years' time?

- Remember that you are talking about the future. As well as the future tense, you could use ***aller*** + infinitive, e.g. ***Je ne vais pas me marier trop jeune.*** To talk about future plans, you could also use ***avoir l'intention de*** or ***compter*** + infinitive, e.g. ***J'ai l'intention de rester célibataire; Je compte avoir deux enfants.***
- You could also give your reasons, e.g. ***parce que je voudrais rester indépendant(e)/j'adore les enfants.***

**5** Is your Second Life family typical? How has family life changed in recent years?

- To give your opinion on whether or not your Second Life family is typical, use ***à mon avis, je pense que, je crois que*** or ***je trouve que.***
- Use the present tense to say what happens today, e.g. ***aujourd'hui, il y a moins de mariages, on divorce plus souvent...***
- If you have already learned it, use the imperfect tense to say what people used to do in the past, e.g. ***on se mariait jeune, on ne divorçait pas,...***

## GRADE TARGET

**To reach Grade C, you need to:**

- speak clearly with a good accent.
- use and pronounce masculine and feminine forms of adjectives correctly, e.g. ***mon père est travailleur, ma mère est travailleuse.***
- use ***parce que*** to give reasons, e.g. ***je m'entends bien avec mon frère parce qu'on est tous les deux bavards et on rigole ensemble.***

**To aim higher than a C, you could:**

- ensure your pronunciation is accurate, paying special attention to ***u/ou*** sounds and nasal sounds such as ***on, an, in***.
- use link words to connect opposing ideas, e.g. ***mais, par contre, pourtant, tandis que.***
- use more than one way to talk about future plans, e.g. ***je vais, j'ai l'intention de, je voudrais, je compte*** + infinitive.

**To aim for an A or A*, you could:**

- use a variety of negatives, e.g. ***on ne se dispute plus, je ne me marierai jamais, elle ne me demande rien...***
- give your opinion in different ways, e.g. ***à mon avis, la vie de famille est moins importante; je pense qu'il n'existe plus de familles typiques; je crois que trop de mères travaillent à l'extérieur.***

# 1B Controlled Assessment: Writing

## TASK: A letter about a social issue

Write a letter to the president of France about a social issue that concerns you. You could include the following:

- Details about yourself.
- A list of problems facing society today.
- A brief outline of the problem that concerns you.
- Why you think it is important and what will happen if no action is taken.
- What you have done to help.
- What you think the government could do to help.

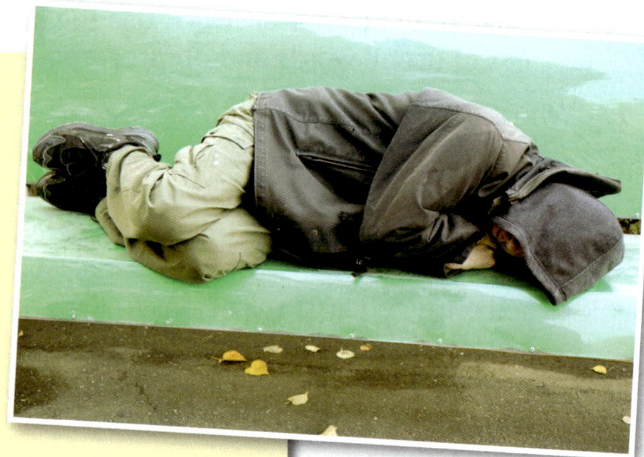

### 1 THINK!

**Start by noting down a few key facts:**

1. Personal details: *nom? âge? nationalité? ville? collège?*
2. Problems: *le vandalisme? la délinquance juvénile? la pauvreté? le chômage? le racisme? la drogue? le SIDA*? les SDF*?*
3. Outline: be sure to choose a subject where you are familiar with the vocabulary, or spend some time looking up key words and phrases. You will need to use French websites to research some basic facts.
4. Why you think it is important: *notre société est menacée, nous sommes tous en danger, c'est inhumain,...*
5. What I have done to help: *j'ai organisé une campagne,...*
6. What the government could do: *informer le public, améliorer l'éducation des jeunes, aider les SDF à trouver un logement,...*

* le SIDA – *AIDS*
les SDF (sans domicile fixe) – *homeless people*

### 2 PLAN!

- **Read the model text.**

Monsieur le Président

Permettez-moi de me présenter. Je m'appelle Ben Green et j'ai seize ans. Je suis anglais et j'habite à Salford, une ville industrielle dans le nord de l'Angleterre.

Aujourd'hui, notre société doit faire face à beaucoup de problèmes comme le racisme, le SIDA, la drogue, le vandalisme et la délinquance juvénile. Mais il y a un problème qui m'inquiète en particulier: la pauvreté.

La France, comme l'Angleterre, est un pays riche, et pourtant il y a des gens qui vivent dans la misère. En France, il y a trois millions de personnes sans logement adéquat. Dans mon quartier, il y a des SDF dans la rue. C'est une honte et la situation empirera si personne ne les aide avec leurs problèmes.

À mon avis, c'est un problème important parce que c'est inhumain de laisser les gens sans logement, nourriture ni chauffage. En plus, cette pauvreté peut être la cause d'autres problèmes comme la dépression et la délinquance juvénile.

Tout le monde doit dire non à la pauvreté. Par exemple, hier, j'ai donné de l'argent à l'organisation Shelter ici en Grande-Bretagne.

Les gouvernements dépensent des millions pour leurs armées, mais par contre il n'y a pas d'argent pour la construction d'appartements pour les familles qui ont le moins d'argent. Je vous demande de construire des logements pour les SDF et de donner plus d'allocations aux familles les plus pauvres.

- Read the text again and note down any opinions or adjectives that you could use. Add these to your list from Step 1.

## 3 ACTION!

**Now prepare what you will write. Use the bullet points below to help you and use your list of useful words and phrases from Steps 1 and 2. Aim to write about 200 words.**

**1** Details about yourself.

- Give your name, age and nationality to provide a context for who you are. If you mention your town or school you could also say where it is, e.g. ***dans le nord de l'Angleterre*** and what type of place it is, e.g. ***une ville industrielle.***
- Avoid personal details that are not relevant to the topic.

**2** A list of problems facing society today.

- Introduce your list with a brief explanatory phrase, e.g. ***la société doit faire face à beaucoup de problèmes comme...***
- Mention at least three relevant social issues.

**3** A brief outline of the problem that concerns you.

- Highlight the problem you are going to talk about, e.g. ***mais le problème qui m'inquiète en particulier, c'est...***
- Make sure you use vocabulary you are familiar with. Try to express your ideas as simply as possible.

**4** Why you think it is important and what will happen.

- You could start ***À mon avis*** or ***Je pense que...***
- ***parce que*** is a simple way to give your reason.
- use ***aller*** + infinitive or a future tense verb to say what will happen if no action is taken, e.g. ***Ça causera d'autres problèmes***.

**5** What you have done to help.

- Provide a past tense example of what you have done, e.g. ***j'ai donné de l'argent à... j'ai organisé une campagne...***

**6** What you think the government could do to help.

- Try to make a couple of points.
- You could use ***il faut*** or ***le gouvernement doit*** + infinitive.
- You could address your suggestion directly to the president, e.g. ***Je vous demande de...***

## GRADE TARGET

**To reach Grade C, you need to:**

- provide all the information you are asked for.
- use the present tense correctly.
- use link words such as ***et, mais, pourtant***.
- check all spellings.

**To aim higher than a C, you could:**

- use more than one tense, e.g. most of the letter will be in the present tense so find an opportunity to say what you did or what people have done in the perfect tense and/or to talk about the future.
- create longer, more complex sentences by using link words to oppose ideas, e.g. ***tandis que..., par contre,*** etc.
- not just stick to the ***je*** form, e.g. ***la société doit faire face..., les gouvernements dépensent...***

**To aim for an A or A*, you could:**

- use negative sentences, e.g. ***On ne pense jamais..., personne ne les aide, ils n'ont plus de travail.***
- use ***qui*** to link phrases, e.g. ***il y a un problème qui m'inquiète en particulier.***
- use 'if' clauses, e.g. ***si on fait un effort, on peut trouver une solution.***

# 1B Vocabulaire

### Comment trouver ton copain idéal

| | |
|---|---|
| le sens de l'humour | *sense of humour* |
| avoir l'air | *to seem* |
| avoir besoin de | *to need* |
| avoir tendance à | *to have a tendency to* |
| être un peu... | *to be a bit...* |
| il/elle peut être | *he/she can be* |
| aventureux/aventureuse | *adventurous* |
| drôle | *funny* |
| égoïste | *selfish* |
| fidèle | *loyal/faithful* |
| généreux/généreuse | *generous* |
| sensible | *sensitive* |
| têtu(e) | *stubborn* |
| timide | *shy* |
| travailleur/travailleuse | *hard-working* |
| À mon avis | *In my opinion* |
| Je trouve que... | *I find that...* |

### Comment discuter de ta vie de famille

| | |
|---|---|
| l'ambiance (*f*) | *atmosphere* |
| le bonheur | *happiness* |
| le changement | *change* |
| le conflit/la dispute | *conflict/argument* |
| le demi-frère | *half-brother* |
| le rapport/la relation | *relationship* |
| le soutien | *support* |
| comprendre | *to understand* |
| conseiller | *to advise* |
| se disputer avec | *to argue with* |
| garder les enfants | *to look after the children* |
| adopté(e) | *adopted* |
| exigeant(e) | *demanding* |
| heureux/heureuse | *happy* |
| monoparental(e) | *single-parent* |
| parfait(e) | *perfect* |
| tendu(e) | *tense* |
| actuellement | *at the moment, currently* |

### Comment dire si le mariage est pour toi

| | |
|---|---|
| Tu es pour ou contre le mariage? | *Are you for or against marriage?* |
| Est-ce que tu vas te marier plus tard? | *Are you going to get married later on?* |
| Crois-tu qu'il est possible de trouver ton/ta partenaire idéal(e) sur le web? | *Do you think it's possible to find your ideal partner on the web?* |
| Je n'ai pas l'intention de me marier. | *I don't intend to get married.* |
| l'âge (*m*) moyen du mariage | *the average age for getting married* |
| un couple sur deux divorce | *one out of every two couples gets divorced* |
| un défaut | *fault* |
| un site de rencontre en ligne | *online dating site* |
| hors marriage | *outside marriage* |
| célibataire | *single* |
| solitaire | *lonely* |
| veuf/veuve | *widowed* |
| avoir des enfants | *to have children* |
| se marier | *to get married* |
| tomber amoureux/amoureuse | *to fall in love* |

### Comment en savoir plus sur un ado en prison

| | |
|---|---|
| un ado (adolescent) | *teenager* |
| une bêtise | *stupid thing* |
| une cellule | *cell* |
| un délit | *crime* |
| une douche | *shower* |
| un entretien | *interview* |
| le quartier des mineurs | *the young offenders' section* |
| la vie quotidienne | *daily life* |
| le vol | *theft* |
| avoir le droit de | *to have the right to* |
| se comporter | *to behave* |
| condamner | *to convict* |
| s'ennuyer | *to be bored* |
| rester enfermé | *to stay locked up* |

### Comment parler du problème de la pauvreté

| | |
|---|---|
| une allocation | *allowance/grant* |
| le chauffage | *heating* |
| les chômeurs (*mpl*) | *unemployed people* |
| la construction d'appartements | *the building of flats* |
| le logement | *housing* |
| la misère | *poverty* |
| la nourriture | *food* |
| la pauvreté | *poverty* |
| les retraités (*mpl*) | *retired people* |
| autour de nous | *surrounding us* |
| exclu(e) | *excluded* |
| grave | *serious* |
| mal logé | *badly housed* |
| partout | *everywhere* |
| dépenser | *to spend* |
| financer | *to finance* |
| promettre | *to promise* |

# 2A Passe-temps et médias

## Sais-tu comment...

- ❑ choisir une nouvelle activité de loisir?
- ❑ parler «musique»?
- ❑ être chic pour pas cher?
- ❑ comparer les loisirs: passé/présent?
- ❑ se protéger sur le Net?

## Controlled assessment

- **An interview about computers and the internet**
- **A letter about how you spend your free time**

Ton passe-temps préféré, c'est quoi?

## Stratégies

### À l'écrit

When writing, how do you...

- use a variety of different structures to give reasons?
- make the most of synonyms?
- keep to the point?
- use a dictionary to look up verbs?

### À l'écoute

When listening in French, how do you...

- convert common word endings from French to English?
- use related words to deduce meaning?
- spot link words that change meaning?

## Grammaire active

As part of your French language 'toolkit' can you...

- use the comparative/superlative?
- use possessive pronouns?
- use direct and indirect object pronouns?
- use modal verbs correctly?
- form the imperfect tense?

# 2A Comment choisir une nouvelle activité de loisir

(G) Le comparatif, le superlatif; les pronoms possessifs (V) Les loisirs

(S) Expliquer pourquoi; ne pas s'éloigner du sujet; traduire les terminaisons de mots

A

B

C

D

E

**VOCABULAIRE**

Faire de la danse hip-hop
Faire de la randonnée
Écrire un blog sur Internet
Jouer d'un instrument
Faire de l'astronomie

## Forum-Internet

**Lili, Chambéry:**

Je ne pars pas pendant les grandes vacances cette année. La télé, ça m'ennuie et je voudrais trouver un nouveau passe-temps pour m'amuser. Alors, répondez le plus vite possible à mes questions! J'attends vos suggestions.

1 Quel est ton passe-temps préféré?
2 Tu le pratiques où? Quand?
3 Quel matériel faut-il?
4 Quels sont les avantages et les inconvénients?

**Kenny, Dax:**

Moi non plus, je ne pars jamais pendant les vacances, mais il y a beaucoup de passe-temps que tu pourrais faire. Le mien, c'est la randonnée. J'en fais parce que j'adore le plein air et aussi pour faire un peu d'exercice. Quand il fait beau, je prends un bus et je vais à la campagne. J'ai toujours une bonne carte avec moi afin de ne pas me perdre, et il faut aussi de solides chaussures de marche comme les miennes. J'ai des Berghaus parce qu'elles protègent mieux. Les avantages? L'exercice, c'est bon pour la santé, ça ne coûte pas cher et on est dans la nature! Et en marchant, on a une sensation de liberté. Un seul inconvénient: quand il pleut, c'est moins agréable.

**Samira, Paris:**

Mon passe-temps préféré, c'est jouer de la guitare. Ma sœur joue aussi et je joue beaucoup moins bien qu'elle mais ça m'amuse! J'ai appris toute seule avec un DVD. J'apprends en jouant. Je joue le soir dans ma chambre. J'apprends plus facilement comme ça. Il faut une guitare (au début, ma sœur m'a prêté la sienne) mais comme la guitare est un instrument populaire, on peut facilement acheter un instrument d'occasion*. Une guitare, c'est pas cher, c'est portable et on peut jouer seul ou avec des amis. Mais attention! C'est assez difficile si tu n'as pas l'oreille musicale et ça fait mal aux doigts.

* second-hand

**1** Trouve le nom des passe-temps sur les photos.
*Exemple*: **A** Écrire un blog sur Internet

**2** Lis les phrases. Choisis un mot de l'encadré pour compléter chacune.

**a** J'écris *** sur Internet.
**b** J'adore ***. J'ai un téléscope pour regarder le ciel la nuit.
**c** Je joue du saxophone dans ***.
**d** Avec mes copains, on fait de *** hip-hop.
**e** La randonnée, c'est super pour *** comme moi.

un orchestre   un blog   un sportif
la danse   l'astronomie

**3** Lis le message de Lili. Explique-le en anglais.

**4** Lis et écoute Kenny, page 48. Ensuite écoute les questions a–f. Réponds aux questions.

**STRATÉGIES**

To give reasons, use:
- *parce que* or *car* – because
- *pour* + infinitive – (in order) to
- *afin de* + infinitive – in order to

Remember to use a variety of structures when you write!

**5** Recopie les trois phrases où Kenny, page 48, donne ses raisons et traduis-les en anglais.

**6** Lis le message de Samira, page 48. Comment dit-elle...?

**a** *I taught myself*
**b** *my sister lent me hers*
**c** *if you are not musical*

**GRAMMAIRE**

**Comparing adverbs using *plus/moins/aussi... que...***

*Elle lit plus rapidement que moi.* – She reads more quickly than I do.

*C'est lui qui chante le plus fort.* – He sings the loudest.

Exception: *bon - mieux/le mieux*
*Tu chantes **mieux** que moi, mais c'est Léa qui chante **le mieux**.*

**7** Trouve des exemples du comparatif/superlatif dans les trois messages, page 48, et traduis-les.
*Exemple*: Lili écrit: Répondez le plus vite possible - *Reply as quickly as possible.*

**GRAMMAIRE**

**Possessive pronouns**

| | masc. sing. | fem. sing. | masc. pl. | fem. pl. |
|---|---|---|---|---|
| *à moi* (mine) | *le mien* | *la mienne* | *les miens* | *les miennes* |
| *à toi* (yours) | *le tien* | *la tienne* | *les tiens* | *les tiennes* |
| *à lui/elle* (his/hers) | *le sien* | *la sienne* | *les siens* | *les siennes* |

Can you find any examples in the texts on page 48?

**8** À deux. Jeu de rôle: **A** pose les questions de Lili, **B** est Kenny et répond. Ensuite, **B** pose les questions et **A** répond pour Samira.

**9** À deux. **A** lit trois phrases dans les messages, page 48, à **B**. **B** les écrit, sans regarder le livre. (**B**⟷**A**). Vérifiez que vous n'avez pas fait d'erreurs.

**STRATÉGIES**

Keep to the point when writing. It is good to include plenty of detail, but only if it is relevant!

**10** Écoute les interviews (1–3) et prends des notes pour répondre aux questions de Lili, page 48. Ensuite, écris leurs suggestions.

**STRATÉGIES**

When listening or reading, know how to convert some common French word endings into English, e.g.:

| French | English | Example |
|---|---|---|
| present participles ending ***-ant*** | -ing | *arrivant*/arriving |
| adverbs ending ***-ment*** | -ly | *rarement*/rarely |
| adjectives ending ***-aire*** | -ar or -ary | *militaire*/military |
| nouns ending ***-é*** or ***-ée*** | -y | *armée*/army |

Find an example of each on page 48.

## À vous!

**11** Write a speech bubble (50 words) for one of the people in the photos on page 48. Do NOT write the name of the activity. Swap with a partner who must read it and guess which person is speaking.
*Exemple*: Je fais ce passe-temps pour m'amuser avec mes copains. C'est une activité que j'adore car...

**12** Write your own reply to Lili persuading her of the advantages of one of your interests. Be sure to include answers to all of her questions.

# 2A Comment parler «musique»

(G) Les pronoms compléments d'objet direct (V) Opinions sur la musique et les chanteurs
(S) Les synonymes

## A Sondage: Les jeunes et la musique

**Quel est ton style de musique préféré? (944 votes)**

| | |
|---|---|
| Rap/RnB (466) | 49,4% |
| Pop/Rock (196) | 20,8% |
| Hard Rock/Métal (78) | 8,3% |
| Techno (60) | 6,4% |
| Variétés françaises (52) | 5,5% |
| Reggae (32) | 3,4% |
| Variétés étrangères (24) | 2,5% |
| Electro (22) | 2,3% |
| Disco (8) | 0,8% |
| Classique (6) | 0,6% |

**Tu écoutes ta musique avec... (912 votes)**

| | |
|---|---|
| un lecteur MP3 standard? (564) | 61,8% |
| un iPod? (244) | 26,8% |
| ton téléphone? (104) | 11,4% |

**D'où provient ta musique? (922 votes)**

| | |
|---|---|
| de téléchargements gratuits (422) | 45,8% |
| d'achats de CD/DVD (234) | 25,4% |
| d'échanges avec les amis (210) | 22,7% |
| d'enregistrements radio/TV (36) | 3,9% |
| de téléchargements payants (20) | 2,2% |

Sondage auprès de jeunes de 12 à 25 ans

**B**

L'orchestre était bon, la musique était bonne, les chanteurs étaient bons et les chansons étaient... euh... bonnes!

**D**

J'aime beaucoup la musique rock parce que ça m'éclate! Mon groupe préféré, c'est le groupe de rock français Les Hushpuppies. Mon frère les adore aussi – ils sont vraiment super. Je voudrais savoir s'ils ont un fan club. Par contre, je n'aime pas du tout la techno parce que c'est trop répétitif. Ça m'énerve.

**C**

Pour moi, la meilleure musique, c'est le rap. C'est génial. Je l'adore parce que quand je l'entends, j'ai envie de danser. Le meilleur rappeur français, c'est Rohff. Je vais à tous ses concerts. Ma copine et moi, nous téléchargeons toutes ses chansons. Nous les écoutons tous les jours. J'ai horreur de la musique classique parce que c'est monotone. Ça m'endort.

**E**

Moi, j'adore le reggae. Ça me détend et ça me met de bonne humeur. C'est très rythmé. C'est très agréable à écouter. Mon chanteur préféré, c'est Charly B. Il chante en français et en anglais. J'ai tous ses CD – je les adore! – et j'ai un poster de lui dans ma chambre. Je n'aime pas beaucoup le hard rock ni le métal parce que la musique est trop rapide et violente. Ça te rend sourd*!

* it makes you deaf

**1** Lis le sondage A, page 50, et trouve l'équivalent en français.

**a** *classical music* **c** *recordings*
**b** *free downloads* **d** *swapping with friends*

**2** Écoute. Ils aiment quelle musique? Recopie et coche la grille.

| | rap | pop/rock | metal | classical |
|---|---|---|---|---|
| **Hugo** | | | | |
| **Cécile** | | | | |
| **Moussa** | | | | |
| **Salifa** | | | | |

**3a** Écoute les réponses de Karima and Nico au sondage. Qui aime le plus la musique?

**3b** Réécoute et prends des notes. Ensuite, avec un(e) partenaire, jouez les rôles de Nico et de Karima et recréez les interviews en utilisant vos notes.

**4** Lis les textes de Cyrielle, Sam et Magali (C, D, E), page 50. Complète les phrases.

*Exemple*: **a** *...it makes her want to dance.*

**a** *Cyrielle likes rap music because...*
**b** *She and her friend...*
**c** *She thinks classical music...*
**d** *Sam wants to know...*
**e** *He thinks techno music...*
**f** *Magali likes reggae because...*
**g** *She thinks metal music...*

**5** La musique a quel effet? Dans les bulles, page 50, trouve des expressions pour continuer les listes.

*Exemple*:

| Effet positif | Effet négatif |
|---|---|
| j'ai envie de danser | ça m'endort |

**GRAMMAIRE**

**Direct object pronouns**

You have met *le*, *la*, *l'* and *les* ('the') as determiners in front of nouns. But what if they are not followed by a noun? They can also be used alone as **pronouns**, to avoid repeating a noun that is not the subject of the verb.

The pronoun is masculine or feminine, singular or plural, to match the noun it replaces.

**6** Trouve les phrases avec des pronoms compléments d'objet direct dans les bulles, page 50. Donne l'équivalent en anglais.

*Exemple*: Je **l'**adore – *I love **it***

**7** Tu aimes les styles de musique du sondage (A), page 50? Pourquoi? Ils ont quel effet sur toi? Écris une ou deux phrases pour chaque style.

*Exemple:* J'aime beaucoup le classique parce que ça me détend. Mon compositeur préféré, c'est Mozart.

**STRATÉGIES**

**Synonyms**

Try to use a range of vocabulary to make what you write or say more colourful and interesting. Why not keep a note of possible variations in your vocabulary notebook?

e.g. *ennuyeux – monotone, répétitif, ...*

**8** Dans les bulles, page 50, trouve les synonymes des expressions suivantes:

**a** je déteste **c** ça me fait dormir
**b** c'est relaxant **d** c'est ennuyeux

**9** Lis la bulle B, page 50. Trouve des synonymes pour le mot «bon». Écris cinq phrases similaires mais avec des adjectifs différents.

*Exemple*: **1** L'orchestre était génial, la musique était sensationnelle...
**2** L'orchestre était excellent...

## À VOUS!

**10** Organise your own music survey.

- Draw up a questionnaire.
  *Exemple:* Pour toi, quel est le meilleur groupe?
- Ask your classmates the questions and record the answers.
- Present your findings to the class. Compare with the findings of the French survey.

**11** Write a message for a French internet forum about your favourite band or singer. Include a profile of the band/singer (name, appearance, etc.), explain the type of music and why you like them. Say what you do to support them (download songs, go to gigs, buy CDs, etc.)

*Exemple:* Pour moi, le meilleur groupe, c'est Sensorium. Ce sont cinq jeunes Écossais qui...

# 2A Comment être chic pour pas cher

(G) Les pronoms compléments d'objet indirect (V) L'argent, la mode, le shopping

(S) Faire des associations de mots pour mieux comprendre

**A**

**Le look sport?**
**Le look décontracté?**
**Le look glamour?**
**Le look gothique?**

**B**

**Emma:** **Je n'ai pas beaucoup d'argent de poche (ma mère me donne quarante euros par mois). Comment être à la mode sans trop dépenser?**

**Hugo:** Tu peux **[1]** des vêtements au marché ou au supermarché où les prix sont raisonnables et il y a un bon choix.

**Alicia:** Les **[2]** sont chers, alors achète des accessoires et des bijoux. Je fais pratiquement tous mes achats sur Internet parce que c'est moins cher d'acheter en ligne. J'adore ebay!

**Karima:** J'achète toujours mes vêtements dans un magasin. Je préfère **[3]** les vêtements avant de les acheter. Achète en solde, quand les prix sont réduits.

**Thomas:** Je déteste le shopping, mais j'ai un look original. J'échange des vêtements avec mes copains. Pour moi, ce n'est pas important si c'est démodé. Mélange les **[4]** – c'est rigolo!

**Zoé:** Demande à tes parents de t'offrir des vêtements à Noël ou pour ton **[5]**.

**Magali:** Les magasins d'occasion ont souvent de bonnes affaires. Avec mon argent, je préfère acheter du maquillage, des livres ou des petits gadgets, la **[6]** ne m'intéresse pas beaucoup.

**C**

## Jeu-test: Spécial shopping

**1** C'est ton anniversaire. Tes grands-parents demandent ce que tu voudrais comme cadeau.

♥ Tu leur téléphones pour demander de l'argent, comme ça tu peux acheter ce que tu veux.

▲ Tu leur écris un petit mot* pour demander un nouveau portable.

**2** Ta petite sœur n'a rien à mettre pour une fête.

♥ Tu lui suggères de faire du shopping ensemble.

▲ Tu lui proposes de lui prêter ton T-shirt favori.

**3** Ta copine veut acheter exactement le même jean que toi.

♥ Tu lui demandes de choisir un style différent.

▲ Tu ne lui dis rien... ça n'a pas d'importance.

* a little note

**1** Trouve les noms des vêtements sur les photos A, page 52.

*Exemple:* **1** une casquette

un T-shirt un jean une mini-jupe
une casquette des chaussures un collier
des lunettes de soleil un sac un sweat à capuche

**2** Vous avez cinq minutes. À deux, faites une liste de tous vos vêtements et accessoires. Utilisez un dictionnaire si nécessaire. Ensuite, comparez avec une autre paire. Qui a la liste la plus longue?

**3** Écoute (1–4). Ils aiment le look de Christina et de Grégor? Pourquoi? Prends des notes.

**4** Et toi? Que penses-tu du look de Christina et de Grégor? Discute avec un(e) partenaire.

**5** Lis la question d'Emma (B) et les réponses, page 52. Remplace les numéros par les bons mots. (Attention! Il y a deux mots de trop.)

styles couleur acheter essayer
anniversaire mode habiller vêtements

**6** Écoute pour vérifier.

**7a** Relis le texte B, page 52. Comment dit-on...?

- **a** *40 euros a month*
- **b** *without spending too much*
- **c** *it's cheaper to buy online*
- **d** *buy in the sales*
- **e** *second-hand shops often have bargains*
- **f** *fashion doesn't interest me much*

**7b** Qui l'a dit?

- **a** *I don't get much pocket money.*
- **b** *I hate shopping.*
- **c** *Ask your parents for clothes for Christmas.*
- **d** *You can buy clothes at the supermarket.*
- **e** *Buy online.*

**STRATÉGIES**

To help work out the meaning of a new word, check if it is related to others you know. For example: *inoubliable* (unforgettable) is from the same family as *oublier* (to forget).

**8** Dans le texte B, page 52, trouve les mots associés aux mots a–d et donne les équivalents en anglais.

*Exemple:* choisir → un choix (*to choose/a choice*)

**a** choisir **b** acheter
**c** la mode **d** réduction

**9** Et toi? Qu'est-ce que tu fais pour être chic sans trop dépenser? Écris +/- 100 mots.

**GRAMMAIRE**

**Indirect object pronouns**

These pronouns are used instead of direct object pronouns when the verb is followed by a **preposition** (*usually* ***à***): *parler* ***à****, donner* ***à****, demander* ***à***, etc.

| | | | |
|---|---|---|---|
| ***me/m'*** | to me | ***nous*** | to us |
| ***te/t'*** | to you | ***vous*** | to you |
| ***lui*** | to him, it (masc.) | ***leur*** | to them |
| ***lui*** | to her, it (fem.) | | |

*Tu ne* ***lui*** *dis rien.* — You don't say anything **to him** (or **her**).

*Tu* ***leur*** *demandes de l'argent.* You ask **them** for money.

**10** Trouve des exemples de «lui» et «leur» dans le jeu-test, page 52. Écris la phrase avec le pronom et ensuite avec «à + nom».

*Exemple:* Tu leur téléphones./Tu téléphones à tes grands-parents.

**11** Écoute. Lève la main quand tu entends «lui» ou «leur».

## À VOUS!

**12** Record an interview with a friend about his/her views on fashion. Find out:

- their favourite look (and why)
- what clothes they like to wear
- what they do to look good without spending a lot.

**13** Write an article for a French magazine. Explain the advantages and disadvantages of internet versus regular shopping in your area. Write about 100 words. You could mention:

- les magasins près de chez toi
- le choix/les styles/les prix
- les vendeurs: ils aident ou pas? Attitude?
- la livraison (*delivery*) etc.

# 2A Comment comparer les loisirs: passé/présent

(G) L'imparfait (V) Les loisirs du présent et du passé (P) Verbes à l'imparfait
(S) Utiliser un dictionnaire à l'écrit

1 Écouter des cassettes sur un baladeur

2 Acheter des DVD ou des disques Blu-ray

3 Avoir la télé avec peu de chaînes

4 Jouer aux jeux électroniques simples comme Pacman et Tetris

5 Écouter de la musique sur son MP3

A

B

6 Écrire une lettre à une copine

7 Avoir la télé numérique, câblée ou par satellite

8 Regarder les cassettes vidéo sur un magnétoscope

9 Envoyer un SMS à un copain

10 Aller au petit cinéma du coin

11 Jouer aux jeux électroniques sophistiqués, même sur son portable

12 Voir un film dans un cinéma multiplex

**1** Les deux photos représentent quelles activités?

**2a** Les activités 1–12 sont du présent ou du passé? Écris des phrases au présent ou à l'imparfait.

| *Exemple*: | Dans les années 80 | Aujourd'hui |
|---|---|---|
| | On écoutait des cassettes. | On achète des DVD ou des disques Blu-ray. |

**2b** Écoute pour vérifier.

**3** À deux. **A** pose les questions, **B** répond. (**B**⟷**A**)

**a** À six ans, tu savais lire et écrire?
**b** Qu'est-ce que tu aimais faire quand tu étais petit(e)?
**c** On avait des jeux électroniques il y a cent ans*?
**d** Est-ce que les punks avaient un look élégant?

* 100 years ago

**GRAMMAIRE**

**Imperfect tense**

In French, the imperfect tense is used to say **what used to happen** or **what things were like** in the past:

e.g. *je jouais aux cartes* I used to play cards

| | |
|---|---|
| *je jou**ais*** | *nous jou**ions*** |
| *tu jou**ais*** | *vous jou**iez*** |
| *il/elle/on jou**ait*** | *ils/elles jou**aient*** |

To find out how to form the imperfect tense, see *Grammaire active*, page 59.

**4a** Recopie en mettant les verbes à l'infinitif à l'imparfait.

*Exemple*: Quand j'étais jeune...

Quand j'**[être]** jeune, on n'**[avoir]** pas la télévision. Le soir, je **[faire]** mes devoirs et j'**[aider]** ma mère à la cuisine ou nous **[jouer]** aux cartes. Tous les samedis, on **[aller]** danser. Il y **[avoir]** souvent des bals. C'**[être]** super! L'été, les gens ne **[partir]** pas souvent. Par contre, ils **[faire]** des excursions à la campagne ou au bord de la mer. Et moi, j'**[adorer]** faire du vélo.

**4b** Traduis ton paragraphe de l'activité 4a en anglais.

**STRATÉGIES**

The endings of imperfect tense verbs all **sound** the same except for the *nous* and *vous* forms, even though the spellings are different. It makes life a bit easier!

**5** Écoute (a–l). Imparfait (i) ou passé composé (pc)?

*Exemple*: **a** pc

**STRATÉGIES**

**Looking up verbs in the dictionary**

In the dictionary, verbs are listed in the infinitive form (typical endings: ***-er***, ***-ir***, ***-re***). So work out what the infinitive is and look that up, e.g.

***ils ne bougent plus*** – look up ***bouger***

Reflexive verbs are listed under the first letter of the main verb.

So look up *s'allonger* under **A**, not **S**.

**Tip!** You can get help with different parts of the verb and tenses in the **verb tables** in the middle or at the end of most dictionaries.

**6** Lis le texte «Les nouvelles technologies», sans dictionnaire. Ensuite, écoute et réponds aux questions (1-6).

*Exemple*: **1** Les magnétoscopes étaient populaires dans les années 80.

## Les nouvelles technologies

Dans les années 80, c'était la mode du magnétoscope. Maintenant, les cassettes vidéo sont démodées: elles ont fait place aux DVD et aux disques Blu-ray.

Les films sortent de plus en plus rapidement en DVD et on peut voir les sorties les plus récentes presque immédiatement, sans aller au cinéma, même sur son ordinateur portable. Notre façon de vivre a été radicalement changée par Internet: c'est là qu'on fait ses achats ou qu'on communique par la messagerie instantanée.

Un inconvénient: les jeunes ne bougent plus. Ils s'allongent devant la télé ou ils s'adonnent à des jeux vidéo de plus en plus violents. Alors, pour ou contre la technologie moderne?

## À vous!

**7** Make up a true/false puzzle. Write a list of statements about what you used to do in your free time when you were at primary school – nine true, three false. Use the imperfect tense. Swap with a partner who guesses which are the three false statements.

*Exemple:* J'avais un vélo rouge et je faisais du vélo tous les week-ends.

**8** Fast forward 20 years! How would you describe what you do now in your free time? Write a description (100 words) using the imperfect tense for regular activities and the perfect tense for one-off events.

*Exemple:* Quand j'avais 16 ans, ma passion, c'était la musique hip-hop. J'écoutais mon iPod nano le plus souvent possible. Les meilleurs chanteurs étaient... Je suis allé à un concert...

# 2A Comment se protéger sur le Net

G Vouloir, pouvoir, devoir V Réseaux sociaux: avantages et inconvénients S Conjonctions contradictoires

82% affichent leur prénom.

29% indiquent leur nom de famille.

49% indiquent le nom de leur école.

## Cyberpage – votre réseau social...

79% affichent des photos d'eux-mêmes.

61% indiquent la ville où ils habitent.

**Jeanne-Marie Fabre**
Sexe féminin
17 ans
Nantes, France
Dernière connexion 5/5/20XX

40% attachent des clips audio ou MP3.

**Mes émissions favorites**
La nouvelle star
X factor
Tournez manège
Koh-Lanta

**Mes personnages favoris**
Camille
Christophe Dechavanne
Arthur
Denis Brogniart

2% mettent le numéro de leur portable.

**Mon profil:**
Je suis en 1ère au lycée Éric-Tabarly à Nantes. Envoyez-moi un message instantané à jmf1992 ou un mail à *jmfabre@hotmail.com*

40% donnent leur nom d'utilisateur.

29% donnent leur adresse email.

Le dernier billet de Jeanne-Marie

S'abonner à mon blog

Voir tous les billets sur mon blog

39% mettent un lien pour leur blog.

**Qui j'aimerais rencontrer:**
des gens cool – mais en priorité des filles qui s'appellent Jeanne-Marie

66% affichent des photos de leurs amis.

**Amélie**

Toutes mes copines sont sur Facebook. Comme ça, je peux rester en contact avec elles quand je veux. Depuis mon téléphone portable, je me connecte tous les soirs, sauf le samedi quand je sors ou en semaine quand je dois faire mes devoirs. Je tchate et je regarde les profils.
C'est pratique et c'est amusant. Sur Facebook, il y a tout sur ma vie privée, mais je limite quand même l'accès à mon profil à mes copines en me rendant dans la rubrique «confidentialité». J'ai un seul regret – à mon avis, on passe trop de temps dans ce monde virtuel. Moi, j'y perds des heures et ça limite le temps que je passe avec mes copines dans le «vrai» monde!
Pour moi, c'est le danger le plus grave.

**Mohammed**

Facebook, c'est génial; néanmoins on doit faire attention quand on l'utilise. Vous pouvez tout mettre sur votre page si vous voulez: vos photos, des messages d'autres membres, etc. Mais attention! Vous ne devez jamais inscrire votre adresse ni votre numéro de téléphone. Les jeunes doivent comprendre que tout sur Facebook est accessible à tous. Mon copain a affiché son adresse et les dates de ses vacances et des voleurs en ont profité pour cambrioler sa maison! On ne peut pas non plus diffuser des musiques, des vidéos ni des photos protégées par le droit d'auteur. Je déteste les alertes et les mises à jour pour dire à tous ce qu'on fait à chaque minute – c'est dérangeant. Je préfère le courrier électronique car je peux envoyer des mails sans risques. En revanche, je ne dis mon mot de passe à personne.

**1a** Lis et écoute les bulles, page 56. De quoi ça parle?

**1b** À deux. A dit un pourcentage, B dit le reste de la phrase. (B↔A) Ensuite, B ferme son livre et répond de mémoire.

*Exemple:* A 61%... B indiquent la ville où ils habitent.

**2** Écoute. Choisis a ou b.

1 *Alizé thinks the biggest danger of sites like Facebook is*
 a *giving away too many personal details*
 b *spending too much time on them.*
2 *Manu is concerned about*
 a *identity theft* b *losing friends.*
3 *Claire mentions*
 a *sexual predators* b *online bullying.*

**3** La classe discute des dangers des réseaux sociaux et classe les risques par ordre de gravité.

**4** Tu fais ça? Écris une phrase pour chaque bulle. (Invente si tu n'es pas inscrit(e) à un réseau.) Explique pourquoi.

*Exemple:* J'affiche mon prénom. Je n'indique pas mon nom de famille parce que...

**5** Lis les messages d'Amélie et de Mohammed, page 56. De quoi parlent les deux messages?

a Les cybercafés
b Les réseaux sociaux
c Le courrier électronique

**6** Relis les deux messages, page 56. Réponds en anglais.

a *When and why does Amélie go on Facebook?*
b *When and why doesn't she go on?*
c *What does she do on Facebook?*
d *How does she limit access to her page?*
e *What does Mohammed think of Facebook?*
f *What details does he say you should not put online?*
g *How does Mohammed prefer to communicate?*
h *What does he keep secret?*

**GRAMMAIRE**

**Modal verbs**

These verbs are almost always followed by an infinitive.

| | | |
|---|---|---|
| ***pouvoir*** = to be able to | ***Je peux*** | **+ infinitive** |
| ***vouloir*** = to want | ***Je veux*** | |
| ***devoir*** = to have to | ***Je dois*** | |
| ***savoir*** = to know how to | ***Je sais*** | |

See also the Grammar Bank, page 183.

**7** Relis les messages, page 56. Recopie toutes les phrases avec des verbes modaux et traduis-les en anglais.

*Exemple:* Comme ça, je peux rester en contact avec elles quand je veux. – *That way, I can stay in contact with them when I want.*

**8** Retrouve dans les messages les conjonctions (soulignées) qui veulent dire:

a *except*
b *in contrast*
c *but all the same*
d *nonetheless*

**STRATÉGIES**

Some connectives have a dramatic effect on the meaning of a sentence. If you read or hear: *J'aime tous les réseaux sociaux...*('I like all social networking sites') you might think you have a clear idea of what the speaker likes. But if the sentence continues: *sauf Facebook* ('except Facebook'), then you have a different view. So make sure you learn these little words! Why do you think the words in activity 8 have been used in the messages? What effect do they have?

**9** Écoute et réponds en anglais. (Attention aux «petits mots»!)

a *Does Anna only use her computer for word processing* (le traitement de texte)?
b *Does she really put everything on Skyrock? How do you know?*
c *What does she think of the quizzes? Does she do them?*
d *Does she take the tests seriously?*

pourtant – *however*
par contre – *on the other hand*

## À VOUS!

**10** How do young people in your country use the internet to communicate? Which are the most popular social networking sites? Do you use them? When? How? Why? With a partner, record an interview for a French school's radio station.

**11** Write an article explaining the advantages and disadvantages of social networking sites like Facebook (about 120 words). Score points for each of the following connectives you use correctly:

1 point – *et, mais, ou*
3 points – *sauf, pourtant, néanmoins, par contre*

# 2A Grammaire active

## DIRECT OBJECT PRONOUNS

Direct object pronouns replace a word that is the object of the verb.

| | | | |
|---|---|---|---|
| *me** | me | *nous* | us |
| *te** | you | *vous* | you |
| *le** | him, it (masc.) | *les* | them |
| *la** | her, it (fem.) | | |

* *m', t'* or *l'* before words that start with a vowel or 'h'

These **pronouns** go before the verb:
*Je **l'**adore.* I love it.
*Je **les** écoute.* I listen to them.

In verb + infinitive structures, the **pronouns** go before the infinitive:
*On va **les** regarder.* We are going to watch them.
*Tu veux **le** lire?* Do you want to read it?

Preceding direct object: in the perfect tense, object pronouns usually come before the part of *avoir* or *être* and **the past participle must agree with it**:
*Mon mot de passe? Je l'ai oublié.* My password? I've forgotten it.
*Ses textos? Je ne les ai pas vus.* Her texts? I didn't see them.

**1a** Rewrite the following sentences replacing the underlined words with direct object pronouns. (Make past participles agree with feminine and/or plural nouns where necessary. Unsure of the gender of the nouns? Check in the dictionary.)

*Exemple:* **a** Je ne les aime pas beaucoup.

- **a** Je n'aime pas beaucoup les jeux.
- **b** Mon père lit toujours ses emails.
- **c** J'adore la musique classique.
- **d** Tu connais ce site?
- **e** On va regarder ma boîte à lettres électronique.
- **f** Tu as vu la page d'accueil?
- **g** J'ai lu tous tes textos.

**1b** Translate your sentences from activity 1a into English.

*Exemple:* **a** I don't like them very much.

## INDIRECT OBJECT PRONOUNS

These replace a word that is the object of the verb and which is linked to the verb by a preposition, usually *à*, e.g. *parler à, donner à*.

| | | | |
|---|---|---|---|
| *me** | to me | *nous* | to us |
| *te** | to you | *vous* | to you |
| *lui* | to him, it (masc.) | *leur* | to them |
| *lui* | to her, it (fem.) | | |

The position of these pronouns is the same as for direct object pronouns (see left).

*Elle ne **m'**écris pas.* She doesn't write to me.
*Je **leur** ai téléphoné.* I phoned them.

**2** Compare the direct and indirect object pronouns. Only three are different – which are they?

**3** Rewrite the following sentences replacing the underlined words with indirect object pronouns.

*Exemple:* **a** Je lui expliquerai le problème.

- **a** J'expliquerai le problème à Valérie.
- **b** Il va dire à Max et Joe de venir.
- **c** On a montré au prof le nouveau réseau social.
- **d** Elle téléphone souvent à Anna et moi.

## STRATÉGIES

In a positive command, the **pronoun** comes after the verb:
*Regarde-**le**/**la**!* *Donne-**lui** le journal.*

**More than one pronoun in the same sentence?**

Learn the order – it's a bit like the layout on a football pitch!

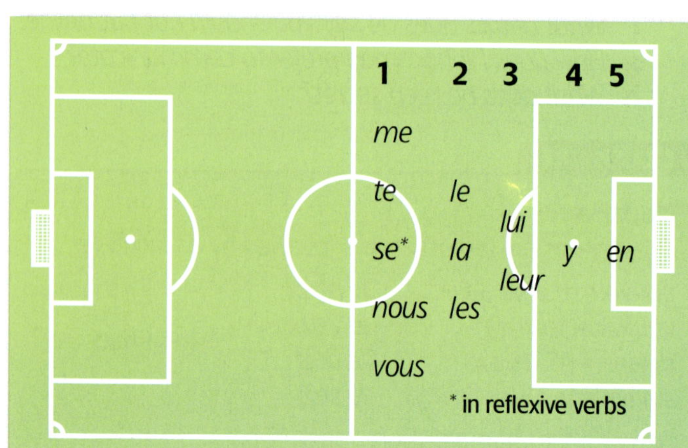

## 4 Rearrange the words and write out the sentences. Then translate them into English.

*Exemple*: **a** Elle me le donne. *She gives it to me.*

**a** Elle donne me le
**b** Je en parlais lui
**c** Tu dis demain me le?
**d** On la demandée leur a
**e** Ils envoyé ont te l'
**f** Qui donnés a les lui?

**Le lièvre et la tortue**

La tortue voulait absolument participer aux Jeux Olympiques alors, elle s'entraînait tous les jours. C'était dur! Pendant qu'elle s'entraînait, le lièvre se reposait. Il trouvait ça super!

### WHEN TO USE THE IMPERFECT TENSE

- To describe what something was like in the past.
  ***C'était** dur.* It was hard.
- To give an opinion in the past.
  *Il **trouvait** ça super!* He thought that was great!
- To describe a regular action in the past.
  *Elle **s'entraînait** tous les jours.* She trained/used to train every day.
- To describe what was happening at the same time as something else was going on.
  *Pendant qu'elle **s'entraînait**, le lièvre **se reposait**.*
  While she was training, the hare was resting.

### HOW TO FORM THE IMPERFECT

1 Take the *nous* part of the present tense*
***faire*** = *(nous) faisons*

2 Take off the –*ons* ending and keep the stem.
***fais~~ons~~***

3 Add imperfect endings:

| | |
|---|---|
| *je fais**ais*** | *nous fais**ions*** |
| *tu fais**ais*** | *vous fais**iez*** |
| *il/elle/on fais**ait*** | *ils/elles fais**aient*** |

* The only exception is **être**, which has the stem ***ét-***

## 5 Which of these sentences are in the imperfect? Translate each into English.

**a** Est-ce qu'il veut venir au concert avec nous?
**b** Il faisait froid à Noël.
**c** Quand elle était petite, elle jouait du piano.
**d** Elle a acheté un joli pull bleu.
**e** Je voudrais jouer dans l'équipe de France.
**f** Ils aimaient bien écrire un blog sur Internet.

## 6 Fill the gaps with the correct imperfect form of the verbs given in brackets (see Grammar Bank, page 187).

*Exemple*: ... j'étais vraiment déçu!

Salut Max!

J'ai regardé le match France-Hollande avec mon père hier soir. J' ..... vraiment déçu **(être)**! Nous, les Français, nous ..... nuls! **(être)**. Il ne se ..... rien **(passer)**! On ..... presque à la fin de la première mi-temps **(dormir)**! Les Bleus ..... faute après faute **(faire)**. Tu ne ..... pas ça lamentable **(trouver)**? Quand quelqu'un ..... de marquer **(essayer)**, personne ne l'..... **(aider)**. En plus, le gardien néerlandais ne ..... rien passer **(laisser)**! Et la défense? Nulle. Les Hollandais ..... avancer sans problème **(pouvoir)**, on ne les ..... pas **(arrêter)**. Pathétique!

À bientôt,

Thomas

## 7 Complete these sentences and make them true for you. Use the imperfect when needed.

*Exemple*: Avant, je ne faisais pas de sport mais maintenant, je joue au rugby.

**a** Avant, je ne... pas mais maintenant, je...
**b** Avant, je... par contre maintenant, je ne... plus.
**c** Quand j'étais petit(e), je...
**d** L'année dernière,...

# 2A Controlled Assessment: Speaking

## TASK: Computers and the internet

Your teacher is going to interview you about computers and the internet.
Your teacher will ask you the following:

- What do you use a computer for?
- Are you going to use a computer this evening?
- Do you use any social networking sites, and how often?
- Are sites like Facebook and MySpace a good thing? Why?
- Have you ever put personal details on your web pages, and why/why not?
- Do you download music? If so, what type of music?
- How did people communicate before the invention of computers?
- !

*(! Remember: at this point, you will have to respond to something you have not prepared.)*

The dialogue will last between 4 and 6 minutes.

### 1 THINK!

**Read the phrases below. Write down any others that you might find useful for the speaking task.**

- ☐ **Use of computer:** faire mes devoirs, surfer le web, envoyer/lire des mails, télécharger de la musique,...
- ☐ **How often:** quand j'ai le temps, tous les jours, une ou deux fois par semaine,...
- ☐ **Advantages of social networking sites:** rester en contact avec les amis, lire les profils de stars ou d'organisations que j'aime, faire partie d'une communauté,...
- ☐ **Have you given personal details?:** prénom, nom de famille, âge, adresse,...
- ☐ **Reasons: parce que** c'est dangereux, **pour** limiter l'accès à mes amis seulement, **afin de** respecter les règles de mes parents,...
- ☐ **Music:** les téléchargements gratuits/payants, le rap, la musique pop, le rock,...
- ☐ **In the past:** téléphoner, écrire des lettres,...

**! *Can you predict what the unexpected question might be?***

Do you have a computer at home? In which room? What is your favourite website?

**Add to your list any language you would need to answer these questions too.**

### 2 PLAN!

- **Listen to the model conversation. Your teacher has the script.**
- **Listen again and note down any phrases you could use or adapt. Add these to your list from Step 1.**

## 3 ACTION!

**Now prepare your answers. Use the bullet points below to help you and your list of useful words and phrases from Steps 1 and 2.**

**1** What do you use a computer for?

- There are lots of possible answers here so give several.
- Add some details or examples, e.g. ***Je trouve l'ordinateur utile pour faire mes devoirs – par exemple, pour faire des recherches sur Internet.***
- You will mostly be using the present tense to say what you do regularly, but earn extra marks by using a past tense to give an example of what you have done, e.g. ***Par exemple, hier soir, j'ai fait des recherches sur Internet pour mon devoir de géographie.***

**2** Are you going to use a computer this evening?

- Use ***aller*** + infinitive to say what you are going to do, e.g. ***Je vais faire mes devoirs sur l'ordinateur***.

**3** Do you use any social networking sites, and how often?

- You can keep the answer simple: ***oui*** or ***non*** + a time expression.

**4** Are sites like Facebook and MySpace a good thing? Why?

- You can give positive or negative comments, or a mixture of both.
- Use a variety of structures to give your opinion, e.g. ***Je pense que..., Je trouve que..., À mon avis,..., Il me semble que...***
- Think of varying the way you give your reasons, e.g. ***parce que je préfère sortir avec mes amis, car on peut rester en contact, ça me permet d'avoir des amis partout dans le monde...***
- If you want to oppose ideas, use connectives like ***pourtant, par contre, d'un côté... de l'autre...***

**5** Have you ever put personal details on your web pages, and why/why not?

- Don't just give a yes/no answer. Remember to list which details.
- If the question is in the perfect tense, you will need to answer in the perfect tense, e.g. ***Tu as mis...? Non, je n'ai jamais mis...***
- ***Parce que*** is an easy way to give a reason but don't forget to try other ways too, e.g. ***pour*** + infinitive, ***afin de*** + infinitive.

**6** Do you download music? If so, what type of music?

- You could name more than one type of music.
- If you don't download music, extend your answer by saying why not, e.g. do you buy CDs, or do you not like music?
- Other ways to extend your answer: say when, how often, why you download, e.g. ***Je télécharge de la musique au moins une fois par semaine parce que...***

**7** How did people communicate before the invention of computers?

- Use the imperfect to describe what used to happen regularly in the past, e.g. ***On écrivait des lettres,...***
- The imperfect can be used to describe what it was like too, e.g. ***c'était lent***.

### GRADE TARGET

**To reach Grade C, you need to:**

- keep to the point, but give some opinions or examples.
- use the main tenses correctly. Most of your answers here will be in the present tense. Make sure you understand when to use the perfect tense (completed action in the past – what you did) and when to use the imperfect tense (e.g. to say what people used to do).
- use ***aller*** + infinitive to say what you are going to do.

**To aim higher than a C, you could:**

- use synonyms to add variety. How many different words can you find to replace the word ***super (Ce site web est super)***?
- use modal verbs accurately, e.g. to say what you can do or have to do.
- speak with a good French accent – you will be marked for accuracy and pronunciation.

**To aim for an A or A*, you could:**

- use pronouns, e.g. ***J'adore recevoir des mails. Je les lis sur l'ordi ou sur mon portable. J'ai une correspondante en France et je lui envoie un mail toutes les semaines.***
- make more complex sentences by contrasting ideas, using connectives such as ***par contre, pourtant, néanmoins,*** etc.

# 2A Controlled Assessment: Writing

## TASK: Writing about what you do in your free time

Write a letter or email to a French penfriend explaining what you do in your free time. You could include the following:

- Your favourite leisure activity: why you like it, when and where you do it, who with, etc.
- Details of any other activities you do.
- Details of music, TV programmes, films or books you like, and why.
- What you think of clothes, fashion, shopping.
- What you did last weekend.
- What you are going to do in the summer holidays.

### 1 THINK!

**Start by noting down a few useful words and phrases. Add to this list:**

1 Activities: *le sport? la danse? le cinéma? les jeux de console? la photographie?*
2 Why: *pour faire un peu d'exercice, parce que j'adore les comédies, ça me détend,...*
3 When: *le samedi matin? tous les week-ends? de temps en temps?*
4 Where: *dans un club? en ville? au collège? chez moi? dans un centre sportif?*
5 Likes: *j'adore, j'aime beaucoup, ma passion, c'est..., l'activité que j'aime le plus, c'est...*
6 Opinions: *c'est génial, je trouve ça intéressant, je pense que c'est bon pour la santé...*

### 2 PLAN!

- **Read the model text.**

Chère Alizé

Je vais te parler un peu de ce que je fais pendant mon temps libre. Mon passe-temps préféré, c'est le cinéma. Je vais au cinéma en ville une ou deux fois par semaine avec ma mère, mes copines ou mon petit copain. J'adore surtout les films romantiques, mais j'aime bien aussi les films d'action ou les films comiques. Ça me détend et ça me met de bonne humeur.

Le mercredi après-midi, je fais du judo dans un club au centre sportif. Je fais du judo depuis cinq ans et je fais ça pour prendre un peu d'exercice. De temps en temps, j'écoute de la musique sur mon iPod. Ma musique préférée, c'est la musique pop, mais j'aime aussi le rap et la musique classique. Je regarde la télé tous les soirs, surtout les vieux films ou les feuilletons.

Quand j'ai le temps, je lis les romans historiques.

Je déteste faire du shopping et je ne suis pas la mode. J'ai un look décontracté parce que je préfère les vêtements confortables.

Samedi dernier, j'ai fait du vélo avec mon petit copain et le soir, je suis allée à un concert au collège où mon petit frère jouait de la trompette.

Pendant les vacances d'été, j'ai l'intention de faire un stage d'art dramatique parce que je m'intéresse aussi au théâtre.

Amicalement

Sophie

- **Read the text again and note down any useful words or phrases you could use or adapt. Add these to your list from Step 1.**
- **Remember:** present tense for what you do regularly – ***je fais... j'aime...***
  perfect tense for completed actions – ***j'ai fait..., je suis allé(e)...***
  to talk about the future – ***je vais..., j'ai l'intention de...*** + infinitive
- **Note how the letter starts and ends.**

## 3 ACTION!

**Now prepare what you will write. Use the bullet points below to help you and use your list of useful words and phrases from Steps 1 and 2. Aim to write about 200 words.**

**1** Start and end in a way suitable for a letter or email.

- Start: ***Cher*** (for a boy) or ***Chère*** (for a girl) + penfriend's name.
- Finish ***Amicalement*** or ***Ton copain*** (for a boy) / ***Ta correspondante*** (for a girl) + your own name.

**2** Your favourite leisure activity: why you like it, when and where you do it, who with, etc.

- Introduce your favourite activity, e.g. ***Mon passe-temps préféré, c'est...*** or ***Ma passion, c'est...***
- Add the extra detail as suggested, e.g. ***J'adore le foot parce que je suis très sportif et j'aime beaucoup les jeux d'équipe. Je fais de l'entraînement au collège le jeudi soir avec...***

**3** Other activities.

- Mention several different activities: sport, music, TV, reading, going to gigs, etc.
- Give some extra detail (as in 2 above) for each one.
- Use synonyms to add variety, e.g. ***Je regarde les documentaires parce qu'ils sont amusants/ intéressants/instructifs/éducatifs.***

**4** What you think of clothes, fashion, shopping.

- Start with ***Je pense..., Je trouve que...*** or ***À mon avis,...*** to give your opinion.
- Think of interesting adjectives or expressions you could use, e.g. ***Le shopping, c'est un cauchemar..., La mode, c'est important, passionnant, super...***

**5** What you did last weekend.

- Mention at least two or three different things.
- Use the perfect tense to say what you did, e.g. ***J'ai aidé mon père dans le jardin, je suis allé(e) en ville pour acheter des chaussures,...***
- To be more impressive, use the imperfect tense to describe what it was like, e.g. ***il faisait beau, c'était sympa,...***

**6** What you are going to do in the summer holidays.

- Start: ***Pendant les vacances d'été*** and then try to give a couple of activities.
- Use ***Je vais*** + infinitive, or synonyms like ***j'ai l'intention de*** + infinitive.

## GRADE TARGET

**To reach Grade C, you need to:**

- use a variety of verbs to describe your activities, e.g. ***jouer, faire, écouter.***
- use verb + infinitive correctly, e.g. ***j'aime aller au cinéma, je voudrais faire du ski,...***
- add detail, e.g. ***tous les jours, le lundi soir, parce que j'adore les jeux,*** etc.

**To aim higher than a C, you could:**

- use modal verbs correctly, e.g. ***je peux aller en ville le samedi soir mais je dois rentrer avant minuit.***
- use synonyms to add variety to your opinions.
- not limit yourself to the ***je*** form: use ***on*** or ***nous*** to say what you do with others, e.g. ***on a joué... nous sommes allés...***

**To aim for an A or A*, you could:**

- use object pronouns to avoid repetition, e.g. ***Je lis régulièrement des magazines de mode. Je les lis parce que...*** Remember that the pronouns come before the verb.
- use present tense + ***depuis*** to say how long you have been doing an activity, e.g. ***Je fais du karaté depuis deux ans.***

# 2A Vocabulaire

## Comment choisir une nouvelle activité de loisir

| | |
|---|---|
| Je voudrais trouver un nouveau passe-temps. | *I'd like to find a new hobby.* |
| Tu pourrais... | *You could...* |
| écrire un blog sur Internet | *write a blog on the internet* |
| faire de l'astronomie | *take up astronomy* |
| faire de la danse hip-hop | *do break dancing* |
| faire de la randonnée | *go hiking* |
| jouer d'un instrument | *play an instrument* |
| Quel est ton passe-temps préféré? | *What is your favourite hobby?* |
| Quel matériel faut-il? | *What equipment do you need?* |
| Quels sont les avantages et les inconvénients? | *What are the advantages and disadvantages?* |
| Tu le pratiques où? Quand? | *Where do you do it? When?* |
| afin de + *infinitive*/pour + *infinitive* | *in order to* |
| le mien, la mienne, les miens, les miennes | *mine* |

## Comment parler «musique»

| | |
|---|---|
| Quel est ton style de musique préféré? | *What is your favourite type of music?* |
| Tu écoutes ta musique avec un lecteur MP3? | *Do you listen to your music with an MP3?* |
| D'où provient ta musique? | *Where does your music come from?* |
| le classique/la musique classique | *classical music* |
| la disco/la pop | *disco music/pop* |
| le hard rock/le métal/ le rap/le rock | *hard rock/heavy metal/rap/rock* |
| l'échange (*m*) avec amis | *swap with friends* |
| l'enregistrement (*m*) | *recording* |
| le téléchargement gratuit | *free download* |
| le téléchargement payant | *paid-for download* |
| Ça me détend | *It relaxes me* |
| Ça me donne envie de danser | *It makes me feel like dancing* |
| Ça m'énerve | *It gets on my nerves* |
| Ça me met de bonne humeur | *It puts me in a good mood* |
| C'est ennuyeux/monotone | *It's boring/monotonous* |
| C'est (trop) répétitif/rapide/ violent | *It's (too) repetitive/fast/violent* |

## Comment être chic pour pas cher

| | |
|---|---|
| le look décontracté | *the relaxed style* |
| le look glamour | *the glamorous style* |
| le look gothique/sport | *the gothic/sporty style* |
| les magasins (*mpl*) d'occasion | *second-hand shops* |
| les prix réduits (*mpl*) | *reduced prices* |
| Demande à tes parents... | *Ask your parents...* |
| J'achète toujours mes vêtements... | *I always buy my clothes...* |
| Je n'ai pas beaucoup d'argent | *I don't have a lot of money* |
| Je préfère acheter... | *I prefer to buy...* |
| Ils me donnent... | *They give me...* |
| Ma mère me donne... | *My mother gives me...* |
| démodé(e) | *out of fashion* |

## Comment comparer les loisirs: passé/présent

| | |
|---|---|
| Les films sortent de plus en plus rapidement en DVD. | *Films come out more and more quickly on DVD.* |
| Maintenant on écoute de la musique sur son MP3 ou iPod. | *Now people listen to music on an MP3 player or iPod.* |
| On écoutait des cassettes sur un baladeur. | *People used to listen to cassettes on a Walkman.* |
| Quand j'étais jeune, il n'y avait pas la télévision. | *When I was young, there was no television.* |
| avoir la télé avec peu de chaînes | *to have TV with few channels* |
| avoir la télé numérique, câblé ou par satellite | *to have digital, cable or satellite TV* |
| aller au petit cinéma du coin | *to go to the little local cinema* |
| envoyer un SMS à un copain | *to text a friend* |
| jouer aux jeux électroniques sophistiqués | *to play sophisticated electronic games* |
| regarder les cassettes vidéo sur un magnétoscope | *to watch videos on a video player* |
| voir un film dans un cinéma multiplex | *to see a film in a multiplex cinema* |
| dans les années 80 | *in the 1980s* |

## Comment se protéger sur le Net

| | |
|---|---|
| cambrioler | *to burgle* |
| dérangeant | *disturbing* |
| le droit d'auteur | *copyright* |
| le mot de passe | *password* |
| le réseau | *network* |
| le vol d'identité | *identity theft* |
| afficher leur prénom | *to post/display their first name* |
| indiquer leur nom de famille | *to post/display their surname* |
| donner leur nom d'utilisateur | *to give their user name* |
| donner leur adresse email | *to give their email address* |
| indiquer le nom de leur école | *to give their school name* |
| mettre le numéro de leur portable | *to give their mobile number* |
| rester en contact | *to stay in contact* |
| tchater | *to chat online* |
| en revanche | *on the other hand* |
| par contre | *on the other hand* |
| quand même | *all the same* |
| néanmoins | *nevertheless* |

# 2B Voyages et vacances

## Sais-tu comment...

- ❑ choisir une destination sympa?
- ❑ ne jamais te perdre?
- ❑ proposer une sortie?
- ❑ organiser une excursion?
- ❑ raconter un voyage?

## Controlled assessment

- **Have a conversation about holidays**
- **Write an account of a recent holiday for a travel blog**

Qu'est-ce que tu aimes faire?

## Stratégies

### À l'écoute

When listening in French how do you...

- distinguish between questions and statements?
- predict the words that will come up?
- listen for particular tenses?

### Lecture

When reading in French, how do you...

- skim for information?
- exploit contextual clues?
- deal with words you don't know?

## Grammaire active

As part of your French language 'toolkit', can you...

- use the future tense correctly?
- give instructions using the imperative?
- use modal verbs in the conditional to make suggestions?
- use the preposition 'à' correctly?

# 2B Comment choisir une destination sympa

(G) Les mots interrogatifs (V) Destinations de vacances (S) L'intonation: question ou affirmation?

Monsieur Diallo adore voyager. Il s'intéresse à l'histoire et aux visites culturelles. Pour lui, le confort est important et un bon restaurant est essentiel.

Madame Diallo aime le soleil. Son rêve: une journée reposante à la plage ou à la piscine. Elle ne veut absolument pas faire la cuisine!

Djibril a 18 ans. C'est un vrai sportif. Il aime la nature, le plein air et l'aventure… et aussi les boîtes de nuit.

Macky a 10 ans. Il adore les parcs d'attractions et les jeux à la plage. Il n'aime pas visiter les musées ni les monuments.

Toly a 15 ans. Ses sports préférés sont la natation et l'équitation. Elle est sociable et aime se faire des amis pendant les vacances.

**1**

Passez vos vacances dans un parc d'attractions! L'hôtel des Trois Hiboux***, sur le site du Parc Astérix, est situé dans un cadre exceptionnel. Le parc n'est pas loin de Paris et quand vous quittez le parc, vous trouverez à l'hôtel une salle de jeux pour les enfants, une bibliothèque et un bar avec terrasse.

**Notre avis: Une idée intéressante pour des vacances originales mais la destination n'est pas recommandée pour ceux qui veulent se reposer. Il ne fait pas toujours chaud en été.**

**2**

Village de Vacances en bord de mer Méditerranée, près de la ville de Nice

Ouvert de février à octobre. Séjour en pension complète ou demi-pension. Chambres de bon confort. Services sur place: accueil, restaurant panoramique, bar et discothèque, salon de détente, salle d'animation, clubs enfants. Piscine ouverte de mai à octobre.

**Notre avis: Le village de vacances est un bon truc pour découvrir le pays et faire des activités sportives et culturelles. Le climat méditerranéen est très agréable en été.**

**3**

**Hôtel Restaurant Brise de Mer**

dans un cadre pittoresque sur la côte ouest de l'île de la Corse

Chambres tout confort (avec balcon, douche ou bain, téléphone, télévision, coffre-fort) – restaurant avec vue panoramique sur le golfe – point de départ de nombreuses excursions – activités sportives (volley, tennis, cheval) – à 150 mètres de la plage.

**Notre avis: La Corse est une région de France qui mérite une visite pour la beauté de sa nature et pour son histoire. Normalement, en été, il fait très chaud.**

**4**

*Camping Les Chadenèdes*

Petit camping familial à la campagne, avec piscine, proche des 3 rivières: la Beaume, le Chassezac et l'Ardèche. Idéalement situé entre le pays des Vans, connu pour ses superbes sites d'escalade, et les Gorges de l'Ardèche, le camping vous offre des vacances au soleil et en plein air.

**Notre avis: L'Ardèche est une région sauvage, pour ceux qui préfèrent la nature à la ville. En plus, au camping, vous vivrez en plein air. Climat agréable mais risque de pluie*.**

*rain

**1** Lis tes textes sur la famille Diallo, page 66. Traduis-les en anglais.

**2** Écoute (1–5). C'est quel membre de la famille Diallo?

**3a** Lis les annonces, page 66. Les destinations sont en France ou dans différents pays d'Europe?

**3b** Relis et trouve dans le texte l'équivalent en français.

- **a** *not recommended for those who want to rest*
- **b** *full-board or half-board*
- **c** *in a picturesque setting*
- **d** *which is worth a visit*
- **e** *you will live outdoors*

**3c** Réponds.

- **a** Où se trouve Brise de Mer?
- **b** Quand est-ce que le village de vacances est ouvert?
- **c** Le camping est près de combien de rivières?
- **d** Pourquoi Toly aimerait-elle une piscine?
- **e** Quelles destinations ont des activités pour enfants?

**GRAMMAIRE**

| Question words | |
|---|---|
| place | *où?* |
| time | *quand?, à quelle heure?* |
| duration | *combien de temps?* |
| number/cost | *combien?* |
| reason | *pourquoi?* |
| how | *comment?, de quelle manière?* |
| people | *qui?, qui est-ce qui?* |
| things | *qu'est-ce que?, qu'est-ce qui?, quoi?, quel/quelle/quels/quelles?* |

**4** Écoute et réponds.

**5** Écris huit questions sur les textes, page 66. Utilise au moins cinq mots interrogatifs différents. Échange avec ton/ta partenaire qui répond.

*Exemple:* Où se trouve le village de vacances?

**6** Écoute. Recopie et complète la grille pour chaque personne (1–6).

*Exemple:*

| Destination | Reason |
|---|---|
| 1 campsite | has 5 children/cheaper |

**7a** À deux, discutez et choisissez la destination idéale (parmi les quatre, page 66), pour chaque membre de la famille Diallo.

*Exemple:*

**A** Je pense que Macky aimerait le village de vacances parce qu'il y a un club pour enfants et...

**7b** Mettez-vous d'accord sur une des destinations pour toute la famille. Expliquez pourquoi.

*Exemple:*

**A** Le camping serait idéal pour Djibril parce qu'il aime le plein air. Par contre, son père aime...

**STRATÉGIES**

**Question or statement?**

To tell if someone is asking a question, listen out for:

- question words: *qui? quand?* etc. These usually come at the beginning or end of the sentence.
- *est-ce que* at the start: *Est-ce qu'il y a une piscine?*
- subject pronouns that come after the verb: *Veux-tu faire du camping?*
- rising intonation (voice going up at the end of a sentence): *Il y a un bar?*

**8a** Écoute Djibril et sa mère. Qui préfère le village de vacances?

**8b** Réécoute. Tu entends combien de questions?

## À vous!

**9** Write a survey to find out which ingredients make a perfect holiday. Use each of the question words in the grammar panel (left) at least once. Try out your questions on your classmates.

*Exemple:* **Qu'est-ce que** tu préfères: les activités sportives ou les activités culturelles? **Qui** serait ton compagnon de vacances idéal?

**10** Choose a destination on page 66 for your own holiday with family or friends. Explain why you chose it. Say how it compares with the other places in the ads and why it suits each member of your group.

*Exemple:* Au village de vacances, il y a une piscine tandis qu'à l'hôtel, il n'y a pas de piscine. Mon petit frère aimerait bien...

# 2B Comment ne jamais te perdre

(G) L'impératif (V) Demander et indiquer le chemin (S) Prévoir le vocabulaire utilisé

## Arles, Provence: ville d'art et d'histoire

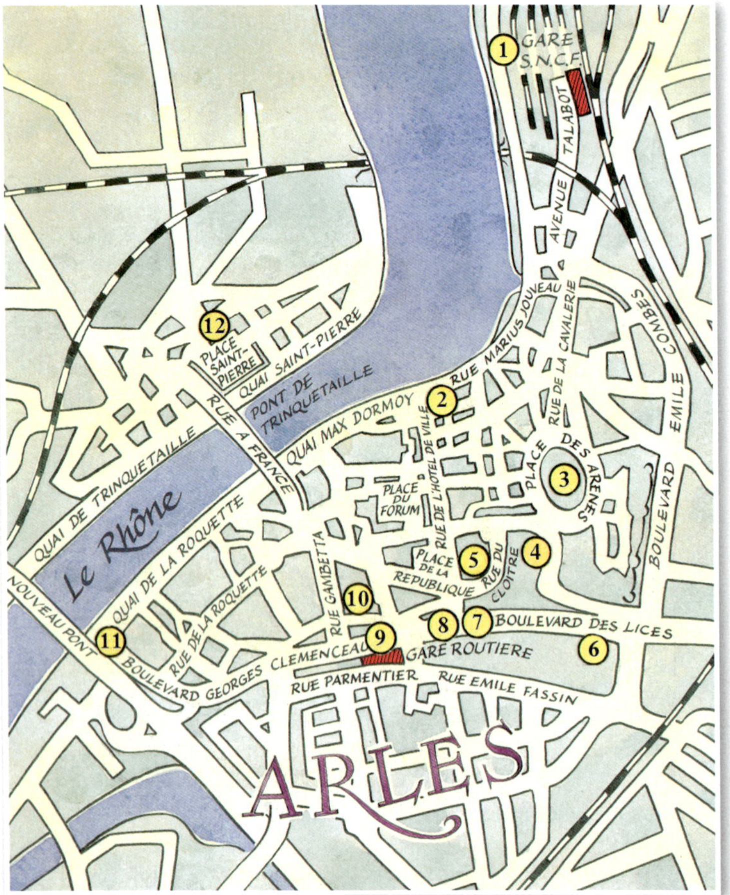


**Plan d'Arles – Légende**

1 Gare SNCF
2 Musée Réattu
3 Arènes
4 Théâtre antique
5 Église et cloître St-Trophime
6 Poste de police
7 Office du tourisme
8 Poste
9 Gare routière
10 Médiathèque-Espace Van Gogh
11 Tour de l'Écorchoir
12 Église St-Pierre

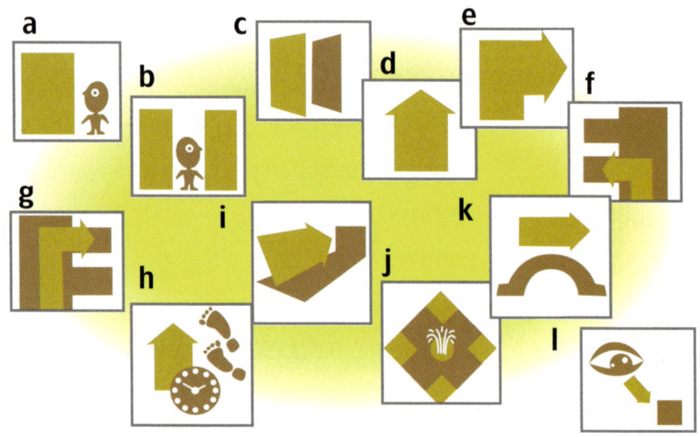

B

A

C

E

D

F

**VOCABULAIRE**

1 Allez tout droit.
2 Tournez à droite.
3 Prenez la première (rue) à gauche.
4 Continuez jusqu'au bout de la rue.
5 Il faut prendre la deuxième à droite.
6 Traversez la rue/le pont.
7 Ne traversez pas la place.
8 C'est à 10 mn à pied.
9 Vous trouverez/verrez le/la/les...
10 à côté du/de la/des...
11 entre le/la/les... et le/la/les...
12 en face du/de la/des...

**1** À deux. Regardez les photos d'Arles, page 68. C'est quel numéro sur la légende? Discutez. (**B**↔**A**)

*Exemple:* La photo A, c'est le numéro 3, parce que ce sont des arènes. Tu es d'accord?

**2** À deux: reliez les symboles a-l aux expressions 1–12. **A** dit la lettre d'un symbole, **B** dit l'expression qui correspond. (**B**↔**A**)

*Exemple:* **A** c **B** 12 En face de

**STRATÉGIES**

To help you understand when listening to an item on a specific topic, think of key words and phrases you know relating to that topic and which you think are likely to come up in the listening, e.g. phrases 1-12 on page 68.

**3a** Écoute les conversations (1-5) à l'office du tourisme. Recopie et complète les questions.

1 Où est la... la plus proche, s'il vous plaît?
2 Excusez-moi, où sont...?
3 ..., c'est par où? C'est loin?
4 Pour aller à..., s'il vous plaît?
5 Vous pouvez me dire comment aller au...?

**GRAMMAIRE**

**The future tense**

| | |
|---|---|
| *Vous trouverez/tu trouveras* | you'll find |
| *Vous verrez/tu verras* | you'll see |

See *Grammaire active*, page 77.

**GRAMMAIRE**

**The preposition *à* – at, to**

***à la** gare* (f)

***à l'**église* (before a m or f noun starting with a vowel or h)

***au** stade* (m)

***aux** arènes* (m or f plural)

**3b** Recopie les expressions 1–12, page 68. Écoute encore et coche quand tu les entends.

**3c** Réécoute. Suis les indications avec ton doigt sur le plan. L'hôtesse de l'office du tourisme fait une erreur. Laquelle?

**4** Écoute (1–6) et note les instructions en anglais.

*Exemple:* **1** *take the first street on the right*

**5** Jeu de rôle. Vous êtes au poste de police (6 sur le plan). **A** pose des questions (1–5, activité 3a) et **B** répond (expressions 1–12, page 68). (**B**↔**A**)

*Exemple:* **A** Pour aller au Musée Réattu, s'il te plaît?
**B** Tourne à gauche, continue tout droit...

**6** Lis cet extrait d'un guide sur Arles. Trouve les endroits A et B.

Quand vous quittez la gare routière, traversez la rue, passez devant l'office du tourisme, continuez tout droit sur le boulevard des Lices. Après le poste de police, traversez et prenez la première rue à gauche. Allez tout droit. À gauche, vous verrez **A**.

Sortez de **A**, tournez à gauche, puis à gauche et encore à gauche. Allez tout droit et vous trouverez **B** sur votre droite.

**GRAMMAIRE**

**The imperative**

Remember the two forms of address:

***vous*** – for adults you don't know

***tu*** – for friends, adults you know very well and children

Use the imperative to give directions or commands.

| Vous | Tu |
|---|---|
| *Allez* | *Va* |
| *Tournez* | *Tourne* |
| *Prenez* | *Prends* |
| *Traversez* | *Traverse* |
| *Continuez* | *Continue* |

See also *Grammaire active*, page 76.

## À vous!

**7** Draw a map of your town or neighbourhood. Include a key. Use your map to write an itinerary for a tour of your town.

*Exemple:* Ton point de départ est la gare. Sors de la gare et tourne à droite.

**8** Write and record a podcast of a guided tour to your town for French visitors and record it using the OxBox software. Explain what there is to do and see and include an itinerary and practical information such as opening hours and prices.

# 2B Comment proposer une sortie

(G) Vouloir, devoir, pouvoir + infinitif (V) Inviter, accepter/refuser une invitation (S) Survol d'un texte*

* skimming a text

## Où aller à Marseille?

*En vacances, Jonas fait la connaissance de Gaëlle.*

**J:** **Tu es libre mercredi après-midi? Si on sortait? Tu veux aller au cinéma?**
**G:** Ah, je suis désolée. Je voudrais bien mais mercredi je ne peux pas. On doit faire une excursion à Arles. C'est dommage...
**J:** **Jeudi alors?**
**G:** D'accord. Mais tu sais, il n'y a pas de bons films en ce moment. Si on faisait autre chose?
**J:** **On pourrait aller à la plage s'il fait beau. Ça te dit?**
**G:** D'accord. Je veux bien.
**J:** **Où est-ce qu'on se retrouve? Je pourrais passer au camping, si tu veux.**
**G:** Non, ce n'est pas la peine. On peut se retrouver au café de la plage, non?
**J:** **Comme tu veux. À quelle heure?**
**G:** À deux heures? Mais tu sais, je n'aime pas attendre... tu ne dois pas être en retard!
**J:** **OK! Ben, je vais essayer! À jeudi! Salut!**

### 1 Le parc balnéaire du Prado

**Plages du Roucas Blanc**: Piste de vélocross, jeux d'enfants, jeu de boules, jeu de volley-ball, solarium.

**Plages Escale Borély**: Spot remarquable pour la pratique de la planche à voile. Restaurants, matelas et parasols, piscine, boutiques.

**Plages de Bonneveine**: Zone de jeux, location de scooters et ski nautique.

### 2 Le Bowl Marseillais

**(Gratuit et non couvert)**

Considéré comme un des plus importants d'Europe!

Le Skate Park, d'une surface de 700m$^2$, est chaque année fréquenté par les passionnés de roller et de skateboard. Au Skate Park, on peut aussi faire d'autres sports tels que le roller, le bicross, le V.T.T. et la patinette.

### 3 Le musée boutique de l'OM

Il retrace le parcours de l'Olympique de Marseille lors d'expositions, etc.

### 4 Cinéma Pathé Madeleine

36, avenue Foch - 13004 Marseille 8 salles, 1373 places

**Mamma Mia ! Le Film - VF**

Comédie musicale de Phyllida Lloyd

avec Amanda Seyfried, Meryl Streep, Pierce Brosnan...

Durée : 1h48

### 5 Espace Julien - Marseille : les prochains concerts

Je **01 août**

Nada Surf + Underground Railroad + Kim Novak en concert
Espace Julien - Marseille - 20h30
\+ d'info & billetterie

Ve **02 août**

Chaos Fest
Espace Julien - Marseille - 20h
\+ d'info & billetterie

### 6 Le Millénium

Sortir » Clubs & Boîtes de Nuit à Marseille

Route Léon Lachamp, Entrée 20 € (le vendredi et samedi avec deux conso), 13 009 Marseille

Pour ma part, c'est une des meilleures boîtes de Marseille. Malgré le problème de la distance (la boîte est relativement loin du centre ville... **plus...**

**Exit Café**

Bar & Pub » Bars » Bars Lounge à Marseille | Restaurant » Restaurant Terrasse à Marseille

12, quai de Rive Neuve, Vieux Port, 13001 Marseille

**Couscous** ••••

Cet établissement situé sur le vieux port de Marseille est très fréquenté par la jeunesse marseillaise. Le fond de musique électro très sympathique... **plus...**

**1** Explique chaque panneau en anglais.

*Exemple:* **a** *shop*

a

b

c

d

e

f

**STRATÉGIES**

When you first read a text, skim it for information. Let your eyes flow over it to get a general idea of what it is about. Illustrations and headings can give you clues.

**2** Qu'est-ce qu'on peut faire à Marseille? Lis rapidement les annonces, page 70. Écris une liste en anglais pour un copain qui ne comprend pas le français.

**3** Écoute et lis la conversation entre Gaëlle et Jonas, page 70. Ils vont où? Où vont-ils se retrouver? Quel jour? À quelle heure?

**GRAMMAIRE**

**Modal verbs**

***je veux*** (I want) }
***je peux*** (I can) } + infinitive
***je dois*** (I must) }

Use the conditional of these verbs to be more polite: *je voudrais* – I would like, *on pourrait* – we could, etc.

Find and translate all the examples of these verbs in the dialogue, page 70 (there are 11).

See pages 195–196 for how to form *vouloir*, *pouvoir* and *devoir*.

**4** Note les expressions utilisées dans la conversation, page 70, quand:

**a** Jonas propose une sortie.
**b** Gaëlle refuse.
**c** Jonas propose une autre activité.
**d** Gaëlle accepte.

**5** À deux. Jouez les rôles de Gaëlle et Jonas.

**GRAMMAIRE**

**Suggestions**

To make a suggestion, use:

- *Tu veux...?* or *Tu voudrais...?* + infinitive OR
- *Si* + imperfect tense verb, e.g.

*Si on allait au café?* How about going to the café?

**6a** Écoute les conversations 1–4. Recopie et complète la grille.

| Activité proposée | Acceptée ou refusée? | Autre activité proposée? |
|---|---|---|
| 1 aller à la plage | | |

**6b** Réécoute 1 et 4. Note le lieu et l'heure de chaque rendez-vous.

**7** Relie les débuts et fins d'excuses. À toi d'inventer d'autres excuses! (au moins cinq)

*Exemple:* **1 e** Je n'ai pas d'argent.

| | |
|---|---|
| **1** Je n'ai pas | **a** avec Luc. |
| **2** Je dois | **b** préférée à la télé. |
| **3** Je déteste | **c** me laver les cheveux. |
| **4** Je sors déjà | **d** le rap. |
| **5** Il y a mon émission | **e** d'argent. |

**8** À deux. Imaginez que vous êtes à Marseille. **A** téléphone à **B** et propose une sortie. **B** refuse (et donne ses raisons) et propose une autre activité. Mettez-vous d'accord. Fixez une heure/un endroit pour vous retrouver. (**A**↔**B**)

*Exemple:* **A** Salut, Amy! Ici Nikki. Tu veux aller au Skate Park cet après-midi?

**B** Non, je ne peux pas, je dois faire...

## À vous!

**9** With a partner, write a scene for a French sitcom. A very shy (or very persistent) person is asking a boy/girl out but the latter is making up excuses to avoid going.

**10** What is there to do in Annecy, Dieppe or Blois? Choose a town. Use the internet to find out. Write an email (100 words) suggesting things to do there to a French friend.

*Exemple:* Tu veux...? Tu voudrais...? On pourrait... Si on allait/faisait...?

# 2B Comment organiser une excursion

(G) Verbe + à/de + infinitif (V) Les renseignements touristiques (S) Aborder les mots nouveaux d'un texte

Le Grand Parc du Puy du Fou invite les visiteurs à voyager dans l'histoire. Ici, pas d'attractions à sensations fortes mais des spectacles uniques et révolutionnaires, des animations ludiques pour petits et grands, et des reconstructions à l'identique pour remonter dans le temps: du Bourg 1900 au Village du 18ème siècle, des Mousquetaires du Roi aux Chevaliers du Donjon, de la Cité Médiévale au Fort de l'An Mil avec l'attaque des Vikings, jusqu'aux combats de Gladiateurs dans les arènes gallo-romaines. Un spectacle de fauconnerie immanquable permet d'observer des oiseaux de proie de très près. Éventuellement, on peut assister à la Cinéscénie, le plus grand spectacle historique nocturne au monde, qui a lieu le week-end. Une dizaine de nouveautés sont actuellement en préparation. Nous vous recommandons de prolonger le voyage dans le temps en passant la nuit dans une villa romaine. Commencez à préparer votre visite au Grand Parc en consultant **www.puydufou.com.**

**1** Lis les infos, page 72. Réponds aux questions d'un ami anglais.

**a** *Where is this park?*
**b** *Are there any rides?*
**c** *Why is this park special?*
**d** *What do you do there?*

**STRATÉGIES**

When reading a text with unfamiliar words, remember:

1. look for words that are similar in English and French, e.g. *invite*.
2. beware of false friends, e.g. *éventuellement* = 'possibly', not 'eventually'.
3. think of other words in the same family: *révolution-naire*.
4. remember sound-spelling links and read texts aloud or in your head, e.g. *oi* = 'wa' sound.

**2** Trouve d'autres mots du texte pour illustrer les stratégies 1–4.

*Exemple:* **1** visiteurs - *visitors*

**3** Écoute des touristes parler du Puy du Fou (1-5). Ont-ils une opinion favorable (F), défavorable (D) ou entre les deux (D/F)? Explique pourquoi.

*Exemple:* **1 F** – Elle a adoré le spectacle des oiseaux.

**4** À deux. Discutez d'une attraction touristique que vous avez visitée. Utilisez le passé composé.

*Exemple:* **A** Tu es déjà allé(e) à Alton Towers?
**B** Oui, j'y suis déjà allé(e).
**A** Qu'est-ce que tu as le plus aimé?
**B** Ce que j'ai le plus aimé, c'est...

**5** Lis les questions 1-12. Utilise les stratégies 1–4 ci-haut pour les mots nouveaux. Puis invente des réponses aux questions.

1. Est-ce qu'il y a des restaurants (dans le parc)?
2. Est-ce qu'on peut pique-niquer?
3. Est-ce qu'il y a une banque?
4. C'est où, la poste?
5. Je voudrais prendre le train. Il y a une gare ici?
6. À quelle heure est le prochain train?
7. Où sont les toilettes les plus proches?
8. Je peux avoir un plan et les horaires des spectacles?
9. Il faut réserver les places?
10. C'est combien, la nuit à l'hôtel? Il y a des tarifs enfants?
11. Les parkings sont-ils payants ou gratuits?
12. Quels sont les horaires d'ouverture des magasins?

**GRAMMAIRE**

**Verb + *à* or *de* + infinitive**

When there are two verbs together, the second is in the infinitive, e.g. *On peut assister...*

Some verbs must add *à* or *de** before the infinitive, e.g.

*inviter **à** venir* – to invite to come

*permettre **de** faire* – to allow to do

* becomes *d'* before a vowel

See also page 141.

**6a** Dans le texte, page 72, trouve des phrases contenant un verbe + ***à*** ou ***de*** + infinitif. Traduis-les en anglais.

**6b** Invente une phrase avec chacun des verbes suivants:

(avec **à**) aider, continuer, apprendre, réussir
(avec **de**) refuser, décider, dire, essayer, oublier
*Exemple:* refuser – J'ai refusé de sortir avec lui.

**7** Écoute les visiteurs (1–12) au Point Infos du parc. Note les réponses de l'hôtesse.

*Exemple:* **1** Oui; cinq restaurants + plusieurs fast-foods

**8** Jeu de rôle: **A** est le visiteur et **B** travaille à l'office du tourisme de votre ville. Posez les questions 1–12 et répondez. (**B**↔**A**)

*Exemple*:
**A** Il y a des restaurants?
**B** Oui, il y a trois restaurants et un fast-food.

## À VOUS!

**9** Post a message (100 words) on a French forum describing a visit to a theme park. Say what you saw/did/thought about it.

*Exemple*: Pendant les vacances, je suis allé(e) à Windsor et j'ai visité Legoland...

**10** Prepare a FAQ page for the website guide of your town or your favourite theme park: write questions and answers for French visitors.

*Exemple*:
**Q** Y a-t-il des parkings gratuits?
**R** Non, les parkings du centre-ville sont payants.

# 2B Comment raconter un voyage

G Si + conditionnel   V Raconter un voyage   S Le temps des verbes

Noémie, 15 ans

## FORUM DES JEUNES GLOBE-TROTTERS

**Mon séjour en Tunisie**

Normalement, on ne part pas pendant les vacances, mais l'année dernière, je suis allée en Tunisie. C'est un pays très intéressant en Afrique du Nord. Je suis partie avec ma famille le 15 juillet. Nous sommes restés deux semaines. Nous avons pris l'avion pour Tunis.

Après être arrivés à Tunis, nous sommes allés à l'Hôtel Oasis. L'hôtel était assez vieux mais confortable. Mes parents avaient une jolie chambre avec un petit balcon et vue sur la vieille ville. Par contre, ma chambre n'avait ni balcon ni vue!

Il faisait beau et il y avait du soleil tous les jours. Nous avons fait beaucoup d'excursions. Nous avons visité Tunis, la médina (la vieille ville), les souks (marchés arabes) et les mosquées. C'était super mais il y avait beaucoup de monde partout. Nous avons aussi visité le musée du Bardo où il y avait des collections de mosaïques romaines. Comme je n'y connais rien, j'ai trouvé ça inintéressant. En plus, il faisait vraiment très chaud ce jour-là, c'était pénible.

Par contre, j'ai adoré l'excursion en car à Sidi Bou Saïd, un petit village bleu et blanc très pittoresque à l'est de Tunis, et la visite du site historique de Carthage. C'était passionnant. J'ai aussi aimé prendre le train pour aller à Sousse au bord de la mer.

J'ai beaucoup aimé mon séjour en Tunisie. Si je pouvais, j'y retournerais le plus vite possible. Cette année, on ne part pas, mais si c'était moins cher, on partirait tous les ans. L'année prochaine, si j'avais le choix, j'irais au Mexique!

**1** À deux, lisez le texte. Discutez de ce que vous ne comprenez pas. Cherchez le minimum de mots dans le dictionnaire. Résumez le texte en exactement 30 mots.

**2** Trouve et note toutes les expressions positives et toutes les expressions négatives du texte.

*Exemple:* **Positif** C'est un pays très intéressant
**Négatif** assez vieux

**3** Lis le premier paragraphe. Choisis la phrase fausse.

**a** *Noémie doesn't usually go on holiday.*
**b** *She went to Tunisia last June.*
**c** *Tunisia is in North Africa.*
**d** *The weather was good.*

**Sondage**

**a** Pendant les vacances, tu es allé(e) où?
**b** Tu es parti(e) avec qui?
**c** Tu as voyagé comment?
**d** Tu es resté(e) combien de temps?
**e** Tu as dormi où?
**f** Quel temps faisait-il ?
**g** Qu'est-ce que tu as fait?
**h** C'était comment?

**4** Écoute Noémie (**1–7**). Elle répond à quelles questions du sondage?

*Exemple:* **1** – c, ...

**5** À deux: **A** pose les questions du sondage, **B** joue le rôle de Noémie et répond.

**6** Écoute Marie, Seb et Zoé. Résume leurs réponses aux questions du sondage en anglais.

*Exemple:* **Marie**: *seaside, western France, ...*

**GRAMMAIRE**

**If ... then ...**

For unlikely situations, use ***si*** + imperfect + **conditional**.

***Si** j'avais le choix, **j'irais** au Mexique.*

If I could choose, I would go to Mexico.

This example is taken from Noémie's text. Read it through again. Find another example and translate it.

**7** Écoute les huit personnes. Ils aimeraient visiter quels pays? Pourquoi? Et toi?

**STRATÉGIES**

**Listen out for verb tenses**

The tense of a verb affects meaning, so practise listening out for typical verb endings. How would you **hear** which of these had already happened?

*Je visite le musée. / J'ai visité le musée. / Je visiterai le musée.*

The future and conditional forms often sound very similar: *je ferai / je ferais.*

**8** Écoute et choisis la bonne traduction.

**a** *is visiting Scotland / has visited Scotland*
**b** *went to Paris / is going to go to Paris*
**c** *has been to Italy / would like to go to Italy*
**d** *would like to go to Australia / has been to Australia*

**9** Relis le texte de Noémie. Trouve et explique pourquoi il y a des verbes:

**a** au présent
**b** au passé composé
**c** à l'imparfait
**d** au conditionnel

*Exemple:* Normalement, on ne part pas = *present tense because it is something that happens regularly*

**STRATÉGIES**

**Vary your tense**

To get top marks in your exam, you need to find ways to use a variety of tenses. How did Noémie do this in her text? How could you create opportunities to use different tenses if you were writing about your hobbies?

Revise *Grammaire active*, page 22.

## À vous!

**10** Think of someone famous and imagine where they might have gone on holiday. Put yourself in their place and write a report of the trip (+/- 150 words). Say:

- where you went and when
- who you went with
- what you did
- what the weather was like
- what you thought of it

*Exemple:* Je m'appelle James Bond. L'année dernière, je suis allé à...

**11** Do a personality test. Write ten questions about hypothetical situations, such as the examples given below. Write your answers to the questions on a sheet of paper. Then use the questions to interview two different people. Whose answers are closest to your own?

*Exemples:*

- Si tu avais le choix, tu visiterais quel pays?
- Si les voitures n'existaient pas, que ferais-tu?
- Si tu parlais au Premier Ministre, que dirais-tu?

# 2B Grammaire active

## HOW TO ASK QUESTIONS

| There are three ways of asking 'yes' or 'no' questions. | |
|---|---|
| 1 Form a normal sentence and raise your voice. | *Tu aimes les pommes?* |
| 2 Add **est-ce que** at the beginning of the sentence. | *Est-ce que tu aimes les pommes?* |
| 3 Reverse the order of the subject of the verb, adding a hyphen (more formal). | *Aimes-tu les pommes?* *Mange-t-il de la viande?* * |

*Add *t* to help pronunciation.

**1** Ask the following questions in two other ways.

*Exemple:* **a** Tu veux jouer au volley?/Veux-tu jouer au volley?

- **a** Est-ce que tu veux jouer au volley?
- **b** Aime-t-il la natation?
- **c** On fait du shopping?

## QUESTION WORDS

For other questions, you need to use a question word:

who – ***qui*** what – ***que/qu'est-ce que/qu'est-ce qui/quoi***
when – ***quand*** how much/many – ***combien***
how – ***comment*** why – ***pourquoi*** where – ***où***

| **Which?** | singular | plural |
|---|---|---|
| masculine | **quel** | **quels** |
| feminine | **quelle** | **quelles** |

To sound more French, use ***est-ce que*** after a question word: *Où/Quand/Pourquoi... est-ce que tu manges?*

**What**

Before the verb, use ***que/qu'est-ce que***:

***Que** fais-tu pendant les grandes vacances?*

***Qu'est-ce que** tu fais pendant les grandes vacances?*

After the verb, use ***quoi***:

*Pendant les grandes vacances, **tu fais quoi**?*

**2** Write 12 questions for your partner using all of the question words above. Then answer their questions. (**B↔A**)

*Exemple:* **A** Quel sport aimes-tu faire?
**B** J'adore faire du...

## THE IMPERATIVE

Use this form of the verb to give an order, an instruction or a piece of advice.

– for people you normally speak to as *tu*:
use the *tu* form of the verb, remove the *tu* and the final *–s* for *–er* verbs

***écouter → tu écoutes → Écoute!***
***venir → tu viens → Viens!***

– for people you normally speak to as *vous*:
use the *vous* form of the verb, without using the word *vous*

***écouter → vous écoutez → Écoutez!***
***venir → vous venez → Venez!***

To say not to do something, put ***ne/n' ... pas*** around the verb:

***N'**écoute **pas!*** ***Ne** venez **pas!***

**Les huit commandements de l'éco-touriste**

1. Utiliser l'*** avec modération,
2. prendre le ***, c'est plus malin.
3. Oublier la *** et protéger la nature,
4. faire du ***, c'est plus sage.
5. Aller à *** pour la santé,
6. et à *** quand il fait beau.
7. En ville, choisir le ***, c'est écolo,
8. et prendre le ***, la bonne astuce!

**3** Read the charter for green travellers. Fill in the correct form of transport and it will rhyme!

voiture avion métro vélo
bus train pied covoiturage*

* car sharing

**4** Rewrite the charter using the verbs in the imperative, first with the second person singular (*tu*), then the second person plural (*vous*).

*Exemple:* **1** (tu) Utilise l'avion.../(vous) Utilisez l'avion...

### TALKING ABOUT THE FUTURE

There are several ways to talk about something in the future:

- **the present tense** to talk about events which are certain to happen very soon:
  ***Je pars*** *ce soir.* — **I'm leaving** tonight.
- ***aller*** + infinitive to talk about something that is going to happen in the near future:
  ***Il va*** *travailler ce week-end.* — **He's going** to work this weekend.
- **the conditional** to talk about future plans which are not certain (wishes, ambitions or dreams):
  ***Tu aimerais*** *habiter en France?* — **Would you like** to live in France?

But there is also a special tense:

- **the future tense**

The future tense describes what will happen in the future. To form the future tense, add these endings to the infinitive (if the infinitive ends in *-e*, take off the *-e* first):

| | | | |
|---|---|---|---|
| *je* | *-ai* | *nous* | *-ons* |
| *tu* | *-as* | *vous* | *-ez* |
| *il/elle/on* | *-a* | *ils/elles* | *-ont* |

***J'habiterai*** *une grande maison.* I **shall live** in a big house.

*Mes parents* ***passeront*** *trois jours au bord de la mer.*
My parents **will spend** three days at the seaside.

**5** Find the five future tense verbs in the box below.

je partais elle sortira je choisirai vous racontez
ils perdront tu proposeras elles comparent
on a parlé nous organiserons

**6** Rewrite the sentences changing the underlined verbs into the future tense. Then translate them into English.

*Exemple:* Je parle français. → Je parlerai français. / *I shall speak French.*

**a** On part pour Paris dans deux semaines.
**b** Nous y restons quatre jours.
**c** Je visite tous les monuments.
**d** Tu sors le soir?
**e** Mon copain m'attend au café.
**f** Mes grands-parents prennent le train.

### IRREGULAR FUTURES

Some verbs form their future with an irregular stem instead of an infinitive.

Here are some common examples:

| | |
|---|---|
| *avoir* → *j'aurai* | *pouvoir* → *je pourrai* |
| *aller* → *j'irai* | *savoir* → *je saurai* |
| *devoir* → *je devrai* | *venir* → *je viendrai* |
| *être* → *je serai* | *voir* → *je verrai* |
| *faire* → *je ferai* | *vouloir* → *je voudrai* |

See pages 195–196 for the full pattern of these verbs.

**7** Read Alizé's bubble. Note all the examples of *aller* + infinitive and replace them with future tense verbs.

Dans 20 ans, je vais être reporter pour le journal 'le Monde'. Je vais avoir un petit appartement à Paris et je vais faire beaucoup de voyages. De temps en temps, je vais venir en Angleterre en vacances et nous allons pouvoir faire des excursions ensemble. On va s'amuser!

# 2B Controlled Assessment: Speaking

## TASK: Holidays

You are going to have a conversation with your teacher about holidays.
Your teacher will ask you the following:

- What do you usually like doing during the summer holidays?
- Do you prefer to go away or stay at home? Why?
- What is your ideal type of holiday and why?
- What will you do this summer?
- When and where was your last holiday?
- Who did you go with and what did you do?
- !

*(! Remember: at this point, you will have to respond to something you have not prepared.)*

The dialogue will last between 4 and 6 minutes.

## 1 THINK!

**Read the phrases below. Write down any others that you might find useful for the speaking task.**

- ☐ **Free time activities**: retrouver mes amis, faire du sport, regarder la télé...
- ☐ **Advantages of staying at home**: plus relaxant, moins cher,...
- ☐ **Advantages of going away**: plus intéressant, une autre façon de vivre,...
- ☐ **Justifying your choice**: parce que, car, ça me permet de...
- ☐ **Ideal holidays**: au bord de la mer, à la montagne, un pays chaud, un hôtel moderne...
- ☐ **Giving reasons**: pour me reposer, parce que j'aime la vie en plein air, comme j'adore le ski...
- ☐ **Details of past holiday**: chez ma grand-mère, faire du camping, faire un échange...
- ☐ **Useful perfect tense verbs**: je suis allé(e), je suis parti(e), je suis resté(e), j'ai vu...
- ☐ **Useful imperfect tense verbs**: c'était (intéressant), il y avait (du vent)...

***! Can you predict what the unexpected question might be?***

Do you think school summer holidays are too long? Have you ever been abroad?
**Add to your list any language you would need to answer these questions too.**

## 2 PLAN!

- **Listen to a model conversation. Your teacher has the script.**
- **Listen again and note down any phrases you could use or adapt. Add these to your list from Step 1.**

# 3 ACTION !

**Now prepare your answers. Use the bullet points below to help you and your list of useful words and phrases from Steps 1 and 2.**

**1** What do you usually like doing during the summer holidays?

- Use the present tense to say what you usually do, e.g. ***J'aime retrouver mes amis. Souvent on va au cinéma.***
- Mention several different activities.
- Add a little extra detail to make it more interesting, e.g. ***Quand il fait beau, je vais à la pêche. Je joue au tennis avec ma copine.***

**2** Do you prefer to go away or stay at home? Why?

- Choose ***Je préfère rester à la maison*** or ***Je préfère partir***. Give reasons to justify your choice.
- Remember: ***plus*** + adjective = more, ***moins*** + adjective = less, e.g. ***c'est plus relaxant, c'est moins intéressant***.
- Give different reasons, e.g. ***parce que je n'aime pas quitter mon chien, car c'est moins cher, ça me permet de me faire des amis***.

**3** What is your ideal type of holiday and why?

- You could start ***Pour moi, les vacances idéales, c'est*** ... and follow with as much detail as you like: place, type of destination, who with, how long you would stay, e.g. ... ***trois semaines au bord de la mer à Tahiti avec mon petit copain***.
- Use the conditional ***Je voudrais*** or ***J'aimerais***, e.g. ***J'aimerais faire de la planche à voile. Je voudrais faire du camping***.
- Give reasons for your choice, e.g. ***pour voir la tour Eiffel, comme j'ai toujours voulu visiter l'Afrique***.

**4** What will you do next summer?

- Make up details if necessary.
- Use ***aller*** + infinitive or the future tense to say what you will do, e.g. ***Je vais rester chez moi, J'irai en Irlande...***

**5** When and where was your last holiday?

- If you haven't been away, make up the details.
- Remember how to say 'to' a place: ***à*** + town, ***en*** + feminine countries, ***au*** + masculine countries, ***aux*** + plural countries, e.g. ***Je suis allé(e) à Paris / en Espagne / au Portugal / aux États-Unis***.
- You need to say when as well as where, e.g. ***l'année dernière, en avril, en 2009***.
- You could add an opinion too, e.g. ***C'était génial / un voyage intéressant***.

**6** Who did you go with and what did you do?

- Vary the verbs you use. Here, you could use ***Je suis parti(e) avec*** instead of ***Je suis allé(e) avec***, just to show off the range of your vocabulary.
- Mention several things you did, using perfect tense verbs, e.g. ***on a mangé***.
- Link your ideas together, e.g. ***Un jour j'ai visité un château, et après, on a mangé des crêpes***.

## GRADE TARGET

**To reach Grade C, you need to:**

- speak clearly with a good accent.
- use the main tenses correctly (e.g. present tense for what you usually do, perfect tense for what you did in the past).
- use ***parce que*** to justify your choices and give reasons.

**To aim higher than a C, you could:**

- use a greater variety of tenses, e.g. use the imperfect to give an opinion in the past or a conditional to say what you would like.
- use link words to create longer, more complex sentences.
- use a range of expressions of time or frequency, e.g. ***d'habitude, souvent, de temps en temps, un jour***.

**To aim for an A or A*, you could:**

- use a '***si***' clause, e.g. ***s'il pleut, je reste à la maison / si j'avais beaucoup d'argent, j'aimerais partir en Australie***.
- use a perfect infinitive, e.g. ***après avoir visité tous les monuments, on est allés à Disneyland Paris***.

# 2B Controlled Assessment: Writing

## TASK: An account of a recent holiday

Write an account of a recent holiday or day trip you have been on for a travel blog.

You could include the following:

- Where you went, the time of year and how long you stayed.
- How you got there and who you travelled with.
- Where you stayed and what it was like.
- What you did and what you enjoyed most/least.
- What the weather was like.
- Your opinion.
- Whether you will go again and why (or why not).

## 1 THINK!

**Start by noting down a few key facts:**

1. destination: *un pays étranger? la mer? la montagne? un village de vacances?*
2. when: *le mois (juillet? août?) ou la saison (au printemps? en été?)*
3. how long: *un jour? quelques jours? deux semaines?*
4. who you went with: *ta famille? tes copains? tes camarades de classe?*
5. transport: *l'avion? le train? le vélo?*
6. accommodation: *un camping? un hôtel? un appartement?*
7. activities: *des excursions? bronzer sur la plage? un bon livre?*
8. weather: *du soleil? des nuages? de la neige?*

## 2 PLAN!

- **Read the model text.**

L'année dernière, au mois d'août, je suis allée à Royan. Royan est une assez grande ville au bord de la mer dans l'ouest de la France. Je suis partie avec ma mère et mes deux demi-sœurs. On est allées en voiture et on a pris le bateau à Portsmouth. La traversée en bateau était très longue et j'ai eu le mal de mer. C'était horrible.

Une fois arrivées à Royan, nous avons trouvé le camping où nous avons passé quinze jours. J'étais déçue parce que c'était un petit camping pas très joli.

Ma mère et mes demi-sœurs voulaient seulement aller à la plage et bronzer. Je n'ai pas vraiment aimé les journées à la plage parce que je me suis ennuyée.

C'était nul. J'ai nagé un peu dans la mer, j'ai lu deux gros romans et j'ai mangé des glaces.

On a fait deux ou trois excursions dans la région qui est assez belle. C'était intéressant. Ce que j'ai préféré, c'est jouer au volley ou au ping-pong avec des copains au camping. Heureusement, il y avait du soleil et il faisait chaud tous les jours.

J'ai trouvé mon séjour un peu ennuyeux. À mon avis, les journées à la plage étaient une perte de temps.

Je ne retournerai pas à Royan parce que je préfère les vacances plus actives et j'aimerais visiter une autre région la prochaine fois que j'irai en France.

- **Read the text again and note down any opinions or adjectives that you could use. Add these to your list from Step 1.**
- **Look carefully at the verbs used and make a note of any you could reuse:**
  perfect tense for completed actions – ***j'ai nagé…, je suis allé(e)…***
  imperfect tense for opinions and descriptions – ***c'était nul, il y avait du soleil***
  future tense for what you will do – ***j'irai, je retournerai***
  conditional for what you would like – ***j'aimerais…, je voudrais…***

## 3 ACTION!

**Now prepare what you will write. Use the bullet points below to help you and use your list of useful words and phrases from Steps 1 and 2. Aim to write about 200 words.**

**1** Where you went, the time of year and how long you stayed.

- Use the perfect tense. Remember that many verbs of movement make the perfect tense with ***être***, e.g. ***je suis allé, je suis parti***.
- As well as naming the place you went to, e.g. ***Blackpool***, you could say where it is, e.g. ***dans le nord-ouest de l'Angleterre*** and what type of place it is, e.g. ***une assez grande ville au bord de la mer***.

**2** How you got there and who you travelled with.

- Give means of transport/describe your journey. You could add extra detail, e.g. ***On est allés à Newcastle en taxi et puis on a pris le train jusqu'à…*** or an opinion, e.g. ***Le voyage était un peu long mais j'ai écouté mon iPod, alors je ne me suis pas ennuyé(e)***.
- Mention who you travelled with.

**3** What you did and what you enjoyed most/least.

- Use ***J'ai préféré*** to say what you liked best.
- ***Je n'ai pas vraiment aimé*** is a simple way to say what you liked least.

**4** What the weather was like.

- Try to give a couple of details, e.g. ***Il y avait du soleil, mais le soir, il faisait assez froid.***

**5** Your opinion.

- Make a couple of points and introduce them in a different way to show off what you know, e.g. ***J'ai trouvé le parc d'attractions super. À mon avis, c'était un séjour sympa.***

**6** Whether you will go again and why.

- To talk about the future, use the future tense or ***aller*** + infinitive, e.g. ***je retournerai, l'année prochaine, on va aller….***
- Give a reason using ***parce que***, e.g. ***parce qu'il y a toujours quelque chose à faire***.

### GRADE TARGET

**To reach Grade C, you need to:**

- include adjectives for descriptions and opinions, using ***c'était*** if you are talking about the past, e.g. ***c'était intéressant***.
- use the perfect tense correctly.
- check all spellings.

**To aim higher than a C, you could:**

- use a greater variety of tenses, e.g. use the present to say what you normally like or do, or the conditional to say what you would do another time.
- Create longer, more complex sentences by using link words.
- Don't just stick to the ***je*** form: use ***on*** or ***nous*** when talking about 'we' (e.g. ***on a visité… nous sommes allés…***)

**To aim for an A or A*, you could:**

- use less common connectives and include negatives to create complex sentences, e.g. ***Je n'ai pas fait de sport parce que je ne suis pas du tout sportive, tandis que ma sœur a joué au volley ou au tennis tous les jours***.
- use 'if' clauses with the conditional, e.g. ***si je pouvais, j'irais à l'étranger l'année prochaine***.

# Vocabulaire

## Comment choisir une destination sympa

| | |
|---|---|
| le camping | *campsite* |
| la chambre | *room* |
| la douche | *shower* |
| l'équitation (*f*) | *horse-riding* |
| l'escalade (*f*) | *rock-climbing* |
| l'île (*f*) | *island* |
| le musée | *museum* |
| la natation | *swimming* |
| le parc d'attractions | *theme park* |
| la piscine | *swimming pool* |
| la plage | *beach* |
| le séjour | *stay* |
| le village de vacances | *holiday village* |
| demi-pension/pension complète | *half-board/full-board* |
| en plein air | *in the open air, outdoors* |

## Comment ne jamais te perdre

| | |
|---|---|
| Où est le... le plus proche, s'il vous plaît? | *Where is the nearest... please?* |
| ..., c'est par où? C'est loin? | *Which way is...? Is it far?* |
| Pour aller à..., s'il vous plaît? | *Which way is it to..., please?* |
| Allez tout droit. | *Go straight on.* |
| Tournez à droite. | *Turn right.* |
| Prenez la première (rue) à gauche. | *Take the first on the left.* |
| jusqu'au bout de la rue | *to the end of the road* |
| Traversez la rue/le pont. | *Cross the road/the bridge.* |
| C'est à 10 minutes à pied. | *It's a 10 minute walk.* |
| Vous trouverez/verrez le/la/les... | *You'll find/see...* |
| à côté du/de la/des... | *next to the...* |
| entre le/la/les... et le/la/les... | *in between the... and the ...* |
| en face du/de la/des... | *opposite the* |
| l'église (*f*) | *church* |
| la gare routière | *coach station* |
| la médiathèque | *media library* |
| le poste de police | *police station* |

## Comment proposer une sortie

| | |
|---|---|
| On peut aller... | *You can go...* |
| On pourrait (regarder un DVD). | *We could (watch a DVD).* |
| Si on allait (au café)? | *How about going (to a café)?* |
| Si on faisait autre chose? | *How about doing something else?* |
| Tu es libre (vendredi soir)? | *Are you free (on Friday evening)?* |
| Tu veux (aller au café)? | *Do you want to (go to the café)?* |
| Ça te dit? | *Do you fancy that?* |
| D'accord! Bonne idée. | *OK! Good idea.* |
| On doit (faire une excursion). | *We have to (go on an excursion).* |
| Je ne peux pas. | *I can't.* |
| Je sors déjà avec (Luc). | *I'm already going out with (Luc).* |
| Je suis désolé(e) mais... | *I'm sorry but...* |
| Je veux bien. | *I'd like that.* |
| Je voudrais bien mais... | *I'd like to but...* |
| Où est-ce qu'on se retrouve? | *Where shall we meet?* |
| À quelle heure? | *At what time?* |
| On se retrouve (à six heures/ au café de la plage.) | *Let's meet (at six o'clock/ at the beach café.)* |
| le rendez-vous | *date* |
| la sortie | *outing* |

## Comment organiser une excursion

| | |
|---|---|
| Est-ce qu'il y a des restaurants? | *Are there restaurants?* |
| C'est où, la poste? | *Where is the post office?* |
| Il y a une gare ici? | *Is there a station around here?* |
| À quelle heure est le prochain train? | *What time is the next train?* |
| Où sont les toilettes les plus proches? | *Where are the nearest toilets?* |
| Je peux avoir un plan et les horaires des spectacles? | *May I have a map and a timetable for the shows?* |
| Il faut réserver les places? | *Do we have to book tickets?* |
| C'est combien, la nuit à l'hôtel? | *How much is a night at the hotel?* |
| Il y a des tarifs enfants? | *Are there discounts for children?* |
| Les parkings sont-ils payants ou gratuits? | *Are the car parks free or paying?* |
| Quels sont les horaires d'ouverture des magasins? | *What are the opening hours of the shops?* |
| l'aire (*f*) de pique-nique | *picnic area* |
| la boîte aux lettres | *post box* |
| le distributeur de billets | *cashpoint machine* |
| le point infos | *information point* |

## Comment raconter un voyage

| | |
|---|---|
| Je suis allé(e) en Tunisie. | *I went to Tunisia.* |
| Je suis parti(e) avec mes parents. | *I went with my parents.* |
| On a pris l'avion/le train/le car. | *We went by plane/train/coach.* |
| Tu es resté(e) combien de temps? | *How long did you stay?* |
| Je suis resté(e) deux semaines. | *I stayed for two weeks.* |
| Tu as dormi où? | *Where did you sleep?* |
| Dans un hôtel/un camping/ une auberge de jeunesse. | *In a hotel/at a campsite/ at a youth hostel.* |
| Quel temps faisait-il? | *What was the weather like?* |
| Il faisait beau et il y avait du soleil tous les jours. | *The weather was nice and it was sunny every day.* |
| Qu'est-ce que tu as fait? | *What did you do?* |
| J'ai fait des excursions. | *I went on excursions.* |
| C'était comment? | *What was it like?* |
| C'était super/pas mal. | *It was great/not bad.* |
| Si je pouvais, j'y retournerais. | *If I could, I would go back there.* |

# 3A Chez moi et aux alentours

## Sais-tu comment...

- ❑ raconter une fête familiale?
- ❑ échanger ta maison?
- ❑ devenir l'ambassadeur de ta région?
- ❑ trouver la ville jumelle idéale?
- ❑ découvrir Madagascar?

C'est comment, chez toi?

## Controlled assessment

- **Talk about a special occasion you celebrated with your family**
- **Write a letter describing your home town**

## Stratégies

### Lecture

When reading, how do you...

- make sense of new words?
- work out people's opinions?
- look out for words which reverse meanings?

### À l'oral

In French, how do you...

- practise your pronunciation by reading aloud?
- make sure you have the right words at your disposal?
- build longer sentences?

## Grammaire active

As part of your French language 'toolkit' can you...

- use the pluperfect tense?
- use emphatic pronouns?
- use *depuis* correctly?
- use demonstrative adjectives?
- use relative pronouns?

# 3A Comment raconter une fête familiale

**G** Le plus-que-parfait **V** Raconter un évènement **S** Reconnaître l'intonation (question, exclamation, etc.) **P** Lire à haute voix pour améliorer la prononciation

## Forum-Internet

Fichier Actions Outils ?

**Sam, Limoges:**

**A** Une fête inoubliable pour moi, c'était quand Bastien, un copain, m'a invité à Noël chez lui, en Provence. Je suis musulman et donc je n'avais jamais fêté Noël avant ça. En plus, je vis seul avec ma mère, alors je n'étais jamais allé à une vraie fête de famille.

**B** Le Noël Provençal, c'est vraiment génial! Quand je suis arrivé, Bastien et ses petites sœurs étaient allés au Marché de Noël et ils avaient acheté des décorations: ils avaient fait une crèche avec des santons. Les parents de Bastien avaient préparé les sept plats du repas traditionnel de Noël. Ils avaient aussi posé les Treize Desserts traditionnels sur la table.

**C** On est tous allés écouter les chants de Noël à l'église puis quand on est revenus, on a mangé. Ensuite, on a fait la fête. C'était super! Et toi? Tu as eu des fêtes familiales inoubliables dans ta vie? Raconte-moi!

1 **Ta meilleure fête familiale, c'était quand? Quoi? Où?**
2 **Qu'est-ce que tu as fait?**
3 **C'était comment?**
4 **Est-ce qu'on avait fait des préparatifs à l'avance?**

**Marion, Bordeaux:**

Moi, la fête que je n'oublierai jamais, c'est la fête d'anniversaire pour mes 16 ans, l'année dernière. Mon frère et ma sœur avaient organisé une surprise pour moi à la maison. Ils avaient décoré le séjour avec des ballons et des banderoles et ils avaient fait un super gâteau. Ils avaient invité tous mes copains: ils s'étaient tous cachés derrière les rideaux alors moi, je ne les avais pas vus en entrant! Quelle surprise quand ils sont tous sortis! J'ai eu de super cadeaux. J'ai adoré le cadeau de mon frère, qui est illustrateur: il avait dessiné une caricature vraiment drôle de moi! Tout le monde avait apporté des plats et des boissons donc on a fait un grand repas! Ensuite, des copains, qui avaient apporté leurs instruments en cachette, ont joué de la musique et on a dansé jusqu'à trois heures du matin! C'était une vraie surprise-partie, parce que moi, je n'avais rien vu venir!

**1a** Écoute et lis le message de Sam, page 84. Choisis quatre phrases vraies sur Sam.

- **a** *Sam lives with his mum and brothers and sisters.*
- **b** *He normally spends Christmas with his family.*
- **c** *Sam spent Christmas with a friend in Provence.*
- **d** *Sam had never celebrated Christmas before.*
- **e** *He took part in the Christmas preparations.*
- **f** *Bastien's family had prepared everything when Sam arrived.*
- **g** *The traditional Christmas meal in Provence has seven dishes and seven desserts.*
- **h** *Sam went to church and ate with Bastien's family afterwards.*

**1b** Relis le texte. Explique en anglais pourquoi cette fête était inoubliable pour Sam.

**2** Écoute et lis le message de Marion, page 84. Réponds aux questions en anglais.

- **a** *How old was Marion on her last birthday?*
- **b** *Who organised the party?*
- **c** *What had they done beforehand to prepare for it?*
- **d** *Why didn't Marion see her friends at first?*
- **e** *What was she given?*
- **f** *What did they do at the party?*

### STRATÉGIES

French has more than one word to translate 'then':

- *Ainsi, alors* and *donc* are mainly used to explain the consequences or effect of an action.
- *Après, ensuite* and *puis* are used to indicate the order of events.

Can you find examples of any of these in the texts?

### GRAMMAIRE

**Tenses**

| **In the past** | | **Now** |
|---|---|---|
| pluperfect ← | perfect ← <br> imperfect | present |

Use the pluperfect to say that something had (already) happened.

The pluperfect is a bit like the perfect tense. It is made up of two parts:

*avoir* or *être* in the imperfect + a past participle.

| | |
|---|---|
| *j'avais oublié* | I had forgotten |
| *j'étais allé(e)* | I had been to/gone to |

See *Grammaire active* on page 94.

**3** Relis les textes, page 84. Trouve les phrases avec des verbes au plus-que-parfait et traduis-les.

*Exemple:* Je n'avais jamais fêté Noël avant ça. – *I had never celebrated Christmas before that.*

**4** Comment dire en français...?

- **a** *I had never eaten 13 desserts before that!*
- **b** *She had gone to the market when I arrived.*
- **c** *They had brought food and drink.*

### STRATÉGIES

To improve your pronunciation, practise reading aloud so you get used to making French sounds and hearing yourself speak. Try reading aloud Sam's and Marion's messages before doing activity 5 and see if it helps.

**5** Jeu de rôle: **A** pose les questions de Sam, **B** est Marion et répond. Ensuite, **B** pose les questions et **A** répond pour Marion.

**6** Écoute d'abord l'exemple. Puis, écoute 1–9 et note si c'est une affirmation (.), une question (?) ou une exclamation (!).

*Exemple:* **1** (.)

## À VOUS!

**7** Write your own message for the forum. Describe an unforgettable day you have had (you can invent one if you prefer). Answer Sam's questions. Say:

- what/when/where the special occasion was celebrated
- what you did
- what it was like
- whether you had made any preparations beforehand

**8** With a partner, prepare a list of questions and record an interview about a special occasion families celebrate in your country as a guide for French visitors. Be careful to make your pronunciation as authentic as possible.

*Exemple:* **A** Qu'est-ce qui se passe dans ton pays le 25 janvier?

**B** On fête *Burns Night*.

**A** Que fête-t-on ce jour-là? etc.

# 3A Comment échanger ta maison

(G) Les pronoms emphatiques; les adjectifs démonstratifs (V) La maison et le voisinage
(S) Préparer le vocabulaire utile

**Pour les vacances, échangez votre maison!**
**Passez une annonce sur www.échange-de-maisons.com**

1. *Habitez-vous dans une maison ou un appartement?*
2. *Combien de pièces y a-t-il?*
3. *Où est-il/elle situé(e)?*
4. *Qu'est-ce que vous recherchez?*

**1** *dans le quartier de Bercy, à Paris*

**2** *en Bretagne*

**3** *en Guadeloupe*

**4** *dans les Alpes*

**A** maison ancienne, à la campagne
rez-de-chaussée: cuisine avec coin salle à manger, séjour
premier étage: trois chambres, salle de bains-WC
grand jardin, garage pour 2 voitures
**Contactez:** M. Le Guen – 06 17 65 45 78
**Recherche:** maison ou appartement (bord de mer)

**B** chalet traditionnel, à la montagne
rez-de-chaussée: deux chambres, une salle de bains
premier étage: deux chambres, douche, grande cuisine équipée, salon avec balcon; garage, jardin
**Contactez:** Mme Duval – s.duval@clubinternet.fr
**Recherche:** appartement en ville

**C** appartement moderne, en ville, 2ème étage, salon, salle à manger, grand balcon, trois chambres, cuisine équipée, salle de bains, WC, place de parking
**Contactez:** M. et Mme Thomas – 01 45 63 98 76
**Recherche:** maison avec jardin et piscine si possible (campagne ou mer)

**D** villa, au bord de la mer, deux chambres, petite cuisine, terrasse, salle de bains avec douche et WC, piscine dans le jardin
**Contactez:** Firmine Justin – f.justin@wanadoo.fr
**Recherche:** maison ou appartement (montagne ou campagne, en France ou à l'étranger)

**1** Relie les annonces et les photos.

**STRATÉGIES**

When dealing with a new topic, make sure you have the right vocabulary at your disposal: scan through your vocabulary lists for useful words and phrases you already know and look up any other words you need in a dictionary.

For example, if you are describing your house, make sure you know words for some rooms and features: sitting room, garden, countryside, seaside, etc.

**2** Relis les annonces et trouve les mots français:

*Exemple:* **1** ancienne

**a** *old*
**b** *in the country*
**c** *ground floor*
**d** *kitchen-diner*
**e** *first floor*
**f** *looking for*
**g** *in the mountains*
**h** *in town*
**i** *toilet*
**j** *by the sea*
**k** *shower*
**l** *swimming pool*

**3a** Qui parle à l'employé d'*échange-de-maisons.com*? Mme Duval, Firmine Justin ou Mme Thomas?

**3b** Réécoute et réponds aux questions 1–4 pour cette personne.

**4a** Lis la conversation de M. Le Guen avec *échange-de-maisons.com*.

– Bonjour. Je voudrais passer une annonce.
– Oui. Habitez-vous dans une maison ou un appartement?
– Alors, moi, j'habite dans une maison.
– Combien de pièces y a-t-il chez vous?
– Chez nous, il y a six pièces: une cuisine avec coin salle à manger, un séjour, trois chambres et une salle de bains-WC. Il y a aussi un jardin et un garage.
– Où est-elle située?
– C'est à la campagne.
– Et vous, qu'est-ce que vous recherchez?
– Alors moi, je recherche une maison ou un appartement au bord de la mer.

**GRAMMAIRE**

**Emphatic pronouns**
These add emphasis to the subject that follows.
***Moi***, *j'habite...*
***Vous***, *vous recherchez...*
Use them after a preposition too, e.g. *c'est comment chez* ***vous****?*
See the Grammar Bank, page 189.

**4b** Imagine la conversation d'un autre propriétaire avec *échange-de-maisons.com*. Adapte le modèle de l'activité 4a.

*Exemple:*

**A** Bonjour. Je voudrais passer une annonce.
**B** Oui. Habitez-vous dans une maison ou un appartement?
**A** Moi, j'habite dans un appartement, etc.

**GRAMMAIRE**

**Demonstrative adjectives**
These are are useful in descriptions.
To say 'this/that' or 'these/those' use: ***ce*, cette, ces***
(* *cet* is used in front of masculine words starting with a vowel or 'h')
NB: Beware! *cet/cette* sounds like number 7!
See the Grammar Bank, page 189.

**5a** Lis la description de Léa. Complète avec «ce», «cet», «cette» ou «ces».

**5b** Écoute pour vérifier.

Je m'appelle Léa Thomas. J'habite dans un appartement moderne, situé dans le quartier de Bercy. *** quartier moderne est dans le centre de Paris et il y a des magasins et des restaurants pas loin.

Nous habitons au quatrième étage. *** appartement a une jolie vue et il est très confortable. Il y a sept pièces et *** pièces sont très grandes: il y a un salon, une salle à manger avec un grand balcon, trois chambres, une grande cuisine équipée, une salle de bains, et bien sûr des toilettes. Il n'y a pas de cave mais il y a une place de parking. *** place est réservée pour nous. Il n'y a pas de jardin mais il y a un joli parc pas loin.

Nous recherchons une maison pour trois personnes, si possible avec jardin et piscine, au bord de la mer! Moi, mon rêve, c'est une maison créole aux Antilles!

**6** Traduis en français.

**a** *I love these houses!*
**b** *I live in this room.*
**c** *There is a lovely view from this balcony.*
**d** *There is no lift on this floor.*

**7a** Recopie les phrases de Léa avec les bons éléments.

**a** J'habite dans un appartement/une maison ancien(ne)/moderne/traditionnel(le).
**b** Il est situé dans la banlieue/au centre de Paris.
**c** C'est au rez-de-chaussée/au quatrième étage.
**d** Il y a cinq/sept pièces: il y a un salon, etc.
**e** Il est près/loin des magasins/de la mer.

**7b** Adapte les phrases a–e de l'activité 7a pour parler de chez toi.

## À VOUS!

**8** Choose a home from the ones on page 86 for a house swap. Write a letter to the owner describing your own house/flat and explaining the reasons for your choice. (100–150 words).

**9** Imagine you have just spent a holiday in one of the houses on page 86. Make up an account of your stay and give the agency some feedback (email or phone message).

# 3A Comment devenir l'ambassadeur de ta région

(G) Les pronoms relatifs (V) Décrire un endroit (S) Mieux comprendre les mots nouveaux

1

2

3

4

5

6

7

8

9

10

11

12

## Le loto des régions

1 Choisis 6 des 12 cases et note les numéros.
2 Écoute et coche les numéros des photos.
3 Tu as 6 numéros cochés: Loto!

La Vendée, moi, j'adore!

Depuis deux ans, je vis à Chambretaud, une petite ville de Vendée, dans l'ouest de la France. Avant, j'habitais dans une banlieue industrielle de Paris, que je n'aimais pas du tout, qui était très sale et très polluée et où il y avait trop de monde et trop d'usines.

L'endroit où je vis maintenant est campagnard. Il n'y a pas de grandes agglomérations et les villes sont agréables. L'hiver ici, c'est mort et ce n'est pas génial mais par contre j'adore l'été qui est très animé: pas loin de chez moi, il y a la mer, avec de super plages.

La Vendée est une région riche en histoire où on trouve beaucoup de monuments historiques et de musées. Il y a aussi le grand parc de spectacles historiques, le Puy du Fou, que j'aime beaucoup. C'est une région très dynamique et il y a beaucoup de choses à faire pour les jeunes qui aiment le sport et la nature: il y a des activités nautiques, il y a des promenades dans la nature, par exemple en canoë dans les marais, qui sont uniques en France! Le temps n'est pas toujours fantastique ici: il pleut assez souvent. Par contre, les gens sont vraiment très sympa!

Sylvain

**1** À deux. Associez ces mots aux photos, page 88.

*Exemple:* **A** Le numéro 1, c'est la campagne.
**B** Oui, c'est calme.

la montagne la campagne le bord de mer la forêt le lac la rivière l'île la plage la ville la banlieue le village beau calme pollué mort rural historique pittoresque industriel animé

**2** Écoute. Joue au loto avec les photos, page 88.

**3** À deux. Jouez au Morpion (*noughts and crosses*) avec les photos, page 88: pour gagner, faites une phrase avec les expressions a–e et des mots associés à la photo.

*Exemple:* **c + 3** Près de chez moi, il y a un lac.

- **a** J'habite…
- **b** Là où j'habite, c'est/ce n'est pas…
- **c** Près de chez moi, il y a/il n'y a pas de…
- **d** J'aime bien/Je n'aime pas vraiment… parce que…
- **e** Par contre, c'est/ce n'est pas… il y a/il n'y a pas de…

**STRATÉGIES**

To make clever guesses about the meaning of words, consider the context, e.g. *banlieue industrielle* will help understanding *usines* (factories). Also think of other words from the same family, e.g. *campagnard* comes from *campagne*.

**4a** Lis le message de Sylvain, page 88. Traduis en anglais les mots soulignés mais sans le dictionnaire.

**4b** Relis. Réponds aux questions par vrai ou faux.

- **a** *There are no big cities in Vendée.*
- **b** *Summers and winters are alike in Vendée: boring.*
- **c** *Vendée is home to many historical places and has a lot to offer young people.*
- **d** *The weather is always fantastic whatever the season.*

**GRAMMAIRE**

***depuis* – for/since**

*Depuis* is used with the present tense in French.

| | |
|---|---|
| *J'habite ici depuis un an.* | I have been living here for a year. |
| *J'habite ici depuis 2005.* | I have been living here since 2005. |

**5** Relis le message. Réponds pour Sylvain.

*Exemple:* **a** J'habite à Chambretaud.

- **a** Tu habites où et depuis quand?
- **b** C'est comment, là où tu habites?
- **c** Qu'est-ce que tu aimes dans ta région?
- **d** Qu'est-ce que tu n'aimes pas? Pourquoi?

**6a** Écoute Manon. Choisis la bonne réponse.

1. *Manon lives in a* **a)** *large town* **b)** *village*
2. *Her place is* **a)** *close to* **b)** *far from the sea*
3. *She finds the Vendée region* **a)** *very lively* **b)** *very dull*
4. *She likes where she lived before because there was* **a)** *lots to do* **b)** *the sea*

**6b** Réécoute Manon. Prends des notes et réponds pour elle aux questions a–d (activité 5).

*Exemple:* **a** J'habite en Vendée.

**7** À deux, répondez oralement aux questions a–d de l'activité 5. (**B↔A**)

*Exemple:* **A** Tu habites où? **B** J'habite à Brighton.

**GRAMMAIRE**

**Relative pronouns: *qui, que, où***

These refer to a person, a place or a thing that has already been mentioned:

| | |
|---|---|
| *J'habitais dans* ***une banlieue…*** | I used to live in a suburb… |
| ***que*** *je n'aimais pas du tout* | which I didn't like at all |
| ***qui*** *était très sale* | which was very dirty |
| ***où*** *il y avait trop de monde.* | where there were too many people. |

**8** Relis l'email de Sylvain. Trouve tous les pronoms et traduis les phrases en anglais.

*Exemple:* L'endroit **où** je vis… *The place where I live…*

## À VOUS!

**9** 'Is your region cool or rubbish?' Choose a point of view and prepare your arguments. Use the vocabulary on page 100 and the expressions below. Have a class discussion and decide who wins the debate.

**10** The tourist office in your region is looking for a young ambassador. To be chosen you need to write a fantastic article about your region (150–200 words) for a brochure to appeal to young French visitors.

# 3A Comment trouver la ville jumelle idéale

(G) Le pronom «y» (V) En ville (S) Identifier les opinions exprimées oralement

## A Pontivy

Pontivy, petite ville de 15 000 habitants, **est située** au centre de la Bretagne, à 110 km à l'ouest de Rennes. C'est une ville agréable et assez touristique: un canal la traverse et il y a des petites rues très pittoresques, des chapelles et un château médiéval. Pontivy est aussi une ville moderne et dynamique: **on y trouve** un cinéma multiplex, deux salles de spectacles et une médiathèque. On peut faire des courses dans plus de quatre cents magasins et une quarantaine de supermarchés. Le lundi, un marché attire des gens de toute la région. **On peut y faire** beaucoup de sports puisque la ville possède un gymnase et une piscine. Pontivy n'est pas près de la mer, mais il y a un lac pas loin où on peut faire des activités nautiques.

L'été, **il s'y passe beaucoup de choses**: des festivals de musique et des fêtes bretonnes traditionnelles en plein air, les fest-noz, vraiment intéressantes pour les visiteurs et tellement agréables quand il fait beau et chaud. L'hiver, il ne fait pas trop froid mais il pleut assez souvent. Ce n'est pas vraiment un problème: on peut aller manger et boire des spécialités locales réellement délicieuses, les crêpes et le cidre, dans les crêperies de la ville. On y mange très bien!

## B Pointe-à-Pitre

Pointe-à-Pitre, capitale du département français de la Guadeloupe, se trouve à 7000 km des côtes de la métropole. C'est une ville moyenne avec une population de 21 000 habitants. Dans la journée, Pointe-à-Pitre est [1] vivante. **On peut visiter** les quartiers historiques qui possèdent [2] de belles maisons coloniales et deux musées [3] intéressants. **On peut** [4] **faire du shopping** dans les magasins de la ville moderne ou au marché Saint-Antoine, [5] pittoresque. **Il est aussi possible de se promener** au port ou sur la marina, d'aller boire ou manger dans les cafés et les restaurants qui offrent des spécialités locales, comme le ti-punch au rhum et les accras de morue. Il y a deux centres culturels où **on peut assister à** des spectacles de musique. Le soir, par contre, c'est calme, les Pointois n'aiment pas [6] sortir le soir. En janvier, **on peut participer** aux fêtes du Carnaval qui sont [7] fantastiques! Là, on s'amuse [8]! Et bien sûr, il y a les plages de rêve où **on peut faire des sports** nautiques et il y a la campagne où **on peut faire des randonnées** en forêt ou sur un volcan. Et ici, il fait beau toute l'année: il y a du soleil mais il ne fait pas [9] chaud!

**1** **Lis les textes A et B, page 90. Note ce qu'il y a dans chaque ville. Compare avec ton/ta partenaire.**

*Exemple:* Pontivy – il y a un canal, des chapelles...

**STRATÉGIES**

You might not always understand every word in a text, but often you don't need to. Really concentrate on what the task is asking you to do, e.g. in activity 2, to find details on four specific points.

**2** **Note les informations (a–d) pour les deux villes.**

*Exemple:* Pontivy: **a** centre Bretagne, 110 km à l'ouest de Rennes **b** 15 000 habitants

**a** situation **b** population
**c** climat **d** à voir et à faire

**3a** **Trouve l'équivalent français de ces adverbes dans le texte A.**

*Exemple: very* – très

*very a lot of also too really/truly (x2) fairly so well*

**3b** **Lis le texte B à haute voix et remplace [1–9] par les adverbes d'intensité ci-dessous. Il y a plusieurs possibilités.**

*Exemple:* Pointe-à-Pitre est **assez** vivante.

**GRAMMAIRE**

**Adverbs of intensity**

Use adverbs to emphasize what you say and to sound more convincing! Here are a few useful ones:

*assez aussi bien beaucoup réellement tellement très trop vraiment*

**3c** **Écoute et note les adverbes dans l'ordre.**

*Exemple:* **1** très

**4** **Relis les textes A et B. Recopie les expressions en caractères gras et traduis-les en anglais.**

*Exemple:* est située – *is situated*

**GRAMMAIRE**

**Pronoun *y***

*y* refers back to a place that has already been mentioned and is normally translated by 'there'.

*J'habite **à Paris**. J'**y** habite depuis un an.* (*y* = Paris)

I live in Paris. I've been living there for a year.

See the Grammar Bank page 185.

**5a** **Transforme ces phrases: remplace les mots soulignés par le pronom *y*.**

*Exemple:* **a** Ma ville est agréable parce qu'on y fait ...

**a** Ma ville est agréable **parce que** dans ma ville, on fait beaucoup d'activités sportives.
**b** C'est la ville idéale **puisqu'**on trouve de tout dans cette ville.
**c** J'aime bien ma ville en été; **par contre**, dans ma ville, il ne se passe rien en hiver.
**d** Je n'aime pas Paris; **pourtant**, on peut faire beaucoup de choses à Paris.
**e** Pontivy semble être une ville agréable **mais** je ne vais pas aller à Pontivy cette année.

**5b** **Traduis ces phrases en anglais. Attention aux mots de liaison (en caractères gras).**

*Exemple:* **a** *My town is pleasant because you can do lots of sporting activities there.*

**STRATÉGIES**

To make sure you understand people's opinions properly when listening, be aware that some little words may affect meaning:

negatives: *il y a/il n'y a pas de; c'est/ce n'est pas*
adverbs: *trop/assez*
comparisons: *plus/moins... que*
prefixes: *im/possible; dés/agréable*
link words: *mais, par contre, puisque, parce que*
phrases: *je pense que.../je ne sais pas si...*

**6** **Écoute les membres d'un comité de jumelage parler des deux villes candidates (1–14). Qui exprime une opinion favorable (F) ou défavorable (D)? Réécoute pour vérifier.**

*Exemple:* **1** F

## À VOUS!

**7** **Choose a town from page 90 to be twinned with your town. Write reasons for your choice and have a group discussion. The class votes for their favourite town.**

**8** **Write an advert proposing your town for twinning (200-250 words). Use the vocabulary, the adverbs and the link words on pages 90 and 91 to explain why your town would be the ideal candidate. Write very enthusiastically! The class chooses the best advert.**

# 3A Comment découvrir Madagascar

G Les pronoms relatifs V Un pays francophone S Faire des phrases longues et détaillées

Globe-Trotter

## Madagascar

Sylvana, 16 ans, est d'origine malgache*. Elle nous parle de Madagascar où elle est née. Cet été, elle y est retournée pour un mois. Elle voulait revoir ses grands-parents, qu'elle adore et qu'elle n'avait pas vus depuis longtemps puisqu'elle n'était pas retournée sur l'île depuis son arrivée en France, à six ans. Elle répond aux questions de Globe-Trotter.

**Globe-Trotter: Où est Madagascar?**

**Sylvana:** Madagascar se situe à 10 000 km de la France et à 400 km à l'est de l'Afrique. C'était une colonie française jusqu'en 1960 et on y parle encore français. C'est une grande île (plus grande que la France) d'environ 20 millions d'habitants, dont la capitale s'appelle Antananarivo ou Tananarive en français.

**GT: Comment est Madagascar?**

**S:** Au centre de l'île, du nord au sud, il y a des montagnes et des forêts, avec des paysages fantastiques. À l'ouest, il y a des plaines et de belles plages exotiques dont rêvent les touristes, avec du sable blanc et des cocotiers*. À l'est, la côte est plus abrupte et plus rocheuse*.

**GT: Où habite ta famille et c'est comment, chez eux?**

**S:** Mes grands-parents habitent dans une petite ville sur la côte nord-est, région célèbre pour ses plantations de vanille. Ils habitent dans une de ces maisons sur pilotis* typiques, fabriquées en bois et en matières végétales, que l'on voit surtout sur la côte est. Il y a un niveau avec une seule grande pièce qui sert de chambre, de séjour et de cuisine. C'est rudimentaire*, mais confortable même si c'est très différent des maisons en France!

**GT: C'est comment, la vie de famille à Madagascar?**

**S:** La vie de famille est très traditionnelle: elle tourne autour du respect des anciens. Il y a beaucoup de cérémonies pour célébrer les ancêtres. Le plus important pour une famille, c'est que toutes les générations se retrouvent le plus souvent possible ensemble pour les repas de tous les jours et pour les fêtes de famille. C'est très différent d'en France.

* malgache – *from Madagascar*
cocotiers – *coconut trees*
rocheuse – *rocky*
pilotis – *stilts*
rudimentaire – *basic*

**1** Écoute et lis l'article, page 92. Lis les questions et choisis la bonne option (a–c).

1 *Sylvana left Madagascar*
  - a *six years ago.*
  - b *ten years ago.*
  - c *last summer.*

2 *She has*
  - a *never been back to Madagascar before last summer.*
  - b *returned a few times to Madagascar.*
  - c *gone back to live there.*

3 *Madagascar is*
  - a *an island off the coast of Africa.*
  - b *a French colony and has been since 1960.*
  - c *the French name for Antananarivo.*

4 *Sylvana's grandparents live*
  - a *on a vanilla plantation.*
  - b *in the capital city.*
  - c *on the north-eastern coast.*

5 *Their house has*
  - a *three rooms.*
  - b *one large room.*
  - c *two storeys.*

6 *In Madagascar, whole families gather*
  - a *only to worship the ancestors.*
  - b *for meals whenever possible.*
  - c *only on special occasions.*

**2** Relis l'article, page 92. Réponds en anglais et trouve une phrase du texte pour illustrer.

- a *Why did Sylvana want to go back to Madagascar?*
- b *Why is it that people speak French in Madagascar?*
- c *What is the difference between the east and the west coasts?*
- d *What is the north-eastern region well known for?*
- e *What are the typical houses there made of?*
- f *What is at the heart of family life in Madagascar?*
- g *What is one difference between family life in Madagascar and in France?*

**GRAMMAIRE**

**Relative pronouns: *qui, que, où, dont***
These link two parts of a sentence to avoid repetition:

- to replace the subject of the verb:
  use ***qui*** (who, which, that)
- to replace the object of the verb:
  use ***que*** (who, whom, which, that)
  ***où*** (where/when)
  ***dont*** (whose, about/of whom, about/of which)

For other pronouns, see the Grammar Bank, page 189.

**3** Relis l'article, page 92. Trouve des exemples de chaque pronom. Explique et traduis en anglais.

*Exemple:* ...Madagascar **où** elle est née = où refers to *Madagascar* = *...Madagascar, where she was born*

**4** Complète avec «qui», «que», «où» ou «dont». De qui ou de quoi parle-t-on?

*Exemple:* que (ses grands-parents)

- a Ce sont des gens ___ Sylvana aime beaucoup.
- b C'est la région ___ on produit de la vanille.
- c C'est une ville ___ s'appelle Tananarive en français.
- d C'est un pays ___ la capitale est Paris.

**5** Écris quatre phrases sur ta région avec «qui», «que», «où» et «dont».

*Exemple:* À Brighton, il y a la plage que les touristes adorent.

**STRATÉGIES**

Try to use relative pronouns to extend your sentences when speaking or writing. This allows you to make what you say and write more interesting as it adds information and detail.

## À VOUS!

**6** Globe-Trotter has asked you to write a short article (150–200 words) about the area your family is from. Start by listing useful vocabulary and phrases. Use Sylvana's answers as a model.

*Exemple:* Mes grands-parents maternels sont écossais. Ils viennent de l'île de Skye. C'est une île qui se trouve sur la côte ouest de l'Écosse. On peut y aller par un pont ou en ferry, etc.

**7** With a partner, research another French-speaking area on the internet and do a presentation to the class. Mention where it is, its size and population, the languages spoken, the capital city, its links to France, the types of landscape and houses and typical family life.

*Exemple:* La Réunion est une île, à 10 000 km de la France, à l'est de Madagascar. C'est un département français d'outre-mer, etc.

# 3A Grammaire active

## THE PLUPERFECT TENSE

Quand je suis arrivée à l'arrêt ce matin, **le bus était déjà parti!**

*When I arrived at the bus stop this morning, the bus had already left.*

The pluperfect allows you to describe an action in the past that happened before another past action. Like the perfect tense, it is in two parts, but *avoir/être* are in the imperfect:
Perfect tense: *avoir/être* in the present + past participle
Pluperfect tense: *avoir/être* in the imperfect + past participle.

**How to form the pluperfect**

| with *avoir* | | with *être* | |
|---|---|---|---|
| *j'avais* | *vu* | *j'étais* | *arrivé(e)* |
| *tu avais* | *vu* | *tu étais* | *arrivé(e)* |
| *il/elle/on avait* | *vu* | *il/elle/on était* | *arrivé(e)(s)* |
| *nous avions* | *vu* | *nous étions* | *arrivé(e)s* |
| *vous aviez* | *vu* | *vous étiez* | *arrivé(e)(s)* |
| *ils/elles avaient* | *vu* | *ils/elles étaient* | *arrivé(e)s* |

See page 186 for a list of the verbs which use *être*.

As for the perfect tense, the past participle only agrees with the **subject** of the verb when it is used with *être* and with a reflexive verb:

*Il (Elle) était allé(**e**) en France avant d'apprendre le français.*

It agrees with the **direct object** of a verb used with *avoir* ONLY when the object is placed in front of the verb:

*Voici **la chemise** qu'il avait acheté**e**.*

**1** Change the verbs from the perfect or imperfect to the pluperfect.

*Exemple:* **a** J'avais acheté

**a** J'achetais
**b** Tu as voulu
**c** Elles sont parties
**d** Ils entraient
**e** Nous lisions
**f** On a pu

**2** Write out the sentences, changing the infinitives in brackets to pluperfect verbs.

*Exemple:* **a** J'avais invité tout le monde...

**a** Je (inviter) tout le monde au repas de famille.
**b** On (mettre) de beaux vêtements pour la fête.
**c** Il m'a dit qu'il (arriver) hier soir.
**d** Ils (visiter) toute la région à vélo.
**e** Quand je l'ai appelée, elle (sortir).

**3** Translate these sentences into French, using a verb in the pluperfect.

*Exemple:* **a** Il avait déjà visité...

**a** He had already visited the Eiffel Tower.
**b** She was sad because the cat had eaten the hamster.
**c** She had never eaten in a fast-food place before.
**d** When I came back, he had washed my car.
**e** My mum said that she didn't like the flats which she had visited.

## *DEPUIS* AND THE PRESENT TENSE

To say how long something has been going on (and still is), use the present tense and *depuis*.

*Depuis* translates as 'for' (when referring to a duration) and 'since' when referring to an event or a specific point in time.

*On habite à Londres depuis cinq ans.*
We have been living in London for five years.
*J'apprends le français depuis que j'ai six ans.*
I have been learning French since I was six.

**4** Translate these sentences into French.

**a** I have been living in France for five years.
**b** She has been doing her homework since four o'clock.
**c** My brother has been walking for an hour.
**d** My sister has been going to school for five years.

**5** Write sentences using the details below and *depuis*.

**a** my brother – playing football – 5 years
**b** my grandparents – living in new flat – 2 months
**c** my parents – holidays in Tunisia – 2003
**d** my sister – cooking on her own – since age 7
**e** you – learning French – (own answer)

## RELATIVE PRONOUNS

Relative pronouns link two parts of a sentence, to avoid repetition. They refer to nouns and add information.
The ones you have come across in this unit are:

| | |
|---|---|
| *qui* | who, which, that |
| *que/qu'* * | who, whom, which, that (* in front of a vowel or 'h') |
| *où* | where |
| *dont* | whose, about whom/which, of whom/which |

Use *qui* when the noun to be replaced is the subject of the verb:
*J'ai un frère. Mon frère s'appelle Ahmed.*
*J'ai un frère* ***qui*** *s'appelle Ahmed.*
I have a brother **who**'s called Ahmed.

Use *que/qu'* when the noun to be replaced is the object of the verb:
*J'ai un frère. J'aime beaucoup mon frère.*
*J'ai un frère* ***que*** *j'aime beaucoup.*
I have a brother **whom** I love very much.

Use *où* to mean 'where':
*J'habite dans un village. J'aime le village.*
*J'aime le village* ***où*** *j'habite.*
I love the village **where** I live.

Use *dont* to mean 'whose', 'about whom/which', 'of whom/which':
*Ce sont les nouveaux voisins. Je t'ai parlé des nouveaux voisins.*
*Ce sont les nouveaux voisins* ***dont*** *je t'ai parlé.*
They're the new neighbours I told you about (about whom I told you).

*Au village, il y a huit maisons. Six de ces maisons sont en bois.*
*Au village, il y a huit maisons,* ***dont*** *six sont en bois.*
There are eight houses in the village, of which six are made of wood.

**6** Read the mad professor's speech bubble. Select the correct relative pronouns.

Bonjour, la classe! Je me présente: Professeur Rambeau. C'est moi **qui/que** suis le prof de français **dont/qu'**on vous a parlé et **où/que** vous attendez avec impatience! Bienvenue dans la jungle de la grammaire française **où/qui** vous allez survivre grâce à moi!

**7a** Match the two halves of these clues.

*Exemple:* **a** 3

- **a** Ce sont des spécialités que
- **b** Ce sont des petits personnages qu'
- **c** C'est une région où
- **d** C'est une ville dont
- **e** C'est un pays qui

1. on fête Noël avec sept plats et treize desserts.
2. les habitants s'appellent les Pointois.
3. nous mangeons dans les crêperies.
4. on met dans la crèche.
5. était français jusqu'en 1960.

**7b** The clues in activity 7a all refer to things that have been mentioned in this unit. Can you work out what they are?

*Exemple:* **a** 3 = les crêpes

la Provence
les santons
Pointe-à-Pitre
Madagascar
les crêpes

**7c** Translate the clues into English. Then look at the English and translate them back into French. Remember to use a relative pronoun, even if it is not used in English! Check against the originals.

*Exemple:* **a** 3 They are a speciality you eat in a pancake restaurant.

**8** Now it's your turn to write clues for your partner to work out. For an extra challenge, try using four different relative pronouns.

*Exemple:* C'est une tour célèbre qui se trouve à Paris (la tour Eiffel).

**9** Complete the sentences with the correct pronouns *qui, que (qu'), dont, où.*

- **a** Mon père a visité l'endroit ___ il est né.
- **b** La fougasse, c'est une spécialité provençale ____ on mange à Noël.
- **c** J'habite dans une maison ancienne ____ date de 1860.
- **d** Je vais souvent voir mes grands-parents ___ j'adore.
- **e** Je pense beaucoup à mes grands-parents ___ habitent loin.
- **f** C'est une région de France ____ on entend beaucoup parler.

# 3A Controlled Assessment: Speaking

## TASK: A special occasion

You are going to have a conversation with your teacher about a special occasion you recently celebrated with your family. Your teacher will ask you the following:

- What sort of celebration was it?
- Where did it take place?
- Who was there?
- What did you prepare?
- What happened and what did you think of it?
- Will you be celebrating again next year?
- !

(! Remember: at this point, you will have to respond to something you have not prepared.)

The dialogue will last between 4 and 6 minutes.

## 1 THINK!

**Read the phrases below. Write down any others that you might find useful for the speaking task.**

- **What and why?** Is it a traditional celebration? A religious one? Other?
- **When?** Celebrated when and how often? Was it a one-off? Was it a regular event? Will you celebrate it again?
- **Where?** Where did the celebration take place? If a regular event, do you go there every time?
- **Who?** Explain who was there, whether they come every time, who could not make it, etc.
- **How:** what was done in advance of the day? What happened on the day (e.g. order of events, etc.)?
- **Your opinion:** Did you enjoy it? Why?

***! Can you predict what the unexpected question might be?***

What is your best/worst memory of the day?
What is your favourite celebration and why?

**Add to your list any language you would need to answer these questions too.**

## 2 PLAN!

- **Listen to the model conversation. Your teacher has the script.**
- **Listen again and note down any phrases you could use or adapt. Add these to your list from Step 1.**

## 3 ACTION!

**Now prepare your answers. Use the bullet points below to help you and your list of useful words and phrases from Steps 1 and 2.**

**1** What sort of celebration was it?

- Use the perfect tense to speak about what happened in the past, e.g. ***on a fait une fête...; on est allés...; ma famille est venue...***
- Use *depuis* + present tense to speak about how long something has been going on: ***Depuis 2005, on fait la fête tous les ans.***
- Add a little extra detail to make it more interesting, e.g. ***On célèbre cette fête musulmane parce que nous sommes turcs.***

**2** Where did it take place?

- If it is celebrated in a home, explain where and describe it, e.g. ***le jardin qui est très grand, le salon où on peut danser.***
- Try explaining in different ways, e.g. ***on a organisé la fête chez ma grand-mère parce que c'est grand chez elle; on n'a pas de jardin alors on va au parc.***

**3** Who was there?

- Use the imperfect tense for descriptions in the past, e.g. ***on était environ trente; il y avait mes parents, mes grands-parents.***
- Use ***aussi*** and ***non plus***, e.g. ***ma copine aussi était là; mon père n'était pas là, mon demi-frère non plus.***

**4** What did you prepare?

- This is your chance to show off your use of the pluperfect tense. If you haven't done anything, just make it up!
- Mention several things you did, using pluperfect tense verbs, e.g. ***j'avais acheté des chips, j'avais préparé des sandwiches, je m'étais bien habillé(e).***
- Use words to link your ideas together, e.g. ***Comme je ne suis pas bonne cuisinière j'avais acheté des sandwiches.***

**5** What happened on the day and what did you think of it?

- This is your chance to show off a variety of tenses, e.g. ***Comme il pleuvait, on n'a pas fait de pique-nique, c'était dommage!***
- To give a simple opinion in the past, use the imperfect, e.g. ***C'était super! J'étais content(e).***

**6** Will you celebrate next year?

- Show how you can speak about the future using ***aller*** + infinitive and the future tense, e.g. ***L'année prochaine, on va faire la fête. Ce sera chez nous,*** etc.

### GRADE TARGET

**To reach Grade C, you need to:**

- have a variety of vocabulary at your disposal; revise your word lists as often as possible.
- use the main tenses correctly (e.g. present tense for what you usually do, perfect tense for what you did in the past; imperfect for description and opinion in the past).

**To aim higher than a C, you could:**

- use a greater variety of tenses, e.g. use the imperfect, the pluperfect and a future tense, e.g. ***j'avais fait des gâteaux; personne n'aimait mes gâteaux! Je ne ferai plus de gâteaux!***
- create longer sentences, e.g. ***parce que, comme, avant de..., depuis, puisque.***
- use the pronoun ***y***, e.g. ***on est allés au restaurant: on y a bien mangé.***

**To aim for an A or A*, you could:**

- use ***'si'*** clauses, e.g. ***s'il fait beau, on fera un pique-nique.***
- use direct object pronouns ***le/la/les*** and ***en***, e.g. ***j'avais fait des gâteaux, personne ne les a aimés! Je n'en ferai plus!***
- use a variety of relative pronouns: ***qui/que/où/dont***, e.g. ***c'est une sainte dont on célèbre la fête le 15 août.***

# 3A Controlled Assessment: Writing

## TASK: Writing to a visiting penfriend

A French teenager from your twin town will be staying with you for a week. You have been asked to write to him telling him about your town in French so that he will feel at home when he arrives.

You could cover the following points:

- What kind of town you live in.
- What is good/not so good for young people there.
- Suggest a few places you will be visiting in the area.
- Describe an event you recently attended in your town.
- Describe your family and your home.

### 1 THINK!

**Start by researching and noting down a few key facts and phrases:**

1 Your town's characteristics: *petite/grande/ancienne/moderne/industrielle,* etc.

2 Facilities for young people: What can they do there? Sports and leisure facilities?

3 Visiting the area: think of different types of tourist attractions: natural (beaches, etc.) or cultural (museums, etc.)

4 A celebration in the town: *un carnaval/festival; la fête de la musique,* etc.

5 Family and home: type of house you live in, who lives there, where his room will be.

### 2 PLAN!

- **Read the model text.**

Bonjour, c'est Bruno! Je vis à Hyères, une ville moyenne très agréable, située dans le sud de la France où il fait toujours beau! C'est une ville touristique avec un centre historique très pittoresque et une partie moderne, où j'habite depuis six ans.
À mon avis, Hyères est une ville idéale pour les jeunes: c'est très animé, avec des clubs sportifs où on peut pratiquer beaucoup de sports, des cinémas, des magasins et des cafés sympa où on peut se retrouver entre copains.
Il y a beaucoup de choses à voir et à faire dans la région. Toulon, à 20 minutes en voiture, est une très grande ville qui a des musées fascinants. On va faire des randonnées dans les collines et des excursions en bateau à Porquerolles. Sur cette île, on trouve des plages vraiment magnifiques! On fera peut-être des sports nautiques au port et du vélo sur les pistes cyclables le long des plages.
Il y a aussi des fêtes absolument fantastiques à Hyères. Le mois dernier, c'était le Carnaval. J'ai défilé dans les rues avec des copains. On avait trouvé de super déguisements. Ensuite, on est allés au grand pique-nique. C'était très sympa.
J'habite dans une petite maison moderne entre le centre-ville et la plage, avec mes parents, mes deux petits frères et ma grand-mère. Comme nous n'avons que quatre chambres, tu dormiras dans ma chambre, qui a un balcon avec vue sur la mer!
À bientôt! Bruno

- **Read the text again and note down any words or phrases that you could use. Add these to your list from Step 1.**
- **Look carefully at the tenses used and make a note of any you could reuse:**
  present tense for descriptions – ***il fait beau, j'habite, on peut se retrouver...***
  perfect tense for completed action – ***J'ai défilé...***
  imperfect for description in the past and opinion on past events – ***c'était; il y avait...***
  pluperfect tense for actions completed before another action in the past – ***on avait trouvé...***
  future tense for what will happen in the future – ***on va faire, tu dormiras***.

## 3 ACTION !

**Now prepare what you will write. Use the bullet points below to help you and use your list of useful words and phrases from Steps 1 and 2. Aim to write 200–250 words.**

**1** Your town
- ***petite/grande? ancienne/moderne? industrielle?***
- Mention its geographical situation and the impact on its character, e.g. the weather.

**2** Facilities for young people
- ***il y a/il n'y a pas de/d'... activités/piscine/club sportif/terrain de foot/cinéma/cafés...***
- Make more elaborate descriptions by using a relative pronoun, e.g. ***des cafés où on se retrouve.***

**3** Visiting the area
- ***à voir et à faire; plages, randonnées, musées, monuments...***
- Use ***on peut*** + infinitive to explain what is available: ***On peut faire des randonnées.***
- Use ***on va*** + infinitive or a verb in the future tense to say what you will be doing.

**4** A celebration in the town
- ***un carnaval/festival; la fête de la musique...***
- Use the perfect tense for actions that took place in the past and are now over: ***j'ai participé.***
- Use the imperfect to describe what it was like at the time or to give an opinion: ***il y avait du monde; C'était amusant!***
- Use the pluperfect for actions prior to that: ***je n'avais encore jamais participé à un festival, j'y étais déjà allé(e) l'an dernier.***

**5** Family and home
- ***j'ai un grand appartement moderne dans la banlieue; j'y habite avec mes parents, mes deux sœurs et mon chien; tu dormiras dans ma chambre...***

## GRADE TARGET

**To reach Grade C, you need to:**
- make sure you can spell all basic vocabulary correctly.
- use the present and perfect tenses and the future with ***aller*** + infinitive correctly.
- use ***c'était*** + adjective to give an opinion.

**To aim higher than a C, you could:**
- use a variety of tenses including a pluperfect to describe actions prior to others in the past, e.g. ***j'avais invité des amis.***
- use the pronoun ***y*** to avoid repetition: ***C'est une ville géniale; j'y habite depuis...***
- say how long something has been going on using a present tense, e.g. ***je vis ici depuis six ans.***

**To aim for an A or A*, you could:**
- use a variety of more unusual vocabulary, e.g. ***pittoresque*** for ***jolie***; ***fascinant*** for ***intéressant***.
- Use adverbs to emphasize what you say and sound more convincing, e.g. ***absolument, vraiment.***
- create complex sentences by using relative pronouns: ***où, qui, que, dont***.

# 3A Vocabulaire

## Comment raconter une fête familiale

| | |
|---|---|
| une fête inoubliable pour moi | *an unforgettable celebration for me* |
| Ta meilleure fête familiale, c'était quand? Quoi? Où? | *When, what, where was your best family celebration?* |
| Qu'est-ce que tu as fait? | *What did you do?* |
| C'était comment? | *What was it like?* |
| Est-ce qu'on avait fait des préparatifs à l'avance? | *Did you make any preparations in advance?* |
| c'était quand... | *it was when...* |
| en cachette | *in secret* |
| je n'avais jamais fêté | *I had never celebrated* |
| ils avaient décoré le séjour | *they had decorated the living room* |
| ils s'étaient cachés | *they had hidden* |
| je suis allé(e) à... | *I went to...* |
| tout le monde avait apporté des plats | *everyone had brought dishes* |
| un copain m'a invité | *a friend invited me* |
| ensuite, puis | *then* |

## Comment échanger ta maison

| | |
|---|---|
| Chez nous il y a... | *Our house has...* |
| Je voudrais passer une annonce | *I'd like to place an advert* |
| Habitez-vous dans une maison ou un appartement? | *Do you live in a house or a flat?* |
| Combien de pièces y a-t-il? | *How many rooms are there?* |
| Où est-il/elle situé(e)? | *Where is it?* |
| Qu'est-ce que vous recherchez? | *What are you looking for?* |
| à la campagne | *in the country* |
| à la montagne | *in the mountains* |
| au bord de la mer | *at the seaside* |
| dans le quartier... | *in the ... district/area* |
| un chalet traditionnel | *a traditional chalet* |
| une cuisine equipée | *a fitted kitchen* |
| une maison ancienne | *an old house* |
| le rez-de-chaussée | *ground floor* |
| le premier étage | *first floor* |

## Comment devenir l'ambassadeur de ta région

| | |
|---|---|
| C'est comment, là où tu habites? | *What is it like where you live?* |
| Là où j'habite, c'est/ce n'est pas... | *Where I live is.../isn't...* |
| Qu'est-ce que tu aimes dans ta région? | *What do you like about the area where you live?* |
| Près de chez moi, il y a/il n'y a pas... | *Where I live, there is/are...; there isn't/aren't...* |
| Qu'est-ce que tu n'aimes pas? Pourquoi? | *What don't you like? Why?* |
| Avant, j'habitais... | *Before, I used to live...* |
| C'était... | *It was...* |
| Il y avait ... | *There was/were...* |
| J'habite ici depuis deux ans. | *I have been living here for two years.* |
| la banlieue | *suburb* |
| le bord de mer | *seaside* |
| la campagne | *countryside* |
| la forêt | *forest* |
| l'île (*f*) | *island* |
| le lac | *lake* |
| la montagne | *mountain* |
| la plage | *beach* |
| la rivière | *river* |
| animé(e) | *lively* |
| calme | *quiet* |
| historique | *historic* |
| industriel(le) | *industrial* |
| mort(e) | *dead* |
| pittoresque | *picturesque* |
| pollué(e) | *polluted* |

## Comment trouver la ville jumelle idéale

| | |
|---|---|
| Ma ville est située... | *My town is situated...* |
| On y trouve... | *There you can find...* |
| On peut y faire... | *There you can do...* |
| ...du shopping/du sport/des randonnées | *shopping/sport/rambling* |
| Il s'y passe beaucoup de choses | *There is a lot happening there* |
| On peut visiter... | *You can visit...* |
| Il est possible de se promener | *You can go for walks* |
| On peut assister à... | *You can attend/go to...* |
| On peut participer à... | *You can take part in...* |
| J'y habite depuis un an. | *I have been living there for one year.* |
| assez | *rather* |
| aussi | *also/too* |
| bien | *well* |
| réellement | *truly* |
| tellement | *so, so much* |
| trop | *too much* |
| vraiment | *really* |

## Comment découvrir Madagascar

| | |
|---|---|
| Où est Madagascar? | *Where is Madagascar?* |
| Comment est Madagascar? | *What is Madagascar like?* |
| C'est comment, la vie de famille? | *What is family life like?* |
| C'est une colonie française. | *It's a French colony.* |
| C'est différent d'en France. | *It's different from in France.* |
| l'est/l'ouest | *east/west* |
| au centre | *in the centre* |
| sur la côte nord-est | *on the north-east coast* |
| les plantations (*fpl*) de vanille | *vanilla plantations* |

# 3B Notre monde

## Sais-tu comment...

- ❑ exprimer tes soucis pour la planète?
- ❑ être écolo?
- ❑ voyager écolo?
- ❑ faire de l'écotourisme?
- ❑ parler des initiatives écologiques?

## Controlled assessment

- **Present your eco credentials for a Mr/Ms Green World competition**
- **Write an advert for an eco-tourism holiday**

**Tu es un bon citoyen/une bonne citoyenne du monde?**

## Stratégies

### Lecture

When reading, how do you...

- decode unfamiliar vocabulary?
- avoid word for word translations?
- get the maximum marks for each question?

### À l'écoute

When listening, how do you...

- get the most out of listening more than once?
- use reported speech in your answers?
- get the maximum marks for each question?

## Grammaire active

As part of your French language 'toolkit', can you...

- recognise and use the subjunctive?
- compare things?
- use adverbs of time?

# 3B Comment exprimer tes soucis pour la planète

**G** Identifier le type de mot qui manque dans une phrase **V** L'environnement: problèmes

**S** Déchiffrer les mots inconnus

1

2

3

## Projet écolo au collège André-Malraux

Pour moi, le plus grand problème environnemental, c'est l'énergie. J'ai peur des effets du réchauffement climatique, mais je voudrais continuer à chauffer ma maison, à prendre l'avion pour aller en vacances et à acheter de nouveaux vêtements de temps en temps. Est-ce qu'on peut faire tout cela avec les énergies renouvelables? J'en doute!

*Saïd*

La disparition des forêts m'inquiète beaucoup. Nos forêts sont importantes pour des raisons écologiques, pour sauvegarder la biodiversité de notre planète. Mais j'ai lu que 80% de nos forêts originelles ont déjà disparu. Nous devons absolument agir, sinon il y aura une crise pour les générations futures. Oui, la bonne santé de nos forêts est vitale.

*Louisa*

Les mers et les océans constituent plus de 70% de la superficie terrestre, mais nous ne les protégeons pas. Qu'est-ce qui provoque la pollution marine? L'un des problèmes c'est la surpêche, les grands bateaux de pêche industrielle qui ne respectent pas les limites imposées. Puis, il y a la chasse aux baleines, qui est interdite, mais qui ne s'arrête pas. Oui, il faut absolument prendre des mesures pour protéger notre écosystème marin.

*Thomas*

**1a** Recopie et choisis un mot de la poubelle pour finir chaque phrase.

*Exemple*: **a 5**

**a** Mettre vos déchets à la...

**b** Ne pas gaspiller...

**c** Respecter la...

**d** Toujours éteindre les...

**e** Recycler vos journaux et vos...

**f** Trier vos...

**1b** Traduis les six phrases en anglais.

*Exemple*: **a** *Put your rubbish in the bin.*

**2** Écoute Zoé, Max et Yann. Relie chaque personne à une photo (1–3).

**STRATÉGIES**

When you first look at an unknown text which might be difficult to read, get all the help you can! Start by looking at the pictures, title and introduction and see if you can work out roughly what the text is going to be about.

**3a** Lis l'article, page 102, puis relie chaque photo au texte approprié.

**STRATÉGIES**

When you read through a new text, don't stop at every unknown word! Skim-read it and try to get a general sense of what each paragraph is about.

**3b** Traduis le titre de l'article, page 102, en anglais. Il y a un mot inconnu? Peux-tu deviner?

**STRATÉGIES**

Try to guess what a word might mean before looking up everything in a dictionary. Is it related to an English word or another French word that you know? Can you guess the meaning of the word based on what the rest of the sentence means?

**4** À deux. Choisissez un paragraphe et relisez-le. **A** explique à **B** en anglais ce qu'il/elle a compris. (**B↔A**) Pour finir, comparez vos idées avec une autre paire.

**5a** Relis le paragraphe de Louisa et écris six mots que tu ne connais pas, mais qui ressemblent à des mots anglais.

*Exemple*: écologiques

**5b** Travaillez en groupe. Chacun choisit un paragraphe et fait une liste des mots qui sont faciles à deviner. Puis, comparez vos listes.

**5c** Recopie et remplis la grille.

| Mot du texte | Mot de la même famille | Traduction |
|---|---|---|
| chauffer | chaud | to heat |
| le réchauffement climatique | chaud | |
| renouvelables | | |
| agir | action | |
| terrestre | | |

**5d** Peux-tu deviner la traduction anglaise pour chaque mot souligné?

- **a** La disparition des forêts m'inquiète beaucoup.
- **b** Qu'est-ce qui provoque la pollution marine?
- **c** On nous dit que l'énergie nucléaire peut remplacer les autres formes d'énergie.
- **d** Mais les déchets resteront radioactifs pendant des milliers d'années.

**6** Relis tous les textes, page 102, puis complète les phrases avec tes propres mots.

*Exemple:* **a** *global warming*

- **a** *Saïd says he is worried about...*
- **b** *But he admits that he still likes to... and...*
- **c** *He's not sure we can solve this problem with...*
- **d** *Louisa is worried that 80%...*
- **e** *She thinks if we don't act now, then...*
- **f** *Thomas thinks we don't do enough to protect...*
- **g** *There is over-fishing because people don't...*
- **h** *Although it is banned, people still...*

**7** Un défi! Peux-tu comprendre le sens général de ce texte qui vient du site web du groupe *Les Amis de la Terre?*

Notre climat change et la montée des océans, les bouleversements* des éco-systèmes et la multiplication d'évènements climatiques extrêmes vont toucher toute l'humanité. Il est urgent d'agir!

Les Amis de la Terre

* disruptions

## À VOUS!

**8** Do some research into ecology in France on the internet. Choose some interesting facts and write them out as a *vrai/faux* style quiz for a partner to try. You will need to add negatives or change the statistics of some of the information to make it false. Provide answers and correct versions of the statements which are false.

*Exemple*: Il n'y a pas de centrales nucléaires en France. (Faux)

**9** Choose an aspect of the environment which interests you and make an information leaflet on it in French. Include both facts and your own opinions (remember to justify them).

# 3B Comment être écolo

**G** Le subjonctif **V** L'environnement; solutions **S** Écouter; obtenir les meilleures notes

La classe de monsieur Youssef a dressé une liste de petits gestes que tout le monde peut faire pour protéger l'environnement.

1 *Il faut fermer le robinet quand on se brosse les dents.*
2 *Il est important de baisser le chauffage central.*
3 On doit éteindre les lumières.
4 *On devrait se déplacer à pied ou à vélo quand on peut.*
5 Il ne faut pas laisser de déchets sur la plage.
6 *On doit acheter des produits d'entretien bio.*
7 Il ne faut pas trop voyager en avion.
8 *Il faut recycler ses journaux et ses magazines.*
9 Il est important de planter des arbres.
10 *On devrait se doucher au lieu de prendre un bain.*

A

B

C

D

**1a** Lis la liste et relie chaque dessin (A–D) à une suggestion (1–10).

Moi, j'ai deux passions: le shopping et l'environnement! Je ne crois pas qu'il soit difficile de concilier les deux. D'abord, je n'achète pas trop de choses, et puis j'achète toujours des produits équitables* quand je peux. Chez nous, il y a un petit magasin qui vend de super produits équitables – des bijoux, par exemple – et c'est là que je vais si je veux acheter un cadeau. Je choisis toujours des produits recyclés quand c'est possible, et j'achète aussi des produits bio*. Enfin, j'évite les produits avec trop d'emballages* et je n'utilise jamais les sacs en plastique. Il faut que tout le monde fasse un effort!

* équitable – *fairtrade*
bio – *organic*
les emballages – *packaging*

**1b** Classe les suggestions en trois groupes.

**A** La conservation d'énergie
**B** La protection des forêts
**C** La conservation de l'eau

**2** Lis le texte de Lucie et écris une liste en anglais de tout ce qu'elle fait pour réconcilier sa passion du shopping avec son désir de protéger l'environnement.

*Exemple: She doesn't buy too much.*

**3** À deux. Discutez de ce que vous faites pour protéger l'environnement et pourquoi.

*Exemple:* **A** Moi, je recycle les journaux et je ferme le robinet quand je me brosse les dents. Et toi?
**B** Je recycle aussi, mais je ne me douche pas parce que je n'aime pas ça. Je prends un bain. Et toi?

**STRATÉGIES**

These expressions are useful for saying what must be done or what ought to happen. Each one is followed by a verb in the infinitive.

| | |
|---|---|
| *Il faut...* | *Il est important de...* |
| *On doit...* | *On a besoin de...* |
| *On devrait/Nous devrions...* | |

**4** Écris six choses qui sont importantes pour la protection de l'environnement à ton avis. Utilise les expressions de l'encadré Stratégies et justifie ton opinion.

*Exemple:* Moi, je pense qu'il est important de se déplacer à pied quand on peut parce que c'est plus écolo.

**GRAMMAIRE**

**The subjunctive**

Certain phrases in French are followed by a special form of the verb called the subjunctive. The subjunctive is used to express something that isn't real or is desired, e.g. 'If I **were**...' in English.

There are two examples in Lucie's text: *je ne crois pas que* and *il faut que*. They are followed by verbs which look different in the subjunctive – *soit* instead of *est* and *fasse* instead of *fait* – but many subjunctive forms look similar to the ordinary form.

*Je ne crois pas qu'il* ***soit*** *difficile de concilier les deux.*

*Il faut que tout le monde* ***fasse*** *un effort!*

**5a** Recopie et souligne les verbes au subjonctif.

**a** Il faut que je prenne une douche au lieu d'un bain.
**b** Je ne pense pas que les emballages soient nécessaires.
**c** Il faut que tout le monde soit végétarien!

**5b** Traduis les phrases en anglais. Choisis des phrases de l'encadré pour t'aider.

*Exemple:* **a** *I should take a shower, not a bath.*

*everyone should...* *I don't think that...* *I should...*

**STRATÉGIES**

**Listening skills**

Always listen to a text once through and try to understand the gist of it before tackling the questions. It will be easier to guess unknown words if you know roughly what the passage is about. Also, look at the number of marks given for each question and be sure you write enough detail to get them all.

**6a** Écoute les cinq élèves. Recopie et remplis la grille.

| | Est-ce un(e) bon(ne) écolo? (oui/non) | Nombre d'exemples donnés |
|---|---|---|
| 1 Saïd | non | 3 |
| 2 Louisa | | |
| 3 Thomas | | |
| 4 Audrey | | |
| 5 Ameen | | |

**6b** Réponds aux questions en anglais.

**a** *Name two reasons why Saïd is not very green.* (2)
**b** *What does Louisa do to help the environment?* (2)
**c** *What is Thomas' contribution?* (3)
**d** *What does Audrey do which is not very green?* (2)
**e** *What does Ameen do that is positive?* (3)

## À VOUS!

**7** Take it in turns to convince the class (or group) that you are environmentally aware by telling them what you do to be green and what your opinions on environmental issues are. Everyone has 90 seconds to speak, then you should vote to decide who wins.

**8** Write two diary extracts – one by someone who is very environmentally aware and one by someone who doesn't care about such things. Write about 100 words for each.

# 3B Comment voyager écolo

G Le comparatif; les adverbes V Les transports S Comprendre un texte de façon globale et dans le détail

A

**Les transports quotidiens**

En France, 69% des utilisateurs de transports en commun se déplacent en bus au moins une fois par semaine pour les trajets domicile-travail. 45% prennent le métro, 28% le RER*, 18% le tramway, 16% le car et enfin les trains de la SNCF* (13% le TER*, 5% le train Corail* et 3% le TGV* ).

92% des utilisateurs de transports en commun vont aussi au travail à pied au moins une fois par semaine et 62% en voiture. Par contre, seulement 7% y vont à vélo ou à moto et 3% utilisent les rollers ou le skateboard.

**Les transports pour aller en vacances**

Moyens de transport préférés des Français pour leurs vacances à l'étranger:

la voiture (78,3%), le train (10,8%), l'avion (6,9%), le car (2,2%), le bateau (0,56%), autres (1,2%).

*RER – *high speed link to Paris suburbs*
SNCF – *national railway*
TER – *local and regional train*
Corail – *national train*
TGV – *high speed national train*

B **L'empreinte écologique des transports en commun**

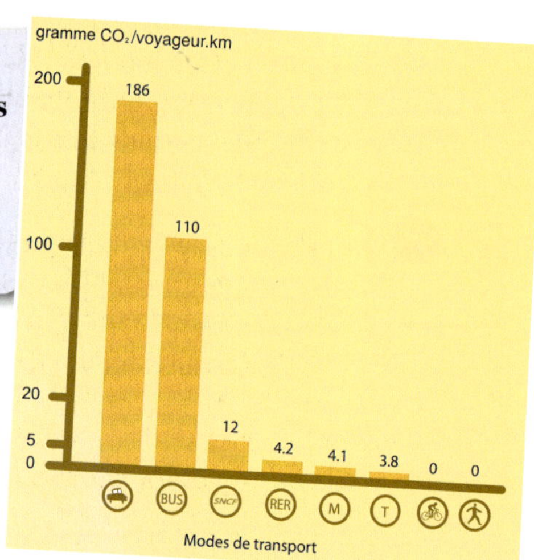


**1** Écoute (1–6) et note le moyen de transport mentionné.

*Exemple:* **1** *boat*

**2** Lis l'article A et réponds aux questions.

*Exemple:* **a** le bus, le métro, etc.

- **a** Quel est le moyen de transport en commun préféré des Français?
- **b** Quel est le moyen de transport préféré des Français pour aller en vacances?
- **c** À ton avis, quels sont les «autres» moyens de transport possibles pour aller en vacances?

**GRAMMAIRE**

**Comparative and superlative**

| | |
|---|---|
| more/less than | *plus/moins* (adjective) *que* ... |
| as... as | *aussi* (adjective) *que* ... |
| the most | *le plus* (adjective) |
| the least | *le moins* (adjective) |

**3** Regarde le graphe de pollution (B). Recopie et complète les phrases avec «plus», «moins» ou «aussi».

*Exemple:* **a** Le tramway (T) est moins polluant que le métro (M).

- **a** Le tramway est... polluant que le métro.
- **b** Le bus est... écologique que le train.
- **c** Le vélo est... écologique que la marche à pied.
- **d** Le transport le... polluant, c'est la voiture.
- **e** Le vélo est le moyen de transport le... polluant.

**4a** Écoute (1-3). Quels adjectifs entends-tu?

polluant écolo cher économique rapide lent confortable inconfortable pratique

**4b** Réécoute. Note comment chaque personne va au collège et explique son choix.

*Exemple:* **1** En voiture, c'est plus pratique

**5** Fais un sondage en classe.

- **a** Comment allez-vous au collège? Pourquoi?
- **b** Quel est votre moyen de transport préféré pour aller en vacances? Pourquoi?

*Exemple:* **a** J'y vais à pied ou bien je prends le métro parce que c'est plus rapide et moins polluant que le bus.

## Comment devenir un éco-voyageur? Lisez ce témoignage!

«Juste avant et pendant la Seconde Guerre mondiale, il n'y avait plus d'essence pour les voitures et les taxis, alors, en ville, on prenait des vélo-taxis. Après, dans les années 50, comme les gens préféraient les voitures, les vélo-taxis ont disparu. Aujourd'hui, ils reviennent dans le centre des grandes villes: ils ne sont pas chers (1,5 euro par km), et surtout, ils sont 100% écologiques! J'ai pris un vélo-taxi quand j'ai visité Paris la dernière fois. C'était fantastique! On a visité la ville sans se fatiguer et sans bouchons*! Bientôt, plus de cent vélo-taxis vont circuler dans Paris. Super idée, non? À partir d'aujourd'hui, je vais circuler uniquement à vélo ou en vélo-taxi! Il faut s'habituer maintenant à circuler sans voiture, parce que plus tard, elles n'existeront peut-être plus!»

**Cécile**

* traffic jams

**STRATÉGIES**

Read the questions carefully then read through the text once for gist, keeping in mind what you are asked to focus on; look for key words and identify the main ideas. Then read a second time, focusing more on specific details.

**6** Lis rapidement le message de Cécile. Choisis la meilleure option.

1 De quoi parle Cécile?
   **a)** de la Seconde Guerre mondiale
   **b)** des vélo-taxis en ville
2 Pourquoi pense-t-elle que c'est une bonne idée pour Paris?
   **a)** ils ne polluent pas et ne sont pas chers
   **b)** il n'y a plus assez d'essence
3 Que fera Cécile plus tard?
   **a)** elle circulera en voiture
   **b)** elle n'utilisera que le vélo ou le vélo-taxi

**7** Trouve les réponses dans le texte.

*Exemple:* **a** Il n'y avait plus d'essence pour les voitures.

- **a** Pourquoi y avait-il des vélo-taxis pendant la guerre?
- **b** Pourquoi ont-ils disparu après la guerre?
- **c** Où les vélo-taxis roulent-ils maintenant?
- **d** Cite quatre avantages des vélo-taxis.
- **e** Il y a combien de vélo-taxis à Paris?

**GRAMMAIRE**

**Adverbs of time**

Use adverbs to give an indication of time:

*avant après la dernière fois maintenant aujourd'hui plus tard bientôt à partir de maintenant*

**8** Relis le texte. Retrouve ces adverbes en français.

*before now today/nowadays later on after last time soon from now on*

**9** Trouve et note tous les verbes aux temps suivants: *present, imperfect, perfect, future.*

*Exemple: present* – ils sont

## À VOUS!

**10** Are you an eco-tourist? Which forms of transport do you use and why? Explain what you used to do, what you do now and what you intend to do in the future (50-150 words).

**11** Prepare a customer satisfaction questionnaire on public transport in your town or local area for French visitors. Mention the different types of transport and ask which they have used, why they used them and what they were like (service, comfort, price, speed, etc.). Exchange questionnaires with a partner and answer the questions for yourself.

# 3B Comment faire de l'écotourisme

(V) L'écotourisme (S) Éviter les traductions mot à mot

## Les vacances: qu'est-ce qui est bon pour l'environnement?

a partir en avion ❑
b partir à vélo ❑
c loger dans un gîte ❑
d loger dans un hôtel de luxe ❑
e faire du camping ❑
f faire des randonnées ❑
g faire du shopping ❑
h aller dans une grande ville ❑
i jouer à la plage ❑
j aller au parc d'attractions ❑

**1** Tu veux prendre des vacances vertes. Choisis les cinq meilleures activités.
*Exemple:* **b**

**Monsieur Youssef va partir une semaine avec sa classe faire un voyage d'étude. Il leur a demandé de faire des recherches sur l'écotourisme. Voici quelques documents présentés à la classe par Saïd et Lucie.**

1

2

3

**A**

### L'écotourisme, c'est quoi?

C'est une forme de voyage responsable qui contribue à la protection de l'environnement.

Vous voulez passer de bonnes vacances, mais sans détruire notre monde? Vous adorez visiter la campagne et les forêts, mais vous désirez que la nature reste naturelle? Vous êtes un voyageur responsable, donc vous faites de l'écotourisme.

**B**

### Amusez-vous bien en Cévennes.

- faites une randonnée dans nos montagnes spectaculaires. Vous trouverez un vrai sentiment de liberté.
- faites du VTT dans un esprit de découverte de notre belle région.
- faites des randonnées en compagnie des ânes* qui portent les bagages et deviennent vite des copains. Ânes sellés* pour enfants de moins de 12 ans.

* ânes - *donkeys*
sellés - *saddled*

**C**

### Logement à la ferme

Sur la ferme de Ribevenes:

- camping à la ferme (6 emplacements) au bord d'une petite rivière, dans la nature, au calme.
- une salle commune avec bibliothèque.
- petit troupeau de brebis*, légumes, petits fruits (fraises, framboises), oies, poules, chien, chats.

* brebis – *sheep*

**2** Choisis la bonne photo pour chaque texte.

**3** Relis les textes A–C, page 108. Comment dit-on en français...?

*Exemple:* **a** voyage responsable

**a** *responsible travel*
**b** *to destroy*
**c** *farm accommodation*
**d** *in a spirit of discovery*
**e** *by a little river*

Voy... peut provoquer un tas de pro... pour l'environnement, mais l'écotourisme est beaucoup plus res...

Je crois que l'écotourisme encourage les gens à mieux apprécier la nat... Si on fait du cam... au lieu de loger dans un hô... de luxe, on montre plus de res... envers la campagne.

Pour les vac... comme pour tellement d'autres choses, il faut que nous changions nos hab... Ça veut dire ne pas laisser ses dé... dans la nature, res... les animaux qu'on rencontre à la campagne et être sen... à son nouvel environnement.

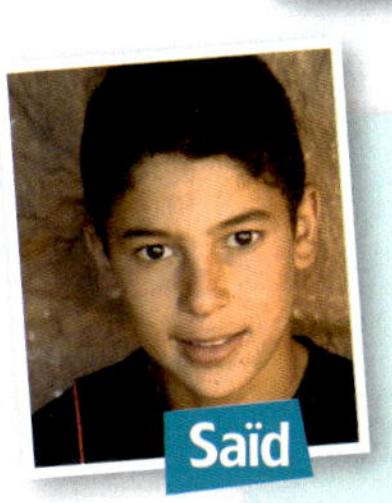


C'est plutôt des ran... en montagne qu'une visite dans un parc d'attractions. Il faut penser à l'en... à tout moment – pour son voy... son log... les activités qu'on choisit de fa... les sou... qu'on achète. Tout cela est important.

**4a** Lis les opinions de quatre membres de la classe. À deux. Pouvez-vous deviner les mots qui manquent?

**4b** Écoute (1–4) pour vérifier.

**4c** Résume l'opinion de chaque personne en anglais.

*Exemple: Lucie thinks ecotourism is more responsible.*

**STRATÉGIES**

You can't always translate a phrase word for word from English into French. You have to know the French expression which conveys the same meaning.

**5** Choisis la bonne traduction pour chaque phrase.

**1** Vous allez faire du camping?
- **a**) *Are you going to the camping?*
- **b**) *Are you going camping?*

**2** Oui, pour visiter la campagne sans la détruire.
- **a**) *Yes, to visit the country without destroying it.*
- **b**) *Yes, to visit the country without to destroy it.*

**3** Moi, je préfère les vacances dans la nature.
- **a**) *I prefer holidays in the nature.*
- **b**) *I prefer holidays in a natural environment.*

## À VOUS!

**6** **Design an advert for *des vacances vertes*, perhaps on a farm, in the countryside or in the mountains. Use expressions from the page to help you.**

**7** **Work in pairs and discuss a holiday you plan to take after the exams. You have very different ideas and must each try to persuade the other that your plan is better! Try to use as many conjunctions as possible to make your sentences longer and more detailed.**

**A** wants a luxury holiday – flight to somewhere hot, expensive hotel, evenings in restaurants or nightclubs.

**B** prefers an eco-holiday – 'green' travel, campsite or gite accommodation, sports or country activities.

*Exemple:*

**A** Alors, si on partait en Thaïlande?

**B** Ah non, c'est très loin. Le voyage sera cher et durera longtemps et, tu sais, ce n'est pas bon pour l'environnement de faire un si long trajet en avion. Donc, je préférerais mettre nos vélos dans le train et aller peut-être en Bretagne ou en Normandie.

**A** Mais c'est fatigant, ton idée, et en plus... Pourquoi pas...?

# 3B Comment parler des initiatives écologiques

(G) Interrogatifs (V) L'environnement (S) Maximiser tes notes à l'examen

Il ne manque pas d'initiatives écolo au Sénégal. Notre reporter, Bernard Goba, nous a envoyé trois reportages très différents, mais qui ont tous pour thème l'importance de protéger la planète.

1

A

### Sénégal: produire local et consommer local

Acheter des produits locaux, c'est bon pour l'environnement et ça encourage l'agriculture locale. Voilà pourquoi on a installé des kiosques pour vendre du riz partout dans la Vallée du Fleuve, au nord du Sénégal.

On veut aussi créer des emplois, surtout pour les jeunes.

2

B

### Portable et environnement: le Sénégal donne l'exemple

On lance une campagne de récupération des vieux portables au Sénégal. Pourquoi? Pour protéger l'environnement. Un opérateur de téléphonie mobile pour la région de l'Afrique de l'Ouest organise cette initiative.

Cette campagne aura deux phases. La première consiste à 'convaincre les populations de ne pas jeter leurs vieux portables dans la nature' et la deuxième à 'indiquer les centres de recyclage'. Il y en aura dans toutes les régions du Sénégal.

3

C

### De l'eau pour la population rurale

L'objectif d'un nouveau projet au nord-ouest du Sénégal est d'améliorer* la santé et la qualité de vie des populations rurales. Comment? En leur donnant un meilleur accès à l'eau potable… en utilisant les énergies renouvelables.

10 villages seront équipés d'une pompe à eau éolienne* ou solaire, selon le choix du village. Il faut que l'eau soit destinée à l'usage de toute la communauté.

* améliorer – *to improve*
éolienne – *wind-power*

**1a** Lis les trois titres, puis travaille avec un partenaire pour deviner le sujet de chacun. Écris des idées en anglais.

*Exemple: Text A might be about producing food locally.*

**1b** Relie les photos aux textes.

**STRATÉGIES**

Use vocabulary clues for matching questions. In activity 2, the verbs *boire* and *faire la lessive* link with the idea of *eau potable* (drinking water) in the text. Try using this approach with other words you don't understand.

**2** **Choisis la citation appropriée pour chaque texte, page 110.**

**1** Maintenant on peut boire, faire la lessive et faire la cuisine beaucoup plus facilement.

**2** J'espère travailler comme producteur ou vendeur et donc gagner de l'argent.

**3** J'allais jeter mon portable, mais c'est mieux de le recycler.

**3** **Relis le texte A et choisis les quatre phrases qui sont vraies.**

- **a** *Buying local produce is good for the environment.*
- **b** *It is also good for local farmers.*
- **c** *The* Vallée du Fleuve *is in the south of Senegal.*
- **d** *In the* Vallée du Fleuve, *kiosks have been set up to sell rice.*
- **e** *This creates jobs for young people.*
- **f** *The rice is very expensive.*

**4** **Relis le texte B, puis décide si les phrases sont vraies (V) ou fausses (F).**

- **a** Cette campagne est nouvelle.
- **b** C'est l'idée du gouvernement.
- **c** Il s'agit de protéger l'environnement.

**5** **Relis le texte C. Réponds en anglais.**

- **a** *In what part of Senegal is the new project?*
- **b** *Is it for people in cities or in the country?*
- **c** *What will it give people access to?*
- **d** *As well as wind-power, what other type of power may be used for the pumps?*
- **e** *Who will be able to use the water?*

**6a** **Lis les questions. Recopie les mots en gras et traduis-les en anglais.**

*Exemple:* **quelle date** – *what date*

- **a** On parle de **quelle date**?
- **b** **Comment** décrit-on cette région?
- **c** **Qu'est-ce qu'**on a fait ce jour-là?
- **d** Il s'agit de **combien** d'arbres?
- **e** Pour **quels produits** le jatropha est-il utile?

**6b** **Relis les questions. Pour quelle question y a-t-il plus d'un renseignement à noter? Pourquoi?**

**STRATÉGIES**

In listening exercises, be especially careful to answer the question precisely, rather than just noting down what you hear. Which question words are used in the questions? Are you asked to give more than one detail?

**6c** **Écoute le reportage sur la journée de l'arbre à Diourbel au Sénégal et réponds aux questions de l'activité 6a.**

## À VOUS!

**7** **Prepare a PowerPoint® presentation on an aspect of life in a French-speaking country or area. Research some facts and statistics on the internet and choose some pictures to illustrate your presentation. Include your opinion on what it would be like to live there. Deliver your presentation in front of the class.**

**Possible countries:** la Martinique, le Cameroun, la Côte d'Ivoire, le Canada, l'Algérie, le Tchad, le Luxembourg, Monaco, le Bénin, le Togo, l'Île Maurice

**Possible topics:** la musique, le sport, la cuisine, la francophonie, la peinture, les personnes célèbres

**8** **Write a report in French on your research, explaining why you chose the topic and giving facts and examples, and adding illustrations such as photos, drawings or maps. Try to write around 300 words.**

# 3B Grammaire active

**CONJUNCTIONS**

Remember to use conjunctions to link ideas and add variety to your sentences.

**1** **Unjumble the letters to form conjunctions, then match them to the translations in the box.**

*Exemple:* **a** *mais* – but

**a** s a m i

**b** c n o d

**c** s p i u

**d** a r c

**e** m m o e c

because   so   as   but   then

**2** **Fill the gaps with a word from the box below.**

*Exemple:* **a** mais

**a** Prendre l'avion c'est rapide,... ça coûte cher à l'environnement.

**b** Les visiteurs contribuent à l'économie d'une région,... on veut les encourager.

**c** Les touristes laissent leurs déchets partout... ils salissent nos plages.

**d** ..., il y en a quelques-uns qui sont plus responsables.

**e** Un hôtel? Non merci, je préfère un camping... un gîte rural.

**f** On peut visiter une région... la détruire.

et   ou   donc   mais   cependant   sans

**3** **Match the two parts of each sentence.**

*Exemple:* **1c**

**1** La plage est belle, mais...
**2** Il faut protéger les pandas parce qu'ils...
**3** On peut voyager en bus ou...
**4** C'est une région où...
**5** J'aime voyager en avion, cependant...
**6** J'essaie d'aller partout à pied, parce que...

**a** on peut se détendre.
**b** c'est mieux pour l'environnement.
**c** l'eau est polluée.
**d** sont rares.
**e** je ne le fais pas souvent.
**f** à vélo.

**4** **Copy each sentence beginning and complete it in your own words.**

**a** Je voudrais être un bon écolo, cependant...
**b** Je devrais prendre les transports en commun au lieu de...
**c** Je devrais acheter plus de produits équitables, mais...
**d** Je pourrais manger bio et...
**e** Je sais qu'il faudrait se déplacer à pied ou...
**f** Mais je suis paresseuse et donc...

**COMPARING – A QUICK GUIDE**

| | + verb | + noun | + adjective | + adverb |
|---|---|---|---|---|
| more | *il recycle* ***plus que...*** | *il y a* ***plus de*** *vent* ***que...*** | *il fait* ***plus*** *chaud* ***que...*** | *il pollue* ***plus*** *souvent* ***que...*** |
| less | *il recycle* ***moins que...*** | *il y a* ***moins de*** *vent* ***que...*** | *il fait* ***moins*** *chaud* ***que...*** | *il pollue* ***moins*** *souvent* ***que...*** |
| the same | *il recycle* ***autant que...*** | *il y a* ***autant de*** *vent* ***que...*** | *il fait* ***aussi*** *chaud* ***que...*** | *il pollue* ***aussi*** *souvent* ***que...*** |

See pages 184–185 for further information and examples.

**5a** **Translate these sentences into English.**

**a** Je suis plus écolo que mes parents.
**b** Pourtant, mon frère est aussi conscient des problèmes environnementaux que moi.
**c** Dans les années 90, on recyclait moins de verre qu'aujourd'hui.
**d** La disparition des forêts est aussi dangereuse que le réchauffement climatique.
**e** Tu fais autant d'efforts que lui.

**5b** Use *plus/moins/aussi/autant... que* to translate these sentences into French.

- **a** You recycle less paper than me.
- **b** The bike is more environmentally-friendly than the car.
- **c** Planting trees is as important as conserving energy.
- **d** He has as many good ideas as her.
- **e** We are using less water than last year.

Il faut qu'on plante des arbres.

**THE SUBJUNCTIVE**

After certain phrases in French you have to use the subjunctive.

These include phrases expressing emotion, such as: *préférer que*, *regretter que*, *avoir peur que*, *être content que*.

The subjunctive is also needed after *il faut que* and after expressions of doubt such as *je ne crois pas que, je doute que* and *je ne suis pas sûr que*.

*Exemples:*

*Il faut qu'on soit à l'heure.* We have to be on time.

*Je regrette qu'il ne fasse pas beau aujourd'hui.*
I'm sorry the weather isn't nice today.

*Je ne crois pas que ce soit une bonne idée.*
I don't think that's a good idea.

**6a** Copy out each sentence, underlining the phrase which needs the subjunctive and circling the verb which is in the subjunctive.

*Exemple:* **a** Je préfère que tout soit recyclé.

- **a** Je préfère que tout soit recyclé.
- **b** Oui, il faut qu'on emporte tout au centre de recyclage.
- **c** Je regrette qu'on continue comme ça!
- **d** Je ne crois pas qu'on fasse assez d'efforts pour l'environnement.
- **e** Eux, ils ont peur qu'on ne respecte pas les limites concernant la surpêche.
- **f** Je suis content que tant de gens écrivent au ministre.
- **g** Je ne suis pas sûr qu'on sauvegarde la biodiversité.

**6b** Translate the sentences into English.

**FORMATION OF THE SUBJUNCTIVE**

To form the subjunctive of regular verbs, take the 3rd person plural form of the present tense, remove the *-ent* and add the endings *-e, -es, -e, -ions, -iez, -ent*.

*Exemples:*

*aimer* → *aiment* → *que j'aime*

*écrire* → *écrivent* → *que nous écrivions*

*lire* → *lisent* → *qu'il lise*

Some common verbs have irregular subjunctive forms. Learn the *je* form and you can usually add the same endings as above, but check in a verb table for a few which vary.

*Exemples:*

*être* → *que je sois* *avoir* → *que j'aie*
*aller* → *que j'aille* *faire* → *que je fasse*
*pouvoir* → *que je puisse*

**7a** Each of these sentences needs the subjunctive. Copy them out and choose the correct form of the verb.

*Exemple:* **a** ce soit

- **a** Je ne crois pas que (c'est/ce soit) dangereux.
- **b** Il a peur qu'on ne (prenne/prend) pas l'environnement au sérieux.
- **c** Il faut qu'on (fasse/fait) un effort.
- **d** Il préfère qu'on (écrit/écrive) tout de suite.
- **e** Je regrette que l'enfant ne (comprend/comprenne) pas.
- **f** Il faut que nous (allons/allions) tout de suite à la déchèterie.

**7b** Explain to a partner why the subjunctive is needed in each of the sentences above.

*Exemple:* **a** – after *je ne crois pas que*

# 3B Controlled Assessment: Speaking

## TASK: Being environmentally friendly

You are going to be interviewed by your teacher. You are a contestant in this year's Mr/Ms Green World competition. You have to show how environmentally-friendly you are. Your teacher will ask you the following:

- What do you do to be environmentally-friendly at home?
- Are you a 'green' shopper?
- What do you eat and drink?
- How do you travel?
- What are your hobbies/interests?
- What sort of holidays have you taken/would you like to take?
- !

*(! Remember: at this point, you will have to respond to something you have not prepared.)*

The interview will last between 4 and 6 minutes.

## 1 THINK !

**Read the phrases below. Write down any others that you might find useful for the speaking task.**

- ☐ **At home:** recycler les journaux et les magazines, éteindre les lumières, trier les déchets, baisser le chauffage central,...
- ☐ **Shopping:** acheter des produits recyclés/bio/équitables, éviter les emballages,...
- ☐ **Food and drink:** être végétarien(ne), manger les légumes de saison,...
- ☐ **Travel:** utiliser les transports en commun, aller au collège à pied, prendre le vélo au lieu de la voiture,...
- ☐ **Hobbies/interests:** lire des articles sur l'environnement, faire du jardinage, membre de l'association Les Amis de la Terre,...
- ☐ **Holidays:** faire de l'écotourisme, faire du travail bénévole à l'étranger,...

**! *Can you predict what the unexpected question might be?***

What is your main concern for the future of the planet? What is your top tip for being green? How can we encourage children to be green?

**Add to your list any language you would need to answer these questions too.**

## 2 PLAN !

- **Listen to the model conversation. Your teacher has the script.**
- **Listen again and note down any phrases you could use or adapt. Add these to your list from Step 1.**

# 3 ACTION!

**Now prepare your answers. Use the bullet points below to help you and your list of useful words and phrases from Steps 1 and 2.**

**1** What do you do to be environmentally-friendly at home?

- There are lots of possible answers here so give several.
- Add a few details (when, how, why) or examples, e.g. ***Je baisse le chauffage en hiver, On économise l'eau en prenant moins de bains, J'éteins les lumières pour conserver l'énergie...***
- You will mostly be using the present tense to say what you do regularly, but earn extra marks by using a past tense to give an example of what you have done, e.g. ***Par exemple, on a installé des panneaux solaires...***

**2** Are you a 'green' shopper?

- Avoid yes/no answers. Expand using: ***Oui, bien sûr/absolument!, Je pense que oui...,*** etc.
- Follow with a couple of examples to support your view (invent if necessary), e.g. ***Je n'utilise jamais de sacs en plastique, Je n'achète pas trop de vêtements et souvent j'achète des vêtements d'occasion...***

**3** What do you eat and drink?

- This is not just a general question: think how it relates to the topic of the interview.
- Use the present tense to say what you regularly eat/drink. However, here is another chance to earn extra marks by using a past tense to give an example of what you have eaten, e.g. ***Par exemple, hier, j'ai mangé une salade de fruits et j'ai bu de l'eau.***
- You could even use the imperfect to contrast what you used to eat with what you eat now, e.g. ***Quand j'étais petit(e), je mangeais beaucoup de chocolat et de bonbons, tandis que maintenant, je mange...***

**4** How do you travel?

- Mention several means of transport.
- Give your reasons, e.g. ***parce que c'est moins polluant que la voiture, pour être le plus écolo possible, afin de conserver l'énergie...***

**5** What are your hobbies/interests?

- Mention a couple that relate to the topic. It is OK to invent some interests in order to sound more impressive, e.g. ***J'écris un blog sur mes inquiétudes pour la planète.***
- Use the present tense for what you do regularly and the perfect tense to talk about events in the past, e.g. ***L'année dernière, je suis allé(e) à un camp environnemental...***

**6** What sort of holidays have you taken/would you like to take?

- Remember the context for the question and relate what you say to environmental concerns, e.g. ***On a fait le tour de la région des lacs à vélo, Je voudrais faire de l'écotourisme,...***
- If the question is in the perfect tense, you will need to answer in the perfect tense, e.g. ***Tu as fait...? Non, je n'ai jamais fait...***
- Use the conditional (followed by an infinitive) to say what you would like to do, e.g. ***J'aimerais faire du camping au lieu d'aller à l'hôtel,...***

## GRADE TARGET

**To reach Grade C, you need to:**

- keep in mind the topic you are being asked to focus on and give relevant examples.
- use the main tenses correctly. Most of your answers here will be in the present tense. Use the perfect tense to give an example of what you have done in the past.
- use adverbs of time accurately, e.g. ***avant, après, maintenant, aujourd'hui.***

**To aim higher than a C, you could:**

- use verb + infinitive expressions accurately, e.g. ***Il faut, on doit, on devrait, il est important de...***
- use comparatives, e.g. ***le vélo est plus écolo que la voiture, le moins écolo...***
- practise speaking with a really convincing French accent – marks are awarded for pronunciation as well as content. Remember that words that are spelled the same in French and English are not usually pronounced in the same way!

**To aim for an A or A*, you could:**

- use a variety of conjunctions to make longer sentences, e.g. ***et, ou, mais, donc, cependant, sans...***
- include an example of the subjunctive to show off your grammatical knowledge, e.g. ***Il faut qu'on fasse un plus grand effort, j'ai peur qu'on ne prenne pas le problème au sérieux, bien que ce soit cher,*** etc.

## TASK: Writing a leaflet for an eco-tourism holiday

You are going to write a publicity leaflet advertising an ecotourism holiday in a French-speaking country.

You could include details of the following:

- The location and surroundings.
- Accommodation where tourists will stay.
- Meals.
- The activities on offer.
- The advantages of this kind of holiday.

### 1 THINK!

1 Choose where (*la Nouvelle-Calédonie? le Sénégal? Tahiti?*) and what kind of holiday to write about.

2 Do some research about ecotourism projects of this type on the internet and at your local travel agent's so that you will be able to make your leaflet as realistic as possible.

3 Note down a few useful words and phrases. Add to this list:

location: *à la campagne? dans un village? au bord de la mer? dans une région rurale?...*

accommodation: *chez l'habitant? dans un camp? dans un camping? à la ferme?*

meals: *des produits locaux? des repas simples? viande? poisson? légumes?*

activities: *une randonnée dans les montagnes? du travail bénévole? un tour à vélo?*

advantages: *la protection de l'environnement, la proximité de la nature, des vacances plus responsables,...*

### 2 PLAN!

- **Read the model text.**

#### Faites de l'écotourisme!

Vous voulez visiter l'Afrique, mais pas comme un touriste? Alors, pour des vacances originales, choisissez le campement de la Palangrotte afin de découvrir la vraie vie au Sénégal.

Palangrotte est située dans le village de N'Dangane, à 160 kilomètres au sud de Dakar, la capitale du Sénégal. C'est tout près de la mer. Mais ce n'est pas un endroit touristique comme les autres. Ici, on fait du tourisme équitable et solidaire. Un pourcentage de l'argent des visiteurs étrangers va directement aux associations du village et donc le visiteur participe au développement local, par exemple en aidant à la protection de l'environnement local.

Les touristes dorment dans des cases traditionnelles. Il y a l'eau et l'électricité mais l'hébergement est simple. Il y a un bloc sanitaire avec deux WC, deux douches et deux lavabos. On prend les repas dans une case communale: vous mangerez du riz local ou du mil avec des légumes comme la patate douce. On sert aussi du poisson local, du poulet et quelquefois du mouton et de la chèvre.

Passez de super vacances en aidant les gens du village ou en faisant des visites inoubliables. Vous pouvez aussi apprendre la langue locale (le wolof) ou à faire la cuisine.

Il faut que tout le monde vienne à la Palangrotte: on découvre vraiment un pays fascinant, on aide les gens du village… et on s'amuse! Qu'attendez-vous?

- **Read the text again and note down any useful words or phrases you could use or adapt. Add these to your list from Step 1.**
- **Note how the leaflet starts and ends. Look carefully at how the text involves the reader:**
  use of imperatives – ***faites..., choisissez..., passez...***
  use of questions – ***vous voulez...?, qu'attendez-vous?***

## 3 ACTION !

**Now prepare what you will write. Use the bullet points below to help you and use your list of useful words and phrases from Steps 1 and 2. Aim to write about 200 words.**

**1** Introduction

- Start in a way that will attract the reader's attention. Use imperatives or questions to draw the reader in.

**2** Location and surroundings

- As well as the country name, try to provide a more precise geographical location: ***au nord de la capitale, à 50 kilomètres de la frontière avec...***
- Add detail of the surroundings as suggested, e.g. ***à la montagne, en Kabylie, une région montagneuse d'Algérie...***

**3** Accommodation

- Mention the type of accommodation and then focus on arrangements for sleeping and eating.
- You can talk to the reader directly, e.g. ***Vous dormirez... Vous mangerez...*** or indirectly, e.g. ***On dort..., Les touristes/visiteurs dorment...***

**4** Meals

- Mention whatever you think most interesting: when, where, what the tourist will eat.
- To be more impressive, you could describe what a dish is made of, e.g. ***le pain patate, qui est un plat typiquement haïtien composé de patates douces avec...***

**5** Activities

- Mention several of the most interesting or unusual activities, e.g. ***on peut faire des promenades dans la nature à dos d'âne, faire du kayak de mer,...***
- You could extend your answer by adding in adjectives to make the activities sound more attractive, e.g. ***faire une randonnée inoubliable dans ce paysage spectaculaire.***

**6** Advantages

- Try to sum up the advantages in two or three phrases.
- You could use ***C'est*** + adjective: ***C'est écolo/pas cher/intéressant*** or list what the visitor can do: ***On peut partager les traditions...***

**7** Conclusion

- End in a suitably persuasive way.

## GRADE TARGET

**To reach Grade C, you need to:**

- cover all the points suggested. You can't get full marks unless you do.
- use adjectives to add detail, e.g. ***un logement économique, des lits confortables, une visite intéressante,*** etc. Check the adjectives agree with the noun they describe (masculine or feminine, singular or plural) and are in the correct position (usually after the noun they describe).

**To aim higher than a C, you could:**

- use more than one tense correctly. The future tense (or ***aller*** + infinitive) could be used here to show what tourists will do, e.g. ***vous allez faire des visites, on mangera des plats typiques...***
- use a variety of structures, e.g. vary question formats: ***Vous voulez partir? Est-ce que tu préfères la vie en plein air?***
- Use intensifiers to be more precise, e.g. ***assez/vraiment bon.***

**To aim for an A or A*, you could:**

- use superlatives, e.g. ***la région la plus pauvre, les gens les plus sympa, le paysage le plus spectaculaire...***
- use an example of the subjunctive to impress the examiner, e.g. ***bien qu'il ne fasse pas beau tout le temps, si tu préfères que tout soit authentique,...***

# 3B Vocabulaire

### Comment exprimer tes soucis pour la planète

| | |
|---|---|
| la canette alu | *aluminium can* |
| la chasse aux baleines | *whale-hunting* |
| la crise | *crisis* |
| les déchets (*mpl*) | *rubbish* |
| la disparition | *disappearance* |
| la lumière | *light* |
| la poubelle | *dustbin* |
| le réchauffement climatique | *global warming* |
| la surpêche | *over-fishing* |
| agir | *to act* |
| chauffer | *to heat* |
| disparaître | *to disappear* |
| éteindre | *to put out* |
| gaspiller | *to waste* |
| protéger | *to protect* |
| provoquer | *to cause* |
| recycler | *to recycle* |
| respecter | *to respect* |
| sauvegarder | *to save* |
| trier | *to sort (out)* |
| renouvelable | *renewable* |

### Comment être écolo

| | |
|---|---|
| les emballages (*mpl*) | *packaging* |
| le jardinage | *gardening* |
| les petits gestes (*mpl*) | *small actions* |
| baisser le chauffage | *to turn the heating down* |
| faire un effort | *to make an effort* |
| fermer le robinet | *to turn off the tap* |
| mettre un pullover | *to put on a jumper* |
| produire | *to produce* |
| sauver | *to save* |
| utiliser | *to use* |
| bio | *organic* |
| équitable | *fair-trade* |
| recyclé(e) | *recycled* |
| végétarien/végétarienne | *vegetarian* |
| au lieu de | *instead of* |

### Comment voyager écolo

| | |
|---|---|
| les transports en commun | *public transport* |
| (la marche) à pied | *on foot/walking* |
| le car | *coach* |
| le métro | *underground* |
| la moto | *motorbike* |
| le RER | *Paris fast suburban rail link* |
| le tramway | *tram* |
| écolo(gique) | *green, ecological* |
| économique | *economical* |
| polluant(e) | *polluting* |
| pratique | *handy* |
| rapide | *fast* |
| plus (*adjective*) que... | *more... than* |
| moins (*adjective*) que... | *less... than* |
| aussi (*adjective*) que... | *as... as* |
| le plus (*adjective*) | *the most...* |
| le moins (*adjective*) | *the least...* |
| à partir de maintenant | *from now on* |
| après | *after* |
| avant | *before* |
| aujourd'hui | *today* |
| bientôt | *soon* |
| la dernière fois | *last time* |
| maintenant | *now* |
| plus tard | *later* |

### Comment faire de l'écotourisme

| | |
|---|---|
| les bagages (*mpl*) | *luggage* |
| la découverte | *discovery* |
| l'écotourisme (*m*) | *ecotourism* |
| le gîte | *country holiday home/gite* |
| la liberté | *freedom* |
| la randonnée | *walk, hike* |
| le sentiment de liberté | *feeling of freedom* |
| le voyage d'étude | *study trip* |
| apprécier | *to appreciate* |
| détruire | *to destroy* |
| loger | *to stay (in a hotel, etc.)* |
| responsable | *responsible* |
| sensible | *sensitive* |

### Comment parler des initiatives écologiques

| | |
|---|---|
| la communauté | *community* |
| l'eau (*f*) potable | *drinking water* |
| les produits (*mpl*) locaux | *local products* |
| le puits | *well* |
| convaincre | *to convince* |
| encourager | *to encourage* |
| financer | *to finance* |
| installer | *to install* |
| travailler ensemble | *to work together* |
| francophone | *French-speaking* |
| meilleur(e) | *better* |
| accès à | *access to* |

# 4A La vie à l'école

## Sais-tu comment...

- ❑ parler de tes matières préférées?
- ❑ parler de ton école?
- ❑ parler de la scolarité à l'étranger?
- ❑ combiner l'école et le boulot?
- ❑ surmonter le stress au lycée?

Que ferais-tu pour améliorer ton école?

## Controlled assessment

- **Have a conversation about part-time jobs**
- **Write an article about how to improve your school**

## Stratégies

### À l'écoute

When listening, how do you...

- predict the answers to questions?
- check that your answers are correct?
- recognise false friends?

### À l'écrit

In French, how can you...

- give detailed answers?
- use a variety of structures?
- write sophisticated sentences?

## Grammaire active

As part of your French language 'toolkit' can you...

- compare and contrast?
- use 'depuis' with the correct tense?
- use the passive?
- recognise and use the perfect infinitive?

# 4A Comment parler de tes matières préférées

(V) Les matières (G) Adjectifs (S) Deviner les réponses

**A** Thomas Lemaire, Lycée Victor-Hugo, Rennes. Classe de seconde

| | LUNDI | MARDI | MERCREDI | JEUDI | VENDREDI | SAMEDI |
|---|---|---|---|---|---|---|
| 8.30-9.30 | histoire-géo | physique-chimie | physique-chimie | informatique | anglais | français |
| 9.30-10.30 | anglais | maths | maths | ECJS (éducation civique, juridique et sociale) | physique-chimie | anglais |
| 10.30-11.00 | RÉCRÉATION | | | | | |
| 11.00-12.00 | sciences économiques et sociales | atelier artistique | français | atelier artistique | maths | histoire-géo |
| 12.00-14.00 | DÉJEUNER | | | | | |
| 14.00-15.00 | français | histoire-géo | | maths | français | |
| 15.00-16.00 | SVT (sciences de la vie et de la terre) | sciences économiques et sociales | | EPS (éducation physique et sportive) | création-design | |
| 16.00-17.00 | permanence | permanence | | EPS | création-design | |

**A**

**B**

**C**

**D**

**E**

**F**

**G**

**H**

**I**

**J**

**K**

**L**

**M**

**N**

**B**

Thomas Lemaire

Salut! Je m'appelle **[1]**. Je vais au lycée Victor-Hugo à **[2]**. Ma matière préférée c'est **[3]** car je suis très fort en sport. J'en fais deux fois par semaine. Mon sport préféré est le **[4]**. J'aime aussi le **[5]**, l'histoire-géo et la **[6]**. Je n'aime ni les **[7]** économiques et sociales ni l'anglais car je trouve ça inutile. Je suis relativement faible en **[8]**. Je trouve que c'est **[9]** et le prof n'est pas **[10]**.

**1a** **Regarde l'emploi du temps de Thomas, page 120. Trouve les 14 matières illustrées.**

*Exemple:* **A** maths

**1b** **Lis l'emploi du temps et trouve l'équivalent en français.**

**a** *free period* **c** *ICT*
**b** *PSHE* **d** *life sciences*

**2** **Compare le texte A, page 120 avec ton propre emploi du temps. Note les matières que tu as en commun avec Thomas, et les matières différentes.**

*Exemple:* J'ai maths. Thomas aussi a maths, etc. Thomas fait de l'histoire. Moi, je n'en fais pas.

**STRATÉGIES**

A key listening skill is prediction – guessing from context and your own experience what someone is likely to say. Use the information on the page opposite and your own predictions to help you.

**3a** **Lis le texte B, page 120. Remplace [1]–[10] par le bon mot. Écoute pour vérifier.**

*Exemple:* **[1]** Thomas

français sympa Thomas rugby création-design difficile Rennes maths sciences l'éducation physique

**3b** **Fais une liste des adjectifs que Thomas emploie pour décrire ses matières. Attention aux terminaisons! Ajoute trois adjectifs positifs et trois adjectifs négatifs. Cherche-les dans le dictionnaire si nécessaire.**

*Exemple:* préférée – *favourite*

**4** **Écoute. Thomas fait un sondage pour découvrir les matières les plus populaires (1-4). Recopie et complète la grille.**

| Ami(e)s | Aime | N'aime pas | Pourquoi |
|---|---|---|---|
| Aurélie | | | |
| | | | très utile |
| | | ni les langues ni les maths | |
| Kim | | | forte en langues, mais... |

**5** **Fais une liste des matières que tu étudies. Note si tu aimes la matière ou pas et donne une raison.**

*Exemple:* J'aime bien les maths. Je crois que c'est ma matière préférée, parce que...

**6** **À deux. Parlez de vos matières. Prenez des notes et comparez vos opinions.**

*Exemple:* **A** Je déteste l'histoire parce que j'ai toujours de mauvaises notes.
**B** J'aime l'histoire, car je trouve le travail facile.

**7** **Écoute trois lycéens parler de la vie au lycée. Recopie la grille et complète-la en anglais.**

| | does not like | would prefer |
|---|---|---|
| Kévin | 1 | 2 |
| Sophie | 3 | 4 |
| Mélanie | 5 | 6 |

## À VOUS!

**8** **Post a message of about 150 words on a French forum explaining the differences between a French school day and your school day. Say which system you prefer and why.**

*Exemple:* En France, dans certains lycées, on doit aller en cours le samedi matin. Moi, je n'ai pas besoin d'aller au lycée le samedi matin. Je préfère avoir un week-end de deux jours.

- samedi matin: libre?
- mercredi après-midi: cours?
- déjeuner: longueur? cantine ou maison?
- permanence
- fin de la journée
- uniforme?

**9** **Conduct a survey in French on your classmates' views of the subjects they study and their opinions on the school day. In each case ask for reasons, positive or negative. Note down your conclusions.**

*Exemple:*

- La matière la plus populaire, c'est... parce que...
- Les matières les moins populaires sont... parce que...
- Ils travaillent en moyenne... heures par jour.
- Les lycéens trouvent la journée scolaire trop longue/courte, etc.

# 4A Comment parler de ton école

(G) Comparer et contraster (V) Mon lycée (P) Les verbes au pluriel
(S) Bien lire les questions pour bien répondre

**Je m'appelle Matthew. Je suis en Year 11 (en seconde) à Malvern High School. J'étudie neuf matières et en général je les aime bien, sauf les maths. Je trouve les devoirs de maths difficiles.**

**Malvern est un lycée très moderne avec mille cinq cents élèves âgés de 11 à 18 ans. Il y a beaucoup de salles de classe, un grand hall, un CDI (centre de documentation et d'information), une cantine, des laboratoires, un gymnase et une piscine.**

**Les cours commencent à neuf heures moins le quart. Nous avons deux heures de cours, une récré et puis encore deux heures de cours. Tous les cours durent une heure et je trouve ça trop long. Le déjeuner est à une heure et demie et on mange à la cantine.**

**Le dernier cours commence à deux heures trente et finit à trois heures trente. Après ça il y a beaucoup de clubs pour les élèves. Si on aime le sport, il y a des clubs de foot, tennis, rugby, etc. Moi, j'aime aller au club de foot parce que le foot est ma passion. Pour les élèves qui aiment la musique, il y a un orchestre, une chorale et un club de jazz.**

| Les systèmes scolaires | | |
|---|---|---|
| **En France** | **Âge** | **En Grande-Bretagne** |
| ***Collège*** | | |
| la sixième | 11-12 | year 7 |
| la cinquième | 12-13 | year 8 |
| la quatrième | 13-14 | year 9 |
| la troisième | 14-15 | year 10 |
| ***Lycée*** | | |
| la seconde | 15-16 | year 11 |
| la première | 16-17 | year 12 |
| la terminale | 17-18 | year 13 |

**GRAMMAIRE**

**Contrasting**

Here are some useful phrases when you want to compare and contrast:

*Il est en Year11,* ***moi aussi****.* (He's in Year 11, me too) / ***pas moi*** (I'm not)

*Il n'aime pas les maths,* ***moi non plus*** (neither do I) / ***moi si!*** (I do!)

*Il trouve les maths difficiles,* ***par contre,/tandis que*** *moi, je trouve ça facile.*
He finds maths difficult, whereas/while I find them easy.

*Il trouve les maths difficiles,* ***comme moi / contrairement à moi****.*
He finds maths difficult, I do too / unlike me.

**1a** **Lis le texte de Matthew. Choisis quatre phrases vraies.**

**a** *Matthew likes all of his school subjects.*
**b** *Matthew's school is modern and well-equipped.*
**c** *He thinks that one-hour lessons are fine.*
**d** *He has one hour for lunch.*
**e** *He has school lunches.*
**f** *There are music clubs at lunchtime.*
**g** *Matthew's passion is football and he enjoys football club.*

**1b** **Relis le texte. Contraste avec ta propre vie scolaire.**

*Exemple:* Il étudie 9 matières, par contre, moi, j'étudie...

**STRATÉGIES**

Read the questions carefully before you listen, and make predictions based on these about what you expect to hear.

When listening, remember what you were asked and focus on those aspects. Then check what you hear against your predictions.

After listening, check your answers against the questions. Do they make sense?

**2a** **Lis les questions et les réponses possibles. Essaie de deviner ce que Sophie va dire – a), b) ou c).**

**1** *Sophie is:* **a** *14* **b** *16* **c** *17 years old.*
**2** There are:
**a** *700* **b** *800* **c** *900 students in her school.*
**3** *She is studying:* **a** *9* **b** *10* **c** *16 subjects.*
**4** *Lessons begin at:*
**a** *8.00 am* **b** *8.30 am* **c** *9.00 am.*
**5** *For lunch she usually eats:*
**a** *meat and salad* **b** *soup and a roll*
**c** *a sandwich.*
**6** *Lessons finish at:*
**a** *5 pm* **b** *3.15 pm* **c** *4.30 pm.*
**7** *The buildings are:*
**a** *modern* **b** *old* **c** *futuristic.*
**8** *Next year the school is getting:*
**a** *a swimming pool* **b** *a gymnasium*
**c** *new science labs.*
**9** *She goes to a club for:*
**a** *dance lessons* **b** *swimming* **c** *drama.*
**10** *She enjoys school because:*
**a** *she meets up with friends*
**b** *it's boring at home*
**c** *she likes sitting exams.*

**2b** **Écoute pour vérifier. As-tu bien deviné?**

9–10 bonnes réponses: tu es télépathe!
7–8 réponses: un bon essai!
1–6 réponses: pas de chance!

**3** **Réécoute Sophie. Note les différences entre la vie scolaire de Matthew, page 122, et celle de Sophie.**

**4** **À deux. Posez les questions a-g pour votre lycée et répondez. (B↔A)**

*Exemple:* **A** Combien de matières étudies-tu?
**B** J'étudie dix matières.

**a** Combien de matières étudies-tu?
**b** Quelle est ta matière préférée?
**c** Est-ce que tu aimes (la géo)?
**d** À quelle heure finissent les cours?
**e** Il est comment, ton lycée?
**f** Quels clubs y a-t-il?

**5** **Écris une phrase pour comparer les groupes d'images.**

*Exemple:* **a** Je trouve le français plus difficile que l'anglais.

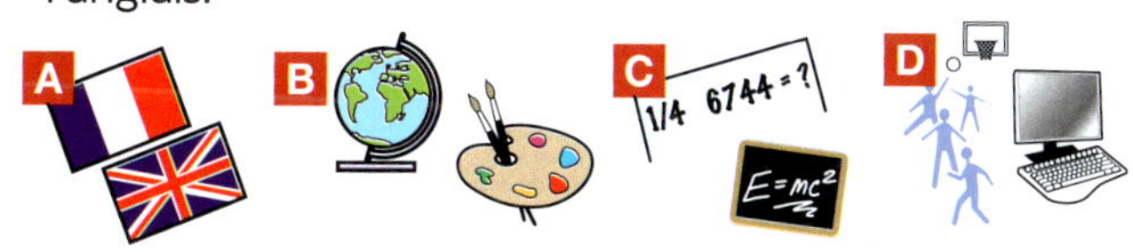


**6** **Écoute Philippe. Note:**

*Exemple:* **a** Il a quinze ans.

**a** son âge
**b** sa matière préférée
**c** l'heure du premier cours
**e** son déjeuner
**f** l'heure de fin des cours

## À VOUS!

**7** **In groups, prepare a FAQ page for a web guide to your school. Write the questions and answers for French visitors.**

*Exemple:* **Q:** Il y a combien d'élèves?
**R:** Il y a neuf cents élèves.

**8** **Describe your ideal school: the buildings, the timetable, the clubs, etc. Aim to give a presentation lasting two to three minutes.**

*Exemple:* Il y aurait une piscine... les cours commenceraient/finiraient à...

# 4A Comment parler de la scolarité à l'étranger

G Depuis + imparfait V La vie scolaire dans un autre pays S Faux amis

Deux lycéens, Julie at César, font un projet sur le Sénégal. Voici des textes qu'ils ont trouvés:

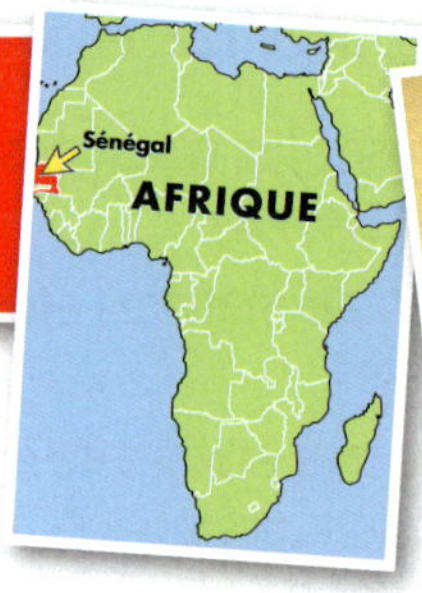

**A**

## Le Sénégal: quelques chiffres

Ancienne colonie française, devenue indépendante en 1960 7 langues officielles, y compris le français, le wolof et le peul

**Population**: 11 millions

**Capitale**: Dakar

**Religion**: musulmane (90%), chrétienne (5%)

**Espérance de vie**: 56 ans (femmes), 54 ans (hommes)

**Population de moins de 15 ans**: 43,1%

**Analphabétisme***: 51,8% (hommes), 71,4% (femmes)

**Scolarisation* des 12–17 ans**: 30%

* analphabétisme – *illiteracy*
scolarisation – *school attendance*

**B**

## À la croisée des écoles Yonne-Sénégal

Le but de notre association: donner aux enfants sénégalais la possibilité d'aller à l'école. Notre priorité, ce sont les enfants qui vivent en brousse*.

Nos deux activités principales sont l'aménagement des salles de classe et l'apport de fournitures* scolaires. Par exemple, pour la rentrée des écoles cette année, l'association a offert à chaque élève d'une école située en brousse:

1 cahier

1 cahier de coloriage* pour les petits

1 ardoise*

1 crayon de papier

1 pochette de crayons de couleurs

1 stylo à bille bleu ou noir

* en brousse – *in the bush*
fourniture – *equipment*
coloriage – *colouring-in*
ardoise – *slate*

**C**

Une étude a montré que sur 6 060 écoles élémentaires au Sénégal, 3 080 (ou 59%) n'ont pas d'eau. Environ 2 850 manquent de blocs sanitaires et 36% ne sont pas clôturées.* Les élèves sénégalais travaillent donc dans des conditions difficiles et un assez grand nombre doivent redoubler* ou choisissent d'abandonner leurs études.

* clôturé – *fenced off*
redoubler – *repeat the year*

**D**

48 millions d'enfants de moins de 14 ans, soit* un tiers* de la population de leur âge, "travaillent" en Afrique sub-saharienne. Et le Sénégal n'est pas une exception. Le scénario classique: un(e) marchand(e) d'esclaves* va voir une famille dans un village pauvre et promet toutes sortes d'avantages aux parents de l'enfant. Les parents lui confient leur enfant en échange de quelques billets. Ils ne le reverront jamais.

Que font ces enfants? On les voit dans les rues, vendant des beignets ou de l'eau fraîche. Quelques-uns mendient* au coin de la rue, ou sont condamnés à servir de guide à un mendiant adulte aveugle. Ce qui est sûr, c'est qu'ils ne vont plus à l'école.

* soit – *i.e.*
un tiers – *a third*
marchand d'esclaves – *slave trader*
ils mendient – *they beg*

**1** Lis le texte A, page 124, puis recopie et complète les phrases.

*Exemple:* **a** *a French colony*

- **a** *The main language spoken in Senegal is French because it used to be...*
- **b** *But there are seven different...*
- **c** *Nine out of ten people in Senegal are...*
- **d** *Life expectancy in Senegal is...*
- **e** *Over half the men and nearly three quarters of the women can't...*
- **f** *Only about one in three teenagers...*

**2** Survole* les textes B–D et écris une phrase en anglais pour résumer chacun.

* scan

**3** Relis le texte B et choisis les bons mots pour compléter les phrases.

1. Cette association veut aider les **a**) parents **b**) familles **c**) élèves au Sénégal
2. Elle veut surtout aider les enfants dans les **a**) régions rurales **b**) grandes villes **c**) villages
3. Elle s'occupe des **a**) salaires des profs **b**) bâtiments scolaires **c**) uniformes scolaires
4. Elle envoie des **a**) vêtements **b**) fournitures scolaires **c**) professeurs

**4** Relis le texte C et note trois choses en anglais que les écoles élémentaires au Sénégal n'ont pas.

**STRATÉGIES**

Watch out for 'false friends' – words which look like an English word, but mean something different. E.g. *redoubler* which means to re-take a school year, not to redouble. Check the meaning of these words if you are unsure: *sympathique, une pièce, un car, sensible, blessé*.

**5** Lis le texte D et décide si les phrases sont vraies (V), fausses (F) ou pas mentionnées (?).

*Exemple:* **a** F

- **a** *Children under the age of 14 are not allowed to work in Sénégal.*
- **b** *Some parents sell their children.*
- **c** *The government tries to monitor those who try to buy and sell children.*
- **d** *Most children who are sold never see their parents again.*
- **e** *Most beggars are children who have been bought and sold.*
- **f** *They go to school when they are not begging.*

**GRAMMAIRE**

***Depuis* + imperfect**

Use *depuis* + the imperfect tense to say how long something **had been** happening.

*L'enfant mendiait depuis l'âge de dix ans.* The child **had been** begging since the age of 10.

See page 94 for how to use *depuis* + present tense to say how long something **has been** happening.

**6** Lis les questions préparées par Julie et César. Puis, écoute un groupe d'élèves en discuter (1–6). Qui répond à chaque question?

*Exemple:* **a** 3

- **a** Peut-on dire que la population sénégalaise a un bon niveau d'éducation?
- **b** Croyez-vous que la population soit en bonne santé?
- **c** Quels problèmes existent dans les écoles au Sénégal?
- **d** Quel rôle joue l'association «À la croisée des écoles Yonne-Sénégal»?
- **e** Qu'est-ce qui montre que les élèves ont des difficultés à l'école?
- **f** Que savez-vous sur le travail des enfants au Sénégal?

## À vous!

**7** Work in pairs. One person asks the questions from activity 6 and the other replies. To prepare, re-read texts A–D, page 124, and listen again to activity 6. Try to include one or two extra questions.

**8** Write about 150 words comparing your life with the life of someone about your age in Senegal. Use these phrases as a starting point:

| | |
|---|---|
| Au Sénégal, la vie est plus... | Par exemple... |
| On a moins de... là-bas | J'imagine que... |
| Les ados au Sénégal... | mais nous, par contre,... |

# 4A Comment combiner l'école et le boulot

G Le passif  V Les avantages et les inconvénients d'un petit boulot  S Donner des réponses détaillées

## *C'est possible de faire son travail scolaire et d'avoir aussi un petit boulot?*

**A**

Mme Boudry

Ma fille Léa aime beaucoup son job au supermarché où elle a beaucoup de copains. Elle y travaille tous les samedis de neuf heures à dix-huit heures et aussi le mardi et le jeudi soir pendant quatre heures. Je trouve que c'est trop parce qu'elle n'a pas le temps de faire son travail scolaire et elle est toujours fatiguée. Ses devoirs sont trop vite faits ou ne sont pas faits du tout. Elle est toujours de mauvaise humeur et elle trouve mon avis ridicule. Mais en tant qu'adulte, je sais qu'il faut réussir aux examens pour avoir un travail intéressant et bien payé un jour. Si elle travaillait moins au supermarché, je n'aurais pas de problèmes avec son job.

**B**

M. Thierry

Mon fils Simon distribue des journaux tous les jours. Il doit se lever à six heures pour être prêt à l'heure et aller chercher les journaux. Il rentre vers sept heures et demie et en principe il a assez de temps pour prendre une douche et quitter la maison à huit heures pour prendre le bus et aller au lycée. Je ne sais pas quoi penser. D'un côté il gagne de l'argent et comprend la valeur de l'argent, d'un autre côté il me semble qu'il se fatigue. En hiver c'est pire parce qu'il fait toujours noir quand il quitte la maison et il fait mauvais. Peut-être que ce serait mieux s'il ne distribuait des journaux que le week-end, comme ça il aurait plus de temps pour faire ses devoirs. Je n'ai pas été content de son travail scolaire cette année. Le travail a été trop vite fait et il n'a pas eu de bonnes notes.

**C**

Quentin

J'ai un petit boulot que je fais trois soirs par semaine et six heures le week-end. Je travaille dans un magasin de bricolage, et mon job, c'est décharger les marchandises des camions. C'est un boulot physiquement très très fatigant. Par exemple, deux tonnes de planches ont été déchargées hier soir! Je n'ai pas vraiment envie de faire ce boulot mais mes parents ne sont pas riches et on a besoin de l'argent. Pendant les vacances, je fais d'autres boulots: je lave des voitures, je distribue de la pub et je fais du baby-sitting. Tout ça me donne de l'expérience. Malheureusement, ça prend sur mon temps de travail scolaire et mes devoirs sont faits à la va-vite*! En plus, le job au magasin est assez mal payé. Je trouve que les jeunes sont exploités par les employeurs parce qu'on fait le même travail que les adultes mais on est moins bien payés de l'heure.

**1** Lis l'opinion des deux parents et trouve l'équivalent en français.

*Exemple:* **a** tous les samedis

**A**
- **a** *every Saturday*
- **b** *her homework is done too quickly*
- **c** *she finds my opinion ridiculous*
- **d** *you need to do well in exams*
- **e** *if she did fewer hours…*

**B**
- **f** *he has to get up*
- **g** *in theory he has enough time*
- **h** *on the one hand he is earning money*
- **i** *in winter it's worse*
- **j** *if he only delivered papers at the weekend*
- **k** *I haven't been happy*
- **l** *the work was done quickly*

* hastily, slapdash

**2** Lis les trois textes. C'est qui: Mme Boudry (B), Léa (L), M. Thierry (T), Simon (S) ou Quentin (Q)?

- **a** *Who works in a supermarket?*
- **b** *Who would prefer not to have a part-time job?*
- **c** *Who thinks working 17 hours a week is too much?*
- **d** *Who thinks working at the weekend is better than during the week?*
- **e** *Who is always in a bad mood?*
- **f** *Who has not been working well at school over the past year?*

**3** Relis. Fais une liste des avantages et des inconvénients des petits boulots. Pense aux horaires de travail, à l'argent gagné, au temps pour les devoirs, à l'expérience que cela apporte.

**4** Trouve la fin pour chaque phrase a–g et traduis-les.

*Exemple:* **a 3** *I find it difficult to have the time to do my homework and my part-time job.*

| | |
|---|---|
| **a** Je trouve difficile d' | **1** on a le reste de la semaine pour faire le travail scolaire. |
| **b** Si on travaille le samedi, | **2** ont besoin de beaucoup de sommeil. |
| **c** Les ados sont fatigués et | **3** avoir le temps de faire mes devoirs et mon petit boulot. |
| **d** J'ai des difficultés à m'endormir | **4** le soir donc je veux faire la grasse matinée le week-end. |
| **e** J'aime bien gagner de l'argent pour | **5** si je travaille bien à l'école. |
| **f** Mes parents me donnent de l'argent | **6** parce qu'il est paresseux. |
| **g** Mon ami n'a pas de travail | **7** m'acheter des habits. |

**GRAMMAIRE**

**The passive**

In a passive sentence, the subject of the verb has something done to it, rather than performing an action itself. The passive is often used when you don't know who did something:

*deux tonnes de planches ont été déchargées*
two tons of planks were unloaded

or to attract attention to the passive role of the person concerned:

*les jeunes sont exploités* young people are exploited

It is formed with the correct part of *être* + past participle. See *Grammaire active*, page 130.

**5** Recherche tous les verbes au passif dans les textes A, B et C. Traduis-les.

*Exemple:* Texte A: Ses devoirs sont trop vite faits – *Her homework is done too quickly.*

**6** Écoute Marion. De quoi parle-t-elle? Note quatre lettres.

- **a** *what job she does*
- **b** *where and when she does it*
- **c** *what exactly her job entails*
- **d** *how long she's been doing it*
- **e** *how much she earns*
- **f** *what she likes about it*
- **g** *what she dislikes about it*

**7** Fais un sondage dans ta classe. Où et quand travaillent les élèves? Combien gagnent-ils? Est-ce que leurs petits boulots ont des inconvénients?

**8** Écoute ces jeunes parler de leurs petits boulots (1–4). À deux, proposez des solutions à leurs problèmes.

*Exemple:* **1** Tu pourrais aider ta mère à la maison et trouver un petit boulot, par exemple, dans un supermarché.

## À VOUS!

**9** Choose the part-time job that you find the most interesting. Write a list of the advantages of this job and give a 90-second presentation to the class. Vote to decide which job wins.

**10** Write an article for a teen magazine. Give your readers advice on how best to combine paid work with school work. Try to include examples of part-time jobs from your classmates in the article.

# 4A Comment surmonter le stress au lycée

(G) Verbes pronominaux au passé; l'infinitif passé (V) Pressions et problèmes scolaires

(S) Varier les structures à l'écrit

## Cyberpage

### Isa

Le gros problème, au lycée, c'est que la discipline est très mauvaise. Je pense que le règlement n'est pas assez strict. Ce matin, deux élèves ont commencé à perturber le cours de français. Je me suis concentrée difficilement parce que la prof n'arrivait pas* à contrôler la classe. Après avoir crié pendant une heure, elle a envoyé ces élèves chez le directeur mais il ne s'est rien passé. Pour moi, c'est inadmissible. Ils ont recommencé la même chose pendant les cours de l'après-midi.

* n'arrivait pas à – *didn't manage to*

### Rico

J'ai souvent peur à l'école parce qu'il y a des élèves qui font du racket et moi, je ne trouve pas normal d'avoir peur à l'école. Selon moi, l'intimidation est un des plus gros problèmes au lycée et pourtant, on ne fait pas grand-chose. Un élève de terminale s'en prend toujours à moi*. Il veut m'attaquer quand je serai seul si je parle à mes parents. J'estime que c'est très grave. Après être allé en parler au conseiller d'éducation qui n'a rien fait, je me suis adressé au directeur. Ce garçon a été renvoyé* pendant trois jours mais il est revenu et il recommence. Je ne sais plus quoi faire!

* s'en prend à moi – *picks on me*
renvoyé – *excluded*

### Lou

Je crois que ce qui me stresse le plus au lycée, c'est l'emploi du temps qui, à mon avis, est trop chargé et les contrôles que je trouve trop stressants. J'ai plus de trente heures de cours par semaine, plus environ quatre heures de travail personnel par jour. Après être rentrée chez moi le soir, après avoir dîné et après avoir aidé aux tâches ménagères, je n'ai pas beaucoup de temps pour les devoirs. J'ai dû abandonner la musique et le sport. Le samedi, j'ai un job. Hier soir, il était minuit quand je me suis couchée parce que je devais réviser pour un contrôle de maths.

**1** **Lis les messages. C'est qui? Trouve les phrases pour justifier ta réponse.**

*Exemple:* **a** Rico – Il y a un élève de terminale qui...

**a** *...is always being bullied by a student at school.*
**b** *...has far too heavy a timetable.*
**c** *...can't focus in class because of other students' bad behaviour.*
**d** *...suffers from the pressure of tests.*
**e** *...resents not having time for leisure activities.*
**f** *...feels the school doesn't do enough to combat bullying.*
**g** *...is shocked that the headteacher is doing nothing.*
**h** *...thinks the main issue is a lack of discipline.*

**STRATÉGIES**

To make your writing more interesting and more sophisticated, use a variety of different structures, e.g. to give your opinion: *je pense/j'estime/je trouve que..., à mon avis...*

Find other structures in the texts above.

**2** Écris ces opinions en utilisant différentes structures.

*Exemple:* J'estime que la principale cause de stress, c'est la pression des parents.

- **a** La principale cause de stress, c'est la pression des parents.
- **b** La pression des examens est insupportable.
- **c** Les relations avec d'autres élèves sont difficiles.
- **d** Le climat au sein du lycée est trop violent.

**3** À deux. Écrivez d'autres raisons pour expliquer le stress au lycée. Échangez vos idées avec d'autres paires et discutez.

*Exemple:* – Je crois que les professeurs sont trop autoritaires.
– Moi, au contraire, je trouve qu'ils ne sont pas assez autoritaires.

**4a** Écoute les conseils d'une conseillère d'éducation. À qui s'adresse-t-elle: Isa, Rico ou Lou?

**4b** Réécoute. Dans quel ordre la conseillère suggère-t-elle de faire les choses? Numérote «1» ou «2».

*Exemple:* Isa: 1 b, 2 a

Isa: **a)** parler au directeur **b)** parler aux profs
Rico: **a)** parler au directeur **b)** parler à la police
Lou: **a)** parler à ses parents **b)** arrêter le job

**GRAMMAIRE**

**The perfect infinitive**

This is formed with the infinitive of *avoir* or *être* + the past participle. It is often used after *après* to link up two sentences and to indicate which action took place before another.

*Je fais mes devoirs. Puis je me couche.* I do my homework. Then I go to bed.
*Après avoir fait mes devoirs, je me couche.* After doing my homework, I go to bed.
*On est sortis de cours. Ensuite on s'est retrouvés au foyer.*
*Après être sortis de cours, on s'est retrouvés au foyer.*
After coming out of lessons, we met up in the common room.

**5** Relis les textes, page 128. Trouve des exemples de l'infinitif passé et traduis-les.

*Exemple:* Après avoir crié pendant une heure, elle a envoyé ces élèves...
*After shouting for an hour, she sent those pupils...*

**6** Réécris ces phrases en utilisant un infinitif passé.

*Exemple:* **a** Après avoir attaqué un élève de sixième, il lui a pris son sac.

- **a** Il a attaqué un élève de sixième et il lui a pris son sac.
- **b** D'abord, elle a fait ses devoirs. Puis elle est partie faire son job au supermarché.
- **c** Il faut d'abord parler au prof. Ensuite on peut aller voir la directrice.

**GRAMMAIRE**

**Reflexives in the perfect**

Reflexive verbs in the perfect use *être* + past participle which agrees with the subject:

*Je me couche.* I go to bed.
*Je me suis couché(e).* I went to bed.

Find all the reflexive verbs in the perfect tense in the texts on page 128.

**7** Réécris au passé composé ce que dit Marina de sa journée au lycée.

*Exemple:* **a** Hier, je me suis levée...

- **a** Je me lève à 6 heures et je me prépare.
- **b** Un élève s'en prend à moi à l'entrée du lycée. Il vole mon sac. J'arrive en retard au cours.
- **c** Le prof se met en colère et me donne une colle après les cours*.
- **d** Le soir, mes parents s'inquiètent parce qu'il est tard quand je rentre.
- **e** J'explique la situation et je me couche, très stressée!

* detention

## À VOUS!

**8** Imagine that when you woke up this morning you had become a French teacher in your school! Invent and describe your day.

*Exemple:* Ce matin, je suis allé(e) au lycée en voiture. Des élèves ont abîmé ma voiture...

**9** Describe a problem you (or someone you know) experienced at school and explain how it was resolved. (250 words)

*Exemple:* L'année dernière, j'ai été victime de la violence de certains élèves qui...

# 4A Grammaire active

### THE PASSIVE VOICE

Use the passive voice to place more emphasis on the action, rather than the subject of the verb:
*Mon lycée a été fermé.* My school has been closed.
It can also be used when we do not know who is performing the action:
*Il a été attaqué.* He was attacked.

**1** **Read the following pairs of sentences. Which of each pair uses the passive?**

*Exemple:* **1a**

**1 a** The library has been closed.
**b** The school has closed the library.
**2 a** Textbooks are being handed out.
**b** Teachers are handing out textbooks.
**3 a** The headteacher excluded two pupils.
**b** Two pupils were excluded.
**4 a** The school will reward good work.
**b** Good work will be rewarded.

### FORMING THE PASSIVE

Use the appropriate tense of *être* plus the past participle of the verb of action.
The past participle must agree with the subject.

**Present passive:** *Les étudiants en difficulté sont assistés par des bourses.* Students in difficulty are helped by grants.

**Perfect passive**
*La fille a été renvoyé**e**.* The girl was excluded.
Note that the past participle adds *–e* to agree with *la fille*.

**Future passive**
*La piscine sera ouvert**e**.* The swimming pool will be opened.

**2** **Now translate each passive sentence from activity 1 into French.**

*Exemple:* **1a** La bibliothèque a été fermée.

### AVOIDING THE PASSIVE

**Use *on* when it's not clear who performed the action**
*On ouvrira la nouvelle bibliothèque.* The new library will be opened.

**Give the verb a subject**
*Ces décisions sont prises par le directeur.* These decisions are taken by the headteacher. →
*Le directeur prend ces décisions.* The headteacher takes these decisions.

**3** **Write these sentences in French avoiding the passive.**

*Exemple:* **a** On a vendu l'appartement.

**a** The flat was sold.
**b** The money was stolen.
**c** I was given a job by the school.
**d** The canteen was opened by the headteacher.

| Past, present, future | |
|---|---|
| 1 Use a verb in the present tense: | – to say what happens now/regularly.<br>– to say what is happening as you speak. |
| 2 Use a verb in the imperfect tense: | – to describe something in the past.<br>– to say what used to happen regularly. |
| 3 Use a verb in the perfect tense: | – to say what happened (as in a sequence of events) in the past. |
| 4 Use *aller* + infinitive: | – to say what you're more or less sure is going to happen soon. |
| 5 Use a verb in the future tense: | – to anticipate what will happen at some point and say how things will be. |

## L'histoire de Hugo

**4** Read *L'histoire de Hugo* on page 130 and find a sentence to illustrate each tense from the table.

*Exemple:* a–4

a **L'année prochaine, je vais** retourner à Paris pour aller à l'université.
b **Quand je serai adulte, j'habiterai** en ville, pas à la campagne!
c **Depuis, j'habite** dans un petit village à la campagne. Je n'aime pas habiter ici parce qu'il n'y a rien d'intéressant à faire pour les jeunes.
d **Quand j'étais petit, j'habitais** à Paris et j'adorais ma ville!
e **J'ai déménagé** l'année dernière parce que mes parents ont changé de travail.

**5a** Copy out the sentences in order to reconstruct Hugo's story. Match the pictures 1–5 to the sentences.

**5b** Use the phrases in bold and adapt sentences a–e to make them true for you.

### TYPICAL VERB FORMS AND ENDINGS

Recognising typical verb endings can help you understand when an action takes place.

| When the verb has one part: | |
|---|---|
| **Present** | *je parle* |
| **Imperfect** | *je parlais* |
| **Future** | *je parlerai* |

| When the verb has two parts: | |
|---|---|
| **Perfect** | *avoir/être* + past participle: *j'ai parlé, je suis allé* |
| **Future** | *aller* + infinitive: *je vais parler* |

| Typical verb endings | | | | |
|---|---|---|---|---|
| **Present** | *je* | ***-e/s/ds/ts/x*** | *nous* | ***-ons*** |
| | *tu* | ***-es/s/ds/ts/x*** | *vous* | ***-ez*** |
| | *il/elle/on* | ***-e/d/t*** | *ils/elles* | ***-ent/ont*** |
| **Imperfect** | *je* | ***-ais*** | *nous* | ***-ions*** |
| | *tu* | ***-ais*** | *vous* | ***-iez*** |
| | *il/elle/on* | ***-ait*** | *ils/elles* | ***-aient*** |
| **Future** | *je* | ***-(i/e)rai*** | *nous* | ***-(i/e)rons*** |
| | *tu* | ***-(i/e)ras*** | *vous* | ***-(i/e)rez*** |
| | *il/elle/on* | ***-(i/e)ra*** | *ils/elles* | ***-(i/e)ront*** |

**6** Match each verb below with one of the tenses in the table on page 130.

*Exemple: allais* – imperfect

**allais** **vas** **habitait** **parleront** **aimiez**
**peux** **prendras** **changerez** **ira** **part**
**allions** **voyageaient** **aimons** **partirons**
**prenez** **décidais** **habiterai** **prennent**

### STRATÉGIES

Knowing when something takes place helps you make sense of what you hear. Listen out for clues such as time phrases, tenses and typical verb endings.

**7** Listen (1–8). What tense is used in each sentence?

*Exemple:* **1** – present

**8a** Listen to the questions (1–8) and work out which tense is being used.

### STRATÉGIES

Always try and use a variety of tenses when answering a question. For example:

Est-ce que tu aimes aller à l'école?

Grade C – *Oui, j'aime aller à l'école./Non, je n'aime pas aller à l'école.*

Grade C–B – *Non, je n'aime pas aller à l'école. J'ai changé d'école l'année dernière. Mon ancienne école était super mais maintenant c'est nul.*

Grade A/A* – *Oui, j'aime bien aller à l'école maintenant. Par contre, l'année dernière, quand j'habitais à Oxford, je n'aimais pas du tout l'école! Les profs étaient très sévères et on avait trop de devoirs. Quand je serai prof moi-même, je serai plus gentil avec mes élèves!*

**8b** Listen again and reply using *oui* and the correct tense.

*Exemple:* **1** – Oui, j'habitais en ville quand j'avais 10 ans.

**9a** Read the questions and listen to the model answers. Identify the different tenses used.

a C'est comment, là où tu habites?
b Qu'est-ce que tu penses de ton école?

**9b** Answer for yourself using at least three tenses.

# 4A Controlled Assessment: Speaking

## TASK: Part-time jobs for students

You are going to have a conversation with your teacher about the pros and cons of having a part-time job while at school. Your teacher will ask you the following:

- What are the best ways of making money when you are still at school?
- What kind of part-time job do you have or would you like to have?
- What are the benefits of having a part-time job, apart from money?
- How much do part-time jobs disrupt school work and social life?
- What would you recommend young people do?
- Will you have a job next year?

*(! Remember: at this point you will have to respond to something you have not prepared.)*

The dialogue will last between 4 and 6 minutes.

## 1 THINK !

**Read the phrases below. Write down any others that you might find useful for the speaking task.**

- ☐ **Making money while at school:** faire du baby-sitting; travailler dans un magasin; distribuer des journaux, etc.
- ☐ **Which part-time job?** J'ai un petit boulot; Je fais.../Je suis...; Je voudrais/ j'aimerais faire... etc.
- ☐ **What are the benefits of a job?** avoir une expérience; devenir plus responsable, etc.
- ☐ **Drawbacks: school work and social life?** moins de temps pour les devoirs; plus fatigué; moins sortir avec les copains, etc.
- ☐ **What would you recommend young people do?** Je recommanderais de...; je ne conseillerais pas de...
- ☐ **Next year?** Je ne vais pas faire de petit boulot...; Je ne travaillerai que le week-end...

**! *Can you predict what the unexpected question might be?***

What do you need to do to find a part-time job?

What do your parents think of you having a part-time job?

**Add to your list any language you would need to answer these questions too.**

## 2 PLAN!

- **Listen to the model conversation. Your teacher has the script.**
- **Listen again and note down any phrases you could use or adapt. Add these to your list from Step 1.**

## 3 ACTION!

**Now prepare your answers. Use the bullet points below to help you and your list of useful words and phrases from Steps 1 and 2.**

**1** How to make money when you are at school?

- Use the modal verb ***pouvoir*** but also try to vary the structures you use: ***on peut*** + infinitive; ***c'est possible de*** + infinitive.
- Remember, in a list, ***et*** comes before the last item: ***distribuer des journaux, faire du baby-sitting et laver des voitures.***

**2** Which part-time job do you have or would you like to have?

- Use the present tense to say which job you have now: ***Je travaille comme...;*** the perfect tense to say which job you had before if applicable: ***j'ai travaillé dans...;*** and the future to talk about a future job you may have: ***j'essaierai de trouver un job...***
- Use the imperfect to describe how things were in the past and to give your opinion in the past: ***c'était nul; j'étais mal payé(e)...***

**3** What are the benefits of a part-time job?

- Use a variety of different expressions and sentence structures to give your opinion: ***je crois/je pense/ j'estime que.../à mon avis/selon moi...***

**4** Drawbacks: school work and social life?

- This is your chance to show off your use of the perfect infinitive to explain what happened after you had done something else: ***après avoir travaillé... j'étais riche/fatigué(e)...***
- Use contrasting sentences to make comparisons: ***Avant j'allais au cinéma, maintenant, j'y vais moins...***

**5** What would you recommend?

- Your chance to use a conditional: ***je conseillerais de.../de ne pas...***
- Try and use a clause with ***si: Si c'est possible, l'idéal serait de...***

**6** What about a job next year?

- This is your chance to use a future tense; say whether you will or won't, and why: ***j'aurai/je n'aurai pas de job parce que qu'il y aura beaucoup de devoirs.***

### GRADE TARGET

**To reach Grade C, you need to:**

- mention a variety of ideas; research the vocabulary beforehand in order to be able to list a few items when asked.
- use the main tenses correctly (e.g. present tense for what you do now, perfect tense for what you did in the past).

**To aim higher than a C, you could:**

- use a greater variety of tenses, e.g. use the imperfect for description and opinion in the past, and the future for what you are planning to do.
- use the conditional to give your opinion or recommendation: ***Pour moi, l'idéal serait de...***

**To aim for an A or A*, you could:**

- create longer sentences, using clauses with ***si*** for instance.
- use a variety of structures to make what you say more sophisticated: ***je trouve que/j'estime que...***
- use the passive voice: ***j'étais bien payé(e); les jeunes sont souvent exploités...***

# 4A Controlled Assessment: Writing

## TASK: An article about your school

You are writing an article (250–300 words) for the next issue of the school newsletter about what you think works and what doesn't work in your school and what improvements you would suggest.

You could include details on the following:

- School facilities.
- School subjects, lesson times, clubs.
- Teachers, staff, students and discipline.
- A specific issue (e.g. a case of bullying) and how it was resolved.
- Improvements you would suggest for the future.

### 1 THINK!

**Start by noting down a few key facts and phrases:**

1. About school facilities and how they affect school life: *les bâtiments modernes/inconfortables; bien/mal équipés,* etc.
2. About a school day and how it is organised, clubs, etc: *les horaires; les heures de cours; les devoirs,* etc. *Les clubs/les sorties/voyages/échanges scolaires...*
3. About people and relationships at school: *le nombre d'élèves par classe, les profs disponibles/autoritaires; le règlement scolaire; les sanctions/punitions,* etc.
4. About a problem, solved or ongoing: *la violence, l'intimidation, le racket; l'insécurité; les sanctions, le renvoi du lycée,* etc.
5. About possible improvements to school life: *on devrait/il pourrait y avoir...; il faudrait; des horaires plus flexibles; moins de devoirs; des espaces plus agréables pour se reposer; plus d'ouverture sur le monde extérieur,* etc.

Notre lycée a une excellente réputation, mais certains aspects de la vie scolaire pourraient, à mon avis, y être améliorés.

Le lycée a été entièrement reconstruit l'année dernière, donc les bâtiments sont neufs. Les classes et les couloirs sont très propres mais ne trouvez-vous pas que ça ressemble un peu à un hôpital?

Les cours et les horaires sont bien. On a 45 minutes pour le déjeuner, pas vraiment assez pour manger et faire des clubs. En plus, il y a peu d'activités pour les non-sportifs.

La discipline est relativement bonne, le directeur est autoritaire et il y a un règlement assez strict. Par contre, comme on est environ 2 200 élèves, les rapports profs-élèves sont très impersonnels.

Il y a peu de problèmes dûs à l'intimidation à l'intérieur du lycée mais il y a souvent des bagarres violentes avec un autre lycée. Récemment, un élève a été attaqué parce qu'il portait notre uniforme. Il va bien, mais maintenant il a très peur. Le directeur dit qu'il ne peut rien faire.

Ce que j'envisagerais pour améliorer la vie au lycée, c'est qu'on autorise aux élèves de décorer les couloirs, par des expositions temporaires de leur choix. Ce serait plus agréable et très motivant! Il faudrait des horaires plus flexibles et un déjeuner plus long: les élèves intéressés pourraient faire plus de clubs et d'activités. En plus, j'aimerais que l'école soit plus ouverte. Moi, je crois que l'école va s'améliorer quand elle s'ouvrira sur l'extérieur et sur le monde du travail, peut-être avec plus de stages. Pour éviter les problèmes de rivalités entre lycées, on supprimera peut-être l'uniforme!

Certaines propositions sont radicales, mais qu'en pensez-vous? Avez-vous d'autres idées à proposer?

## 2 PLAN!

- **Read the model text on page 134.**
- **Read the text again and note down any words or phrases that you could use. Add these to your list from Step 1.**

## 3 ACTION!

**Now prepare what you will write. Use the bullet points below to help you and use your list of useful words and phrases from Steps 1 and 2. Aim to write about 250–300 words.**

**1** Introduction

- Start by giving a short summary of your view of your school, linking it together with connectives such as ***mais, par contre, tandis que...***

**2** Aspects of school and school life

- Present the aspects that you like and dislike about your school, covering the points listed: school facilities, the school day, people at school.
- Address the readers directly by asking questions: ***«Ne trouvez-vous pas que...» or «pensez-vous que...».***

**3** A problem or issue

- Be specific and give a concrete example of a problem, explaining how it was solved or why it wasn't solved.
- Remember to use appropriate tenses when talking about a past event: a perfect tense for a completed action in the past (***il a été attaqué***); an imperfect to describe what it was like or what was happening (***il portait un uniforme***).

**4** Improvements

- Give your personal opinion of how you see the school improving.
- This is an occasion to use verbs in the conditional: ***j'envisagerais, ce serait..., il faudrait..., j'aimerais...***
- This is also an occasion to speak about the future with ***aller*** + infinitive or future tense: ***l'école va s'améliorer... elle s'ouvrira***, etc.

**5** Conclusion

- End on a note which opens out the debate, perhaps with a question to the readers.

### GRADE TARGET

**To reach Grade C, you need to:**

- cover all the points suggested, otherwise you won't get full marks.
- make sure that you make the adjectives agree with the nouns they go with.
- use the correct conjunctions to link your ideas, e.g. ***et*** – and, ***mais*** – but, ***ou*** – or, ***donc*** – so.

**To aim higher than a C, you could:**

- use more than one tense correctly: use the perfect tense and the imperfect tense to talk about a past event.
- use a variety of structures to make suggestions: ***ce serait..., il faudrait..., j'aimerais...*** etc.

**To aim for an A or A*, you could:**

- use examples of the passive voice: ***Le lycée a été entièrement reconstruit, un élève a été attaqué***.
- use an example of the subjunctive to impress: ***j'aimerais que l'école soit plus ouverte.***

# 4A Vocabulaire

## Comment parler de tes matières préférées

| | |
|---|---|
| l'anglais (*m*) | *English* |
| l'atelier (*m*) artistique | *art* |
| l'ECJS (Éducation civique, juridique et sociale) (*f*) | *PSHE/Citizenship* |
| l'EPS (*f*) | *PE* |
| le français | *French* |
| l'histoire-géo (*f*) | *history and geography* |
| l'emploi (*m*) du temps | *timetable* |
| l'informatique (*f*) | *IT* |
| les maths (*fpl*) | *maths* |
| la matière | *subject* |
| la musique | *music* |
| la permanence | *free period* |
| la physique-chimie | *physics and chemistry* |
| les SVT (Sciences de la vie et de la terre) (*fpl*) | *science* |
| les sciences économiques et sociales (*fpl*) | *social sciences* |
| J'ai de bonnes/mauvaises notes | *I get good/bad marks* |
| Le prof n'est pas sympa | *the teacher isn't nice* |
| être faible en/fort en... | *to be bad at/good at...* |
| utile | *useful* |

## Comment parler de ton école

| | |
|---|---|
| le bâtiment | *building* |
| le CDI | *school library* |
| la cantine | *canteen* |
| la chorale | *choir* |
| le club d'échecs | *chess club* |
| le cours | *lesson* |
| le déjeuner | *lunch(time)* |
| les devoirs (*mpl*) | *homework* |
| mon ancienne école (*f*) | *my former school* |
| l'élève (*m/f*) | *pupil* |
| le gymnase | *gym* |
| le laboratoire | *laboratory* |
| le lycée | *secondary school* |
| l'orchestre (*m*) | *orchestra* |
| la pause/la récré | *break* |
| la piscine | *swimming pool* |
| la salle de classe | *classroom* |
| augmenter | *to increase, go up* |
| injuste | *unfair* |
| ailleurs | *elsewhere* |

## Comment parler de la scolarité à l'étranger

| | |
|---|---|
| l'eau (*f*) fraîche | *fresh water* |
| l'esclave (*m/f*) | *slave* |
| les fournitures (*fpl*) scolaires | *school equipment* |
| la langue officielle | *official language* |
| la santé | *health* |
| abandonner les études | *to drop out of school* |
| confier | *to entrust* |
| manquer | *to lack* |
| mendier | *to beg* |
| redoubler | *to retake (the school year)* |
| savoir (lire) | *to know (how to read)* |
| ancien/ancienne | *former* |
| aveugle | *blind* |
| chrétien/chrétienne | *Christian* |
| musulman(e) | *Muslim* |
| pauvre | *poor* |
| sénégalais(e) | *Senegalese* |

## Comment combiner l'école et le boulot

| | |
|---|---|
| le boulot | *job* |
| les habits | *clothes* |
| avoir envie de | *to feel like* |
| décharger | *to unload* |
| se fatiguer | *to get tired* |
| faire la grasse matinée | *to have a lie-in* |
| gagner son propre argent | *to earn your own money* |
| Ses devoirs sont trop vite faits. | *She does her homework too quickly.* |
| il faut réussir aux examens | *you need to do well in your exams* |
| d'un côté... d'un autre côté | *on the one hand... on the other hand* |
| de mauvaise humeur | *bad-tempered* |
| les jeunes sont exploités | *young people are exploited* |
| mal payé | *badly paid* |

## Comment surmonter le stress au lycée

| | |
|---|---|
| le contrôle (de maths) | *(maths) test* |
| un conseiller d'éducation | *equivalent to head of year or person in charge of pastoral care* |
| un élève de terminale | *final year student* |
| la pression des parents | *pressure from parents* |
| la principale cause de stress | *the main cause of stress* |
| l'intimidation (*f*) | *bullying* |
| le racket | *bullying* |
| le règlement | *rules* |
| la sanction | *punishment* |
| les tâches (*fpl*) ménagères | *household tasks* |
| insupportable | *unbearable* |
| stressant(e) | *stressful* |
| trop chargé | *overloaded* |
| s'adresser à quelqu'un | *to speak to someone* |
| attaquer | *to attack* |
| avoir peur | *to feel scared* |
| se concentrer | *to concentrate* |
| perturber | *to disrupt* |

# 4B Gagner sa vie

## Sais-tu comment...

- ❑ trouver du travail?
- ❑ poser ta candidature?
- ❑ briller dans un entretien?
- ❑ décrire ton stage?
- ❑ choisir une carrière?

## Controlled assessment

- **Role play of a job interview**
- **Apply for a summer placement in a French-speaking country**

**Sais-tu quoi faire pour réussir à un entretien?**

## Stratégies

### À l'écrit

In French, how do you...

- make sure that you use the correct accents?
- use capital letters in the right places?
- write a formal letter?

### À l'oral

When speaking, how do you...

- work out the meaning of words from their word family?
- answer questions in the Controlled Assessment?
- cope if you don't know a word?

## Grammaire active

As part of your French language 'toolkit' can you...

- recognise and use the conditional?
- use expressions with the infinitive?
- use a range of different conjunctions?
- form relative clauses?
- use the present participle?

# 4B Comment trouver du travail

**G** Le conditionnel **V** Petites annonces; les métiers **S** Quel contexte?; Les sons et l'orthographe

A

**Étudiants! Vous cherchez un job d'été?**

Nous avons besoin de vendeurs/vendeuses de glaces ici au parc d'attractions du Futuroscope.

Rémunération: SMIC.

3 mois à partir du 15 juin

Possibilité de camping gratuit sur le site.

Envoyez votre CV et lettre de motivation à: stages@futuroscope.fr

B

**VOUS VOULEZ ...**

– gagner de l'argent cet été?

– passer 2-3 mois dans le Val de Loire?

– perfectionner vos connaissances en français?

**VOUS ÊTES ...**

– libre à partir du 1er juillet?

– prêt à travailler avec nos touristes environ 40 heures par semaine?

– capable de parler un minimum de 2 langues?

**CONTACTEZ-NOUS:** jobsdété@valdeloire.fr

C

Vous aimez travailler avec le public? Vous êtes responsable et vous savez cuisiner? Vous avez trois mois de libre? Si vous répondez oui, oui et trois fois oui, vous voulez certainement travailler dans un de nos restaurants. Vous serez nourri, logé et payé!

Adressez-vite votre CV et lettre de candidature à Resto-Rapide, 75019 Paris.

**STRATÉGIES**

**Guessing words from context**

If you have to guess words, use the context to help you. Which four of these words would you be most likely to find in a job advert? Pay, hours, textbook, map, minimum wage, disappointed, available.

**1** Lis les trois petites annonces et écris en anglais une phrase pour chacune qui explique de quel type de travail il s'agit.

*Exemple*: **A** *selling ice creams at Futuroscope.*

**2** À quelle annonce peuvent-ils répondre?

*Exemple*: **a** – **B**

**a** Je suis libre pour huit semaines au maximum.
**b** Je préfère avoir un logement gratuit.
**c** Je ne veux pas faire de vente.
**d** J'espère parler français le plus possible.
**e** J'aimerais travailler dans la restauration.
**f** Cela me plairait de travailler avec les touristes.
**g** Je cherche un poste à Paris si possible.

**3** Écoute trois jeunes qui parlent du travail qu'ils veulent faire (1–3). Quel poste convient à chacun – A, B, C ou aucun?

*Exemple*: **1** – aucun

**4a** Écoute (1–3) et essaie d'écrire les noms des professions que tu entends. Attention aux règles d'orthographe.

**1** -eur **2** -ier **3** -ien

**4b** Écris la traduction anglaise pour chaque métier. Devine, discute avec un(e) partenaire et, si besoin est, cherche dans un dictionnaire.

**5** Recopie avec tes propres exemples.

À l'âge de 6 ans, je voulais être *pompier* ou *médecin*.
Ma mère est *femme au foyer*. Mon père est *ingénieur*. Mon oncle est *au chômage*.
Ma grand-mère était *fleuriste*.
Ma sœur est *cuisinière*.
Il y a trois métiers qui m'intéressent: .................., .................. et ...................Je n'aimerais pas être ..............................

**GRAMMAIRE**

**Conditional**
Use the conditional mood to say what 'would' happen:
*J'aimerais être vétérinaire* – I would like to be a vet.
*Je ne voudrais pas travailler dans un magasin* – I would not like to work in a shop.
See page 148 for how to form the conditional.

**6** À deux. **A** choisit un métier. **B** devine lequel en posant des questions à **A** qui doit répondre uniquement par «oui» ou «non». (**B**⟷**A**)

Tu travailles dans un bureau/un hôpital/en plein air avec des animaux/des enfants/des personnes âgées, etc.?
Tu portes un uniforme?

## Mon métier idéal?

*Je suis fort en maths, en informatique et j'aime aussi la musique parce que je suis très créatif. J'aime travailler en équipe mais j'aime aussi être indépendant. Je pourrais être informaticien ou programmeur, ou je pourrais être ingénieur du son. Ah oui, ce serait peut-être le métier idéal pour moi. Cela m'intéresse beaucoup!*

Lucas

Carine

*Je suis très sportive et je fais partie de plusieurs équipes. Je n'aimerais pas passer huit heures par jour dans un bureau et je ne voudrais pas travailler seule! Mes parents disent que je serais un bon prof de sport, mais moi, je pense plutôt devenir assistante dans un centre de sport, ou peut-être kinésithérapeute. Ce serait mieux pour moi, je pense.*

**7** Lis ce que disent Lucas et Carine. Lis ces phrases. Qui est-ce, Lucas (L) ou Carine (C)?

- **a** ... *would hate to work in an office.*
- **b** ... *would equally work alone or in a team.*
- **c** ... *would prefer a job combining music and ICT.*
- **d** ... *would prefer sport physiotherapy to teaching PE.*
- **e** ... *thinks sound engineer might be the ideal job.*

**8** Relis. Trouve les verbes au conditionnel et fais deux listes: verbes réguliers et verbes irréguliers.

*Exemple*: Verbes réguliers: je n'aimerais pas.

**9a** Tu aimerais quelle sorte d'emploi? Pourquoi? Écris un paragraphe au conditionnel.

*Exemple*: Je voudrais bien travailler dans un hôpital ou une école parce que j'aime travailler avec les enfants. Je porterais un uniforme et je travaillerais...

**9b** Qu'est-ce que tu voudrais faire plus tard? Écris un texte sans mentionner de métier. Demande à des camarades de lire ton texte, de suggérer deux ou trois métiers pour toi et d'expliquer pourquoi.

## À vous!

**10** Work in groups. One person suggests a job and the rest say if they would like it or not, giving their reasons.

*Exemple*: **A** Cuisinier!
**B** Ah oui! Je pourrais être cuisinier. J'adore cuisiner.
**C** Je n'aimerais pas passer huit heures par jour dans une cuisine.

**11** Write a personal statement, explaining what you would like to do in the future. Say what you hope to do and why you have chosen this. Mention your school achievements, personal qualities, tastes and interests.

# 4B Comment poser ta candidature

G Verbe + infinitif V Poser sa candidature; CV S Les majuscules; les accents

**Nous recherchons pour la période estivale...**

**Étudiants parlant deux ou trois langues et désirant travailler dans notre camping pendant au moins 8 semaines**

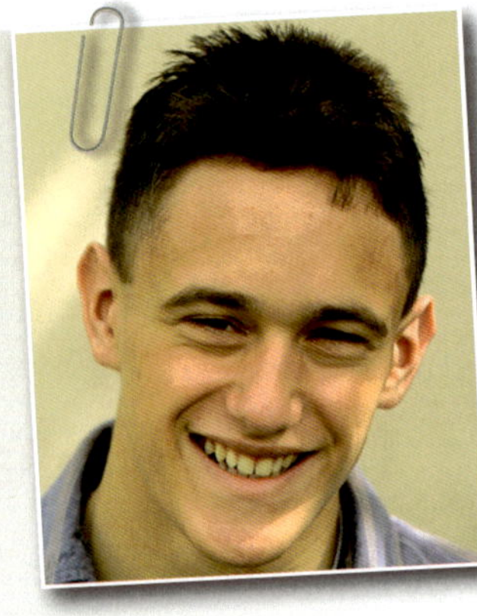

10, Polden Lane
TAUNTON
TA6 9PZ
Grande-Bretagne

Camping Les Pins
Chemin du Bois de la Lande
56760 Pénestin
France

Monsieur,

J'ai vu sur votre site web que vous cherchiez des assistants pour les mois de juillet et août et comme je désire travailler en France cet été, j'ai décidé de poser ma candidature.

J'ai seize ans et mes matières préférées à l'école sont les langues – le français et l'allemand. J'espère continuer les langues et étudier le français à l'université. J'ai donc envie de parler français tout l'été. Je voudrais apprendre à parler couramment.

J'ai déjà un peu d'expérience puisque je travaille dans un salon de coiffure le samedi matin. Je fais aussi du baby-sitting et si possible, je préfère travailler avec des enfants. C'est possible dans votre camping?

J'aimerais commencer à travailler le premier juillet et je dois rentrer chez moi le premier septembre. Pouvez-vous m'envoyer des renseignements supplémentaires sur les horaires, la rémunération et les conditions de travail?

Veuillez agréer, Monsieur, l'expression de mes sentiments les meilleurs.

David Foster

**1a** Vrai ou faux?

*Exemple*: **a** F

**a** David habite à Pénestin.
**b** Il travaille dans un camping en France.
**c** Il ne parle pas français.
**d** Il est fort en langues.
**e** Il a un petit boulot.
**f** Il veut gagner de l'argent cet été.
**g** Il aime les enfants.
**h** Il est libre pour trois mois.

**1b** Corrige les phrases fausses.

*Exemple*: **a** Il habite à Taunton.

**STRATÉGIES**

**Accents**

Be careful of accents! Copy five words from the letter with the *é* sound. Find two words that are written with the *è* sound.

**STRATÉGIES**

**Capital letters**

Which of the following are written with capital letters in French: town names; countries; months; languages; a person's name?

Check in David's letter if you are unsure.

**2** Lis la lettre de David, page 140. Recopie et traduis les phrases ci-dessous.

**a** *to apply for* – poser sa...
**b** *could you send me* – ...
**c** *hours (of work)* –...
**d** *pay* – ...
**e** *working conditions* – ...
**f** *yours faithfully* –...

**GRAMMAIRE**

**Expressions using the infinitive**

Many phrases in the letter contain two verbs. There are different patterns:

- the first verb is followed by an infinitive: *je désire travailler en France*
- the first verb is followed by *à* + an infinitive: *j'aimerais commencer* ***à*** *travailler le premier juillet*
- the first verb is followed by *de* + an infinitive: *j'ai décidé* ***de*** *poser ma candidature*

**3a** Recopie et complète la grille avec les verbes. Regarde la lettre, page 140.

| Followed by an infinitive | Followed by à + infinitive | Followed by de + infinitive |
|---|---|---|
| *désirer* | *commencer* | *décider* |

désirer décider espérer commencer avoir envie vouloir apprendre préférer devoir pouvoir

**3b** Traduis en français.

*Exemple*: **a** Je désire travailler avec les animaux.

**a** *I'd like to work with animals.*
**b** *I'm hoping to study Biology at university.*
**c** *I'd like to learn to speak Chinese.*
**d** *I prefer to work in the evenings.*
**e** *I've decided to live in France.*
**f** *I must return to England in September.*

**4** Écoute Marie. Recopie et complète la grille.

| | |
|---|---|
| name | |
| age and date of birth | |
| address / telephone / email | |
| qualifications | |
| languages spoken | |
| experience | |
| interests | |

## Curriculum vitae

| | |
|---|---|
| **Nom** | Foster |
| **Prénom** | David |
| **Adresse** | 10, Polden Lane, Taunton, TA6 9PZ, Grande-Bretagne |
| **Téléphone** | 01823 445978 |
| **E-mail** | dave999@hotmail.com |
| **Date de naissance** | 02 09 1995 |
| **Enseignement secondaire** | je prépare 10 GCSE |
| **Langues** | français (5 ans), allemand (3 ans) |
| **Expérience** | baby-sitting, travail temporaire dans un salon de coiffure |
| **Centres d'intérêt** | musique (trombone, batterie), sport (1500m, 800m, natation, aïkido) |

**5a** Prépare au minimum dix questions à poser à David dans un interview.

*Exemples*: Où habites-tu?

Quels examens passes-tu cette année?

Est-ce que tu joues d'un instrument de musique?

**5b** Jeu de rôle. **A** joue le rôle de David et **B** lui pose des questions. (**B↔A**)

*Exemple*: **B** Où habites-tu? **A** J'habite à Taunton.

## À vous!

**6** Write a CV, following David's model. Exchange your CVs with each other, then work in pairs to conduct interviews similar to that in activity 5b. Each pupil should base their answers on the CV they have been given.

**7** You have seen an advert for an interesting holiday job in France. Write a letter of application. Use the letter on page 140 to help you.

# 4B Comment briller dans un entretien

**G** Participe présent; qui **V** Un entretien **S** Regrouper les mots

## Jobs d'été Val de Loire

Nous cherchons des étudiants…

- qui parlent français et au moins une autre langue
- qui aiment le contact humain
- capables de créer une ambiance joyeuse pour nos touristes
- responsables
- libres au moins deux mois à partir du premier juillet

**1** Recopie et complète en anglais.

*Exemple*: **a** *two languages*

*To apply for this job, you need to speak at least* **a** .......... *You should get on with* **b** ......... *You should be able to create a happy atmosphere for* **c** ..........., *be* **d** .......... *and must be available for* **e** ........... *from* **f** ............

**GRAMMAIRE**

***Qui***

*Qui* can mean 'who' or 'which'. It can be followed by a verb in the singular or the plural, depending on who *qui* refers to:

- *Nous cherchons* ***des étudiants*** *qui* ***parlent*** *français.*
- *Nous offrons* ***un emploi*** *qui* ***paie*** *bien.*

**2a** Écoute la conversation et note l'ordre des questions posées par Monsieur Simon.

*Exemple*: **e** …

**a** Date de naissance
**b** Libre quand?
**c** Pourquoi ce poste?
**d** Âge
**e** Nom
**f** Langues
**g** Expérience?

**2b** Réécoute. Choisis la bonne réponse: a) ou b).

**1** Le candidat s'appelle **a)** Leon **b)** Liam Clarke?
**2** En juillet, il aura **a)** 15 **b)** 16 ans.
**3** Il parle **a)** deux **b)** trois langues étrangères.
**4** Il travaille dans un supermarché depuis **a)** six semaines **b)** six mois.
**5** Monsieur **a)** va **b)** ne va pas interviewer le candidat.

**3** À deux. **A** essaie de mémoriser les questions **a-g** (voir l'encadré ci-dessous en cas de difficulté). **B** prépare ses propres réponses aux questions **a-g** et écrit quelques mots comme aide-mémoire. Réécoutez l'entretien pour vous inspirer, puis jouez l'entretien. (**B↔A**)

**a** Comment vous appelez-vous?
**b** Quelle est votre date de naissance?
**c** Vous avez quel âge?
**d** Vous parlez quelles langues?
**e** Vous serez libre à partir de quelle date?
**f** Avez-vous déjà de l'expérience? Avez-vous déjà travaillé?
**g** Pourquoi voulez-vous travailler pour nous?

**Comment briller dans un entretien avec Jobs d'été Val de Loire? Voici quelques questions à préparer:**

**A** Pourquoi voulez-vous ce poste?
**B** Quels sont vos atouts?
**C** Avez-vous déjà de l'expérience dans le tourisme?
**D** Comment pourriez-vous améliorer vos connaissances de la langue française avant de nous rejoindre?

## A Pourquoi voulez-vous ce poste?

**4** Fais des phrases pour répondre!

*Exemple*: Parce que j'aimerais passer du temps en France.

Parce que j'aime...
...j'aimerais...
...je voudrais...
...je m'intéresse à...

travailler gagner
perfectionner passer
être avoir

de l'argent indépendant(e) avec les enfants
une nouvelle expérience
mes connaissances de la langue française
du temps en France

## B Quels sont vos atouts?

**5** Choisis des mots de l'encadré et puis donne des explications et des exemples.

*Exemple*: Je pense que je suis travailleur/travailleuse parce que, quand on me donne une tâche, je la finis toujours.

bien organisé(e) responsable
travailleur/travailleuse sociable patient(e)
innovateur/innovatrice créatif/créative honnête
fidèle sûr(e) de moi diplomatique
plein/pleine d'énergie enthousiaste calme

## C Avez-vous déjà de l'expérience dans le tourisme?

**6a** Recopie cette réponse et complète les blancs avec un mot de l'encadré.

*Exemple*: **a** travaillé

Non, mais j'ai déjà **a** .......... dans d'autres secteurs. Par **b** .........., je fais du baby-sitting et j'ai donc appris à être **c** .......... et à bien écouter ce qu'on me dit. En plus, j'ai travaillé l'été **d** .......... dans une supérette. J'ai **e** .......... servir les clients et travailler à la **f** .........., et là, j'ai appris à travailler en **g** .......... avec des jeunes aussi bien qu'avec des adultes.

exemple entreprise dernier équipe boulangerie
travaillé dû patron caisse responsable payé

**6b** Écris maintenant ta propre réponse à cette question.

## D Comment pourriez-vous améliorer vos connaissances de la langue française avant de nous rejoindre?

**GRAMMAIRE**

***En* + present participle**

The construction *en* + present participle is useful for saying how you will do something :

*J'apprends le français* ***en allant*** *à mes cours de français.*

I learn French **by going** to my lessons.

See page 149 for information on forming the present participle.

**7** Traduis en anglais.

*Exemple*: **a** *I learn French by listening to CDs.*

J'apprends le français...

- **a** en écoutant des CD.
- **b** en lisant *AQA GCSE French*.
- **c** en cherchant des mots dans le dictionnaire.
- **d** en parlant avec l'assistante française.
- **e** en faisant des exercices de grammaire.

**STRATÉGIES**

Look out for groups of words which are related. For example, you know *travailler*, so you can guess what someone who is *travailleur* is like. *Créer* is related to *création* and *caissier* to *caisse*. Find at least one word related to each of these: *peintre*, *production*, *paiement*, *nécessité*, *surprise*.

## À VOUS!

**8** Work in groups. You will need a real or imaginary job advert. You each have one minute to explain why you are the best candidate for the job. You can record your explanations on OxBox. Vote to decide who gets the job.

**9** Work with a partner and practise interviews for a summer job with Val de Loire. Use and adapt the questions in activities 4–7.

# 4B Comment décrire ton stage

(G) Conjonctions (V) Décrire un stage (S) Traduire les expressions idiomatiques

**Des élèves du lycée Henri IV de Perpignan viennent de finir leur stage de découverte du monde professionnel. Voici un extrait du rapport de stage que le conseiller d'orientation leur a demandé de remplir.**

## Lycée Henri IV

**Rapport de stage**

1 Tu as travaillé où?
2 Quels étaient tes horaires de travail?
3 Comment était le stage?
4 Comment étaient tes collègues?
5 Qu'est-ce que tu as fait? Coche la liste!

- **a** répondre au téléphone ☐
- **b** servir les clients ☐
- **c** travailler sur l'ordinateur ☐
- **d** vendre des marchandises ☐
- **e** travailler à la caisse ☐
- **f** faire du classement ☐
- **g** mettre le courrier à la poste ☐
- **h** observer les autres ☐
- **i** faire des photocopies ☐
- **j** faire du café ☐
- **k** dessiner des affiches ☐
- **l** participer aux réunions ☐
- **m** taper des lettres ☐
- **n** discuter avec le patron ☐
- **o** nettoyer des machines ☐
- **p** autre (explique) ☐

**1a** Écoute l'un des lycéens parler de son stage. Lis ses réponses au questionnaire ci-dessus. Il a fait deux erreurs – à toi de les corriger.

**1** *dans une boulangerie*
**2** *de 5h30 à 13h*
**3** *fatigant*
**4** *gentils*
**5** *p (préparer du pain), o, l*

**1b** Écoute trois autres lycéens (1-3) et note leurs réponses.

*Exemple*: **1** dans une bibliothèque

**STRATÉGIES**

Notice how Lucas starts and finishes his letter on page 145 and copy the format when you are writing informally.

**Lucas, 15 ans, a fait son stage dans un office du tourisme. Voici la lettre qu'il a écrite à son correspondant britannique pour lui expliquer ce qui s'est passé.**

**A**

**Perpignan, le 5 juin**

Cher Guy,

Comme tu sais, je viens de faire un stage de deux semaines. J'ai passé ces 15 jours à l'office du tourisme ici à Perpignan, et je me suis vite rendu compte qu'il y avait beaucoup de travail à faire.

**B**

Le premier jour, à neuf heures, j'ai d'abord dû ranger toutes les brochures. Ensuite, j'ai observé un collègue à la réception. Entre onze heures et midi, j'ai répondu aux questions des clients, puis je suis allé déjeuner. L'après-midi, j'ai répondu au téléphone et après, à 17 heures, je suis rentré chez moi.

**C**

Le mercredi, j'ai observé une visite organisée avec un groupe de touristes et j'ai répondu à quelques questions. Quand je ne savais pas répondre, j'expliquais que j'étais en stage et que je ne savais pas tout ou je demandais à une collègue! En fait, j'ai beaucoup appris pendant mon stage!

**D**

Mes collègues étaient assez sympa. J'aimais bien le patron parce qu'il était accueillant et j'aimais bien aussi Madame Lafont car elle m'a expliqué beaucoup de choses. J'aimais moins Madame Xavier car elle me faisait un peu peur!

**E**

J'ai appris beaucoup de choses, par exemple comment organiser une visite guidée et où se trouvent les principales attractions de notre région. Mais quand on est en stage, on ne sait pas tout. J'espère pouvoir retravailler à l'office du tourisme l'été prochain… et être payé cette fois!

Lucas

**STRATÉGIES**

Remember to make your writing more interesting by using the perfect **and** imperfect tenses together, adding time phrases and using conjunctions.

**2** Lis la lettre de Lucas. Réponds aux questions sur chaque partie (A–E).

**A** *Where did Lucas do his work placement?*
**B** *How many hours a day did he work?*
**C** *What did he do when he couldn't answer customers' questions?*
**D** *What did Lucas like about his colleagues?*
**E** *What has Lucas learned during his placement?*

**3** Relis la lettre. Trouve:

1. Partie A: une phrase avec le passé composé et l'imparfait et traduis-la en anglais.
2. Partie B: six expressions de temps
3. Partie C: trois conjonctions
4. Partie D: deux conjonctions qui expliquent «pourquoi»

**4** Recopie et complète chaque phrase avec tes propres mots.

**a** Le travail était intéressant parce que…
**b** J'aimais mes collègues car…
**c** Mais je n'aimais pas mon patron car il…

**5** Recopie et mets un de ces mots dans chaque blanc: où, comment, pourquoi, quand, qui.

*Exemple*: **a** C'est le patron qui…

**a** C'est le patron ………… m'a tout expliqué.
**b** J'ai dû apprendre ………… trouver les brochures.
**c** Je ne comprends pas ………… certains visiteurs étaient si impolis.
**d** On m'a demandé ………… je pourrais revenir.

## À VOUS!

**6** Write a letter to a friend to explain what you did during your work experience and if you found it interesting… or not. If you have not done work experience, make something up!

**7** Work in groups. One student thinks of an imaginary work experience placement and the others ask questions. You could use the five questions in the questionnaire on page 144. Whose placement is the most believable and which placement do you think is the most interesting?

# 4B Comment choisir une carrière

**G** Le conditionnel **V** Les avantages et les inconvénients des métiers **S** Réutiliser les mots des questions

## Enquête: *Quel métier choisir?*

**1** Lis les questions 1–4 de l'enquête. Lis les réponses a–l. Qui parle? (Trois personnes parmi A, B, C et D).

*Exemple:* **1a** A

A
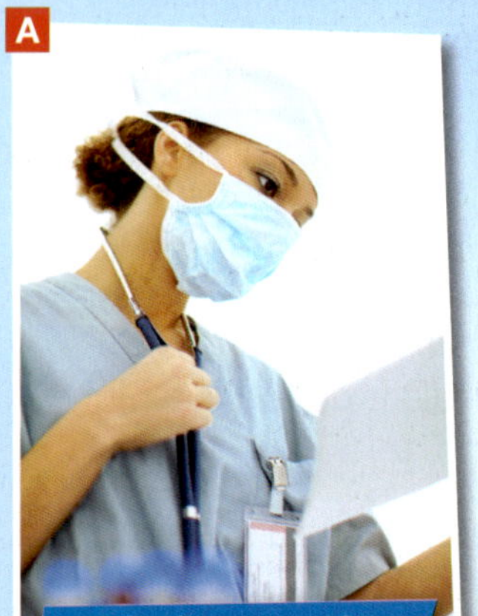
médecin-urgentiste

B
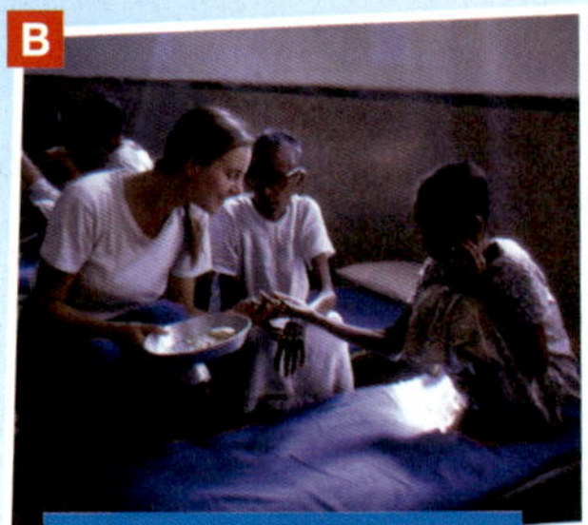
responsable de projet humanitaire

C

chef de cabine

D

animateur/trice 3D

**1 Quel est votre métier?**

**a** «Je travaille au service des urgences de l'hôpital d'une grande ville.»

**b** «Je m'occupe de missions humanitaires que j'organise pour une organisation non-gouvernementale.»

**c** «Je crée des personnages pour des jeux dans une société de jeux vidéo.»

**2 Pourquoi l'avez-vous choisi?**

**d** «Quand j'étais petit, je rêvais qu'un jour, je ferais des dessins animés comme ceux de Disney, que j'adorais!»

**e** «J'ai toujours voulu faire un métier où je voyagerais, où j'habiterais à l'étranger et où j'aiderais les gens des pays défavorisés.»

**f** «Je voulais faire un métier où je me sentirais utile aux gens, où je travaillerais en équipe plutôt que seule et où je n'aurais pas besoin de voyager car je déteste prendre l'avion!»

**3 Quels sont les avantages?**

**g** «Pour moi, c'est pouvoir utiliser mon imagination, créer des personnages virtuels et travailler dans une bonne ambiance avec des gens créatifs et sympa.»

**h** «En faisant ce métier, on peut être utile aux autres et se développer soi-même en découvrant le monde, d'autres pays et d'autres cultures.»

**i** «Pour moi, c'est un métier passionnant et très gratifiant parce qu'on aide les gens. C'est très varié puisqu'aucun cas n'est le même. En plus, c'est bien payé.»

**4 Quels sont les inconvénients?**

**j** «On se trouve parfois dans des situations très dangereuses où on risque sa vie, quand on est dans un pays en guerre, par exemple.»

**k** «Les horaires sont très fatigants. On a de grosses responsabilités et parfois des décisions à prendre dans des situations où le patient est entre la vie et la mort.»

**l** «Il n'y a pas beaucoup de travail et ce n'est pas très bien payé. Il y a un autre côté négatif, et c'est qu'on travaille toujours dans un bureau, assis devant un ordinateur. »

**2** Écoute pour vérifier. Note deux infos supplémentaires sur chaque personne.

*Exemple:* **A** fait ce métier depuis 3 ans

**3** Écoute l'interview de la quatrième personne. Réponds en anglais:

**a** *Job?*
**b** *Reasons for choosing the job?*
**c** *Advantages?*
**d** *Disadvantages?*

**STRATÉGIES**

When answering questions in the Speaking Controlled Assessment, you can reuse the wording of the question, e.g.
*Qu'est-ce qui vous a motivé à faire ce métier?*
*Ce qui m'a motivé à faire ce métier, c'est...*

Use the verb in the correct form and correct tense!

*Qu'est-ce que tu **voudrais** faire comme métier?* (would like)
*Je **voudrais** être professeur.*

*Qu'est-ce que tu **voulais** faire comme métier?* (wanted)
*Je **voulais** être acteur!*

**4** Voici un «interview» pendant un examen. Écoute les questions et utilise les notes pour répondre après le signal. Puis écoute les réponses.

*Exemple:* **1** Comme métier, je suis professeur.

1. professeur langues / collège
2. travailler avec enfants / langues = passionnant
3. vétérinaire / ♥ animaux
4. métier stable, sûr / longues vacances
5. stress, fatigue / salaire bas
6. si... utiliser langues / voyager: interprète / guide touristique

**5a** Lis ces descriptions d'activités professionnelles. Pour toi, avantages ou inconvénients? Discute avec un(e) partenaire.

*Exemple:* Pour moi, avoir des horaires fixes, c'est un avantage, surtout quand on a des enfants jeunes.

avoir des horaires fixes/flexibles
travailler à la maison
avoir beaucoup de déplacements
être autonome et indépendant(e)
faire partie d'une équipe
avoir un travail répétitif mais stable
avoir un travail varié mais imprévisible

**5b** À deux, ajoutez d'autres avantages ou inconvénients.

*Exemple:* Avantages: faire un travail qui me passionne.
Inconvénients: ne pas avoir beaucoup de vacances

**GRAMMAIRE**

**The conditional**

**1** Use it to express a wish or a desire:
***J'aimerais** être astronaute.*

**2** A condition (usually dependent on a *si* clause):
*Si j'étais astronaute, j'**irais** sur Mars.*

**3** It can also be used to express a future-in-the past:
*J'ai toujours rêvé qu'un jour je **voyagerais** dans l'espace.*
I've always dreamt that one day **I'd travel** into space.

**6** Complète ces phrases avec des expressions de l'activité 5 au conditionnel.

*Exemple:* **a** ...où j'aurais des horaires fixes.

**a** Je voudrais faire un métier où...
**b** Je ne voudrais pas faire un métier où...
**c** J'ai toujours voulu faire un métier où...

**STRATÉGIES**

If you don't know how to say something try using:

- a definition: *c'est le métier où on coupe les cheveux (coiffeur).*
- an approximation with *un peu comme...*: *un peu comme une hôtesse dans un hôtel (réceptionniste).*

**7** Écris des devinettes pour un(e) partenaire!

*Exemple:* C'est un métier où on conduit une voiture le jour ou la nuit pour transporter des gens. (chauffeur de taxi)

## À VOUS!

**8** Choose your ideal job and prepare a presentation about it, saying what it is, its advantages and disadvantages and why you would like to do it.

*Exemple:* J'aimerais devenir acteur/actrice parce que c'est un métier où...

**9** Discuss with a partner the pros and cons of working abroad. Then, one of you writes a short passage giving all of the advantages and the other writes a passage giving the disadvantages. Try to use as many verbs in the conditional as possible.

*Exemple:* pros: on pourrait découvrir une nouvelle culture, etc. / cons: on serait loin de sa famille, etc.

# 4B Grammaire active

**HOW TO FORM THE CONDITIONAL**

The endings are the same as for the imperfect tense.

*je* **–ais** *tu* **–ais** *il/elle/on* **–ait**
*nous* **–ions** *vous* **–iez** *ils/elles* **-aient**

Either add them to the infinitive, remembering to drop the final *-e* of *-re* verbs:

***aimer + -ais = aimerais***
***sortir + -ais = sortirais***
***prendr + -ais = prendrais***

(There are a few exceptions: *avoir, être, aller, faire, devoir, pouvoir, venir, vouloir,* etc.)

Or think of verbs in the future tense (including the irregular ones) as the stems are the same:

***j'aimer-ai/j'aimer-ais***
***je sortir-ai/je sortir-ais*** ***je prendr-ai/je prendr-ais***
***avoir: j'aur-ai/j'aur-ais*** ***être: je ser-ai/je ser-ais***

**1a** Read the picture story above. Which verbs are in the conditional?

*Exemple:* Je voudrais

**1b** Which verbs are in the conditional in this list?

adorais adoreraient détesterait préparions étudieriez travaillerai croira choisiront voyageait aidait ferions utiliserez pourrais

**2** Copy the conversation on the right and complete the sentences with the verbs in the conditional.

*Exemple:* **a** aimerais

**a** Max – J'[aimer] bien voir ce film mais je n'ai pas assez d'argent.
**b** Sam – Dommage! Je pense que tu [devoir] trouver un job! À ta place, je [laver] des voitures le samedi.
**c** Max – Bonne idée! J'[aller] faire ça sur le parking du supermarché, si j'ai le droit. Tu [venir] avec moi?
**d** Sam – Je [vouloir] bien mais... je fais mes devoirs le samedi.
**e** Max – Et le dimanche, tu [avoir] le temps de m'aider?
**f** Sam – En fait, euh... tu sais, j'ai assez d'argent.
**g** Max – Ah! Super! Je savais que tu [pouvoir] m'inviter au ciné! Merci!

**WHEN TO USE THE CONDITIONAL**

**A** to express a wish, a desire or make a polite request
**B** to make a suggestion or give advice
**C** to say what would happen if a condition was met
**D** to express a future in the past

**3a** In the cartoon above, which use do the verbs in the conditional illustrate (A, B, C or D)?

*Exemple:* Je voudrais – **A**

**3b** Write an ending for each sentence using the conditional.

*Exemple:* **a** Plus tard, j'aimerais voyager autour du monde!

**a** Plus tard, j'aimerais...
**b** Si j'avais plus d'argent, je...
**c** Je savais qu'un jour, je...
**d** Personnellement, je pense que...

### *SI* CLAUSES

Use *si* to express possible or hypothetical situations. Remember the use of tenses:

*Si* + present followed by future:
*Si tu travailles, tu réussiras.*
If you work, you'll succeed.

*Si* + imperfect followed by conditional:
*Si tu travaillais, tu réussirais.*
If you worked, you would succeed.

## 4 Fill in the missing verbs in these sentences.

*Exemple:* **a** donnerai; **b** donnerais

- **a** Si je gagne à la loterie, je te ... l'argent. [donner]
- **b** Si je gagnais à la loterie, je te ... l'argent. [donner]
- **c** Si tu cherches bien, tu ... un job. [trouver]
- **d** Si tu ... un peu plus, tu trouverais un job. [chercher]
- **e** Si tu parlais plusieurs langues, tu ... plus de chance de trouver du travail. [avoir]
- **f** Tu ... plus facilement du travail si tu parles plusieurs langues. [avoir]

### VERB PHRASES

When there are two verbs together, the second one is in the infinitive. There are different patterns, as the second verb can be:

1. just an infinitive: *Tu dois **arriver** à l'heure.*
2. *à* + infinitive: *Il apprend **à faire** du classement.*
3. *de* + infinitive: *Qu'est-ce que tu as décidé **de faire**?*

See page 191 for more information.

## 5 Copy the sentences, putting the right preposition in the gap. Watch out for sentences where no preposition is needed.

*Exemple*: **a** de

- **a** Vous me permettez ... commencer plus tard demain?
- **b** Tu as appris ... utiliser le traitement de texte?
- **c** Voulez-vous ... travailler jusqu'à 17 heures?
- **d** Qu'est-ce que tu as choisi ... faire?
- **e** Je n'aime pas ... répondre au téléphone.
- **f** Quand avez-vous commencé ... travailler ici?
- **g** Quand devez-vous ... commencer le matin?
- **h** La patronne a oublié ... m'expliquer tout cela.
- **i** J'espère ... gagner un bon salaire un jour.

## 6 Translate these sentences into French.

- **a** Have you finished reading the report?
- **b** I've forgotten to write the letter.
- **c** Do you want to see the boss?
- **d** She chose to finish at five o'clock.
- **e** They don't like going to meetings.
- **f** We will start doing that tomorrow.

### THE PRESENT PARTICIPLE

The construction *en* + present participle is useful for saying how you will do something

*Je fais une bonne impression **en travaillant** dur.*
I make a good impression by **working hard**.

It is formed by taking the *nous* form of the verb in the present tense, removing the *-ons* from the end and replacing it with the ending *-ant*.

## 7 Write a suitable ending for each sentence.

*Exemple*: **a** Luc va perdre du poids en jouant au tennis.

- **a** Luc va perdre du poids en...
- **b** Caroline va réussir aux examens en...
- **c** Sébastien va gagner de l'argent en...
- **d** Monsieur Levallet va rester en forme en...
- **e** Sa femme va se détendre en...
- **f** Et moi, j'espère apprendre la grammaire française en...
- **g** Julie va améliorer ses connaissances en espagnol en...
- **h** J'espère faire de nouvelles rencontres en...
- **i** Vas-tu élargir tes horizons en...?

# 4B Controlled Assessment: Speaking

## TASK: A job interview

You are going to be interviewed for a job by your teacher. You will play the role of the candidate and your teacher will be the interviewer. Your teacher will ask you the following:

- Your personal details.
- What qualifications you have.
- What languages you speak and how well.
- What work experience you have.
- Why you think you are the best candidate.
- What your ambitions for the future are.
- !

*(! Remember: at this point, you will have to respond to something you have not prepared.)*

The dialogue will last between 4 and 6 minutes.

**Secteur géographique:** Mer
**Activité:** Camping

**L'offre d'emploi**

camping CAMPEOLE recherche un placeur/une placeuse pour la période JUILLET et AOÛT

*Salaire à négocier*

Merci d'envoyer CV par email à l'adresse suivante: campeole@hotmail.com

## 1 THINK !

**Read the phrases below. Write down any others that you might find useful for the speaking task.**

- ☐ **Personal details:** Je m'appelle...; Je suis...; J'ai... (ans); Je viens de...
- ☐ **Qualifications:** Je prépare...; J'ai fait...; J'ai passé...; J'ai réussi...; J'ai obtenu...
- ☐ **Languages:** Je parle...; J'apprends... depuis; Je sais/Je peux...
- ☐ **Work experience:** J'ai travaillé...; J'ai fait...; Je faisais...; J'ai appris à...
- ☐ **Why you?** À mon avis,/Je pense que.../Je suis convaincu(e) que je suis le/la meilleur(e) candidat(e), parce que... je suis... j'ai... je sais... j'ai déjà fait...
- ☐ **Your future plans:** Je voudrais/J'aimerais...; Je vais faire... ce sera...

**! *Can you predict what the unexpected question might be?***

Why do you want the job?

What is more important for you, experience or money?

**Add to your list any language you would need to answer these questions too.**

## 2 PLAN !

- **Listen to the model conversation. Your teacher has the script.**
- **Listen again and note down any phrases you could use or adapt. Add these to your list from Step 1.**

## 3 ACTION !

**Now prepare your answers. Use the bullet points below to help you and your list of useful words and phrases from Steps 1 and 2.**

**1** Personal details

- This will be familiar language, so show off by using your knowledge of the alphabet to spell your name.
- Add a little extra detail to make it more interesting, e.g. where your parents come from if relevant, etc.
- Try to use varied structures: ***je suis britannique/je suis d'origine.../...est originaire de...***

**2** Qualifications

- It is obvious you won't have many at this stage, so make the most of what you have. Find out how to describe in French things like the Duke of Edinburgh award, First aid certificate, music grades, etc.
- Use a variety of tenses: ***cette année, je fais/prépare; l'année dernière, j'ai fait/préparé; l'année prochaine, je commencerai...***
- Use ***si*** clauses, e.g. ***si je réussis mes GCSE cet été, je commencerai à préparer...***

**3** Languages

- Use ***depuis*** with the present tense, e.g. ***J'apprends le français depuis...***
- Try to use direct object pronouns to make what you say sound more sophisticated, e.g. ***J'apprends le français... Je le comprends et je le parle très bien.***

**4** Experience

- This is your chance to show off your use of past tenses, e.g. ***j'ai déjà travaillé...*** (perfect); ***J'aidais...*** (imperfect); ***j'avais fait un stage*** (pluperfect).
- If you don't have a lot of experience, say what you are thinking of doing in the near future, e.g. ***Je n'ai pas encore travaillé mais je vais chercher un stage dans...***

**5** Why you!

- This is your chance to show off! Make sure you sound confident and use a variety of structures to give your opinion, e.g. ***Je suis convaincu(e) que je suis le/la meilleur(e)...; je pense que...; je suis sûr(e) que...***
- After you have said why you are good for the job, point out why the job would be good for you: ***Ce serait fantastique pour moi si j'avais le job parce que je pourrais...***

**6** Your future

- Say what your ambitions for the future are, showing off your knowledge of the future tense: ***Je vais faire/ Je ferai..., Je pourrai..., ce sera super.***

## GRADE TARGET

**To reach Grade C, you need to:**

- speak clearly and confidently, using a variety of structures.
- use the main tenses correctly (e.g. present tense for what you usually do, perfect tense for what you did in the past; future tense with ***aller*** + infinitive for what you are intending to do; conditional for what you would like to do: ***je voudrais*** ).
- use ***parce que*** to give reasons.

**To aim higher than a C, you could:**

- use a greater variety of tenses, e.g. use the perfect, the imperfect, the pluperfect and a future tense, e.g. ***J'ai déjà passé certaines épreuves; J'aidais les clients; je commencerai à préparer...***
- use verbs in the conditional, e.g. ***je voudrais, j'aimerais, je voyagerais...***
- create longer sentences, e.g. ***parce que, comme, avant de..., depuis...*** etc.

**To aim for an A or A*, you could:**

- use ***si*** clauses, e.g. ***si je réussis mes GCSE cet été, je commencerai à préparer...***
- use direct object pronouns ***le/la/les*** and ***en***, e.g. ***J'apprends aussi l'espagnol. Je le parle assez bien. J'adore les langues et je voudrais en apprendre d'autres.***
- use ***en*** + present participle, e.g. ***Je l'ai obtenu en faisant du volontariat, du sport,*** etc.
- use two verbs with or without prepositions, e.g. ***Je viens d'avoir 16 ans; je commencerai à préparer...; J'aidais les clients à trouver....***

## TASK: Writing an application for a summer placement

You are writing a covering letter for an online agency that you are using to find a summer placement in a French-speaking country.

In your letter, you could include the following:

- A brief description of who you are.
- Why you want to go to a French-speaking country.
- Your main qualities and interests.
- Your work experience if any.
- What you expect from the placement and your future plans.

**Franco-stages**
Envoyez votre lettre de motivation et CV à Madame Dutilleul

## 1 THINK!

**Start by researching and noting down a few key facts and phrases:**

1 About you: try to think of something interesting/unusual to say about yourself: where you/your family are from: *j'habite à/en... mais je suis né(e) à/en...;* any special role you have at school (prefect, etc.): *je suis délégué(e), je suis très actif/active au lycée...*

2 Your reason for applying to a French-speaking country: think of why you would want to speak more French: *j'aime le français/je suis fort(e) en français; je voudrais continuer le français,* etc.

3 Your qualities and interests: mention the qualities that you think are relevant to this particular application: *je suis sérieux/euse, je suis sociable,* etc. List your interests and say why they are relevant: *Au lycée, mes matières préférées sont...; je m'intéresse beaucoup à/aux... j'aime beaucoup...*

4 Your experience: mention anything you have done that could be relevant here: *j'ai fait du baby-sitting, j'ai travaillé dans un magasin; j'ai fait un stage...* Don't forget to say why it was a good experience to have: *j'ai découvert la vie en entreprise, le milieu du travail/j'ai appris beaucoup de choses,* etc.

5 Your expectations: mention what you would like to get out of the trip, what you could offer in exchange and what your plans for the future are, e.g. *Faire ce stage me permettrait de...; Si je faisais ce stage, je pourrais... parce que plus tard, j'irai à l'université pour... je vais faire... ce sera...* etc.

Alex Oliver
12, Chambard Avenue
Reading

Madame Dutilleul
Franco-Stages
Reading,
le 9 novembre 2010

Madame,

Je m'appelle Alex Oliver, j'ai 16 ans et je suis britannique. J'habite à Reading mais je suis né en Écosse. Je suis en seconde au lycée et je suis délégué de classe.

Faire un stage dans un pays francophone m'intéresserait beaucoup parce que j'apprends le français depuis 10 ans et que j'envisage de continuer à l'étudier à l'université. J'aimerais plus particulièrement travailler dans un pays africain parce que je connais déjà un peu la France, où j'ai passé des vacances en famille, tandis je ne suis jamais allé en Afrique.

Je suis mûr, sérieux et responsable mais je suis aussi sociable et j'aime bien m'amuser! Au lycée, mes matières préférées sont les langues, la géographie et la psychologie et si je réussis mes examens de A level, je continuerai mes études pour devenir professeur ou psychologue. Je m'intéresse beaucoup aux gens et j'adore le contact, surtout avec les enfants. Comme passe-temps, j'adore la musique et le théâtre.

J'ai un peu d'expérience avec les enfants parce que j'ai souvent fait du baby-sitting pour des amis de mes parents. C'était sympa et bien payé! J'ai également fait un stage d'une semaine dans une école primaire. C'était vraiment stimulant et j'ai appris beaucoup de choses en observant et en aidant le professeur dans la classe.

Je suis convaincu que ce stage dans un pays francophone me permettrait de découvrir une nouvelle culture, ce qui serait passionnant et une excellente expérience à ajouter sur mon CV. Mais avant tout, je pense sincèrement que ce serait pour moi l'occasion de pouvoir aider des gens, et surtout des enfants, dans un pays défavorisé, expérience précieuse que je n'oublierais jamais.

Veuillez agréer, Madame, l'expression de mes sentiments les meilleurs.

*Alex Oliver*

## 2 PLAN!

- **Read the model text and note down any words or phrases that you could use. Add these to your list from Step 1.**
- **Look carefully at the tenses used and make a note of any you could reuse:**
  present tense for descriptions – ***je m'appelle/je suis...; je m'intéresse...***
  perfect tense for completed actions – ***je suis allé, j'ai passé, j'ai fait...***
  future tense for what will happen in the future – ***je continuerai...***

## 3 ACTION!

**Now prepare what you will write. Use the bullet points below to help you and use your list of useful words and phrases from Steps 1 and 2. Aim to write about 200–300 words.**

**1** Personal details: name, age, where you live, the school you go to, etc.

- Concentrate on details that are relevant to your application: ***Je suis dans une école internationale, je vais au club de français, je suis membre du conseil d'école,*** etc.

**2** Reason for applying: ***Le français, c'est ma matière préférée; je voudrais m'améliorer, je pense continuer le français à l'université; Je ne suis jamais allé(e) à l'étranger, c'est une bonne occasion de voyager...***

- Remember to use the present tense with ***depuis***: ***j'apprends le français depuis... ans***.

**3** Qualities and interests: ***Je suis mûr, sérieux,*** etc. ***Je m'intéresse à...; Comme passe-temps, je....***

- Remember to use the correct ending for the adjectives: ***mûr/mûre; sérieux/sérieuse; actif/active,*** etc.

**4** Experience: ***J'ai fait du baby-sitting; je suis allé(e) faire un stage. J'ai travaillé comme... Je n'ai pas fait de petit boulot, mais...***

- Use the perfect tense. Remember the verbs which make the perfect tense with **être**, e.g. ***je suis allé(e)...*** Always try to add your appreciation and/or opinion and if it is in the past, remember to use the imperfect, e.g. ***c'était passionnant/utile; ce n'était pas bien payé.***

**5** Expectations: use a variety of adjectives to add colour to your writing: instead of talking about ***super*** or ***bon***, use words like ***passionnant, excellent, précieux.***

- Try and show off your use of the conditional, e.g. ***ça me permettrait, ce serait,*** etc.
- Express your opinion strongly to be convincing: ***Je suis convaincu(e) que.../Je pense sincèrement que...***
- Use ***aller*** + infinitive or a future tense to speak about what you think you will do, e.g. ***Je vais voyager/ Je voyagerai***.

### GRADE TARGET

**To reach Grade C, you need to:**

- start and finish your letter appropriately.
- use the present, perfect and future tenses correctly.
- make sure adjective agreements are correct.

**To aim higher than a C, you could:**

- know how to use the perfect and imperfect tenses: ***j'ai fait un job, c'était bien payé.***
- use conditional verbs other than ***je voudrais/j'aimerais: ça me permettrait, ce serait,*** etc.
- use ***si*** clauses, e.g. ***si je réussis mes examens de A level, je continuerai mes études.***

**To aim for an A or A*, you could:**

- use a variety of verb forms and tenses, including verb phrases with a verb + preposition: ***j'envisage de continuer à l'étudier.***
- use unusual adjectives and adverbs to give more weight to your argument, e.g. ***précieux, sincèrement,*** etc.
- use extended sentences with more unusual link words like ***tandis que*** (whereas).

# 4B Vocabulaire

## Comment trouver du travail

| | |
|---|---|
| Je cherche un poste | *I am looking for a job* |
| perfectionner ses connaissances d'une langue | *to improve one's knowledge of a language* |
| travailler en équipe/seul(e) | *to work in a team/alone* |
| le chirurgien/la chirurgienne | *surgeon* |
| le cuisinier/la cuisinière | *chef* |
| la femme au foyer | *housewife* |
| le/la fleuriste | *florist* |
| l'ingénieur (*m*) | *engineer* |
| le job d'été | *summer job* |
| la lettre de motivation | *letter supporting your application* |
| le logement gratuit | *free accommodation* |
| l'offre (*f*) d'emploi | *job offer* |
| la petite annonce | *advert* |
| le pompier | *fireman* |
| le poste | *job, post* |
| la restauration | *catering* |
| le salaire | *salary* |
| le traducteur/la traductrice | *translator* |
| le vendeur/la vendeuse | *sales assistant* |
| contacter (par email) | *to contact (by email)* |
| être au chômage | *to be unemployed* |
| être nourri et logé | *to get board and lodging* |

## Comment poser ta candidature

| | |
|---|---|
| améliorer ses connaissances | *to improve one's knowledge* |
| avoir de l'expérience | *to have experience* |
| cela donne l'occasion de | *it gives the opportunity to* |
| consulter un site web | *to check a website* |
| se débrouiller (en + *language*) | *to cope (in a language)* |
| parler (espagnol) couramment | *to speak (Spanish) fluently* |
| passer l'été à/en... | *to spend the summer in...* |
| perfectionner | *to improve* |
| poser sa candidature | *to apply* |
| les atouts (*mpl*) | *skills* |
| le boulot | *job* |
| les conditions (*fpl*) de travail | *working conditions* |
| l'entretien (*m*) | *interview* |
| les horaires (*mpl*) | *hours* |
| les qualités (*fpl*) | *qualities* |
| la rémunération | *pay* |
| la réunion | *meeting* |
| libre (à partir de + *date*) | *free (from + date)* |
| temporaire | *temporary* |

## Comment briller dans un entretien

| | |
|---|---|
| la carrière | *career* |
| le métier | *job, career* |
| la tâche | *task* |
| aimer le contact humain | *to get on well with people* |
| briller | *to shine* |
| bien organisé(e) | *well organised* |
| créatif/créative | *creative* |
| diplomatique | *diplomatic* |
| enthousiaste | *enthousiastic* |
| fidèle | *loyal* |
| honnête | *honest* |
| innovateur/innovatrice | *innovative* |
| plein(e) d'énergie | *energetic* |
| responsable | *responsible* |
| sociable | *sociable* |
| sûr(e) de soi | *confident* |
| travailleur/travailleuse | *hard-working* |

## Comment décrire ton stage

| | |
|---|---|
| faire du classement | *to do the filing* |
| se rendre compte que | *to realise that* |
| répondre au téléphone | *to answer the phone* |
| servir (les clients) | *to serve (customers)* |
| travailler à la caisse | *to work on the till* |
| vendre | *to sell* |
| le/la collègue | *colleague* |
| le conseiller d'orientation | *careers adviser* |
| le patron/la patronne | *boss* |
| (participer à) une réunion | *(to take part in) a meeting* |
| (faire) un stage | *(to do) work experience* |
| accueillant(e) | *welcoming* |
| exigeant(e) | *demanding* |
| gentil(le) | *kind* |
| joyeux/joyeuse | *cheerful* |
| de mauvaise humeur | *bad-tempered* |

## Comment choisir une carrière

| | |
|---|---|
| un dessin animé | *cartoon* |
| un pays défavorisé | *disadvantaged country* |
| un personnage | *character* |
| le service des urgences | *casualty department* |
| c'est un métier passionnant | *it's a fascinating job* |
| ce qui m'a motivé | *what motivated me* |
| il y a un autre côté négatif | *there is another negative side* |
| les horaires sont fatigants | *the hours are tiring* |
| on peut être utile | *you can be useful* |
| on risque sa vie | *you risk your life* |
| avoir des horaires fixes/flexibles | *to have fixed/flexible hours* |
| faire des déplacements | *to go on trips for work* |
| faire partie d'une équipe | *to be part of a team* |
| rêver | *to dream* |
| utiliser mon imagination | *to use my imagination* |

# 1A Écouter et lire: Foundation

***Pour rester en forme quand vous êtes en vacances…***

**1** Listen to the advice about staying healthy whilst on holiday. Look at pictures A–E. In which order is the advice given?

**2** Read the outdoor survival tips. Which of the following paragraphs refers to…

**1** attacks by wildlife?
**2** avoiding dehydration?
**3** avoiding sickness?
**4** finding your way?
**5** keeping warm whilst sleeping?
**6** lighting a fire?

***Pour survivre aux dangers du plein air, voici quelques conseils:***

**A** Si tu es fatigué(e) et que tu as sommeil, il faut faire un lit de branches avant de t'allonger pour ne pas avoir froid.

**B** Si tu as faim et que tu trouves des champignons, il faut vérifier s'ils sont comestibles* ou non. Si tu n'es pas sûr(e), ne les mange pas!

**C** Si tu es perdu(e), essaie de trouver de la mousse* sur les arbres. Elle pousse sur le côté nord du tronc.

**D** Garde toujours des allumettes sur toi – elles sont indispensables pour faire du feu.

**E** Si tu rencontres un animal dangereux reste calme et ne crie pas. Essaie de te retirer en marchant lentement.

**F** Bois toujours suffisamment d'eau. Si tu n'en as pas assez, protège-toi des effets du soleil.

*comestible – *edible*
mousse – *moss*

# 1A Écouter et lire: Higher

**1** **Listen to an interview with David Belle. Answer the questions in English.**

- **a** How does David Belle describe his sport? *(3 details)*
- **b** What two sporting disciplines contribute to his sport and what did he personally want to achieve through his sport?
- **c** How does his sport help him in life in general?
- **d** What are the characteristics of a good practitioner of his sport? *(4 details)*

**David Belle: créateur du Parkour**

## Une interview avec Musclon de Bodibuildos, athlète olympique

*par notre envoyé spécial à Olympie, Grèce – 290 après JC*

– **Musclon, comment êtes-vous devenu athlète olympique?**

– Eh bien, mon père et mon grand-père étaient des athlètes olympiques célèbres. J'ai commencé à faire beaucoup de sport très tôt. À six ans, j'ai commencé à m'entraîner avec mon père.

– **Comment vous entraînez-vous avant les Jeux Olympiques?**

– Alors, je m'entraîne tous les jours pendant 10 mois à Corinthe, là où j'habite, avec mon entraîneur. Après, je vais à Olympie et je m'entraîne un mois avec les autres athlètes. Là, le régime est très strict: on ne doit pas manger de viande – que du pain, des céréales, des noix, des figues et du fromage. C'est dur!

– **Vous avez déjà gagné aux Jeux Olympiques?**

– Eh oui! J'ai déjà gagné la course une fois et cette année, j'ai gagné la course et le pentathlon. Je suis donc double champion olympique!

– **Quelles sont les récompenses pour les vainqueurs?**

– J'ai eu une couronne d'olivier, un grand honneur, et un cadeau très précieux, de l'huile d'olive. En plus, quand je suis rentré chez moi, c'était la gloire populaire: on a fait des chansons sur moi, on a mis des statues de moi dans les villes. Maintenant, je suis invité à beaucoup de compétitions nationales et je gagne beaucoup d'argent! Je suis un héros! Heureusement, je sais rester très modeste…

**2** **Read the text about a fictitious Olympic champion. Answer the questions in English.**

- **a** How did Musclon become an Olympic athlete? *(2 reasons)*
- **b** How is the training organised prior to the games? *(2 details)*
- **c** What sort of diet do the athletes follow?
- **d** Which event(s) did he win this year?
- **e** What did the champion find to welcome him when he got back home? *(4 details)*

# 1B Écouter et lire: Foundation

**1** Listen to Thomas, Sophie, Philippe and Marie talking about their families. Choose the correct answer.

1. Thomas gets on with his sister...
   **a** always **b** most of the time **c** never
2. Sophie has...
   **a** a stepmother **b** a stepfather **c** half-sisters
3. Philippe is...
   **a** untidier than his brother **b** as tidy as his brother **c** tidier than his brother
4. Marie...
   **a** has a sister **b** has a brother **c** is an only child

La vie en famille

## Une journée dans la vie d'une famille monoparentale*

Laurent vit seul avec son fils Aurélien, 7 ans, et sa fille Clémence, 4 ans. Leur mère, Carole, est morte il y a deux ans. Il doit bien s'organiser pour gérer la vie familiale. Voici sa journée typique:

**la veille:** il choisit les vêtements que les enfants vont porter le lendemain et vérifie le contenu des cartables.

**6 heures 30:** il se lève avant les enfants, donc il est plus calme pour se préparer; il se douche et s'habille, consulte son agenda, fait une liste d'achats, prépare le petit déjeuner.

**7 heures:** les enfants se lèvent; Aurélien se prépare; Laurent s'occupe de Clémence. Les enfants se lavent, ils se brossent les dents, ils s'habillent.

**7 heures 20:** ils prennent le petit déjeuner ensemble; la télé est interdite!

**7 heures 45:** ils partent pour l'école.

**8 heures:** ils arrivent à l'école.

**8 heures 30:** Laurent arrive à son bureau où il travaille pendant les heures d'école.

**13 heures:** il déjeune, souvent avec ses collègues, avant de faire des courses en ville.

**16 heures 15:** il va chercher les enfants.

**16 heures 45:** ils rentrent à la maison et Laurent donne leur goûter aux enfants.

**17 heures 30:** il surveille les devoirs en préparant le dîner.

**19 heures:** la famille dîne, les enfants jouent ensemble; Laurent remplit le lave-vaisselle; un quart d'heure de relaxation.

**19 heures 30:** les enfants jouent dans le bain; Laurent leur parle de leur journée.

**20 heures:** les enfants se couchent. Laurent se repose un peu, puis il fait encore deux ou trois heures de travail sur l'ordinateur. Après cela, il recommence pour le lendemain.

* single-parent

**2** Read the text about Laurent's role as a single parent. Answer the questions in English.

**a** Why is Laurent a single parent?
**b** Who is older: his son or his daughter?
**c** What does Laurent do before the children get up?
**d** What is not allowed at breakfast time?
**e** What time does Laurent get to work?
**f** What do the children do while he makes the evening meal?
**g** What does Laurent do in the evening when the children have gone to bed?

# 1B Écouter et lire: Higher

**1** Listen to Céline talking about herself. Copy and complete the table.

| | Qualities | Faults |
|---|---|---|
| 1 | | |
| 2 | | |

**2** Read the texts about family life. Which person – Anaïs, David or Marion – says the following?

**a** I am constantly in touch with my friends.
**b** I don't always get on with my parents.
**c** I have a very close relationship with one of my parents.
**d** I like to talk to another member of my family other than my parents when I am upset.
**e** I look like one of my parents.
**f** I would prefer to consult my friends rather than my parents for an opinion.
**g** There are three generations living in my home.

## La vie en famille

On me dit que je ressemble à ma mère parce que je suis petite et mince comme elle, et j'ai aussi les cheveux mi-longs et bouclés. Nous aimons faire des sorties ensemble, surtout dans les magasins ou au cinéma. Mes copines aussi sont importantes, mais je dirais que ma mère est ma meilleure amie et c'est à elle que je préfère me confier quand j'ai des problèmes. **Anaïs**

Après la mort de mon grand-père il y a deux ans, ma grand-mère ne voulait plus rester chez elle. Alors elle est venue vivre chez nous. Je trouve ça génial! Je m'entends bien avec elle car nous avons les mêmes centres d'intérêt et quand je me dispute avec mes parents, elle m'écoute. Quant à mes parents, eux aussi sont contents parce que ma grand-mère s'occupe de mon petit frère quand ma mère travaille. **David**

Je suis rarement chez moi; je préfère être avec mes copines et sortir avec elles. Pour moi, c'est l'opinion de mes copines qui compte plus que celle de mes parents. Si je suis seule je leur envoie beaucoup de SMS ou bien je leur parle au téléphone. **Marion**

# 2A Écouter et lire: Foundation

**1** **Listen to Élodie, Romain, Manon and Clément talking about their television viewing habits. Who is talking about what they do when...**

**a** they return home?
**b** they don't know what's on TV?
**c** the TV breaks down?
**d** they want to watch a programme that's on late at night?
**e** there is nothing they particularly want to watch on TV?
**f** a friend calls whilst they are watching TV?

**Choose the one correct letter for each person.**

**2** **Read the text about how young French people spend their free time. Choose four sentences which are true.**

**a** Jazz concerts are very popular with young people in France.
**b** The favourite pastime of young people in France is going to see a film.
**c** Young people generally go out on their own in France.
**d** Young people watch more television than their parents.
**e** Young people prefer listening to the radio to watching television
**f** About a quarter of the people questioned read a daily newspaper.
**g** Just over half of the people questioned had read more than two books in the past year.
**h** Non-electronic games are popular amongst the French.

## Spécial loisirs

**Cet article est basé sur un sondage du ministère de la Culture sur les loisirs des Français de 12 à 25 ans.**

**A**

Que font les adolescents français pendant leur temps libre? Ils aiment beaucoup sortir. Et la sortie favorite des jeunes en France est le cinéma. On aime aussi aller aux concerts rock et en discothèque. Le week-end, on va souvent dans un parc de loisirs ou à un match sportif.

Les sorties les moins populaires pour les 12–25 ans sont les spectacles de jazz, de musique classique, de danse et d'opéra. En général, les jeunes ne sortent pas seuls, ils préfèrent les sorties en groupe.

**B**

Et à la maison? Les ados regardent moins la télévision que les adultes. Leur média préféré, c'est les radios jeunes (NRJ, Fun Radio, Skyrock). Ils n'aiment vraiment pas lire: 52% n'ont pas lu plus de deux livres l'année dernière. Par contre, ils lisent des magazines de télé ou consacrés à la musique, au cinéma ou à la mode féminine. Et 26% lisent un journal tous les jours.

Les jeux traditionnels ne sont pas morts en France. Neuf Français sur dix jouent à des jeux de société (cartes, Monopoly, échecs, Scrabble...).

# 2A Écouter et lire: Higher

**1** Listen to a pupil and a teacher giving their opinion on the film *Entre les murs*. Which statement is true for each?

**1** Philippe thinks the film...
- **a** is unrealistic
- **b** gives an accurate portrait of life in a school
- **c** exaggerates school life.

**2** Philippe thinks that the teacher...
- **a** doesn't respect his students
- **b** is too patient with his students
- **c** shouts at his students too much.

**3** Guy Leroy thinks that...
- **a** the actors are very amateurish
- **b** the film recognises the difficult job that teachers do
- **c** the director is paying hommage to one of his old teachers.

**4** Guy Leroy says that...
- **a** the dialogue in the film is an accurate portrayal
- **b** the film does justice to the students
- **c** the dialogue in the film is stilted.

**2** Read the text about *Entre les murs*. Choose four sentences which are true about the film.

- **a** In the film the teacher finds the pupils easy to manage.
- **b** The teacher in the film also wrote a book with the same title.
- **c** The film is about a real school.
- **d** The film is set in an underprivileged part of Paris.
- **e** None of the actors were amateurs.
- **f** The pupils make life difficult for the teacher.
- **g** The viewer experiences all sorts of emotions when watching the film.
- **h** The pupils can do what they like and get away with it.

## Entre les murs

**Ce film français a reçu la Palme d'or au Festival de film de Cannes, 2008.**

Cette comédie dramatique se passe «entre les murs» d'un collège à Paris, dans un quartier multiculturel défavorisé. Un jeune prof de français (joué par François Bégaudeau qui est l'auteur du livre qui a inspiré le scénario) fait face à une classe particulièrement «difficile». Les élèves sont souvent insolents mais il doit assurer la discipline.

C'est de la fiction mais c'est presque un documentaire parce que c'est tellement réaliste.

Les acteurs – qui sont tous non professionnels – nous font rire, pleurer, désespérer. Ils capturent facilement le langage de la rue – les mots, les gestes, les vêtements. L'histoire nous fait comprendre que quand les élèves vont trop loin, cela peut avoir des conséquences très graves.

Cette confrontation constante entre un professeur et ses vingt-quatre élèves est une histoire originale et perturbante.

# 2B Écouter et lire: Foundation

**1** Listen to Guillaume talking about his visit to London. Which four topics does he mention and in what order?

**a** the food
**b** the sightseeing
**c** the weather
**d** the journey
**e** the English people
**f** the accommodation

Guillaume

**2** Read Léna's account of a visit to York. Choose four sentences which are true about her visit.

**a** Léna visited York in the summer.
**b** She went there with her family.
**c** She arrived in York by air.
**d** She stayed with someone of her own age.
**e** The weather was very good during her stay.
**f** She liked sightseeing best of all.
**g** She got on well with all the people she met.
**h** She particularly liked the food she had during her stay.

L'année dernière, en août, j'ai fait un séjour de trois semaines à York, en Angleterre. Je suis partie seule. J'ai pris l'avion jusqu'à Londres, et puis le train. J'étais dans une famille où il y avait une fille de mon âge, Katy. Il faisait beau et chaud presque tout le temps. On a visité la ville de York et on a fait des excursions. Mais ce que j'ai préféré, c'était buller* avec les copines de Katy. On s'est bien entendues et c'était un séjour agréable. Les Anglais sont très polis. Par contre, je n'ai pas beaucoup aimé la nourriture anglaise et je trouve que les Anglais mangent trop entre les repas*.

Léna

* buller – *to hang out*
entre les repas – *between meals*

# 2B Écouter et lire: Higher

**1** Listen to Anne-Cécile talking about her experience as an au pair. Copy and complete the table.

| | Advantages | Disadvantages |
|---|---|---|
| 1 | | |
| 2 | | |
| 3 | | |

## Chemin de fer = tourisme vert!

Vous adorez faire du tourisme à la montagne mais vous trouvez les routes parfois dangereuses, et souvent vraiment trop encombrées? Alors, pensez aux trains touristiques! Ces trains roulent sur d'anciennes lignes ferroviaires qu'on restaure aujourd'hui pour le tourisme. Grâce aux* trains touristiques, on voit les paysages en toute sécurité, sans bouchon et sans polluer l'environnement! Dans certaines régions de haute altitude, vous passerez dans des sites sauvages et magnifiques et, pour certains, inaccessibles aux autres véhicules. Il existe une cinquantaine de ces trains dans toute la France, en montagne, mais aussi à la campagne et au bord de la mer. Sur certaines lignes, des trains ultra-modernes ont remplacé les autorails traditionnels; d'autres, comme le petit train de Corse, ont conservé leurs voitures traditionnelles, ce qui ajoute encore au charme du voyage!

* grâce aux – *thanks to*

**2** Read the text. Answer the questions in English.

- **a** What two reasons are given for why people hesitate to visit mountainous regions by car?
- **b** What two advantages of visiting mountainous regions by train are given?
- **c** What is a further advantage of travelling to places at high altitude by train compared to other means of transport?
- **d** How many tourist trains are there in France, and where can they be found in addition to in the mountains?
- **e** What contributes to the charm of the train in Corsica?

# 3A Écouter et lire: Foundation

**1** Listen to Solène, who talking about a public holiday in France. Answer the following questions.

- **a** What is the date of the holiday she is describing?
- **b** How do her parents often celebrate this day?
- **c** What two things are they going to do this year?
- **d** Where does the military parade take place and how does she get to see it?

Nous, on décore la maison et on a un grand sapin avec des décorations et des guirlandes lumineuses. Les magasins, les villes et les villages sont également illuminés. On échange des cadeaux qu'on a mis près de l'arbre. On fait un grand repas: on a toujours des huîtres pour commencer. Ensuite, on mange de la dinde aux marrons, et comme dessert, il y a une bûche au chocolat.

Anya

J'aime bien cette fête qui a lieu au printemps. On est catholiques, alors on va à la messe le vendredi saint et encore le dimanche. C'est une fête religieuse importante pour les chrétiens. Bien sûr, j'aime bien aussi les œufs en chocolat! Quand j'étais petit, je cherchais dans le jardin des œufs en chocolat ou des sucreries que ma mère avait cachés. Le lundi est jour férié.

Damien

**2** Read what Anya and Damien have to say about a public holiday they enjoy. Who...

- **a** eats chocolate as part of a meal?
- **b** goes to church twice as part of this holiday?
- **c** used to spend part of the holiday looking for things one of his parents had hidden?
- **d** spends time eating a lot of food?
- **e** describes a public holiday which falls in March or April?

# Écouter et lire: Higher

**1** Listen to Tatiana talking about Madagascar.

*Part1*

**Which three sentences are true?**

**a** Tatiana has lived longer in Madagascar than in France.
**b** Madagascar is an island which is bigger than France.
**c** Nobody speaks French in Madagascar.
**d** The beaches in Madagascar are all very beautiful.
**e** Most houses are not very big and are made of wood.

*Part 2*

**Which two sentences are true?**

**a** Tatiana used to live with her grandparents.
**b** Her grandparents came with her family to France.
**c** In Madagascar members of the same family rarely eat together.
**d** A typical family meal in Madagascar would not be suitable for a vegetarian.
**e** In Madagascar animals are never caught and killed.

## Le Nord: mythes et réalités

Quand on dit «le Nord» de la France, beaucoup de gens imaginent une région grise, pas intéressante, avec une population pas très agréable. Cette vision est tout à fait à l'opposé de la réalité!

Si le temps ici est assez imprévisible, il ne pleut pas en permanence! Il y a moins de soleil que dans le sud de la France mais l'air y est beaucoup plus pur.

Il y a bien sûr des traces du passé industriel de la région: les anciennes mines de charbon, et les célèbres corons, les villages de mineurs. Mais le Nord, ce n'est pas uniquement ça. C'est une région moderne et accessible, avec d'excellents moyens de transport, comme le TGV et le Tunnel sous la Manche.

C'est une région très dynamique et le tourisme se développe. Il y a sur la côte des paysages et des plages magnifiques et il y a un grand nombre de châteaux et de vieilles villes historiques dans toute la région.

**2** Read the text about the north of France. Answer the questions in English.

**a** What is the typical image of this region in people's minds? *(2 details)*
**b** How does the climate compare with the south? *(2 details)*
**c** In what way is the north very 'modern' now?
**d** What is there to attract tourists to the north? *(3 details)*

# 3B Écouter et lire: Foundation

1

2

3
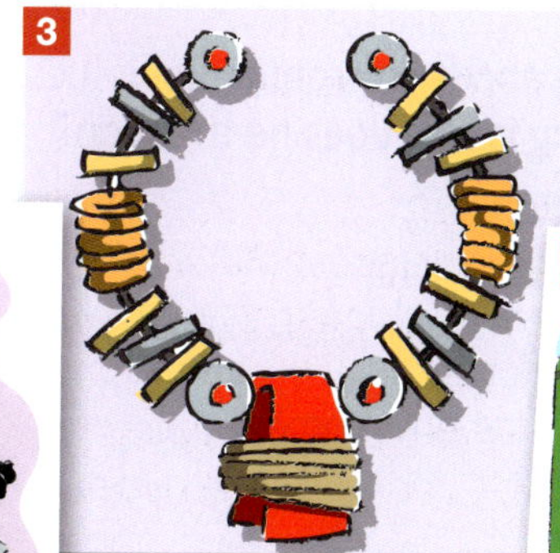

4

**1** Listen to Fabien talking about an environmental project they had at his school. Look at the pictures. In what order does he mention the different aspects of the project?

**2** Read the texts about a project in Martinique. Choose the correct person: Damien, Christelle or Maxime.

- **a** Who is talking about what happened in specific lessons?
- **b** Who mentions what the school wants to do for the next initiative?
- **c** Who tells us who organised this project?
- **d** Who mentions something they did at the school which saved electricity?
- **e** Who describes the benefits of this project for the school?

## Le recyclage en Martinique

Dans mon collège Cassien Sainte-Claire, en Martinique, on vient de faire un projet pour la protection de l'environnement. Le projet était organisé par le directeur, Monsieur Labridy et sa collègue Madame Dol. On voulait que les élèves et les adultes du collège participent ensemble au projet. On a fait beaucoup de choses! **Damien**

On a encouragé des gestes simples: on a éteint les ordinateurs quand on ne les utilisait pas, on a fait des efforts pour réduire les déchets en réutilisant autant de matériaux que possible dans l'atelier artistique, et en cours de sciences on a étudié les problèmes qui menacent la planète comme le réchauffement global. **Christelle**

Le projet a été un formidable succès! Au début, une dizaine d'élèves ont participé à l'initiative de recyclage mais à la fin tout le monde voulait aider et il y a eu une vaste opération de collecte et de tri. On a récupéré des milliers de choses, par exemple des canettes et des emballages. Les résultats sont visibles – l'école est plus propre! – et les élèves sont fiers de leur travail. Le prochain projet? On va créer un jardin créole! **Maxime**

# 3B Écouter et lire: Higher

**1** Listen to Martin talking about environmental issues. Which three of the following issues does he mention?

- **a** alternative energy sources
- **b** biodiversity
- **c** eating habits
- **d** the destruction of the rainforests
- **e** the destruction of the marine environment
- **f** travel
- **g** wasteful packaging

## La rentrée écolo

*CM1 – *Year 2 class, pupils aged 7*
fournitures – *stationery supplies*

La rentrée était un peu différente cette année pour les élèves de CM1.* Leur institutrice, Mary Ann Meurin nous a expliqué qu'elle voulait encourager une attitude responsable envers l'écologie. D'abord, les cahiers ont des pages moins blanches, ce qui a surpris les enfants. Lucas a demandé: 'Ce cahier, il est vieux et déjà usé?'

Les élèves aiment le nouveau matériel écologique. Camille trouve que les stylos sont agréables pour écrire. Maintenant, elle préfère les fournitures* écolo, et Amaury explique que le matériel écolo est 'bien parce que les fournitures sont recyclables'.

Les enfants ont déjà leurs propres idées sur l'écologie. Guillaume et Hugo expliquent qu'il est important de 'fermer le robinet pour se brosser les dents'. Et Marine sait déjà qu'il est important 'de protéger la planète contre le réchauffement climatique'. Son geste écolo à elle, c'est de 'ne pas allumer la lumière des toilettes quand il fait jour'. Luka ajoute qu'il est important de changer nos habitudes 'si l'homme veut continuer à vivre sur Terre' et que chez lui, il y a des 'lumières économiques'.

Laissons le dernier mot à Théo: 'Il faut protéger la planète pour y vivre le plus longtemps possible'.

**2** Read the text and answer the questions in English.

- **a** What was the first change the children noticed when they came back to school this year?
- **b** What did Lucas wonder?
- **c** What did their teacher want to achieve?
- **d** What other new stationery item is mentioned in the second paragraph?
- **e** Name three practical things which children mentioned in the third paragraph say they do.

# 4A Écouter et lire: Foundation

**1** Listen to Félix talking about school life.
Which four topics is he talking about? Choose the correct letters.

**a** break time
**b** choice of subjects in Years 12/13
**c** homework
**d** school rules
**e** teacher absence
**f** uniform

**2** Read the texts. Choose the correct person: Quentin, Lucie or Antoine.

**a** Who can be a bit careless?
**b** Who does not always give their school work top priority at the weekend?
**c** Who does not rush to do their homework?
**d** Who has a relative who helps them with their studies?
**e** Who sometimes plays the role of the teacher?

## Quel type d'étudiant(e) es-tu?

Si j'ai des examens je commence à réviser tout de suite parce que je trouve moins stressant de travailler comme ça. Pour me préparer à un examen oral je m'entraîne avec ma mère. Elle est très patiente. Je préfère toujours faire mes devoirs dès que je rentre chez moi – comme ça j'ai plus de temps pour le reste. **Quentin**

J'ai un petit boulot dans un supermarché. Quand on me demande si je peux travailler aussi le dimanche, je dis "oui", parce que j'ai toujours besoin d'argent, surtout pour payer les frais de mon portable. Parfois je ne fais pas mes devoirs ou bien je les rends en retard! **Lucie**

En général je trouve le travail scolaire facile. Si j'ai un copain qui ne comprend pas ses devoirs de maths, par exemple, je vais l'aider. Je fais mes devoirs tout de suite après l'école et je les fais vite. Quelquefois je les fais trop vite et il y a des erreurs! **Antoine**

# 4A Écouter et lire: Higher

**1** **Listen to Flore talking about her choice of baccalauréat.**

**1 a** What two reasons does Flore give for possibly choosing a literary 'bac'?
**b** What advantage could there be for choosing a scientific 'bac'?

**2 a** What are her feelings about this?
**b** What jobs do her parents do and what is their attitude to her dilemma?

**2** **Read the information about the 'bac'. Choose three statements which are true.**

**a** Students go to a terminal to sit the 'bac'.
**b** Most French students pass the 'bac'.
**c** If you like languages you would choose the literary 'bac'.
**d** You have to study a foreign language in order to sit the 'bac'.
**e** Maths is not compulsory for the 'bac'.
**f** The sciences' 'bac' is more prestigious than the literary 'bac'.
**g** It doesn't matter what type of 'bac' you have if you want to go to one of the more prestigious universities.

## *Le système du baccalauréat*

Presque tous les élèves de terminale passent le baccalauréat quand ils ont 18 ans.

Il y a plusieurs filières du bac, dont:

- le bac scientifique, dont les matières les plus importantes sont les sciences et les maths, mais on étudie aussi le français, une langue étrangère, la philosophie, l'histoire et la géographie.
- le bac littéraire, dont les matières les plus importantes sont la philosophie, la littérature française, l'histoire, la géo et deux langues étrangères. On a aussi quelques heures de maths et de sciences par semaine.

Si on veut aller à l'université, il faut réussir son bac. Si on veut aller dans une grande école*, il faut d'abord faire deux ans de «prépa», ou classes préparatoires. Pour beaucoup de grandes écoles il faut avoir le bac scientifique.

*grande école – *one of France's most prestigious universities*

# 4B Écouter et lire: Foundation

**1** Listen to the statistics about working children. Copy and complete the table with the correct numbers.

1. 127.3 million children in Asia/the Pacific between the ages of ...... and ...... work.
2. In sub-Saharan Africa there are ...... million children working, and in Latin America and the Caribbean ...... million.
3. ...... % of children work in the Middle East and North Africa.
4. ...... million children work in industrialised countries.

**2** Read the text. Which paragraph (A–G) is about...

1. unpaid work by females?
2. children working to support their families?
3. unsafe working conditions?
4. manual labour?
5. children fighting in wars?

## «Non, au travail des enfants»

**A** Près de 218 millions d'enfants et d'adolescents âgés de 5 à 17 ans sont au travail dans le monde.

**B** Les enfants travaillent pour deux raisons principales:
- ils sont exploités.
- ils contribuent simplement au revenu de leur famille.

**C** Ces enfants, qui sont souvent invisibles, travaillent comme employés de maison, dans des ateliers et dans les plantations. 70% au moins travaillent dans l'agriculture.

**D** Près de 171 millions d'enfants travaillent dans des situations ou conditions dangereuses (travail dans les mines, avec des produits chimiques et des pesticides dans l'agriculture, avec des machines dangereuses, etc.).

**E** Des millions de filles travaillent comme domestiques et employées de maison non rémunérées.

**F** Exemples d'exploitation: l'esclavage, la prostitution, la participation à des conflits armés.

**G** Voilà pourquoi on a organisé pour le 12 juin une journée mondiale contre le travail des enfants.

# 4B Écouter et lire: Higher

**1** **Listen to Alexandre talking about doing voluntary work abroad. Answer the questions in English.**

**1** **a** When is it possible for young people to do voluntary work abroad?
**b** How can the volunteer benefit from this experience?
**c** What motives would a volunteer have to do this work?

**2** **a** How long can a volunteer spend on a project? *(2 details)*
**b** What does the fee cover? *(3 details)*
**c** Where are volunteers accommodated?

**2** **Read the text about Léa's time in Morocco. Choose four statements which are true.**

**a** Léa went to Morocco for four weeks.
**b** She spent a year saving up for the trip.
**c** She worked two full days a week in order to earn enough money for the trip.
**d** She has regrets about the amount it cost her to go to Morocco.
**e** She feels she has been privileged in life.
**f** The experience gave Léa the chance to appreciate how fortunate others are.
**g** She found the experience very challenging.
**h** She now knows what she wants to do in life.

**Moi, j'ai travaillé au Maroc.**

L'année dernière, après mes examens, j'ai choisi de passer un mois au Maroc, à travailler comme bénévole dans une école maternelle. J'avais travaillé toute l'année dans une boulangerie le jeudi et vendredi soir pour payer les frais de voyage et d'hébergement au Maroc, mais je n'ai aucun regret. J'ai appris énormément de choses pendant mes quatre semaines avec des orphelins pour lesquels la vie n'offre pas la chance dont moi j'ai toujours profité – la famille, l'éducation, les choses matérielles. J'apprécie beaucoup plus ce que j'ai – j'ai des copains qui ont plus que moi, mais je sais aussi qu'il y a plein d'enfants avec beaucoup moins. Ça me donne une certaine perspective. Le travail même m'a beaucoup plu. J'étais assistante dans une classe primaire et j'ai fait toutes sortes de choses, par exemple, des maths, des petits groupes de français, ou bien on racontait des histoires et écrivait un peu, on faisait des jeux, vraiment tout. Mon ambition maintenant, c'est de devenir institutrice et de retourner travailler dans un pays où on a vraiment besoin de moi et de mes talents.

***Léa***

# Exam Practice

## Listening – Unit 1

- There are 35 marks in the Foundation listening exam and 40 marks in the Higher one. This unit counts for 20% of the final mark.
- No dictionaries are allowed but you will hear each recording twice.
- At Foundation level the test lasts for 30 minutes and at Higher 40. You will be allowed 5 minutes before the recording is played to read the question paper.
- All instructions will be given in English and there may sometimes be an example of the type of answer required.
- Each tier (Foundation or Higher) contains a variety of items of differing lengths. You may be required to fill in a box, complete a form or write fuller answers (these will be in English).
- Three of the texts at Foundation level are the same as the first three texts at Higher level.

### *Foundation tier*

At this level many of the tasks will require you to understand short announcements, conversations, instructions, short news items and telephone messages. There will also be some longer items which refer to past, present and future events. You will be expected to identify the main points and extract details and opinions.

### *Higher tier*

At Higher level you will hear longer texts which contain some complex unfamiliar language. You will need to be able to understand the gist of what you have heard as well as specific details. You will also have to use the context or other clues to work out an answer and to draw conclusions.

## Practice listening questions

### *Foundation level*

**Planning a trip**

You are on an exchange visit. Your partner is talking about some plans for your stay. You will hear each statement twice.

Answer each question **in English** or **in figures**.

**Example:** When are you going to Rouen?
**Answer:** Tomorrow

1 How are you travelling? [1]
2 What will the weather be like? [1]
3 What are you advised to wear? [1]
4 What must you remember to take? [1]

[4 marks]

**Visiting a town**

A

B

C

D

E

F

G

Where are you going in town?
Choose the correct letter.

**Example:** G

5 ☐ 6 ☐ 7 ☐ 8 ☐

[4 marks]

**Free time**

**9** On Saturday morning Aurélie is going to...

A

B

C

Choose the correct letter. ☐

**10** She is going...

A

B

C
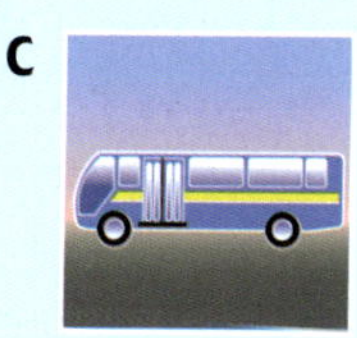

Choose the correct letter. ☐

**11** She needs to buy...

A

B

C

Choose the correct letter. ☐

**12** Her favourite sport is...

**A** 

**B** 

**C** 

Choose the correct letter. ☐

**13** On Sunday evening she is going to...

**A** 

**B** 

**C** 

Choose the correct letter. ☐

[5 marks]

**Taking notes from an answer phone message**
Write down the missing information:

**Example:** First name: *Thierry*

**14.** Surname: ........................................ [1 mark]
**15.** Room for ........................... people [1 mark]
**16.** Date of arrival ............................. [1 mark]
**17.** Room with a view of the ................ [1 mark]

[4 marks]

**Healthy lifestyle**

**A** 

**B** 

**C** 

**D** 

**E** 

**F** 

Choose the correct letter for each action and the correct number for how often he does it.

Write **1** for every day.
Write **2** for regularly.
Write **3** for rarely or never.

| **Example:** | B | 3 |
|---|---|---|
| **18** | | |
| **19** | | |
| **20** | | |

[6 marks]

**Local area**

| | |
|---|---|
| **A** | Transport facilities |
| **B** | Shops |
| **C** | Night life |
| **D** | Sights for tourists |
| **E** | Activities for young people |
| **F** | Climate |

What is Kévin talking about? Choose the correct letter for each thing mentioned.

**21** ☐ **22** ☐ **23** ☐ **24** ☐

[4 marks]

**Living in the country**
Copy and complete the grid.

**Example:**

| Name | Advantage | Disadvantage |
|---|---|---|
| Maxime | *Very picturesque* | *Roads too narrow* |

**25**

| Name | Advantage | Disadvantage |
|---|---|---|
| Sarah | | |

[2 marks]

**26**

| Name | Advantage | Disadvantage |
|---|---|---|
| Hugo | | |

[2 marks]

**Leisure activities**

**27** Sébastien's favourite hobby is

**A** basketball
**B** fishing
**C** football [1]

Choose the correct letter. ☐

**28** Yesterday evening he

**A** did his homework
**B** played computer games
**C** watched TV [1]

Choose the correct letter. ☐

**29** Last weekend he

**A** saw a play
**B** visited his grandparents
**C** watched a lot of TV [1]

Choose the correct letter. ☐

**30** He also went to a

**A** Chinese restaurant
**B** French restaurant
**C** Indian restaurant [1]

Choose the correct letter. ☐

[4 marks]

## *Higher level*

Questions 1–9 are the same as Foundation level questions 18–20 and 25–30.

### Work experience overseas

**10** Which two sentences are true? Choose the correct letters.

| | |
|---|---|
| **A** | Sophie worked in a hospital |
| **B** | She wants to be a doctor |
| **C** | Her work experience was related to what she wants to do in the future |
| **D** | She stayed in the capital city of a West African country |
| **E** | She wanted to visit a school |

☐☐ [2 marks]

**11** Which two sentences are true? Choose the correct letters.

| | |
|---|---|
| **A** | She liked the work |
| **B** | She spent the whole time in the same place |
| **C** | She stayed with some rich people |
| **D** | The family was not very hospitable |
| **E** | She stayed for a month |

☐☐ [2 marks]

**12** What three aspects about her experience did she particularly like? Choose the correct letters.

| | |
|---|---|
| **A** | The food |
| **B** | The markets |
| **C** | The people |
| **D** | The sunbathing |
| **E** | The transport |
| **F** | The weather |

☐☐☐ [3 marks]

### Philippe is talking about his school.

**13** Which **two** words describe his school? Choose the correct letters.

| | |
|---|---|
| **A** | well equipped |
| **B** | dirty |
| **C** | quiet |
| **D** | crowded |
| **E** | clean |

☐☐ [2 marks]

### The environment

These two young people are talking about environmental issues. Choose the correct letter.

**14 (i)** Chloë thinks that the situation is

| | |
|---|---|
| **A** | exaggerated |
| **B** | serious |
| **C** | trivial |

☐ [1 mark]

**14 (ii)** She has made changes

| | |
|---|---|
| **A** | in all areas of her life |
| **B** | in no areas of her life |
| **C** | in some areas of her life |

☐ [1 mark]

**15 (i)** Youssef

| | |
|---|---|
| **A** | agrees with Chloë |
| **B** | disagrees with Chloë |
| **C** | does not do much |

☐ [1 mark]

**15 (ii)** He is reluctant to make changes when it comes to

| | |
|---|---|
| **A** | recycling |
| **B** | buying food |
| **C** | using water |

☐ [1 mark]

**16** He thinks the most pressing problem is

| | |
|---|---|
| **A** | to find energy solutions |
| **B** | to stop deforestation |
| **C** | to stop over fishing |

☐ [1 mark]

### Work experience

Fill in the gaps.

**Example:** Julien did his work experience in a hotel two months ago.

**17 (i)** To begin with Julien's reaction to getting a placement in a hotel was probably one of .................................... [1 mark]

**17 (ii** During his placement he was able to use ............ [1 mark]

**18 (i)** One of the benefits of his work experience was to help him ........................................................................[1 mark]

**18 (ii)** The aspect of his work experience which he disliked the most was ........................................................... [1 mark]

[4 marks]

**Alain Robert is talking about his experience as a climber.**

Answer the questions in English.

**19 (i)** Why did Alain Robert want to become a climber?

[1 mark]

**19 (ii)** Why didn't his parents encourage him to become a climber when he was young?

[1 mark]

**20** What does he say about one of his early experiences of climbing? Give **three** details.

[3 marks]

**21** What have been the high and low points of his career? Give **three** details.

[3 marks]

# Reading – Unit 2

- There are 35 marks in the Foundation tier reading exam and 45 marks in the higher. This unit counts for 20% of the final mark.
- No dictionaries are allowed.
- At Foundation level the test lasts for 30 minutes and at Higher 50 minutes.
- All instructions will be given in English.
- Each tier (Foundation or Higher) contains a variety of question types requiring a non-verbal response (ticking or filling in boxes) or responses in English.
- There are a number of questions which are common to both tiers.

### *Foundation tier*

This paper will test your understanding of short items such as notices, instructions and advertisements, as well as longer extracts from sources such as brochures, websites, and newspapers. These longer items may include reference to past, present and future events and will contain some unfamiliar language. You will be required to identify key points and some specific details.

### *Higher tier*

At this level there will be some items which include complex language, in a range of registers, including non factual and narrative material. You will be expected to use your knowledge of grammar and structure to understand the gist of the text as well as specific details. You will also have to be able to recognise views, attitudes and emotions from what you have read, and to draw conclusions.

## Practice reading questions

### *Foundation level*

Answer **all** questions in English.

**Shops**

**A**

**B**

**C**

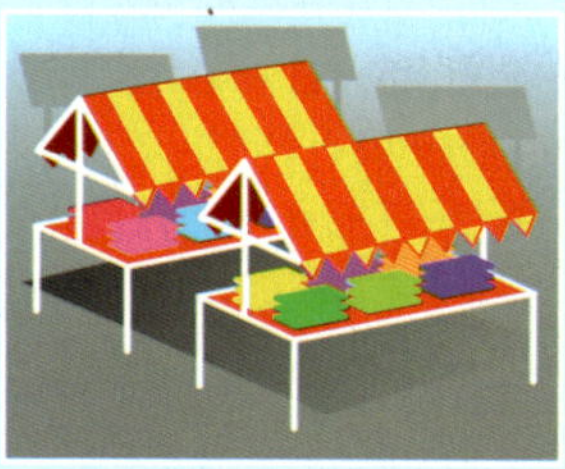

**D**

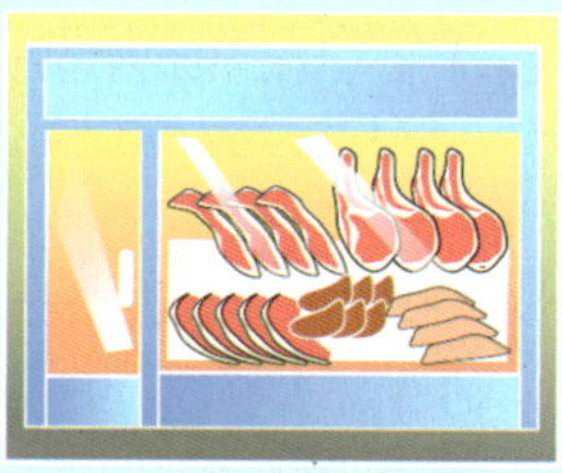

**E**

**F**

**G**

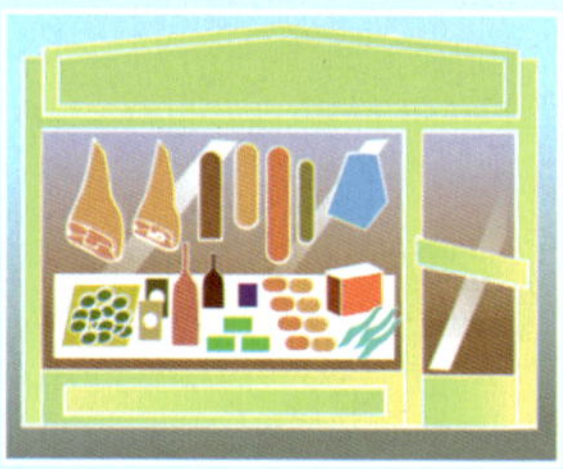

Match the shops with the pictures. Choose the correct letter.

**Example:** Marché [C]

**1a** Librairie [ ]

**1b** Boucherie [ ]

**1c** Pâtisserie [ ]

**1d** Boulangerie [ ]

[4 marks]

**Signs**

You see these signs in France. What do they mean? Write the answer in English .

**Example:** Tirez    Pull

| | | | |
|---|---|---|---|
| **2a** | Piscine | **2c** | Magasin |
| **2b** | Ouvert | **2d** | Ascenseur |

[4 marks]

**Jobs**

You are looking at a French magazine. Some people are describing their jobs.

| | |
|---|---|
| **A** | Chaque jour je m'occupe des gens malades. |
| **B** | Je fais beaucoup de dessins. |
| **C** | Dans mon magasin je vends de la viande. |
| **D** | Je plante des arbres et des fleurs. |
| **E** | Je prépare des repas dans un hôtel. |
| **F** | Les élèves ne sont pas contents quand je leur donne des devoirs. |

What job do they do? Choose the correct letter.

**3a** Philippe is a butcher. ☐

**3b** Amélie is a teacher. ☐

**3c** Pierre is a nurse. ☐ [3 marks]

**Information about a town**

Choose a word from the list to fill the gap.

**Example:** L'office du tourisme est G tous les jours.

**4a** Venez à Dinan, une ☐ pittoresque et médiévale en Bretagne!

**4b** Mangez des ☐ bretonnes! Elles sont délicieuses.

**4c** Réservez des billets pour des spectacles, des ☐ et des concerts à l'office du tourisme.

**4d** À l'office du tourisme on parle anglais, ☐ et espagnol.

| | | | |
|---|---|---|---|
| **A** | rivière | **E** | ville |
| **B** | crêpes | **F** | magasins |
| **C** | excursions | **G** | ouvert |
| **D** | allemand | | |

[4 marks]

**Social and special events**

**A** Mon copain a bien aimé son steak frites, mais mon bœuf bourguignon était trop salé, et le service était trop lent.

**B** Les effets spéciaux étaient fantastiques mais les gens assis à côté ont passé tout le temps à manger des chips. On ne pouvait pas entendre le dialogue. C'était très énervant.

**C** J'ai vraiment eu de la chance. Quand j'ai vu les numéros que j'avais choisis apparaître sur l'écran j'étais très heureuse. Maintenant je peux faire un grand voyage.

**D** Les couleurs dans le ciel noir étaient magnifiques, mais quel bruit!

**E** On a passé une journée agréable à la campagne mais à dix kilomètres de Marseille la voiture est tombée en panne.

**F** Ma mère m'a fait un gâteau formidable avec quinze bougies dessus. On a chanté et j'ai reçu beaucoup de cadeaux.

Choose the correct description for the following events. Choose the correct letter for each.

**5a** A birthday party ☐ [1]

**5b** A firework display ☐ [1]

**5c** A meal out ☐ [1]

**5d** A visit to the cinema ☐ [1]

[4 marks]

**Environmental issues**

What do these people do for the environment? Choose the correct letter for the right sentence ending.

**Example :** Quand je me brosse les dents, je ferme... D

1. Chaque semaine je mets les déchets dans...
2. Quand je sors d'une pièce j'éteins toujours...
3. Quand je fais les courses je n'utilise jamais...

**A** ...les produits bio.
**B** ...des poubelles différentes.
**C** ...de sacs en plastique.
**D** ... le robinet.
**E** ...le jardin.
**F** ...la lumière.

Sentence 1 ☐

Sentence 2 ☐

Sentence 3 ☐ [3 marks]

**Family life**

| | |
|---|---|
| **A** | Il est très bavard et raconte souvent des histoires drôles. |
| **B** | En semaine il est rarement à la maison, mais le week-end je vais toujours au cinéma avec lui. |
| **C** | Il passe beaucoup de temps à faire ses devoirs, mais pour se détendre il aime regarder les comédies. |
| **D** | On ne le voit pas souvent à la maison, car il aime faire des randonnées à la campagne. |
| **E** | Il ne fait rien pour aider à la maison. Il préfère jouer aux jeux en ligne. |

Which member of his family is Martin describing? Choose the correct letter.

**7a** His father likes films but spends a lot of time away from home. ☐

**7b** His older brother is lazy and spends a lot of time on the internet. ☐

**7c** His younger brother talks a lot and has a good sense of humour. ☐

[3 marks]

**An audition**

Je m'appelle Mariama. J'habite dans la banlieue parisienne. J'adore toutes sortes de musique, sauf la musique classique. Je voudrais être chanteuse.

L'an dernier ma mère a vu une petite annonce. On cherchait des concurrents* pour une émission à la télévision. Le gagnant aurait un rôle dans une comédie musicale à Paris.

Le jour de mon audition j'ai dû attendre deux heures dans une queue d'une centaine d'autres concurrents qui espéraient comme moi être la prochaine vedette de l'émission. Nerveuse mais aussi très excitée j'étais le numéro cinquante.

Mon tour est enfin venu. Je suis entrée dans la salle des juges et j'ai commencé à chanter. Tout d'un coup, j'ai oublié mes paroles*. Je me suis arrêtée et j'ai commencé à pleurer. Je pensais que les juges allaient me parler sévèrement mais ils ont été très gentils. Je n'ai pas réussi l'audition mais c'était une bonne expérience quand même.

* concurrents – *competitors*
paroles – *words*

**8** Which four sentences are correct? Choose the correct letters.

| | |
|---|---|
| **A** | Mariama lives in the centre of Paris. |
| **B** | She doesn't like classical music. |
| **C** | There were about 50 people in the queue with her for the audition. |
| **D** | She was in a musical. |
| **E** | Her audition didn't go according to plan. |
| **F** | The judges were as she expected them to be. |
| **G** | The judges were sympathetic. |
| **H** | She took part in a talent show. |

☐ ☐ ☐ ☐

[4 marks]

**School life**

**Philippe**
J'ai quinze ans. J'adore le collège. Normalement j'y vais à pied mais quand il pleut ma mère m'y emmène en voiture. Je n'arrive jamais en retard.

Au collège je peux porter ce que je veux. À mon avis les maths sont importantes mais je ne trouve ça pas facile. Je préfère l'EPS. Par contre, Je n'aime pas tellement les jeux de ballon.

**Bertrand**
J'habite près du collège. Alors je peux me réveiller tard et arriver à l'heure! On n'utilise jamais la voiture. Je dois toujours porter un pantalon noir et une veste grise – c'est pratique! Ma matière préférée – c'est difficile à dire, mais je pense que c'est les maths. Hier je n'ai pas fait mes devoirs. Le collège me plaît beaucoup.

Choose the correct person. Write **P** (for Philippe) or **B** (for Bertrand).

| | |
|---|---|
| **9a** Who doesn't have to get up early to get to school on time? | |
| **9b** Who sometimes travels to school by car? | |
| **9c** Who finds maths difficult? | |
| **9d** Who wears a uniform to school? | |
| **9e** Who is a bit lazy? | |
| **9f** For whom is football not one of their favourite sports? | |

[6 marks]

## *Higher level*

Questions 1, 2 and 3 at this level are identical to questions 5, 8 and 9 on the Foundation paper

**Vegetarianism**

| | |
|---|---|
| Mathieu | Je pense qu'on ne peut plus justifier la production de céréales pour alimenter les animaux. On doit manger moins de viande. |
| Anaïs | Le choix de plats quand on mange au restaurant est limité. Pourtant je trouve que c'est moins cher quand on ne mange pas de viande. |
| Benjamin | Depuis deux ans je ne mange plus de viande. J'ai perdu cinq kilos et je me sens très bien. |
| Céline | À mon avis c'est un régime qui offre peu de variété. Des repas où on ne mange que des légumes, ce n'est pas pour moi. |
| Guillaume | On me dit que c'est un régime extrêmement bon pour la santé. Pourtant il manque des vitamines et minéraux essentiels, à mon avis. |

Are the writers for or against vegetarianism?

Write **P** if you think they have a positive attitude to this issue. Write **N** if you think they have a negative attitude. Write **P/N** if they have a mixed attitude.

**Example** Mathieu P

| | | | | | |
|---|---|---|---|---|---|
| **4a** | Anaïs | | **4c** | Céline | |
| **4b** | Benjamin | | **4d** | Guillaume | |

[4 marks]

**Environmental issues**

| | |
|---|---|
| **1** | Ces produits sont meilleurs pour l'environnement car on n'utilise pas de pesticides artificiels dans leur production. |
| **2** | J'ai peur de la fréquence des inondations et d'autres changements dûs à l'effet de serre. |
| **3** | Il y a la possibilité maintenant de sauvegarder les ressources de la planète en utilisant le vent, le soleil et les marées. |
| **4** | Pour passer des vacances responsables, on peut faire du camping et des randonnées au lieu d'aller dans des établissements de luxe. |

Choose a title for each paragraph. Choose the correct letter.

| | | | |
|---|---|---|---|
| **A** | Ecotourism | **D** | Recycling |
| **B** | Alternative energy | **E** | Deforestation |
| **C** | Organic food | **F** | Global warming |

**5a** Paragraph 1 ☐ **5c** Paragraph 3 ☐
**5b** Paragraph 2 ☐ **5d** Paragraph 4 ☐

[4 marks]

**A visit to a theme park**

Il y a un mois Magali Bréban a visité le Parc Astérix avec ses parents. Le matin, ils sont partis de bonne heure parce qu'ils voulaient éviter les longues queues pour les attractions les plus populaires.

Ce jour-là pourtant il y avait un embouteillage à cause d'un accident sur l'autoroute. Alors ils ont dû prendre une route moins directe, ce qui a prolongé leur trajet d'une heure.

Une fois arrivé au parc, Monsieur Bréban a découvert qu'il avait laissé son portefeuille à la maison. Heureusement, sa femme n'avait pas oublié le sien! Magali voulait absolument essayer le **Tonnerre de Zeus**, la plus grande montagne russe* en bois d'Europe. Elle l'avait aperçue de l'autre côté du lac. Mais elle n'avait pas remarqué que les petits trains ne bougeaient pas – ce qui était évident quand elle est arrivée au point de départ et qu'elle a vu la grande affiche qui disait «En cours de rénovation».

* montagne russe – *rollercoaster*

Read the following sentences.
If you think the sentence is true, write **T**.
If you think the sentence is false, write **F**.
If you think the information is not in the text, write **?** .

**6a** Magali and her parents were involved in a car accident. ☐
**6b** They arrived at the park at the time they intended. ☐
**6c** Magali's mother paid for the tickets. ☐
**6d** Magali was not very observant. ☐
**6e** They had to queue for many rides. ☐
**6f** Magali was able to do everything she wanted to do. ☐

[6 marks]

**Drinking habits**

J'ai commencé à boire à l'âge de treize **[1]**. Au début, c'était le **[2]** du cidre qui me plaisait, mais peu à peu j'ai commencé à le boire pour les **[3]**. Maintenant je bois des mélanges avec mes copains au **[4]** car nous ne sommes pas assez âgés pour aller au bar.

Mes copains disent que je suis dépendant car je ne peux pas **[5]** sans alcool. Si mes parents savaient ce que je faisais ils m'empêcheraient de **[6]** ce mode de vie.

| | | | |
|---|---|---|---|
| **A** | maison | **E** | effets |
| **B** | verres | **F** | poursuivre |
| **C** | ans | **G** | goût |
| **D** | vivre | **H** | parc |

Choose a word from the grid to fill each of the gaps and choose the correct letter for each.

**Example:** 1 C

| | | | | | |
|---|---|---|---|---|---|
| **7a** | 2 | | **7d** | 5 | |
| **7b** | 3 | | **7e** | 6 | |
| **7c** | 4 | | | | |

[5 marks]

### A study trip

Salut, je m'appelle Gabriel et j'habite à Genève en Suisse. Il y a trois mois j'ai fait un stage de langue à Cologne pour perfectionner mon allemand. Je n'apprenais la langue que depuis six mois alors j'avais peur de ne rien comprendre. En plus c'était la première fois que je voyageais à l'étranger sans mes parents.

Les premiers jours ont été vraiment durs. Je logeais chez une famille qui habitait assez loin de l'école. Il me fallait faire un trajet en bus, seul, qui durait normalement trois quarts d'heure. La famille était très sympathique mais tout était nouveau pour moi, surtout la nourriture et les repas.

Cependant le stage – ce qu'on nous a enseigné pendant les cours – était vraiment utile et pratique. Je peux communiquer maintenant avec n'importe qui et je pourrais même trouver un petit travail en Allemagne si je le voulais. C'était obligatoire de parler uniquement l'allemand, et si on parlait une autre langue on devait payer une petite amende! J'ai trouvé cette immersion totale super car je ne suis pas du tout timide, mais pour les étudiants qui manquent d'assurance c'était un cauchemar*! L'an prochain j'irai peut-être en Espagne pour faire un stage semblable.

* cauchemar – *nightmare*

Answer the questions in English.

**8** **(i)** Why was Gabriel a little anxious about this trip before his departure? Give two details. [2 marks]

**8** **(ii)** What difficulties did he experience initially? Give two details [2 marks]

**8** **(iii)** What was he forced to do in lessons? [1 mark]

**8** **(iv)** What particular advantage does he personally feel he has gained from the course? [1 mark]

**8** **(v)** What kind of students would find themselves out of pocket on the course? [1 mark]

**8** **(vi)** What does Gabriel plan to do next year? [1 mark]

### Interview with a wildlife guide in Cameroon

*Alors Njamela, vous travaillez où?*

À Waza, un parc national dans l'extrême nord du Cameroun. Ce n'est pas comme les autres grandes réserves africaines au Kenya ou en Afrique du Sud où on est presque certain de voir des animaux comme des lions sans faire aucun effort, mais Waza offre quand même une grande variété de faune et de végétation, y compris des lions!

**9a** How does the park at Waza compare with game reserves elsewhere in Africa according to Njamela? Give **two** details. [2 marks]

*Parlez-moi des visiteurs qui viennent.*

Je dirais que la majorité vient du Cameroun et des pays voisins, mais on en accueille aussi quelques-uns d'Europe, surtout de France. Il y en a qui sont presque des experts. Ils savent beaucoup de choses: ils ont peut-être visité des parcs ailleurs et cherchent une expérience différente, mais il y en a beaucoup d'autres qui feraient mieux de rester chez eux. Ce sont ceux qui ne comprennent pas qu'il faut respecter les animaux. Il est tout de même évident qu'il faut s'habiller en couleurs neutres et qu'il ne faut pas pousser des cris soudains quand on prend des photos.

**9b** What kind of visitor is Njamela happy to welcome to Waza? Give **two** details. [2 marks]

## Speaking – Unit 3

- There are 60 marks for the speaking assessment (30% of the total GCSE marks).
- You have to do two tasks under controlled conditions.
- Both tasks will be in the form of a dialogue, e.g. conversation or interview.
- You are not allowed to do the same task for both speaking and writing.
- Each task will last between 4 and 6 minutes and may be recorded. You are allowed to prepare for the tasks and to use a dictionary in the preparation. However, you are not allowed to use a dictionary when you are actually doing the task itself.
- The tasks are marked by your teacher and moderated by the exam board.
- Each task is marked for the following:
  1. Communication (the content of what you say) – 15 marks
  2. Range and accuracy of language (Do you use a variety of vocabulary and structures? Is what you say correct or are there mistakes?) – 10 marks
  3. Pronunciation and Intonation (How French do you sound?) – 5 marks
  4. Interaction and Fluency (How responsive are you? Do you hesitate?) – 5 marks

## Examples of assessment tasks

**Example 1: Context: Home and Environment – interview**

You are part of a team on a visit to your twinned town/village. You are trying to persuade more young people from that town to visit your town and are being interviewed. Your teacher will play the part of the interviewer. He/She will ask you:

- Who you are and what your role is
- What kind of town/village you come from
- What the main attractions are
- Why young people should visit
- What are the advantages/disadvantages of living there
- What the transport links are like

- How it compares with other towns/areas
- ! (You will have to respond to something you have not prepared)

**Example 2: Context: Cross context: Home and Environment/ Leisure/Lifestyle – conversation**

You have just arrived at your exchange partner's home. You are being shown around the house and are settling in after the journey. Your teacher will play the part of your exchange partner. He/She will ask you:

- What your journey was like
- How your home compares to his/hers
- What your family is like
- What you want to see/do during your stay
- Whether there is anything you don't like to eat/drink
- What kinds of programmes you like watching on TV
- What you've done recently in your free time
- ! (You will have to respond to something you have not prepared)

**Example 3: Context: Lifestyle – interview**

You have taken part in a sporting event in France/Switzerland/ Belgium, etc. and are being interviewed after the event. Your teacher will play the part of the interviewer. He/She will ask you:

- Who you are (personal details)
- What your training regime is like
- Why you chose this sport
- How your family/school/club has supported you
- What your experience of previous sporting competitions is
- What you think of the benefit/importance of international sporting events and why
- What you think of the importance of diet and a healthy lifestyle and why
- ! (You will have to respond to something you have not prepared)

**Example 4: Context: Leisure – interview**

You have taken part in a music tour in France/Switzerland/ Belgium, etc. and are being interviewed after the event. Your teacher will play the part of the interviewer. He/She will ask you:

- Who you are (personal details)
- What your practice regime is like
- Why you chose a particular instrument
- How your family/school/orchestra/band has supported you
- What was your experience of previous musical events and your opinion of them
- What your plans for future tours/concerts are and why
- What you think the benefit/importance of international musical events is and why
- ! (You will have to respond to something you have not prepared)

**Example 5: Context: Cross context: Leisure/Home and Environment – interview**

Whilst visiting your partner school you are interviewed about an unusual festival or event from your home town/village or country. Your teacher will play the part of the interviewer. He/She will ask you:

- Where you are from
- What the event/festival is like
- What types of people come to the event/festival and why
- What your personal experience of or involvement in the event/festival is
- What the future plans for the event/festival are
- What the problems/benefits associated with the event/ festival are
- What you think the value of such events/festivals is and why
- ! (You will have to respond to something you have not prepared)

**Example 6: Context: Leisure – conversation**

You are travelling around Europe and are staying in a youth hostel in France/Switzerland, etc. and strike up a conversation with another traveller in which you compare notes. Your teacher will play the part of the other traveller. He/She will ask you:

- Who you are/where you are from
- How you are travelling/with whom
- Why you have come to this particular hostel/town
- What you think of it and why
- What were the best/worst moments of your travels so far and why
- What your experiences of previous trips/plans for future trips are
- ! (You will have to respond to something you have not prepared)

**Example 7: Context: Work and Education – interview**

You have applied to do work experience in France/Switzerland, etc. and have been called to interview. Your teacher will play the part of the interviewer. He/She will ask you:

- Who you are (personal details)
- Why you want this work experience
- Why you are qualified for this work experience
- What you can offer
- What your previous experience of work is
- How this work experience can benefit your long term plans
- What you think the advantages/disadvantages of work experience are
- ! (You will have to respond to something you have not prepared)

## Writing – Unit 4

- There are 60 marks for the writing assessment – 30% of the total GCSE marks.
- You have to do two tasks under controlled conditions. Each task must be of a different type to ensure that you use language for a different purpose (e.g. letter, report, story, interview, blog entry, article, etc). The tasks may be based on the contexts below or your teacher may devise a task based on a context relating to your personal interest:
  Context 1 Lifestyle
  Context 2 Leisure
  Context 3 Home and Environment
  Context 4 Work and Education
- Research for the task may take place outside the classroom and you are allowed access to the internet, coursebooks and dictionaries. You are allowed to use a dictionary during the test itself.

- You are allowed no more than 60 minutes for writing the final version of the task.
- If you are aiming for grades A*–C you must write 400–600 words across the two tasks and for grades D–G you must write 200–350 words.

## Examples of assessment tasks

**Example 1: Context 3: Home and Environment – letter**

You and your family are planning to buy a second home in France. You write a letter to an estate agent explaining your requirements. The following are some ideas as to what you could include:

**Grades G–E**

- Who you are and why you are writing
- The location you are looking for and why
- The type of accommodation you are looking for
- When you would be able to view properties

**Grades D–C**

- More detailed information about the type of property you are looking for
- Why you want to live in that particular area
- Previous experience of the area

**Grades B–A***

- Problems that you might encounter
- What you would not consider and why
- How you might contribute to the local community

**Example 2: Context 1: Lifestyle – report**

You have been to the Good Food Show. You send an email about it to your exchange partner or write an account of it on your blog. You could include:

**Grades G–E**

- Who you are
- Your favourite foods and why
- Where/when/with whom you are
- What you see/eat/buy and your opinion about it

**Grades D–C**

- A description of a cooking demonstration
- What you have done/bought/eaten as a result of the show
- Something unusual you saw/tasted/bought

**Grades B–A***

- Your opinion of the value of such events – suggestions for improvement
- The importance of healthy eating and the dangers of poor diet
- Your opinion of celebrity chefs

Note this could also be an event to do with cars/music/gardens, etc.

**Example 3: Context 2: Leisure and entertainment – article**

You have taken part in an online chat forum discussing a book. You are now writing an article about it.

**Grades G–E**

- Some basic information such as title, genre, author
- Description of main character(s)
- Simple account of the plot
- Your opinion

**Grades D–C**

- More detailed descriptions of characters/plot/opinion
- Information about the author
- What you liked/disliked about it and why

**Grades B–A***

- Comparison with other books by the same author
- Why reading is important
- Comparison of book with the film version

Note this could also be about a film/TV programme/concert/play, etc.

**Example 4: Context 2: Leisure – report**

You have been to a festival (music/religious/cultural) in France/Switzerland etc. You write an account of it on your blog.

**Grades G–E**

- Where you are/when/why
- Description of the festival – what you can see/do
- Your accommodation – what's good/bad and why
- Your opinion of the festival – would you return?

**Grades D–C**

- Where you went/when/why
- What you saw/did
- The journey there/back
- The people you met

**Grades B–A***

- Whether you would recommend this event to a friend
- The value of such events

**Example 5: Cross context: Leisure/Home and Environment/Work and Education – letter**

You have returned from an exchange visit and are writing a letter to thank your exchange partner and his/her family.

**Grades G–E**

- Why you are writing
- What you liked in general about your stay
- A specific incident you liked/disliked and why
- What you have been doing since your return
- Your plans for the next few days

**Grades D–C**

- Your journey home
- Your definite plans for your exchange partner's return visit

**Grades B–A***

- Some suggestions for his/her return visit
- What you found most useful about the exchange and why
- Your impressions of your exchange partner's school/town/home/region, etc.
- The value of exchanges

# Grammar Bank

## 1 Nouns

Nouns are words that name a person, place, animal or thing – e.g. doctor, table, brother, cat. You know a word is a noun when you can put 'the' or 'a' before it.

In French all nouns are either masculine or feminine (this is called **gender**), and the words for 'the' or 'a' can be different, depending on their **gender**.

| | indefinite article | definite article |
|---|---|---|
| masculine | *un* | *le / l'* |
| feminine | *une* | *la / l'* |
| masc. & pl. | *des* | *les* |
| fem. & pl. | *des* | *les* |

### Masculine or feminine?

If you look a noun up in the dictionary, it will give the gender – *m* or *f* – after the word.

There are other clues to help you figure out the gender of nouns, e.g.:

**masculine** days, months, seasons
languages
weights and measures
many words ending in *-c, -é, -eau, -ou, -eur*

**feminine** most (but not all) words ending in *-e*
names of rivers
types of shops

**A Spot the nouns, then write their gender.**

1 Lucie
2 stylo
3 au revoir
4 j'habite
5 grand
6 anglaise
7 cinq
8 donné
9 boucherie
10 elle s'appelle

**B Write the correct word for 'the' (*le, la, l'* or *les*).**

1 maison *(house)*
2 parc *(park)*
3 rues *(streets)*
4 frère *(brother)*
5 collège *(school)*
6 magasins *(shops)*

**C Write the correct word for 'a' (*un* or *une*).**

1 appartement *(flat)*
2 gare *(station)*
3 piscine *(swimming pool)*
4 ville *(town)*
5 musée *(museum)*
6 jardin *(garden)*

### Plurals

Most plural nouns end in *-s*, as in English. However, some nouns have irregular plural endings:

| Singular | Plural | Example |
|---|---|---|
| *-al* | *-aux* | *journal / journaux* |
| *-ou* | *-oux* | *genou / genoux* |
| *-eau* | *-eaux* | *manteau / manteaux* |
| *-s* | *-s* | *bras / bras** |
| *-x* | *-x* | *prix / prix** |

* Note that these nouns don't change in the plural.

**D Write the plural form of these nouns.**

1 cadeau
2 animal
3 dos
4 chien
5 croix
6 chou
7 pied
8 gâteau
9 cheval
10 oiseau

## 2 Verbs

Verbs are words that describe an **action** or a **state**. They are sometimes referred to as 'doing words' because many describe what someone or something **does** or **is doing**: I **watch** TV.
You **like** school.
She **is talking**.

Verbs can be **regular** (they follow a set pattern) or **irregular** (they have their own rule).

When you find a verb in the dictionary, you will always find it in its **infinitive** form. This is the original part of the verb that has not been changed in any way, and it usually translates into English as 'to ...' – e.g. *dormir* – to sleep.

All infinitive verbs in French end in *-er, -ir* or *-re*. Removing these endings leaves the **stem** of the verb.

**A Match the following infinitives with their English meaning, then write their stem.**

1 *écouter*
2 *travailler*
3 *finir*
4 *danser*
5 *attendre*
6 *parler*
7 *courir*
8 *habiter*
9 *manger*
10 *vendre*

A to live
B to wait
C to listen
D to sell
E to eat
F to dance
G to run
H to work
I to speak
J to finish

## 3 The present tense

This tense is used when describing something that someone (usually) does or is doing **now**. For example:

*je regarde la télé* I watch / am watching TV

### Formation

To form the present tense of **regular** verbs:

- begin with the **infinitive**
- remove the *-er, -ir,* or *-re* ending – you now have the **stem**
- now add the **present tense endings**. The ending you use depends on the **subject**: who or what is doing the action described.

The present tense endings for **regular** verbs are:

| | **-er** (e.g. ***parler***) | **-ir** (e.g. ***finir***) | **-re** (e.g. ***vendre***) |
|---|---|---|---|
| *je* | *-e* | *-is* | *-s* |
| *tu* | *-es* | *-is* | *-s* |
| *il / elle / on* | *-e* | *-it* | --- |
| *nous* | *-ons* | *-issons* | *-ons* |
| *vous* | *-ez* | *-issez* | *-ez* |
| *ils / elles* | *-ent* | *-issent* | *-ent* |

You can find the present tense of **irregular** verbs in the verb tables on pages 195–196. Even irregular verbs have some patterns – usually it's just the stem that is irregular, with many of the endings the same as for regular verbs.

**A Complete these regular present tense verbs, and translate.**

*Example:* **1** je (parler)
*je parle – I speak / am speaking*

1 je (parler)
2 il (finir)
3 nous (aimer)
4 ils (attendre)
5 elle (descendre)
6 vous (continuer)
7 tu (grossir)
8 elle (vendre)
9 je (répondre)
10 nous (choisir)

## 4 Negative forms

To make verbs negative in the present tense, use:

- ***ne*** + verb + ***pas***
  *Je **ne** regarde **pas*** — I'm not watching
- ***ne*** + verb + ***plus***
  *Je **ne** regarde **plus*** — I'm not watching any more
- ***ne*** + verb + ***personne***
  *Je **ne** regarde **personne*** — I'm not watching anyone
- ***ne*** + verb + ***jamais***
  *Je **ne** regarde **jamais** (la télévision)* — I never watch (television)

**ATTENTION!**

Remember to use ***de*** after a negative to mean 'any':
*Nous n'avons pas **de** lait.* We don't have **any** milk.

**A Write these regular and irregular verbs in the present tense and the negative form, then translate.**

*Example:* **1** tu (finir)
*je ne finis pas* I don't finish / am not finishing

1 tu (finir)
2 elle (aimer)
3 vous (attendre)
4 vous (croire)
5 elle (connaître)
6 nous (écrire)
7 nous (répondre)
8 vous (continuer)
9 tu (grossir)
10 il (savoir)
11 elles (devoir)
12 nous (choisir)

**B Translate into French.**

*Example:* **1** we never visit *nous ne visitons jamais*

1 we never visit
2 they (masc.) don't eat cheese
3 she doesn't play football
4 we never buy any flowers
5 you (pl.) don't like anyone
6 you (sing.) don't live in London any more
7 he never goes shopping
8 it never arrives at 9 o'clock
9 they (fem.) don't work any more
10 I'm not waiting for anyone

## 5 Reflexive verbs

Reflexive verbs describe actions that are usually done to oneself. They have ***se*** before the infinitive. This is called the **reflexive pronoun**, and it changes depending on who is doing the action.

| ***se coucher*** | **to go to bed** |
|---|---|
| *je **me** couche* | I go to bed |
| *tu **te** couches* | you go to bed |
| *il / elle / on **se** couche* | he / she / one goes / we go to bed |
| *nous **nous** couchons* | we go to bed |
| *vous **vous** couchez* | you go bed |
| *ils / elles **se** couchent* | they go to bed |

Note that, before vowels and most verbs starting with 'h', the reflexive pronouns *me*, *te* and *se* are abbreviated to *m', t', s'.* Other useful reflexive verbs include: *se laver* (to wash oneself), *se réveiller* (to wake up), *s'appeler* (to 'call oneself' – i.e. 'my name is ...'), *se doucher* (to shower), *s'habiller* (to get dressed).

### Negative

To make reflexive verbs negative in the present tense, use:

***ne*** + reflexive pronoun + verb + ***pas***

*Je **ne** me couche **pas** avant dix heures*

**A Write the correct present tense form of each reflexive verb.**

1 Vous ............... à quelle heure? (se doucher)
2 Nous ............... vite. (se laver)
3 Je ............... avant de manger. (s'habiller)
4 Mes parents ............... Paul et Marie. (s'appeler)
5 Caroline ............... tard le matin. (se lever)
6 Thomas ............... à minuit. (se coucher)

**N.B.** *pas* always comes immediately after the verb, before an adverb or the rest of the phrase.

**B Make these sentences negative using *ne...pas*.**

1. Il se douche rapidement.
2. Nous nous levons à huit heures.
3. Elle se réveille tôt.
4. Je me couche vers onze heures.
5. Tu t'appelles Sandrine?
6. Elle se déguise en sorcière.

## 6 Modal verbs: *pouvoir, devoir, savoir, vouloir*

The verbs *pouvoir* (to be able to), *vouloir* (to want), *devoir* (to have to) and *savoir* (to know how to) indicate whether you can, must, know how, or want to do something. They are almost always followed by the infinitive of another verb.

***Tu peux sortir** demain soir?*
Can you go out tomorrow evening?

***Nous voulons** faire du surf.*
We want to go surfing.

***Elle doit faire** ses devoirs avant de sortir.*
She has to do her homework before going out.

***Il sait nager.***
He can/knows how to swim.

***Ils savant parler** le français.*
They can/know how to speak French.

Note that modal verbs are used in the conditional to be polite, e.g.
***Je voudrais** des renseignements sur la région s'il vous plaît.*
is more polite than
***Je veux** des renseignements sur la région s'il vous plaît.*

See the full pattern of these verbs on pages 195–196.

**A Insert an appropriate modal verb (*pouvoir, vouloir, savoir* or *devoir*) in the present tense to complete the sentences.**

1. _____-tu parler l'allemand?
2. Je _____ leur parler quand je _____.
3. Les jeunes _____ faire attention de ne pas passer trop de temps dans un monde virtuel.
4. Vous _____ faire ce que vous _____ après avoir fait vos devoirs.
5. Ma petite sœur _____ lire et écrire maintenant.
6. On ne _____ jamais inscrire son adresse sur Facebook.

**B Translate the following sentences into French using modal verbs.**

1. My brother can drive now.
2. Are you (*tu*) allowed to watch television after school?
3. I can't go out as I must do my homework.
4. Young people must be careful when they use Facebook.
5. You (*vous*) can email your friends whenever you want to.
6. We want to be healthy so we must eat lots of fruit and vegetables.
7. She doesn't know where she wants to go on holiday.

## 7 Adjectives

Adjectives are words that **describe nouns**: e.g. a **black** hat. They can be used even when the noun is not present in the sentence: e.g. It's **black**.

### Position

Unlike in English, most adjectives in French go **after** the noun they describe: e.g. a **black** hat = *un chapeau **noir***.

However, a few very common adjectives come **before** the noun. These include:

| | |
|---|---|
| *petit / grand* | small / big |
| *bon / mauvais* | good / bad |
| *nouveau / ancien* | new / former |
| *jeune / vieux* | young / old |
| *beau* | beautiful, nice |
| *autre* | other |

### Formation

Adjectives change their form according to the **gender** of the noun (see **Nouns** on page 181), and according to their **number** – i.e. whether they are singular or plural. Noun and adjective are said to 'agree'. They must agree wherever the adjective is in the sentence:

*une chaise vert**e***   *la chaise est **verte***

Most adjectives change their form in a regular way.
To make regular adjectives agree with nouns:

- add nothing if the noun is masculine
e.g. *un chapeau noir*
- add -*e* if the noun is feminine
e.g. *une robe noir**e***
- add -*s* if the noun is masculine and plural
e.g. *des gants noir**s***
- add -*es* if the noun is both feminine and plural
e.g. *des chaussures noir**es***

However, adjectives that already end in -*e* or -*s* don't add an extra -*e* or -*s* in the feminine or plural forms:

*ma chambre est rouge et mes pantalons sont gris*

**A Put the adjective in the correct form and place.**

*Example: une maison (nouveau) → une nouvelle maison*

1. un crayon (bleu)
2. deux chansons (bon)
3. un ballon (rouge et noir)
4. un ordinateur (grand)
5. des repas (traditionnel)
6. le livre (vieux)
7. la rue (beau)
8. le temps (bon)
9. ma sœur (grand)
10. deux chambres (double)

**B Rewrite, choosing the correct form of the adjective.**

1. Lucie est grand / grande.
2. Ma sœur est petit / petite.
3. J'ai une très grand / grande chambre.
4. Les rues sont étroits / étroites.
5. J'habite une vieux / vieille maison.
6. Elle a de beaux / belles chaussures.
7. L'eau est froid / froide.
8. Nous avons une nouveau / nouvelle voiture.
9. Ma copine Julie est jeune / jeunes.
10. Ma chaise est trop bas / basse.

**ATTENTION!**

Adjectives ending in the following groups of letters have a slightly different form in the feminine singular and feminine plural:

| ending | change (fem.)* | example |
|---|---|---|
| *-eux / -eur* | *-euse* | *heureux / heureuse* |
| *-il / -el* | *-ille / -elle* | *gentil / gentille* |
| *-ien* | *-ienne* | *italien / italienne* |
| *-er* | *-ère* | *cher / chère* |
| *-aux* | *-ausse* | *faux / fausse* |
| *-f* | *-ve* | *actif / active* |
| *-s* | *-sse* | *gros / grosse* |

*For the feminine plural form, just add an *s* to the endings.

A very small number of adjectives are irregular and follow their own pattern:

| masculine | masculine plural | feminine | feminine plural |
|---|---|---|---|
| *beau* | *beaux* | *belle* | *belles* |
| *nouveau* | *nouveaux* | *nouvelle* | *nouvelles* |
| *vieux* | *vieux* | *vieille* | *vieilles* |

Note that the masculine forms of these adjectives change if they come before vowels or the letter 'h': *un* ***bel*** *homme, le* ***Nouvel*** *An, mon* ***vieil*** *ami.*

**C Decide on the correct form of the adjective in brackets.**

1. Mes frères sont (actif).
2. Ma tante est assez (sportif).
3. Ma famille est (ennuyeux).
4. Voici mes sœurs. Elles sont (gentil).
5. Les (nouveau) magasins sont dans cette rue.
6. Sa chemise est (blanc).
7. Tu as mangé la (dernier) tarte aux pommes?
8. Ma cousine n'est pas (gros).
9. La réponse est (faux).
10. Mes parents sont (paresseux).

## 8 Possessive adjectives

Possessive adjectives are used to show to whom or what something belongs:

| | | |
|---|---|---|
| **my** jacket | **his** book | **their** family |
| ***ma*** *veste* | ***son*** *livre* | ***leur*** *famille* |

In French there are different forms of possessive adjectives, depending on the noun they describe:

| | masculine | feminine | plural |
|---|---|---|---|
| my | *mon** | *ma* | *mes* |
| your (sing.) | *ton** | *ta* | *tes* |
| his / her / its | *son** | *sa* | *ses* |
| our | *notre* | *notre* | *nos* |
| your (plural) | *votre* | *votre* | *vos* |
| their | *leur* | *leur* | *leurs* |

* *Mon / ton / son* are also used for feminine nouns that begin with a vowel – e.g. *mon émission préférée.*

**A Rewrite, choosing the correct possessive adjective.**

1. Mon / Mes parents sont stricts.
2. Ses / Sa tante est assez jolie.
3. Dans notre / nos jardin il y a beaucoup de fleurs.
4. Leur / Leurs temps est perdu.
5. Quelle est la date de ton / ta arrivée?
6. Voici mes / ma famille.
7. Ses / Son chemisier est trop grand.
8. Qui a bu ma / mon limonade?
9. Mon / Ma cousine est arrivée en retard.
10. Où sont votre / vos livres?

**B Translate into French.**

1. his friend
2. our feet
3. my job
4. her sister
5. his favourite sport
6. your (sing.) Italian grandmother
7. their little brother
8. our old house
9. my new car
10. his white trainers

## 9 Comparative and superlative adjectives

Adjectives can be used to **compare** things with each other – e.g. I'm **tall** (adjective), a giraffe is **taller** (comparative), the Eiffel Tower is **the tallest** (superlative). In French, the comparative and superlative are formed in the following way:

| | | | |
|---|---|---|---|
| **comparative – more** | *plus* | *elle est* ***plus*** *grande* | she's taller |
| **– less** | *moins* | *elle est* ***moins*** *grande* | she's less tall |
| **superlative – most** | *le / la / les plus* | *c'est* ***la plus*** *petite* | she's the smallest |
| **– least** | *le / la / les moins* | *c'est* ***la moins*** *petite* | she's the least small |

To say something is, for example, bigger or smaller than something else, use ***plus / moins*** ... ***que*** – e.g. he is smaller than me = *il est* ***plus*** *petit* ***que*** *moi.*

To say something is, for example, as big or as small as something else, use ***aussi* ... *que*** – e.g. she is as tall as her brother = *elle est* ***aussi*** *grande* ***que*** *son frère.*

**ATTENTION!**

The comparative and superlative of *bon* (good) is formed differently:

| | comparative | superlative |
|---|---|---|
| *bon(s) / bonne(s)* | *meilleur(e)(s)* (better) | *le / la / les meilleur(e)(s)* (best) |

**A** Translate into English.

1 Lucie est plus grande que Charlotte.
2 Ahmet est aussi intelligent que Julie.
3 Théo est plus petit que Lucas.
4 Flore est la plus intéressante de la classe.
5 Maxime et Paul sont les moins sérieux.
6 Enzo est le meilleur de la classe.

**B** Translate into French.

1 My town is smaller than Lille.
2 Lille is more interesting than Calais.
3 Calais is less quiet than Nice.
4 Nice is as touristy as Marseille.
5 Marseille is the least popular city.
6 Paris is the best!

## 10 The pronoun y

*y* is a very common **pronoun**: a word used instead of a noun. It literally means 'there'. It always goes before all parts of the verb:

*J'adore aller au cinéma. J'**y** vais ce week-end.*
I love going to the cinema. I'm going **there** this weekend.

**ATTENTION!**

If the verb comes in two parts and contains an infinitive, *y* always goes **before the infinitive**:

*Je vais **y** aller ce soir.* I'm going **there** this evening.
*J'aime Paris. On peut **y** visiter le Louvre.*
I love Paris. You can visit the Louvre **there**.

**A** Re-order the sentences, then translate.

1 va on y?
2 on dans ma peut au ville parc aller
3 y peux ne ce je aller pas soir
4 habiter Mathieu voudrait un jour y
5 dernier allé le j' suis week-end y
6 huit je arriver y vais heures vers

## 11 Prepositions – à

Prepositions usually indicate the **position** of places or things. The preposition *à* means 'to' or 'at'. It can also mean 'in' when referring to a town or city.

When *à* comes before *le* in a sentence, the two words combine to make *au*. When *à* meets *les* in a sentence, they combine to make *aux*:

*je vais **au** cinéma* *tournez à gauche **aux** feux*

**A** Insert *à, au, à la, à l'* or *aux*.

1 J'habite .......... Londres.
2 Ce week-end, je vais aller.......... théâtre.
3 J'habite .......... bout de la rue.
4 Traversez la rue .......... feux.
5 J'aime aller .......... piscine.
6 Il travaille .......... hôtel de ville.

## 12 Imperatives

The imperative is used to give commands, instructions or directions.

### Formation

To form the imperative, use the *tu* or *vous* form of the verb in the present tense, but **without** the **pronouns** *tu* and *vous*. In the case of *-er* verbs, drop the final *-s* for the *tu* form.

| | |
|---|---|
| *Lis ton livre!* | Read your book! (sing.) |
| *Mangez!* | Eat! (plural) |
| *Regarde le tableau!* | Look at the board! |

**ATTENTION!**

When using reflexive verbs as imperatives, you replace the **reflexive** pronoun with an **emphatic** one (either ***toi*** or ***vous***). This is placed **after** the verb, to which it is joined by a hyphen.

| | |
|---|---|
| *assieds-**toi**!* | sit down! (sing.) |
| *asseyez-**vous**!* | sit down! (plural) |

**A** Give the following instructions in both the *tu* and *vous* form.

1 Tourner à gauche.
2 Aller jusqu'au bout de la rue.
3 Traverser le pont.
4 Continuer tout droit.
5 Monter la colline.

**B** Give the following instructions in French.

1 Wash the plates! (sing.)
2 Have a shower! (sing.)
3 Go to bed! (plural)
4 Go down the stairs! (sing.)
5 Hurry up! (plural)

## 13 Subject pronouns

A **pronoun** is a word that replaces a noun – e.g. using 'she' instead of 'my sister', or 'they' instead of 'the cats'.

Subject pronouns replace nouns that are doing an action and therefore always need a verb after them.

There are two types of subject pronoun:

- **definite pronouns** – these replace a specific noun, e.g. Thomas, I, you, it. The definite pronouns in French are: *je, tu, il, elle, nous, vous, ils* and *elles*.
- **indefinite pronouns** – these have a more general meaning. The indefinite pronouns in French are: *on* (we/you/one/people), *il* (it), *quelqu'un* (someone) and *ce* (it, as in *c'est*).

**A Which subject pronoun would you use to ...**

1 talk to your friend Lucie?
2 write to a company asking for a job?
3 talk to your parents?
4 write about your family?
5 describe your brother?
6 give a speech to a group of people?

**B Which subject pronoun would you use in the gaps?**

1 ...... habite à Barcelone. (mon copain)
2 ...... travaillent dans une banque. (Charlotte et Ali)
3 ...... sommes espagnols. (moi et toi)
4 ...... suis assez sportif. (moi)
5 ...... parle anglais en Angleterre. (en général)
6 ...... avez vos livres? (toi et ta copine)

## 14 The perfect tense

This tense is used to describe a **completed** action in the past. It is the most commonly used past tense.

*j'ai regardé la télé* I watched TV

The perfect tense has two parts:

the **present tense** of either *avoir* or *être* + the **past participle** of the verb describing the event

### The past participle

The past participle is usually formed as follows:

- *-er* verbs: remove *-er* and add **-é**
  e.g. *j'ai regardé un film*
- *-ir* verbs: remove the *-r*
  e.g. *j'ai fini mes devoirs*
- *-re* verbs: remove the *-re* and add **-u**
  e.g. *j'ai attendu le bus*

**ATTENTION!**

Irregular verbs form their past participles in a different way – e.g. *boire – bu, dire – dit*. See the verb tables on pages 195–196.

### *Être* or *avoir*?

Most verbs use *avoir* in the perfect tense – e.g. *j'ai parlé*.

However, a small group of verbs use *être* in the perfect tense. These verbs are very common and ten of these also form pairs of opposites.

| | | | |
|---|---|---|---|
| ***aller*** | to go | ***venir*** | to come |
| ***arriver*** | to arrive | ***partir*** | to leave |
| ***entrer*** | to go in | ***sortir*** | to go out |
| ***monter*** | to go up | ***descendre*** | to go down |
| ***naître*** | to be born | ***mourir*** | to die |

and

***rester*** to stay ***retourner*** to come back ***tomber*** to fall

**Reflexive verbs** also use *être* (see **Reflexive verbs** on page 182) in the perfect tense. The **reflexive pronoun** goes before the part of the verb *être*:

*il **s'**est couché*
*je **me** suis réveillé*

**ATTENTION!**

With all *être* verbs in the perfect tense, the past participle agrees with the gender of the person or thing that completed the action (the subject). Add *-e* to the past participle, for a feminine subject; add *-s* if it is plural; and add *-es* if it is both feminine and plural:

*Mélissa est sorti**e**.*
*Mes frères sont allé**s** au parc.*
*Claire et Sophie se sont couché**es**.*

**A Complete these perfect tense verbs with the correct part of *avoir* or *être*.**

1 je ........... allé
2 il ........... tombé
3 elle ........... resté
4 vous ........... aidé
5 tu ........... arrivé?
6 Mon copain ........... mangé un sandwich.
7 Mes deux sœurs ........... allées au collège.
8 Maëlle ........... venue chez moi.
9 J'........... aimé le film.
10 Elle ........... regardé le match de rugby.

### Negative

To make verbs negative in the perfect tense, use:

***ne*** + *avoir* or *être* + ***pas*** + past participle

*je **n'**ai **pas** regardé* I didn't look
*il **ne** s'est **pas** couché* he didn't go to bed

Note how, in reflexive verbs, *ne* goes **before** the reflexive pronoun (*me, te, se* ...).

**B Complete these sentences using the past participle of the verb in brackets, then translate.**

1 Elle a .......... du jogging. (faire)
2 Mon père n'a pas .......... (comprendre)
3 Elles ont .......... la table. (mettre)
4 J'ai .......... une carte postale. (écrire)
5 As-tu .......... tes devoirs? (faire)
6 Ma mère a .......... son livre. (lire)
7 Nous avons .......... le bus. (prendre)
8 Élise a .......... son amie à la gare. (voir)
9 Mahmoud a .......... une bonne note. (avoir)
10 Je n'ai pas .......... de carte de Noël. (recevoir)

**C Unjumble the following sentences containing reflexive verbs in the perfect tense, then translate.**

1 mes sont se réveillés neuf parents heures à
2 se levés tard plus ils sont
3 ce je suis me à sept levée matin heures
4 me lavé suis je
5 ma s' levée tard sœur est
6 elle douchée s' tout suite de est
7 me habillé rapidement suis je
8 s' mon pas douché frère est ne
9 s' brossé dents les il est
10 nous couchés sommes nous vers minuit

**D Make these sentences negative.**
*Example: J'ai parlé avec Marie. → Je n'ai pas parlé avec Marie.*

1 J'ai parlé avec Marie.
2 Nous avons fini les devoirs.
3 Elle est allée chez le dentiste.
4 Tu as écrit des cartes postales.
5 Vous avez bu tout le jus d'orange?
6 Ils sont retournés ce matin.
7 J'ai dû partir très tôt.
8 Elles sont venues me voir à l'hôpital.
9 Tu as appris beaucoup de mots nouveaux.
10 J'ai bien aimé le film.

# 15 The imperfect tense

This past tense is used when describing:

- what something **was like**
- what **used to** happen
- what **was** happen**ing**

| | |
|---|---|
| *je regardais la télé* | I was watching / used to watch TV |
| *il faisait beau* | the weather was fine |

### Formation

To form the imperfect tense:

- find the *nous* part of the present tense verb
- take off the *-ons*
- add the **imperfect endings** to the stem.

The imperfect endings are as follows:

| Person | Ending | Person | Ending |
|---|---|---|---|
| *je / j'* | *–ais* | *nous* | *-ions* |
| *tu* | *–ais* | *vous* | *-iez* |
| *il / elle / on* | *–ait* | *ils / elles* | *-aient* |

For example, to form the imperfect of *manger* in the *je* form:

*nous mangeons → mange → + -ais → je mangeais*

**ATTENTION!**

There is one exception! When using *être* (to be), the stem is *ét–*. The imperfect endings are the same.

| | |
|---|---|
| *c'**était** super* | it was great |
| *il **était** content* | he was happy |

**A Change the verb in brackets into the imperfect tense, and translate.**

1 Je (manger) de la salade.
2 Il (sortir) tous les week-ends.
3 Elles (avoir) besoin de pratiquer leur anglais.
4 Nous (lire) des romans.
5 Vous (avoir) raison.
6 Elle ne (boire) jamais de café.
7 Tu (écouter) du rock.
8 Je (avoir) chaud.
9 On (porter) un uniforme au collège.
10 Les maisons (être) belles.

**B Which tense – perfect or imperfect? Rewrite the following text, choosing one of the underlined verbs.**

Le week-end dernier, j'ai décidé / je décidais d'aller en ville parce que j'avais / j'ai eu besoin de faire des courses. Je prenais / j'ai pris le train parce qu'avant, je prenais / j'ai pris le bus et la dernière fois il y avait / il y a eu un gros problème de circulation et le trajet a duré / durait deux heures. Quel désastre! Cette fois, ça a été / c'était beaucoup mieux parce qu'il n'y avait pas / il n'y a pas eu autant de voitures.

# 16 Depuis

*Depuis* can be used in two ways:

- to say how long something **has** been happening (formed with the present tense)
  *j'apprends l'espagnol depuis cinq ans*
  I've been learning Spanish for five years
- to say how long something **had** been happening (formed with the imperfect tense)
  j'apprenais l'espagnol depuis cinq ans
  I had been learning Spanish for five years

**A Translate these sentences into French.**

1. I've been learning French for three years.
2. She's been going out with Jérémy for a month.
3. I had been thinking about living in Paris for a long time.
4. I've been a member of the dance club for 10 years.
5. My mum had been working in an office for a few years.

## 17 Adverbs

An adverb describes a verb: e.g. He sang **loudly**.

In English most adverbs are formed by adding **-ly** to adjectives – e.g. loud – loud**ly**. Most French adverbs are formed in the following way:

- make the adjective **feminine**, then
- add *-ment*

| masculine | feminine | adverb |
|---|---|---|
| *sûr* | *sûre* | *sûrement* |
| *normal* | *normale* | *normalement* |
| *sérieux* | *sérieuse* | *sérieusement* |

**ATTENTION!**

There are exceptions!

- Adjectives ending in *i* or *u* stay in the masculine form:
  *vrai* → *vraiment* *poli* → *poliment*
- Some adjectives need an **acute accent** (é) on the last *-e* when they become adverbs. This makes them easier to pronounce:
  *énorme* → *énormément* *précis* → *précisément*
- Some very common adverbs are not formed with *-ment* at all – e.g.:

| | | | |
|---|---|---|---|
| *bien* | well | *mal* | badly |
| *mieux* | better | *vite* | quickly |
| *tôt / de bonne heure* | early | *en retard* | late |

**A Use these adjectives to form adverbs, and translate.**

1. actif
2. heureux
3. direct
4. doux
5. difficile

**B Rewrite the text in full with the correct adverbs in French.**

Hier, j'ai dû me lever (very early) parce que je voulais (really) aller à Londres. Après le petit déjeuner, j'ai quitté la maison en fermant la porte (quietly) derrière moi.

(Unfortunately) il n'y a pas de bus à cette heure-là, donc je suis parti (on foot). Mais (luckily), j'ai vu un ami qui va souvent en ville de (very) bonne heure, et il m'a (kindly) accompagné à la gare en voiture. Le train était (already) en gare. En repartant il est sorti (slowly) de la gare, et ensuite il est allé (much faster) et je savais que j'arriverais (soon) à Londres. J'étais (quite) content, car le train part (frequently) (late) et le trajet dure (a long time).

## 18 Adverbs of intensity

Adverbs of intensity are used to qualify or emphasize what you say. They are normally placed directly after the verb. Examples of these are:

| | | | |
|---|---|---|---|
| *assez* | quite | *réellement* | truly |
| *trop* | too (much) | *vraiment* | really |
| *aussi* | also | *tellement* | so (much) |
| *bien* | well | | |

| | |
|---|---|
| *il parle* ***trop*** | he talks too much |
| *j'aime* ***bien*** *lire* | I quite like reading |

Note that adverbs of intensity can also be used to describe an adjective, e.g. this film is really great = *ce film est* ***vraiment*** *génial*.

**A Improve these sentences by inserting an adverb of intensity.**

1. J'aime le foot.
2. Londres est une ville animée.
3. Je trouve l'histoire difficile.
4. En été, il fait chaud.
5. Mathieu est sportif.
6. La pollution est un problème.

## 19 Articles

Articles are the small words placed in front of nouns. In English we use either 'the' (**definite article**) or 'a' (**indefinite article**). In French both the indefinite and definite articles change according to their **gender** (see **Nouns** on page 181) and number. There is also something called the **partitive article**, often used when in English we say 'some'.

### The indefinite article

The word for 'a' in French is either *un* (masculine), *une* (feminine) or *des* (plural).

| | |
|---|---|
| *un chat* a cat | *une table* a table |
| *des chats* cats | *des tables* tables |

**A Write the correct word for 'a' for each noun.**

1. pomme *(f)*
2. oiseau *(m)*
3. tableau *(m)*
4. sac *(m)*
5. cousine *(f)*

## 20 The partitive article

The words for 'some' are ***du / de la / des***, depending on whether the noun is masculine, feminine or plural.

They are also used when there is no article in English – e.g. I saw snow outside – *J'ai vu de la neige dehors.*

The *la* part shortens to *l'* if the noun begins with a vowel or a silent *h* and *du* becomes *de l'.*

| | |
|---|---|
| *du thé* (m) | some tea |
| *de la pizza* (f) | some pizza |
| *de l'alcool* (m) | alcohol |
| *de l'eau* (f) | some water |

**ATTENTION!**

When using *de* in a **negative sentence**, the ***de*** does not change in front of feminine or plural nouns:

*je n'ai pas* ***de*** *pommes* I have no apples

**A** **Rewrite the shopping list using the partitive (*du*, *de la* or *des*).**

**1** le lait
**2** l'orangeade
**3** les œufs
**4** le beurre
**5** l'essence

**B** **Write the following in French.**

**1** I eat meat.
**2** I don't like fish.
**3** The children are intelligent.
**4** I don't play golf.
**5** There are some potatoes.
**6** There aren't any bananas.

## 21 Demonstrative adjectives

Demonstrative adjectives refer to a particular place, person or thing. In English we use 'this', 'that', 'these', 'those'. In French, use *ce* (or *cet**), *cette*, *ces*, depending on the noun.

* *Cet* is used for masculine nouns beginning with a vowel or a silent *h*.

| | | |
|---|---|---|
| **masculine** | *ce livre* | this / that book |
| | *cet hôtel* | this / that hotel |
| **feminine** | *cette fille* | this / that girl |
| **plural** | *ces enfants* | these / those kids |

**A** **Add a demonstrative adjective to each sentence after deciding the gender of the nouns.**

**1** J'aime ...... fleurs.
**2** Je voudrais ...... jupe grise.
**3** Je vous recommande ...... vin.
**4** Devant ...... bâtiment, il y a une autoroute.
**5** ...... homme est le patron du café.
**6** ...... enfants sont bruyants.
**7** Je n'aime pas ...... hôpital.
**8** ...... femme chante bien.

## 22 Chaque and quelque

*Chaque* means 'each' or 'every' before a noun:

*chaque jour* every day

*Quelque* means 'some' before a noun. It adds *-s* if the noun is plural.

| | |
|---|---|
| *quelque chose* | something |
| *quelques sandwiches* | some sandwiches |
| *quelquefois* | sometimes |
| *quelqu'un* | someone |

## 23 The pluperfect tense

This tense is used when describing what **had already** happened before a particular past event took place:

*J'avais déjà fini mes devoirs quand j'ai allumé la télé.*

Just like the perfect tense, the pluperfect has two parts:

the **imperfect tense** of either *avoir* or *être* and the **past participle** of the verb describing the event.

See **The perfect tense** on page 186 to revise the verbs that are formed with *être* rather than *avoir*.

**A** **Rewrite these sentences in the pluperfect tense.**

**1** J'aime habiter ici.
**2** Il va au collège.
**3** Nous jouons au foot le week-end.
**4** Mon père travaille dans une banque.
**5** Elle a un bébé.
**6** Charlotte se lève à huit heures.

## 24 Emphatic pronouns

After **prepositions** such as *pour* (for), *avec* (with), *sans* (without), *chez* (at somebody's house), you need to use the following pronouns:

| | | | |
|---|---|---|---|
| *moi* | me | *nous* | us |
| *toi* | you (sing.) | *vous* | you (plural) |
| *lui* | him | *eux* | them (masc.) |
| *elle* | her | *elles* | them (fem.) |

**A** **Translate into French.**

**1** at my house
**2** with her
**3** without us
**4** for you (sing) and me
**5** at their house
**6** with you (plural)

## 25 The pronoun en

*En* means 'of it', 'of them', 'some' or 'any'. It comes **before** all parts of the verb.

*il y* ***en*** *a beaucoup* there are lots of them
*je n'****en*** *ai pas* I haven't any

**A** **Re-order the sentences, then translate.**

**1** en il y a
**2** pas a en y il n'
**3** tu as est-ce en que?
**4** dix en avons nous

## 26 Object pronouns

In French all object pronouns go **before** the conjugated verb. There are two types of object pronouns: **direct** and **indirect**.

### Direct object pronouns

In English, in a sentence such as 'I like chocolate' the noun 'chocolate' is the **direct object**. We can replace the word 'chocolate' with a **pronoun** – 'I like **it**'. 'It' here is an example of a direct object pronoun.

In French the direct object pronouns are:

| | | | |
|---|---|---|---|
| *me** | me | *nous* | us |
| *te** | you (sing.) | *vous* | you (pl.) |
| *le** | him / it | *les* | them |
| *la** | her / it | | |

* *Me, te, le* and *la* become *m', t', l'* before a vowel or silent 'h'.

*J'aime le chocolat* *je l'aime*

**A Place the direct object pronoun (using the noun in brackets) correctly in each sentence.**

*Example: Nous mangeons (les frites).* → *Nous* ***les*** *mangeons.*

1 J'aime (le chocolat).
2 Je porte (ma jupe).
3 Nous voyons (Marion).
4 Mon chat a bu (le lait).
5 Elle cherche (toi).
6 Ils ont trouvé (moi).

### Indirect object pronouns

These are used to mean 'to' along with a pronoun:

He gave the book **to me**.
I loaned my trainers **to him**.

These pronouns are exactly the same as direct object pronouns, except for:

| | |
|---|---|
| *lui* | to him / her / it |
| *leur* | to them |

**B Insert the correct indirect object pronoun.**

*Example: Il ..... donne des bonbons. (to her)* →
*Il lui donne des bonbons.*

1 Il ..... donne son stylo. (to me)
2 Nous ..... avons acheté un cadeau. (to him)
3 Elle ..... a prêté son livre. (to you, sing.)
4 Je ...... ai raconté une histoire. (to you, pl.)
5 Tu ...... as envoyé une lettre? (to me)
6 Vous ..... avez montré vos devoirs? (to us)

**ATTENTION!**

Some sentences contain both direct and indirect object pronouns:

*elle me la donne* she gives it to me
*je le lui envoie* I send it to him

In this case, the order of object pronouns is as follows:

| | | |
|---|---|---|
| *me*<br>*te*<br>*nous*<br>*vous* | *le*<br>*la*<br>*les* | *lui*<br>*leur* |

**C Now try adding the second pronoun correctly and translate.**

*Example: Lucie me donne. (+ la)* *Lucie me la donne* → Lucie gives it to me.

1 Le professeur les donne. (+ lui)
2 Mes copains me prêtent. (+ les)
3 Marie et Julien leur achètent. (+ le)
4 Cécile lui achète. (+ les)
5 Tu les donnes. (+ leur)
6 Il te racontait. (+ la)

## 27 Perfect infinitives

These are verb structures used to mean 'having done'. They usually follow *après* (after):

*Après avoir regardé la télé ...*
(After) Having watched TV ...
*Après être arrivé en retard ...*
(After) Having arrived late ...

Just like the perfect tense, perfect infinitives have two parts:

- the **infinitive** of the auxiliary verb – either *avoir* or *être*
- the **past participle** of the verb describing the event.

*Après avoir* ***visité*** *l'église ...* Having visited the church ...

**A Make the following verbs into perfect infinitives, then translate.**

*Example: finir* → *après avoir fini* (after) having finished

1 aller
2 regarder
3 habiter
4 partir
5 rentrer
6 avoir

**ATTENTION!**

Just as past participles that use *être* in the perfect tense agree with their subjects, so does the past participle in a perfect infinitive taking *être*:

*Après être entrées dans la salle, les filles ...*
(After) Having entered the room, the girls ...

**B Use the perfect infinitive to complete these sentences, using the correct auxiliary verb, *avoir* or *être*.**

1 Après ................ (parler) avec mes parents, j'ai pu aller au cinéma.
2 Après ................ (tomber) dans le lac, elle était complètement mouillée.
3 Après ................ (visiter) la France, je suis allée en Italie.
4 Après ................ (étudier) l'allemand, il va apprendre l'italien.
5 Après ..................... (rester) chez toi, tu ne veux pas sortir ce soir?
6 Après ..................... (manger) du poisson pas frais, j'ai été très malade.

## 28 The passive

The passive is a structure which involves actions being done **to** someone or something, and the verb appears more like an adjective:

I finished my homework – **active**
*j'ai fini mes devoirs*
my homework is finished – **passive**
*mes devoirs sont finis*

**A Active or passive?**

1. Lucie a fait la cuisine.
2. Le repas est préparé.
3. Il recycle beaucoup de papier.
4. Peu de plastique est recyclé.
5. Nous habitons ici depuis deux ans.
6. J'ai cassé mes lunettes.
7. Elles ont été cassées par ma petite sœur.
8. L'acteur célèbre a été vu dans la rue.
9. Elle est très contente.

**B Translate into French using the passive. Be careful to use the right tense!**

1. The shopping centre is open from 8am to 6pm.
2. It will be open this weekend.
3. Lunch was served in the garden.
4. The computer is used by the whole class.
5. The work was done by students.
6. The house is built of concrete.

## 29 The present participle

The present participle translates as ***-ing*** in English. ***En*** + present participle means 'on / by / while ... doing something':

*j'ai dîné **en** regard**ant** la télé*

I had dinner while watching TV

### Formation

To form a present participle:

- take the ***nous*** form of the verb in the present tense
- take off the ***-ons*** ending, and
- add ***-ant***

E.g.: *manger* → *mange**ons*** → *mange**ant***

**ATTENTION!**

There are some irregulars!
*avoir* → *ayant*
*être* → *étant*
*savoir* → *sachant*

**A Translate these sentences using present participles.**

1. On returning home, he saw his friend.
2. While reading my book, I had a coffee.
3. I answered the phone, knowing that it was you.
4. Having eaten lunch, I'm not hungry.
5. I could write while I listen to the radio.
6. By being sensible, she has saved lots of money.

## 30 Relative pronouns – qui and que

Relative pronouns relate to the person, place or thing that has just been mentioned. They mean 'who', 'which', or 'that', and are used to make sentences longer.

- *J'ai un chat qui s'appelle Cléo.*
  (Here *qui* is used because it is the **subject** of the next verb.)
- *J'ai un chien que je n'aime pas.*
  (Here *que* is used because it is the **object** of the next verb.)

**A Choose *qui* or *que* for each sentence.**

1. Je vais au collège qui / que est situé en ville.
2. J'ai acheté un chapeau qui / que j'adore.
3. C'est un genre de musique qui / que je ne connais pas.
4. Ma sœur, qui / que s'appelle Lucie, est jolie.
5. Ça c'est le problème qui / que j'ai eu.
6. J'ai perdu mon passeport, qui / que était dans mon sac.

## 31 Verbs followed by an infinitive

When one verb is followed immediately by a second verb, the second verb must be in the **infinitive**.

The infinitive is used:

- After these verbs:

| | |
|---|---|
| *il faut ...* | it's necessary to ... |
| *devoir* | to have to (must) |
| *pouvoir* | to be able to (can) |
| *savoir* | to know (how to) |
| *vouloir* | to want to |

and also after verbs expressing likes and dislikes – *adorer, aimer, détester* and *préférer*.

- After verbs joined by *à*:

| | |
|---|---|
| *aider à* | to help to |
| *apprendre à* | to learn to |
| *commencer à* | to start / begin (to) |
| *continuer à* | to continue to |

- After verbs joined by *de*:

| | |
|---|---|
| *choisir de* | to choose to |
| *décider de* | to decide to |
| *essayer de* | to try to |
| *refuser de* | to refuse to |

**A Re-order the sentences, then translate.**

1 faut changer il
2 continue il étudier à l'université à
3 dois mes je devoirs faire soir ce
4 dentiste être voudrais je
5 peux aider vous je?
6 décidé le sport de j'ai continuer

**B Translate.**

1 I'd like to go to the theatre.
2 She began to eat.
3 I must finish my work.
4 I'm beginning to like my new job.
5 All the children can swim.
6 It's necessary to drive.

## 32 The immediate future tense

This tense is used when describing what is going to happen in the near future.

*Je vais regarder la télé.* I'm going to watch TV.

### Formation

The immediate future tense has two parts:

- the **present tense** of the verb *aller*, plus
- the **infinitive** of the verb
- Including the **reflexive pronoun** if the verb is reflexive – *je vais me coucher*.

**A Rewrite these sentences in the immediate future.**

1 J'aime habiter ici.
2 Il va au collège.
3 Nous jouons au foot le week-end.
4 Mon père travaille dans une banque.
5 Elle a un bébé.
6 Charlotte se lève à huit heures.

## 33 The future tense

This tense is used when describing something that **will** happen in the future.

*Je regarderai la télé* I'll / I will watch TV

For actions which are sure to happen, the verb *aller* + infinitive is often used instead of the future tense.

### Formation

To form the future tense:

- take the **infinitive***, then
- add the **future endings**

* Except for *-re* verbs, where the final *-e* is dropped in the infinitive before adding the endings, and for some irregular verbs (see below).

The future endings are as follows:

| person | future endings | person | future endings |
|---|---|---|---|
| *je / j'* | *-ai* | *nous* | *-ons* |
| *tu* | *-as* | *vous* | *-ez* |
| *il / elle / on* | *-a* | *ils / elles* | *-ont* |

*je mangerai un sandwich* I'll / I will eat a sandwich
*elle finira ses devoirs* she'll / she will finish her homework

**ATTENTION!**

A few common irregular verbs use irregular stems to form the future. These verbs include:

| infinitive | stem | infinitive | stem |
|---|---|---|---|
| *avoir* | *aur-* | *pouvoir* | *pourr-* |
| *être* | *ser-* | *savoir* | *saur-* |
| *aller* | *ir-* | *venir* | *viendr-* |
| *devoir* | *devr-* | *voir* | *verr-* |
| *faire* | *fer-* | *vouloir* | *voudr-* |

**A Write each verb in the future tense and then translate it.**

*Example:* je (jouer) *je jouerai* I will play

1 je (parler)
2 nous (finir)
3 elle (aller)
4 tu (écrire)
5 vous (boire)
6 ils (retourner)
7 je (devoir)
8 elles (venir)
9 tu (apprendre)
10 je (aimer)

**B Your horoscope. Complete the sentences using the future tense to find out what the future holds.**

1 **Capricorne**: tu ............... organiser ta vie (devoir)
2 **Verseau**: tu ............... plus patient avec un membre de famille (devenir)
3 **Poisson**: tu ............... de la chance en finances (avoir)
4 **Bélier**: tu ............... amoureux (tomber)
5 **Taureau**: tu ............... un roman (écrire)
6 **Gémeaux**: tu ............... un voyage autour du monde (faire)
7 **Cancer**: tu ............... une nouvelle langue (apprendre)
8 **Lion**: tu ............... un vieux copain (voir)
9 **Vierge**: tu ............... plus heureux au travail (être)
10 **Balance**: tu ............... faire des changements (vouloir)
11 **Scorpion**: tu ............... à une question importante (répondre)
12 **Sagittaire**: tu ............... par trouver la solution à un problème grave (finir)

## 34 The conditional

The conditional is used when describing what **would** happen if certain conditions were fulfilled.

*Je regarderais la télé si j'avais le temps.*
I would watch TV if I had time.

### Formation

To form the conditional of regular *-er* and *-ir* verbs:

- take the **infinitive**, then
- add the **conditional endings**

For *-re* **verbs**, the final *-e* is dropped from the infinitive before adding the endings. Some verbs also have irregular stems (see below).

The conditional endings are as follows. Note that they are the same as the imperfect endings:

| person | ending | person | ending |
|---|---|---|---|
| *je / j'* | *-ais* | *nous* | *-ions* |
| *tu* | *-ais* | *vous* | *-iez* |
| *il / elle / on* | *-ait* | *ils / elles* | *-aient* |

| | |
|---|---|
| *je mangerais un sandwich* | I would eat a sandwich |
| *elle finirait ses devoirs* | she would finish her homework |
| *nous répondrions au téléphone* | we would answer the phone |

**ATTENTION!**

The conditional has the same irregularities as the future tense. Use the same irregular stems and add the conditional endings.

**A Write each verb in the conditional and then translate it.**

*Example*: je (jouer) *je jouerais* I would play

1 je (jouer)
2 nous (finir)
3 elle (aller)
4 tu (écrire)
5 vous (boire)
6 ils (retourner)
7 je (devoir)
8 elles (venir)
9 tu (apprendre)
10 je (aimer)

**B Complete these sentences using the conditional of the verb in brackets, then translate.**

1 Il ............ devenir professeur plus tard. (vouloir)
2 Vous ............ recycler plus. (devoir)
3 Tu ............ rester à la maison? (préférer)
4 Mon copain ............ travailler dans une banque. (aimer)
5 Je ............ content d'être riche. (être)
6 Il ............ chez nous en train. (venir)

### *Si* sentences

The **conditional** is very often combined with the imperfect tense to form sentences using ***si*** ('if'):

***Si** j'étais jeune, je **ferais** le tour du monde.*
If I were / was young, I'd do a tour of the world.
*J'**achèterais** un bateau si j'avais l'argent.*
I'd buy a boat if I had the money.

**C Add the missing verbs in the imperfect and conditional.**

*Example*: S'il .......... (pleuvoir), je ne .......... (sortir) pas.
*S'il pleuvait, je ne sortirais pas.*

1 S'il .......... (pleuvoir), je ne .......... (sortir) pas.
2 Si j' .......... (être) riche, j' .......... (acheter) un avion.
3 Si tu .......... (jouer) au foot plus souvent, tu .......... (jouer) mieux.
4 S'il .......... (faire) ses devoirs, il .......... (avoir) de meilleures notes.
5 S'ils.......... (parler) moins, ils .......... (faire) plus de travail.

## 35 The subjunctive mood

The subjunctive is almost always used in connection with ***que***. It is used after the following structures:

| | |
|---|---|
| *pour que* | so that |
| *bien que* | although |
| *il faut que* | it's necessary to / you must |
| *vouloir que* | to want to |
| *il vaut mieux que* | it's better to |

### Formation

To form the present subjunctive, we need to do three things:

- find the ***ils*** / ***elles*** part of the present tense verb
- take off the ***-ent***
- add the subjunctive endings to the stem

The present subjunctive endings are:

| person | subjunctive endings |
|---|---|
| *je / j'* | *-e* |
| *tu* | *-es* |
| *il / elle / on* | *-e* |
| *nous* | *-ions* |
| *vous* | *-iez* |
| *ils / elles* | *-ent* |

**ATTENTION!**

A few verbs form irregular subjunctives, including *faire, être, savoir, avoir, aller* and *pouvoir*. See Verb Tables on pages 195–196 for details.

**A Translate into English.**

1. Je voudrais qu'il m'accompagne à la fête.
2. Il faut qu'on fasse une réservation avant de partir.
3. Bien qu'il y ait du soleil, il fait froid.
4. Il vaut mieux que tu prennes ton parapluie.
5. Pour que tu puisses aller à l'université, il faut que tu travailles bien.
6. Bien que nous ayons une voiture, nous préférons circuler à vélo.

**B Translate into French.**

1. My dad wants me to come home early.
2. It's better that we arrive too early than too late.
3. It's necessary for me to save money to go on holiday.
4. Although I want to stay, I must go.
5. It's necessary to stop smoking so that we can be healthy.
6. Although we travel a lot, it's better to stay at home sometimes.

## 36 Numerals

| | |
|---|---|
| 1 | *un/une* |
| 2 | *deux* |
| 3 | *trois* |
| 4 | *quatre* |
| 5 | *cinq* |
| 6 | *six* |
| 7 | *sept* |
| 8 | *huit* |
| 9 | *neuf* |
| 10 | *dix* |
| 11 | *onze* |
| 12 | *douze* |
| 13 | *treize* |
| 14 | *quatorze* |
| 15 | *quinze* |
| 16 | *seize* |
| 17 | *dix-sept* |
| 18 | *dix-huit* |
| 19 | *dix-neuf* |
| 20 | *vingt* |
| 21 | *vingt et un* |
| 22 | *vingt-deux* |
| 30 | *trente* |
| 40 | *quarante* |
| 50 | *cinquante* |
| 60 | *soixante* |
| 70 | *soixante-dix* |
| 80 | *quatre-vingts* |
| 81 | *quatre-vingt-un* |
| 82 | *quatre-vingt-deux* |
| 90 | *quatre-vingt-dix* |
| 91 | *quatre-vingt-onze* |
| 92 | *quatre-vingt-douze* |
| 100 | *cent* |
| 101 | *cent un* |
| 1000 | *mille* |

Note also the words for 'first', 'second', 'third', and their abbreviations:

| | |
|---|---|
| *premier / première* | *1er/ère* |
| *deuxième* | *2ème* |
| *troisième* | *3ème* |
| *dixième* | *10ème* |
| *centième* | *100ème* |
| *millième* | *1000ème* |

# Verb Tables

| Infinitive | Present | | Perfect | Imperfect | Future | Present subjunctive |
|---|---|---|---|---|---|---|
| **Regular verbs** | | | | | | |
| **-er verbs**<br>parler<br>*(to speak)* | je parle<br>tu parles<br>il/elle/on parle | nous parlons<br>vous parlez<br>ils/elles parlent | j'ai parlé | je parlais | je parlerai | je parle |
| **-ir verbs**<br>finir<br>*(to finish)* | je finis<br>tu finis<br>il/elle/on finit | nous finissons<br>vous finissez<br>ils/elles finissent | j'ai fini | je finissais | je finirai | je finisse |
| **-re verbs**<br>vendre<br>*(to sell)* | je vends<br>tu vends<br>il/elle/on vend | nous vendons<br>vous vendez<br>ils/elles vendent | j'ai vendu | je vendais | je vendrai | je vende |
| **reflexive verbs**<br>se coucher<br>*(to go to bed)* | je me couche<br>tu te couches<br>il/elle/on se couche | nous nous couchons<br>vous vous couchez<br>ils/elles se couchent | je me suis couché(e) | je me couchais | je me coucherai | je me couche |
| **Irregular verbs** | | | | | | |
| aller<br>*(to go)* | je vais<br>tu vas<br>il/elle/on va | nous allons<br>vous allez<br>ils/elles vont | je suis allé(e) | j'allais | j'irai | j'aille |
| avoir<br>*(to have)* | j'ai<br>tu as<br>il/elle/on a | nous avons<br>vous avez<br>ils/elles ont | j'ai eu | j'avais | j'aurai | j'aie |
| boire<br>*(to drink)* | je bois<br>tu bois<br>il/elle/on boit | nous buvons<br>vous buvez<br>ils/elles boivent | j'ai bu | je buvais | je boirai | je boive |
| connaître<br>*(to know a person/place)* | je connais<br>tu connais<br>il/elle/on connaît | nous connaissons<br>vous connaissez<br>ils/elles connaissent | j'ai connu | je connaissais | je connaîtrai | je connaisse |
| devoir<br>*(to have to)* | je dois<br>tu dois<br>il/elle/on doit | nous devons<br>vous devez<br>ils/elles doivent | j'ai dû | je devais | je devrai | je doive |
| dire<br>*(to say)* | je dis<br>tu dis<br>il/elle/on dit | nous disons<br>vous dites<br>ils/elles disent | j'ai dit | je disais | je dirai | je dise |
| dormir<br>*(to sleep)* | je dors<br>tu dors<br>il/elle/on dort | nous dormons<br>vous dormez<br>ils/elles dorment | j'ai dormi | je dormais | je dormirai | je dorme |

| Infinitive | Present | | Perfect | Imperfect | Future | Present subjunctive |
|---|---|---|---|---|---|---|
| écrire<br>*(to write)* | j'écris<br>tu écris<br>il/elle/on écrit | nous écrivons<br>vous écrivez<br>ils/elles écrivent | j'ai écrit | j'écrivais | j'écrirai | j'écrive |
| être<br>*(to be)* | je suis<br>tu es<br>il/elle/on est | nous sommes<br>vous êtes<br>ils/elles sont | j'ai été | j'étais | je serai | je sois |
| faire<br>*(to do/make)* | je fais<br>tu fais<br>il/elle/on fait | nous faisons<br>vous faites<br>ils/elles font | j'ai fait | je faisais | je ferai | je fasse |
| lire<br>*(to read)* | je lis<br>tu lis<br>il/elle/on lit | nous lisons<br>vous lisez<br>ils/elles lisent | j'ai lu | je lisais | je lirai | je lise |
| mettre<br>*(to put/put on)* | je mets<br>tu mets<br>il/elle/on met | nous mettons<br>vous mettez<br>ils/elles mettent | j'ai mis | je mettais | je mettrai | je mette |
| pouvoir<br>*(to be able to)* | je peux<br>tu peux<br>il/elle/on peut | nous pouvons<br>vous pouvez<br>ils/elles peuvent | j'ai pu | je pouvais | je pourrai | je puisse |
| prendre<br>*(to take)* | je prends<br>tu prends<br>il/elle/on prend | nous prenons<br>vous prenez<br>ils/elles prennent | j'ai pris | je prenais | je prendrai | je prenne |
| recevoir<br>*(to receive)* | je reçois<br>tu reçois<br>il/elle/on reçoit | nous recevons<br>vous recevez<br>ils/elles reçoivent | j'ai reçu | je recevais | je recevrai | je reçoive |
| savoir<br>*(to know a fact)* | je sais<br>tu sais<br>il/elle/on sait | nous savons<br>vous savez<br>ils/elles savent | j'ai su | je savais | je saurai | je sache |
| sentir<br>*(to feel)* | je sens<br>tu sens<br>il/elle/on sent | nous sentons<br>vous sentez<br>ils/elles sentent | j'ai senti | je sentais | je sentirai | je sente |
| sortir<br>*(to go out)* | je sors<br>tu sors<br>il/elle/on sort | nous sentons<br>vous sentez<br>ils/elles sentent | je suis sorti | je sortais | je sortirai | je sorte |
| venir<br>*(to come)* | je viens<br>tu viens<br>il/elle/on vient | nous venons<br>vous venez<br>ils/elles viennent | je suis venu | je venais | je viendrai | je vienne |
| voir<br>*(to see)* | je vois<br>tu vois<br>il/elle/on voit | nous voyons<br>vous voyez<br>ils/elles voient | j'ai vu | je voyais | je verrai | je voie |
| vouloir<br>*(to want)* | je veux<br>tu veux<br>il/elle/on veut | nous voulons<br>vous voulez<br>ils/elles veulent | j'ai voulu | je voulais | je voudrai | je veuille |

# Vocabulaire

nm *masculine moun* nf *feminine noun* pl *plural noun* v *verb* adj *adjective* pp *past participle*
* *Adjectives marked with an asterisk do not have a separate feminine form.*

## A

**à peu près** about, roughly
**accomplir** *v* to carry out
d' **accord** OK, agreed
être d' **accord** to agree
l' **accueil** *nm* welcome
**accueillir** *v* to welcome
les **achats** *nm pl* shopping, purchases
**actuellement** at present, presently
une **addition** *nf* a bill
un/une **ado** (short for **adolescent/adolescente**) *nm/nf* teenager
s' **adonner à** *v* to devote oneself to
les **affaires** *nf pl* clothes, stuff; business
une **affiche** *n* a poster
**afin de** in order to
une **agence de voyages** *nf* a travel agency
un **agenda** *nm* a diary
une **agglomération** *nf* a large urban area
il s' **agit de** it's a question of, to do with ...
une **aide-ménagère** *nf* a home help
l' **ail** *nm* garlic
**ailleurs** elsewhere
avoir l' **air ...** to look, seem ... (e.g. tired)
**aisé/aisée** *adj* well-off
les **alentours** *nm pl* surroundings, neighbourhood
**algérien/algérienne** *adj* Algerian
l' **alimentation** *nf* food (shopping)
les **aliments complets** *nm pl* wholefoods
**aller chercher** *v* to collect, fetch
une **allocation** *nf* allowance/grant
s' **allonger** *v* to lie down
**allumer** *v* turn on (a light), light up
**alors que** while, whereas
**améliorer** *v* to improve
une **amende** *nf* fine
**amener** *v* to bring (along)
**amical/amicale** *adj* friendly
l' **amitié** *nf* friendship
l' **amour** *nm* love
s' **amuser** *v* to have fun
un **an** *nm* a year
l' **analphabétisme** *nm* illiteracy
**ancien/ancienne** *adj* (after noun) old; (before noun) former
un **ange** *nm* angel
une **année** *nf* a year
les **années cinquante** the (19)50s
un **anniversaire** *nm* a birthday
une **annonce** *nf* (newspaper) an advertisement
**août** *nm* August
un **appareil photo** *nm* a camera
un **appartement** *nm* an apartment, flat
un **appel** *nm* a (telephone) call
**apporter** *v* to bring
**apprendre** *v* to learn
**appris** *pp* of apprendre
s' **approcher de** *v* to approach
**approfondir** *v to deepen*
**appuyer** *v* to press
**arracher** *v* tear off, out, down; grab
**arrêter de** *v* to stop, give up doing something
s' **arrêter** *v* to stop (e.g. walking)
à l' **arrière** at the back
je n' **arrive plus à** ... I can no longer manage to ...
l' **artisanat local** *nm* local crafts
s' **asseoir** *v* to sit down
**assez** quite
**assis** *pp* of asseoir
être **assis/assise** to be sitting down
**assister à** *v* to attend, be present at
un **atelier** *nm* a workshop, small factory
un/une **athlète** *nm/nf* an athlete
les **atouts** *nm pl* skills
**attendre** *v* to wait
**attendre avec impatience** to look forward to
**attirer** *v* to attract, draw
une **auberge de jeunesse** *nf* a youth hostel
**augmenter** *v* to increase, go up
**auprès de** among
**aur-** future and conditional stem of **avoir**
il y **aurait** there would be
**aussitôt que** as soon as
**autant de** as much, as many
l' **automne** *nm* autumn
**autour de** around
**autrefois** formerly
à l' **avant** at the front
**avant-hier** the day before yesterday
l' **avenir** *nm* future
**aventureux/aventureuse** *adj* adventurous
**aveugle*** *adj* blind
un **avion** *nm* an aeroplane
un **avis** *nm* an opinion
à votre (ton) **avis** in your opinion
**avril** *nm* April

## B

se **baigner** *v* to have a bath
un **bain** *nm* a bath
**baiser** *v* to kiss
**baisser** *v* to lower
une **baleine** *nf* a whale
la **banlieue** *nf* suburbs
en **bas** downstairs
les **baskets** *nf pl* trainers
une **bataille** *nf* a battle
un **bâtiment** *nm* a building
une **batterie** *nf* a battery; drums
**battre** *v* to beat
**beau/bel/belle/beaux/belles** *adj* beautiful, handsome
un **beau-père** *nm* a stepfather
**belge*** *adj* Belgian
une **belle-mère** *nf* a stepmother
le **bénévolat (à l'étranger)** *nm* (overseas) voluntary work
un/une **bénévole** *nm/nf* a voluntary worker
avoir **besoin de** *v* to need
une **bibliothèque** *nf* a library, bookcase
**bien cuit/bien cuite** *adj* well cooked
**bien entendu** of course
**bientôt** soon
à **bientôt!** see you soon!
**bienvenue** welcome
le **bifteck** *nm* a (beef)steak
un **bijou** *nm* a jewel
un **billet** *nm* a ticket
un **billet aller-retour** *nm* a return ticket
**bio** *adj* organic
se **blesser** *v* to get injured
un **bloc sanitaire** *nm* a toilet block
**boire** *v* to drink
un **bois** *nm* a wood
de/en **bois** made out of wood
une **boisson** *nf* a drink
une **boîte** *nf* a box, can
une **boîte de nuit** *nf* a night club
**bon/bonne** *adj* good, right
**bon courage!** take heart!
**bon marché*** *adj* cheap
le **bonheur** *nm* happiness
au **bord de la mer** at the seaside
se **bouger** *v* to move
un **boulot** *nm* a task, job
une **bouteille** *nf* a bottle
une **boutique** *nf* a (small) shop
**branché/branchée** *adj* trendy
**breton/bretonne** *adj* Breton
**briller** *v* to shine
se (faire) **bronzer** *v* to get a tan, sunbathe
se **brosser les dents** to brush one's teeth
**bruyant/bruyante** *adj* noisy
**bu** pp of **boire**
une **bûche au chocolat** *nf* a chocolate log
une **bulle** *nf* a (speech) bubble
un **but** *nm* a goal, aim
**buv-** past imperfect stem of **boire**

## C

**ça m'éclate** I really get a kick out of it!
**ça me plaît** I like it – from **plaire**
**ça ne fait rien!** it doesn't matter!
**ça s'écrit comment?** how do you write it?
**ça se prononce comment?** how do you pronounce it?
**ça suffit!** that's enough!
**ça veut dire** that means

**cacher** *v* to hide
un **cadeau** *nm* a present
un **cadre** *nm* a setting
un **calcul** *nm* a sum
un **calendrier** *nm* a calendar
**calme** *adj* quiet
**campagnard/campagnarde** *adj* rural
une **canette** *nf* a (drink) can
la **cannelle** *nf* cinnamon
**car** because, for
en **caractères gras** in bold
la **carrière** *nf* career
un **cartable** *nm* a schoolbag
un **casse-croûte** *nm* (pl. les casse-croûte) a snack
un **cauchemar** *nm* a nightmare
**c'est-à-dire** that is, that's to say
**ce n'est pas la peine** it's not worth it
**cela m'est égal** I don't mind (either way)
**célibataire** *adj* single
**cent** one hundred
une **centaine de** about a hundred
une **centrale nucléaire** *nf* a nuclear power station
un **centre commercial** *nm* a shopping centre or mall
un **centre de recyclage** *nm* a recycling centre
un **centre-ville** *nm* a town or city centre
**certain/certaine** some, certain
**cesser de** to stop doing something
une **chaîne** *nf* a (TV) channel
la **chaleur** *nf* heat
un **championnat** *nm* a league
un **changement** *nm* a change
se **changer** *v* to get changed
**chaque*** each
la **charcuterie** *nf* cooked meats
le **chauffage central** *nm* central heating
**chauffer** *v* to heat
un **chauffeur** *nm* a driver (male or female)
les **chaussures de marche** *nf pl* walking boots
**cher/chère** expensive; dear (beloved)
**chez Juliette** at Juliette's (house)
un **chiffre** *nm* a number (digit)
un/une **chirurgien/chirurgienne** *nm/nf* a surgeon
un **choix** *nm* a choice
être au **chômage** to be unemployed
une **chorale** *nf* a choral society
**chrétien/chrétienne** *adj* Christian
la **chute libre** *nf* free fall
**ci-dessous** below
**ci-dessus** above
**cinquante** fifty
la **circulation** traffic
**circuler** *v* to go, move (of vehicles)
un/une **citoyen/citoyenne** *nm/nf* a citizen
une **citrouille** *nf* a pumpkin
**cocher** *v* to tick
un **coffre-fort** *nm* a safe
un **coin** *nm* a corner
du **coin** local
un **collège** *nm* a secondary school (11–15)
un/une **collégien/collégienne** *nm/nf* a (secondary) schoolboy/schoolgirl
le/la **collègue** *nm/nf* colleague
une **colline** *nf* hill
**commander** *v* to order (e.g. in restaurant)
**comme** like
**comprendre** *v* to understand
**compris** *pp* of **comprendre**
**compter** v to count
se **concentrer** *v* to concentrate, gather one's thoughts
**condamner** *v* to condemn
un/une **conducteur/conductrice** *nm/nf* a driver
**conduire** *v* to drive
**conduit** *pp* of **conduire**
faire **confiance à** to trust (someone)
**confier** *v* to entrust
un **confort** *nm* a comfort
faire **la connaissance de** to get to know
**connaître** *v* to know (a person, place)
**connu** *pp* of **connaître**
**consacré/consacrée à** *adj* devoted to
se **consacrer à** *v* to devote oneself to
un **conseil** *nm* a piece of advice; a council
**conseiller** *v* advise
un/une **conseiller/conseillère** *nm/nf* a counsellor, adviser
un/une **conseiller/conseillère d'orientation** *nm/nf* a careers adviser
par **conséquence** as a consequence
une **conso (= consommation)** *nf* a drink
**consommer** *v* to consume
**construit/construite en** *adj* built out of
le **contenu** *nm* the contents
le **contrôle (de maths)** *nm* (maths) test
**convaincant/convaincante** *adj* convincing
**convaincre** *v* to convince
un **copain** *nm* a (boy)friend
une **copine** *nf* a (girl)friend
**corriger** *v* to correct
la **côte** *nf* the coast
un **côté** *nm* a side
à **côté de** next to
être **couché/couchée** to be lying down
se **coucher** *v* to go to bed
être en **couple** to be in a couple
**couramment** fluently
**courir** *v* to run
une **couronne** *nf* a crown
le **courrier** *nm* the (day's) post, letters
le **cours** *nm* lesson
une **course (à pied)** *nf* a (running) race
faire les **courses** to do the shopping
**court/courte** *adj* short
un **couteau** *nm* a knife
**coûter** *v* to cost
un/une **créateur/créatrice** *nm/nf* a creator
**crier** *v* to shout
la **crise** *nf* crisis
**croire** *v* to believe
une **croisée** *nf* a crusade
**cru** *pp* of **croire**
**cru/crue** *adj* raw
une **cuiller/cuillère** *nf* a spoon
une **cuillerée** *nf* a spoonful
le **cuir** *nm* leather
**cuisiner** *v* to cook
un/une **cuisinier/cuisinière** *nm/nf* a cook
un/une **cultivateur/cultivatrice** *nm/nf* a farmer

## D

**d'abord** at first
**de bonne heure** early
la **date de naissance** *nf* date of birth
être **debout** to be standing up
**décembre** *nm* December
**décevant/décevante** *adj* disappointing
**décevoir** *v* to disappoint
les **déchets** *nm pl* rubbish
**déclarer** *v* to declare
**découvrir** *v* to discover
**décrire** *v* to describe
un **défilé** *nm* a procession, march
**défiler** *v* to march
**déguster** *v* to taste (for flavour)
**déjeuner** *v* to have lunch (sometimes also: to have breakfast)
un **délit** *nm* crime
**démarrer** *v* to start (a car)
**déménager** *v* to move house
un **demi-frère** *nm* a half-brother
une **demi-sœur** *nf* a half-sister
**démodé/démodée** *adj* old-fashioned
le **dentifrice** *nm* toothpaste
**dépasser les limites** to overstep the mark
**dépendre de** *v* depend on
**dépenser** *v* to spend
se **déplacer** *v* to move around
**depuis** since, for (time)
se **dérouler** *v* to take place
**dès que** as soon as
**descendre** *v* to go down
un **descriptif** *nm* specifications
**désespérer** *v* to despair
**désolé/désolée** *adj* sorry
**dessiner** *v* draw, design
se **détendre** *v* to relax
**détester** *v* to hate
**détruire** *v* to destroy
**deviner** *v* to guess
**devoir** *v* to have to, must
les **devoirs** *nm pl* homework
**devr-** future and conditional stem of **devoir**
**dimanche** *nm* Sunday
**dîner** *v* to have dinner
en **direct** live
**directement** directly
un/une **directeur/directrice** *nm/nf* a (school) head
un/une **dirigeant/dirigeante** *nm/nf* a (company) director, leader
**discuter** *v* to discuss
**disparaître** *v* to disappear
**disparu** *pp* of **disparaître**
**dit** *pp* of **dire**
**divorcer** *v* to divorce
une **dizaine** *nf* ten or so
(c'est) **dommage!** that's a shame!
se **doucher** *v* to have a shower
je m'en **doute!** I can just imagine!
se **douter de** *v* to suspect something
**doux/douce** *adj* sweet, gentle

(tout) **droit** straight on
à **droite** to the right
**dû** *pp* of **devoir**
la **durée** *nf* duration, length

## E

l' **eau potable** *nf* drinking water
un **échange** *nm* an exchange
**échanger** *v* to exchange
les **échecs** *nm pl* chess
**écolo(gique)** *adj* green, ecological
**économiser** *v* to save (money)
**l'écotourisme** *nm* eco-tourism
**écouter** *v* to listen
**écrire** *v* to write
**également** also
une **église** *nf* a church
**égoïste** *adj* selfish
**élargir ses horizons** to broaden one's horizons
les **emballages** *nm pl* packaging
**emballer** *v* to wrap up
**embêtant/embêtante** *adj* annoying
une **émission** *nf* (television) programme
**émouvant/émouvante** *adj* moving
**empêcher** *v* to prevent
un **emplacement** *nm* a site
un **emploi** *nm* a job
l' **empreinte** *nf* a (foot)print
**emprunter** *v* to borrow
s' **endormir** *v* to fall asleep
un **endroit** *nm* a place
**énerver** *v* to get on one's nerves
**s'ennuyer** *v* to be bored
**enregistrer** *v* to record
**enrichissant/enrichissante** *adj* rewarding
un/une **enseignant/enseignante** *nm/nf* a teacher
**ensuite** next
**entendre** *v* to understand, hear
s' **entendre avec** *v* to get on with (a person)
**entouré/entourée de** *adj* surrounded by
**entre** between
d' **entre** among, of
une **entreprise** *nf* a firm (business)
**entrer** *v* to enter, go in
un **entretien** *mn* an interview
**enverr-** future and conditional stem of **envoyer**
avoir **envie de** to want to
**envoyer** *v* to send
**épais/épaisse** *adj* thick
**épaissir** *v* to thicken
une **épingle** *nf* a pin
**éplucher** *v* to peel
**épouvantable*** *adj* frightful
l' **EPS (= éducation physique et sportive)** *nf* PE or PT
**équitable** *adj* fair-trade
l' **équitation** *nf* horse riding
l' **escalade** *nf* (rock) climbing
l' **esclavage** *nm* slavery
un/une **esclave** *nm/nf* a slave
un **espace** *nm* a space
l' **espérance de vie** *nf* life expectancy
**espérer** *v* to hope
l' **espoir** *nm* hope
**essayer** *v* to try
l' **essence (sans plomb)** *nf* (unleaded) petrol
un **établissement** *nm* an establishment
un **étage** *nm* floor, level
l' **été** *nm* summer
**été** *pp* of **être**
**éteindre** *v* to turn off (e.g. the TV)
**s'étirer** *v* to stretch
**étonnant/étonnante** *adj* astonishing
**étranger/étrangère** *adj* foreign, strange
un/une **étranger/étrangère** *nm/nf* a foreigner, stranger
à l' **étranger** abroad
**étroit/étroite** *adj* narrow
une **étude** *nf* study
**étudier** *v* to study
**eu** *pp* of **avoir**
un **événement** *nm* an event
**éventuellement** possibly
**éviter** *v* to avoid
s' **excuser** *v* to apologise
**exiger** *v* to require, demand
**expliquer** *v* to explain
**exprimer** *v* to express

## F

en **face de** opposite
faire **face à** to face, face up to
une **façon** *nf* a way
un/une **facteur/factrice** *nm/nf* a postman/postwoman
**faible*** **(en)** *adj* weak (in) / no good (at)
avoir **faim** to be hungry
**falloir** *v* to be necessary
**fatigant/fatigante** *adj* tiring
la **fauconnerie** *nf* falconry
il **faut** it is necessary to from **falloir**
un **fauteuil** *nm* an armchair
**faux/fausse** *adj* wrong, false
une **femme au foyer** *nf* a housewife
une **fête** *nf* a party
**fêter** *v* to celebrate
le **feu** *nm* fire (in cooking: heat)
une **feuille** *nf* a leaf, sheet of paper
**février** *nm* February
**fidèle*** *adj* loyal, faithful
**fier/fière** *adj* proud
se **figurer** *v* to imagine
à la **fin de** at the end of
**finir** *v* to finish
**foncé/foncée** *adj* dark (of a colour)
le **foot(ball)** *nm* football
le **footing** *nm* jogging
être en **forme** to be fit
**fort/forte (en)** *adj* strong (in), good (at)
**frais/fraîche** *adj* fresh
les **frais** *nm pl* fees
une **fraise** *nf* a strawberry
une **framboise** *nf* a raspberry
**franc/franche** *adj* frank, sincere
**francophone*** *adj* French-speaking
**frapper** *v* to hit
**frisé/frisée** *adj* frizzy
**froid/froide** *adj* cold
avoir **froid** to be cold (of a person)
il fait **froid** it's cold (weather)

## G

**gagner** *v* to win, earn
**gallo-romain/gallo-romaine** *adj* Gallo-Roman
**garder** *v* to look after
un/une **gardien/gardienne (de but)** *nm/nf* goalkeeper
une **gare** *nf* a train station
**gaspiller** *v* to waste
à **gauche** to the left
**généreux/généreuse** *adj* generous
**génial/géniale/géniaux/géniales** *adj* great, brilliant
les **gens** *nm pl* people
**gentil/gentille** *adj* nice
**gérer** *v* to manage
un **geste** *nm* a gesture
le **gîte** *nm* country holiday home/gite
**glisser** *v* to slip, slide
un **goût** *nm* a taste
**grand-chose** much
une **grand-mère** *nf* a grandmother
un **grand-père** *nm* a grandfather
les **grandes vacances** *nf pl* summer holidays
le **gras** *nm* fat
**gras/grasse** *adj* fatty
**gratuit/gratuite** *adj* free (without cost)
**grave*** *adj* serious
**grec/grecque** *adj* Greek
**grimper** *v* to climb
un **grenier** *nm* a loft
une **grille** *nf* a grid
**gros/grosse** *adj* fat
une **guerre** *nf* a war
un/une **gymnaste** *nm/nf* a gymnast

## H

un/une **habitant/habitante** *nm/nf* an inhabitant
**habiter** *v* to live
les **habits** *nm pl* clothes
une **habitude** *nf* a habit
d' **habitude** usually
s' **habituer à** *v* to get used to
un **haltère** *nm* a dumbbell
en **haut** upstairs, at the top
à **haute voix** out loud
la **hauteur** *nf* height
**historique** *adj* historic
l' **hiver** *nm* winter
un **homme au foyer** *nm* a househusband
**honnête** *adj* honest
les **horaires (d'ouverture)** *nm pl* (opening) hours
**hors-piste** *adj & adverb* off-piste
un/une **hôtelier/hôtelière** *nm/nf* an hotelier
une **hôtesse (d'accueil)** *nf* a receptionist
l' **huile (d'olive)** *nf* (olive) oil

## I

**il y a** there is/there are; ago
une **île** *nf* an island
**immanquable*** *adj* unmissable
**impitoyable*** *adj* ruthless
**impoli/impolie** *adj* impolite, rude
**imprévisible*** *adj* unpredictable
**imprimer** *v* to print (out)
**inconfortable*** *adj* uncomfortable
**inconnu/inconnue** *adj* unknown

**incorporer** *v* to fold in
**industriel(le)** *adj* industrial
un/une **infirmier/infirmière** *nm/nf* a nurse
un/une **informaticien/informaticienne** *nm/nf* an IT expert
les **informations** *nf pl* news
l' **informatique** *nf* IT
**injuste** *adj* unfair
**inoubliable*** *adj* unforgettable
s' **inquiéter de** *v* to be worried about
un/une **instituteur/institutrice** *nm/nf* a primary schoolteacher
**insupportable*** *adj* unbearable
**interdit/interdite** *adj* forbidden
un/une **internaute** *nm/nf* a net surfer
**interroger** *v* to question
**l'intimidation** *nf* bullying
**inutile*** *adj* useless
**ir-** future and conditional stem of **aller**

## J

**janvier** *nm* January
le **jardinage** *nm* gardening
un/une **jardinier/jardinière** *nm/nf* a gardener
**jeudi** *nm* Thursday
la **jeunesse** *nf* youth
le **jour des Rois** *nm* Epiphany
un **jour férié** *nm* a holiday, day off
un **journal** (pl. **les journaux**) *nm* a newspaper
une **journée** *nf* a day
la **journée scolaire** *nf* school day
**joyeux/joyeuse** *adj* cheerful
**juillet** *nm* July
**juin** *nm* June
**jumeau/jumelle/jumeaux** *adj* twin
un **jumelage** *nm* town twinning
**jusqu'à** until
**juste*** *adj* fair

## L

**là(-bas)** (over) there
le **lac** *nm* lake
un **lacet** *nm* a (shoe) lace
**laid/laide** *adj* ugly
**laisser** *v* to leave (behind)
une **langue** *nf* a language
se **laver** *v* to get washed
un **lecteur MP3** *nm* an MP3 player
la **lecture** *nf* reading
**léger/légère** *adj* light (weight)
les **légumes** *nm pl* vegetables
le **lendemain** *nm* the day after
**lent/lente** *adj* quick
**faire la lessive** *v* to do the washing
se **lever** *v* to get up
la **liberté** *nf* freedom
le **lieu de naissance** *nm* place of bith
avoir **lieu** to take place
**lire** *v* to read
une **liste d'achats** *nf* a shopping list
**local/locale/locaux/locales** *adj* local
un **logement** *nm* accommodation
**loger** *v* to accommodate
les **loisirs** *nm pl* leisure activities
**long/longue** *adj* long
la **longueur** *nf* length
**lors de** at the time of
**louer** *v* to rent
**lourd/lourde** *adj* heavy
**lu** *pp* of **lire**
la **lumière** *nf* light
**lundi** *nm* Monday
les **lunettes** *nf pl* glasses, spectacles
le **lycée** a sixth-form college (16–18 years); grammar school
un/une **lycéen/lycéenne** *nm/nf* Student at a lycée

## M

un **magnétoscope** *nm* a video recorder
**mai** *nm* May
**maigre*** *adj* thin, skinny
**mal*** *adj & adverb* bad(ly)
faire **mal** to hurt
**malade*** *adj* sick, ill
**malgré** despite, in spite of
une **manière** *nf* a way (e.g. of doing something)
tu me **manques** I miss you
**manquer** *v* to be missing; to lack; to miss (a train)
un/une **marchand/marchande** *nm/nf* dealer, merchant
**mardi** *nm* Tuesday
**marquer un but, un essai** *v* score a goal, a try
**marrant/marrante** *adj* fun
**marron*** *adj* brown (of eyes)
**mars** *nm* March
le **matériel** *nm* equipment
une **matière** *nf* a (school) subject
**mauvais/mauvaise** *adj* bad
un **médecin** *nm* a doctor
une **médiathèque** *nf* a multimedia library
**meilleur/meilleure** *adj* better
un **mélange** *nm* mix
**même** even
la **mémoire** *nf* memory (faculty)
un/une **mendiant/mendiante** *nm/nf* a beggar
**mentionner** *v* to mention
**mercredi** *nm* Wednesday
**merveilleux/merveilleuse** *adj* wonderful
la **messagerie instantanée** *nf* instant messaging
le **métier** *nm* job, career
le **métro** *nm* underground
**mettre** *v* to put
se **mettre d'accord** *v* to agree
la **mi-temps** *nf* half-time
à **midi** at midday
**mille** thousand
des **milliers de** thousands of
au **milieu de** in the middle of
**mince*** *adj* thin, slender
à **minuit** at midnight
**mis** *pp* of **mettre**
la **misère** *nf* poverty
**moche*** *adj* ugly
la **mode** *nf* fashion
à la **mode** fashionable
au **moins** at least (with numbers)
du **moins** at least
le **monde** *nm* the world
**mondial/mondiale/mondiaux/mondiales** *adj* world
la **montagne** *nf* mountain
la **montée des océans** *nf* rising oceans
**monter** *v* to go up
**montrer** *v* to show
un **morceau** *nm* a bit
**mordre** *v* to bite
**mort/morte** *adj* dead; *pp* of **mourir**
une **mosquée** *nf* a mosque
se **motiver** *v* to motivate oneself
une **moto(cyclette)** *nf* a motorbike
un **moule** *nm* a mould
une **moule** *nf* a mussel
**mourir** *v* to die
**moyen/moyenne** *adj* average
en **moyenne** on average
la **musculation** *nf* weight training
un **musée** *nm* museum
un/une **musicien/musicienne** *nm/nf* a musician
**musulman/musulmane** *adj* Muslim

## N

**nager** *v* to swim
la **naissance** *nf* birth
**naître** *v* to be born
la **natation** *nf* swimming
**né/née** *pp* of **naître**
**ne ... jamais** never
**ne ... personne** no one
**ne ... plus** no longer
**néanmoins** nevertheless
la **neige** *nf* snow
il **neige** it's snowing
**n'importe quel** whatever
**ni ... ni** neither ... nor
le **nom de famille** *nm* surname, family name
un **nombre** *nm* a number
la **nourriture** *nf* food
**nouveau/nouvel/nouvelle/nouveaux/nouvelles** *adj* new
**novembre** *nm* November
un **nuage** *nm* a cloud
**nul/nulle** *adj* rubbish, terrible
un **numéro** *nm* a (telephone, bank etc.) number

## O

**obéir** *v* to obey
**occupé/occupée** *adj* busy
s' **occuper de** *v* to see to
**octobre** *nm* October
une **odeur** *nf* a smell
les **œufs brouillés** *nm pl* scrambled eggs
**offrir** *v* to give (as a present); to offer
s' **offrir** *v* to treat oneself to
un **olivier** *nm* an olive tree
une **opération de collecte et de tri** *nf* collect and sort exercise
un **ordinateur** *nm* a computer
un **ordinateur portable** *nm* a laptop
une **oreille** *nf* an ear
s' **organiser** *v* to get organised
un/une **orphelin/orpheline** *nm/nf* an orphan
l' **orthographe** *nf* spelling
**oublier** *v* to forget
l' **ouest** *nm* the west
**ouvert/ouverte** *adj* open

**ouvert** *pp* of **ouvrir**
**ouvrir** *v* to open

## P

une **page de publicité** *nf* a commercial break
**Pâques** *nf pl* Easter
**par contre** on the other hand
il **paraît que** it seems that
un **parc de loisirs** *nm* a leisure park
**paresseux/paresseuse** *adj* lazy
**parfait/parfaite** *adj* perfect
**partager** *v* to share
un/une **partenaire** *nm/nf* a partner
**participer à** *v* to take part in
**partir** *v* to leave
à **partir de** from (time)
**passer** *v* to spend (time); to take (an exam)
se **passer** to happen, occur
**passer une visite médicale** to have a (medical) check-up
une **patate douce** *nf* a sweet potato
**patiner** *v* to skate
un/une **patron/patronne** *nm/nf* a boss
faire une **pause** to take a break
**payer** *v* to pay for
la **pêche** *nf* fishing
une **pêche** *nf* a peach
**pendant** for (time)
se **perdre** *v* to get lost
**perdre du poids** to lose weight
**perfectionner** *v* to improve
la **période estivale** *nf* the summer season
la **permanence** *nf* study period
**permettre** *v* to allow
**persuader quelqu'un de** *v* to persuade someone to
**peser** *v* to weigh
un/une **petit ami/petite amie** *nm/nf* a boyfriend/ girlfriend
un **petit-enfant** *nm* a grandchild
avoir **peur** to be afraid
une **phrase** *nf* a sentence
une **pièce** *nf* a room
une **pierre** *nf* a stone
une **pincée** *nf* a pinch
une **piqûre** *nf* a sting
**pire*** *adj* worst
une **piscine** *nf* a swimming pool
une **place** *nf* a (town) square
faire **place à** to give way to
sur **place** on the spot
une **plage** *nf* a beach
se **plaindre (de)** *v* to complain (about)
**plaire** *v* to please
avec **plaisir!** gladly! with pleasure!
la **planche à voile** *nf* wind surfing
**planifier** *v* to plan
un **plat** *nm* a dish (of food)
**plein/pleine de** full of
en **plein air** in the open air
il **pleut** it's raining (from **pleuvoir**)
**pleuvoir** *v* to rain
la **plongée sous-marine** *nf* (deep-sea) diving
**plu** *pp* of **plaire**
la **plupart** the majority, most
de **plus** more
en **plus** in addition
**plusieurs*** *adj* several
**plutôt** rather
**poli/polie** *adj* polite
un **portable** *nm* a mobile (telephone)
**poser** *v* to put
**poser une question** to ask a question
**posséder** *v* to own, possess
la **Poste** *nf* the post office
un **poste** *nm* a job, position
un **poste de télévision** *nm* a television set
**pourr-** future and conditional stem of **pouvoir**
**pousser** *v* push, grow
**pouvoir** *v* to be able to, can
**préchauffer** *v* to preheat
**préféré/préférée** *adj* favourite
un **prémix** *nm* an alcopop
**prendre** *v* to take
le **prénom** *nm* first name
**près de** close to
un/une **présentateur/ présentatrice** *nm/ nf* a (TV) presenter, newsreader
se **présenter** *v* to introduce oneself
**presque** almost
**pressé/pressée** *adj* in a hurry
**prêter** *v* to lend
le **printemps** *nm* spring (season)
**pris** *pp* of **prendre**
se **priver** *v* to deprive oneself
**prochain/prochaine** *adj* next
**produire** *v* to produce
un **produit** *nm* product
un **professeur** *nm* a teacher, lecturer
**profond/profonde** *adj* deep
la **profondeur** *nf* depth
une **promenade** *nf* a walk
une **promenade en bateau** *nf* a boat trip
**promener** *v* to walk (e.g. a dog)
se **promener** *v* to go for a walk
**promettre** *v* to promise
**promouvoir** *v* to promote
**propre*** *adj* clean
un/une **propriétaire** *nm/nf* an owner
se **protéger** *v* to protect oneself
**provenir (de)** *v* to come (from)
**pu** *pp* of **pouvoir**
la **publicité** nf advert(ising)
**puisque** since
la **puissance** *nf* strength
un **pull** *nm* a pullover, jumper

## Q

**quand même** even so
**quant à** as for
une **quarantaine de** forty or so
**quarante** forty
un **quart d'heure** *nm* a quarter of an hour
**qu'est-ce qu'il y a?** what's the matter?
**quelle blague!** what rubbish!
une **quinzaine** *nf* a fortnight
**quitter** *v* to leave (place)
**quotidien/quotidienne** *adj* daily

## R

**raconter** *v* tell (a story), recount
le **racket** *nm* bullying
**radicalement** *adv* radically
**raide*** *adj* straight (of hair)
avoir **raison** to be right
une **randonnée** *nf* a walk, hike
une **randonnée à cheval** *nf* a (horse or pony) trek
se **rappeler** *v* to remember
**rarement** *adv* rarely
**rater** *v* to miss, fail
**ravi/ravie** *adj* delighted
**récemment** recently
une **recette** *nf* a recipe
**recevoir** *v* to receive, get
le **réchauffement climatique** *nm* global warming
**rechercher** *v* to search for
faire des **recherches (sur)** to do research (on)
**recommander** *v* to recommend
une **récré(ation)** *nf* a (school) break
un **reçu** *nm* a receipt
**reçu** *pp* of **reçevoir**
la **récupération** *nf* recovery; recycling
**recycler** *v* to recycle
**réellement** *adv* truly
se **référer à** *v* to refer to
**regarder** *v* to look at, watch
**régler** *v* to settle (a bill)
les **règles d'or** *nf pl* golden rules
je **regrette** I'm sorry
**régulièrement** *adv* regularly
**rejoindre** *v* to join up with
**relever un défi** to take up a challenge
**remarquer** *v* to notice
**rembourser** *v* to reimburse
**remercier** *v* to thank
**remettre** *v* to put back
**remonter dans le temps** to go back in time
**remplacer** *v* replace
**remplir** *v* to fill (in)
**remporter** *v* to carry back; to win
**remuer** *v* to stir
la **rémunération** *nf* pay
une **rencontre** *nf meeting*
**rendre** *v* to give back
les **renseignements** *nm pl* information
la **rentrée** *nf* the return to school (or work) after the August summer holidays
se **réparer** *v* to mend itself
un **repas** *nm* a meal
**répondre** *v* to reply
un **reportage** *nm* a report
**reposant/reposante** *adj* restful
se **reposer** *v* to rest
le **RER** *nm* Paris fast suburban rail link
un **réseau social** (pl. **réseaux sociaux**) *nm* a social network
la **restauration** *nf* catering
un **résultat** *nm* a result
en **retard** late

se **retrouver** *v* to meet (by arrangement)
**réussir à** *v* to succeed at, in, to pass (exam)
un **rêve** *nm* a dream
se **réveiller** *v* to wake up
**revenir** *v* to come back
**révolutionnaire*** *adj* revolutionary
**rire** *v* to laugh
**risquer de** *v* to risk doing something
une **rivière** *nf* a river
le **riz** *nm* rice
un **robinet** *nm* a tap
un **roi** *nm* a king
**rôti/rôtie** *adj* roasted

## S

**sain/saine** *adj* healthy
un/une **saisonnier/saisonnière** *nm/nf* a seasonal worker
une **salle d'animation** *nf* an activity room
**samedi** *nm* Saturday
**sans** without
un **sapin** *nm* a fir tree
une **saucisse** *nf* a sausage
**sauf** except
**saur-** future and conditional stem of **savoir**
**sauter un repas** to skip a meal
**sauvegarder** *v* to save
**savoir** *v* to know (a fact)
la **scolarisation** *nf* schooling
un **séjour** *nm* a stay; living room
le **sel** *nm* salt
une **semaine** *nf* week
un **sens de l'humour** *nm* a sense of humour
**sensible*** *adj* sensitive
**septembre** *nm* September
**ser-** future and conditional stem of **être**
un/une **serveur/serveuse** *nm/nf* a waiter/waitress
se **servir de** *v* to use
**seul/seule** *adj* alone
**si besoin est** if necessary
un **siècle** *nm* a century
un **signe astrologique** *nm* a star sign
**situé/située** located
**soi(-même)** oneself
avoir **soif** to be thirsty
il/elle/on **soit** present subjunctive of **être**
**soixante** sixty
**solitaire*** *adj* lonely
un **sondage** *nm* a poll, survey
une **sortie** *nf* an exit; trip out
**souligné/soulignée** *adj* underlined
**soupçonner** *v* to suspect
**sourire** *v* to smile
un **souvenir** *nm* a memory
se **souvenir de** *v* to remember
**sportif/sportive** *adj* sports, sporty
un/une **sportif/sportive** *nm/nf* a sportsman/sportswoman
un **stade** *nm* a stadium
un **stage** *nm* an internship
un/une **stagiaire** *nm/nf* an intern
une **station balnéaire** *nf* a seaside resort
**su** *pp* of **savoir**
le **sucre en poudre** *nm* caster sugar
les **sucreries** *nf pl* sweet things
je **suis** I am from **être**
**suivant/suivante** *adj* following
**suivre** *v* to follow
la **superficie terrestre** *nf* the Earth's surface
être **sur le point de** to be about to
**sûr/sure (de)** *adj* sure (about, of)
**surnommer** *v* to nickname
la **surpêche** *nf* over-fishing
en **surpoids** overweight
**surprendre** *v* to surprise
**survivre** *v* to survive
**survoler** *v* to skim over
les **SVT** *nf pl* science

## T

un **tablier** *nm* an apron
les **tâches ménagères** *nf pl* housework
la **taille** *nf* size
**tant de** so many
**tant mieux!** so much the better!
en **tant que** as, in the role of
un **tas** *nm* a pile
un **téléchargement** *nm* a download(ing)
un/une **téléspectateur/téléspectatrice** *nm/nf* a (TV) viewer
**tellement** so
le **témoignage** *nm* an account, testimony
de **temps en temps** from time to time
avoir **tendance à** to tend to
la **tenue** *nf* dress; upkeep
**terminer** *v* to finish
un **titre** *nm* a title
avoir **tort** to be wrong
**tourner un film** *v* to make a film
**tout à coup** suddenly
**tout de suite** immediately
**tout le monde** everyone
**toutefois** nevertheless, however
le **traducteur/la traductrice** *nm/mf* translator
**traduire** *v* to translate
être en **train de** to be in the process of
un **trajet** *nm* a (short) journey
le **tramway** *nm* tram
**travailler** *v* to work
**travailleur/travailleuse** *adj* hard-working
à **travers** across, through
**traverser** *v* to cross
**trente** thirty
**trier** *v* to sort (out)
se **trouver** *v* to be situated
un **truc** *nm* a thing, 'thingummy'

## U

**unique*** *adj* only
une **usine** *nf* factory
**utile** adj useful
**utiliser** *v* to use

## V

un **vainqueur** *nm* a conqueror, victor
une **valise** *nf* a suitcase
il **vaut** *v* it is worth from **valoir**
**vécu** *pp* of **vivre**
une **vedette de cinéma** *nf* a film star (male or female)
la **veille** *nf* the day before
un **vélo** *nm* a bike
un/une **vendeur/vendeuse** *nm/nf* a salesman/saleswoman
**vendre** *v* to sell
**vendredi** *nm* Friday
**venir** *v* to come
**venu/venue** *pp* of **venir**
**vérifier** *v* to check
**verr-** future and conditional stem of **voir**
**vers** towards; around (time)
**verser** *v* to pour
les **vêtements** *nm pl* clothes
**veuf/veuve** *adj* widowed
la **viande** *nf* meat
la **vie** *nf* life
**vieux/vieil/vieille/vieux/vieilles** *adj* old
**vif/vive** *adj* bright (of a colour)
**vilain/vilaine** *adj* ugly, nasty
une **ville jumelle** *nf* a twin town
**vingt** twenty
rendre **visite à** to visit (a person)
une **vitrine** *nf* a shop window
**vivre** *v* to live
un/une **voisin/voisine** *nm/nf* a neighbour
le **vol** *nm* flight; theft
**voler** *v* to fly; to steal
**voudr-** future and conditional stem of **vouloir**
**vouloir** *v* to want
**vrai(e)** *adj* true
**vraiment** *adv* really
**vu** *pp* of **voir**

## Y

**y** *there*
**y compris** *including*

# Vocabulary

## A

to be **able to** pouvoir *v*
**about** environ
to be **about to ...** être sur le point de ...
**about** (approximately) à peu près; (with times) vers
it is **about ...** il s'agit de ...
**abroad** à l'étranger
**access to** accès à
**accommodation** le logement *nm*
**according to** selon
**across** à travers
**actually** en fait
in **addition** en plus
in **advance** à l'avance
**advantage** l'avantage *nm*
**adventurous** aventureux/aventureuse *adj*
**advertising** la publicité *nf*
(piece of) **advice** le conseil *nm*
to **advise** conseiller *v*
an **aeroplane** un avion *nm*
to be **afraid of ...** avoir peur de ...
**after** après (que)
in the **afternoon** l'après-midi *nm*
**ago** il y a
to **agree** être d'accord
**alcohol** l'alcool *nm*
**allergic** allergique *adj*
**almost** presque
**alone** seul/seule *adj*
**also** aussi, également
**always** toujours
**among** parmi
**angel** un ange *nm*
**angry** fâché, fâchée *adj*
to get **angry** (with someone) se fâcher (contre quelqu'un) *v*
**annoying** embêtant(e) *adj*
that **annoys me** ça m'embête
**anxious** anxieux/anxieuse *adj*
an **apartment** un appartement *nm*
to **apologise** s'excuser *v*
**appetite** l'appétit *nm*
an **apprentice** un apprenti *nm*/une apprentie *nf*
an **apprenticeship** un apprentissage *nm*
**appropriate** approprié(e) *adj*
**April** avril *nm*
**around** autour de; (approximately) environ; (time) vers
**as** comme; (while) alors que; (being) en tant que
**as for** quant à
**as soon as** aussitôt que, dès que
to **ask** demander *v*
to **ask a question** poser une question
to be **asleep** dormir *v*
**astonishing** étonnant/étonnante *adj*
**at** à
**at Juliette's (house)** chez Juliette
an **athlete** un/une athlète *nm/nf*
**athletics** l'athlétisme *nm*
**atmosphere** l'ambiance *nf*
to **attach** attacher *v*
to **attend** assister à *v*
**August** août *nm*
**autumn** l'automne *nm*
**average** moyen/moyenne *adj*
on **average** en moyenne
to **avoid** éviter *v*

## B

**bad** mauvais(e) *adj*; (serious) grave* *adj*
**badly** mal
a **bag** un sac *nm*
a **bank** une banque *nf*
a **basement** un sous-sol *nm*
to have a **bath** se baigner *v*
a **bathroom** une salle de bain *nf*
a **battle** une bataille *nf*
a **beach** une plage *nf*
**beard** la barbe *nf*
to **beat** battre *v*
**beautiful** beau/bel/belle/beaux/belles *adj*
**because** parce que, car
**because of** à cause de
to go to **bed** se coucher *v*
**before** avant, avant de, avant que
**beforehand** à l'avance
**behind** derrière
to **believe** croire *v*
the **best** le meilleur *nm*/la meilleure *nf*
**better** (*comparative of* **good**) meilleur/meilleure *adj*; (*comparative of* **well**) mieux
**between** entre
**big** grand/grande *adj*
a **bike** un vélo *nm*
**biology** la biologie *nf*
**birth** la naissance *nf*
a **birthday** un anniversaire *nm*
a **bit (piece)** un morceau *nm*
**black** noir/noire *adj*
a **block of flats** un immeuble *nm*
**blue** bleu/bleue *adj*
a **boat** un bateau (les bateaux) *nm*
**body** le corps *nm*
to **book** (e.g. a room) réserver *v*
a **bookshelf** une étagère *nf*
a **bookshop** une librairie *nf*
**boring** ennuyeux/ennuyeuse *adj*,
to be **born** naître *v* (takes **être**)
a **boss** un patron *nm*/une patronne *nf*
a **bowl** un bol *nm*
a **box** une boîte *nf*
**bread** le pain *nm*
to **break** casser *v*
**breakfast** le petit déjeuner *nm*
to **bring** (a person, animal, vehicle) amener *v*; (an object) apporter *v*
to **broaden one's horizons** élargir ses horizons
**brother** le frère *nm*
**brown** brun/brune *adj*; (of eyes) marron* *adj*
to **brush one's teeth** se brosser les dents
to **build** construire *v*
a **building** un bâtiment *nm*
**bullying** l'intimidation *nf*, le racket *nm*
a **bus** un (auto)bus *nm*
a **bus station** une gare routière *nf*
**business** les affaires *nf pl*
a **businessman** un homme d'affaires *nm*
a **businesswoman** une femme d'affaires *nf*
**busy** occupé/occupée *adj*
**butter** le beurre *nm*
to **buy** acheter *v*

## C

a **cake** un gâteau *nm*
a **calculator** une calculatrice *nf*
a **camera** un appareil photo *nm*
a **career** une carrière *nf*
a **careers adviser** un conseiller d'orientation *nm*/une conseillère d'orientation *nf*
a **car park** un parking *nm*
a **cartoon** un dessin animé *nm*
to **celebrate** fêter *v*
a **century** un siècle *nm*
to get **changed** se changer *v*
a (TV) **channel** une chaîne *nf*
**cheap** bon marché* *adj*
to **check** vérifier *v*; (a ticket) contrôler *v*
**chemical** chimique* *adj*
**chips** les frites *nf pl*
a **choice** un choix *nm*
a **choral society** une chorale *nf*
**Christian** chrétien/chrétienne *adj*
**Christmas** Noël *nm*
happy **Christmas!** joyeux Noël!
a **church** une église *nf*
a **citizen** un citoyen *nm*/une citoyenne *nf*
a **city** une grande ville *nf*
a **city centre** un centre-ville *nm*
**clean** propre* *adj*
to **clear the table** débarrasser la table
**close to** près de
**clothes** les vêtements *nm pl*
a **coach** (sports) un entraîneur *nm*/une entraîneuse *nf*, (transport) un car *nm*
the **coast** la côte *nf*
**cold** froid/froide *adj*
to be **cold** (of a person) avoir froid
it's **cold** (weather) il fait froid
a **colleague** un(une) collègue *nm/f*
to **come** venir *v* (takes **être**)
to **come back** revenir *v*
**comfortable** confortable* *adj*
to **complain** (about) se plaindre (de) *v*
a **computer** un ordinateur *nm*
to **condemn** condamner *v*
a **counsellor** un/une conseiller/conseillère *nm/nf*
as a **consequence** par conséquent
to **cook** faire la cuisine, cuisiner *v*

a **cook** un cuisinier *nf*/une cuisinière *nm*
to **cost** coûter *v*
a **country** un pays *nm*
the **country(side)** la campagne *nf*
in the **country(side)** à la campagne
**crisis** la crise *nf*
to **cross** traverser *v*
to **cry** pleurer *v*
a **cup** une tasse *nf*
to **cut** couper *v*
**cute** mignon/mignonne *adj*

## D

**daily** quotidien/quotidienne *adj*
**dancing** la danse *nf*
**date of birth** la date de naissance *nf*
**daughter** la fille *nf*
a **day** un jour *nm*, une journée *nf*
the **day after** le lendemain *nm*
the **day after tomorrow** l'après-demain *nm*
the **day before** la veille *nf*
the **day before yesterday** avant-hier
**dead** mort(e) *adj*
**December** décembre *nm*
**delighted** ravi(e) *adj*
that **depends** ça dépend
to **describe** décrire *v*
a **desk** (in office) un bureau *nm*; (for pupil) un pupitre *nm*
**despite** malgré
to **die** mourir *v* (*takes* **être**)
a **digital camera** un appareil photo numérique *nm*
a **dining room** une salle à manger *nf*
**dinner** le dîner *nm*
to have **dinner** dîner *v*
a **director** (e.g. of a company) un dirigeant *nm*/une dirigeante *nf*
**dirty** sale* *adj*
to **disappear** disparaître *v*
to **disappoint** décevoir *v*
**disappointing** décevant(e) *adj*
to **discover** découvrir *v*
a **dish (of food)** un plat *nm*
a **district** un quartier *nm*
**diving** la plongée *nf*
to **divorce** divorcer *v*
a **doctor** un médecin *nm* / une femme médecin *nf*
a **double bed** un grand lit *nm*
to **download** télécharger *v*
**downstairs** en bas
**drama** (subject) l'art dramatique *nm*
a **dream** un rêve *nm*
a **drink** une boisson *nf*, une conso(mmation) *nf*
to **drink** boire
**drinking water** l'eau potable *nf*
to **drive** conduire *v*
a **driver** (of a taxi, lorry, bus) un chauffeur; (of a car) un conducteur *nm*/une conductrice *nf*
a **driving licence** un permis de conduire *nm*

## E

**email** le courrier électronique *nm*
**each** chaque*
**early** de bonne heure
to **earn** gagner *v*
**east** l'est *nm*
**Easter** Pâques *nf pl*
Happy **Easter!** Joyeuses Pâques!
**education** l'éducation *nf*
**educational** éducatif/éducative *adj*
an **egg** un œuf *nm*
**eighty** quatre-vingts
**elsewhere** ailleurs
**elder** aîné/aînée
at the **end of** à la fin de
to **enjoy oneself** s'amuser *v*
to **enter** entrer *v* (*takes* **être**)
**equipment** le matérial *nm*
an **establishment** un établissement *nm*
**even** même
**even so** quand même
**evening** le soir *nm*; la soirée *nf*
an **event** un événement *nm*
**everybody/everyone** tout le monde
an **exam(ination)** un examen *nm*
**except** sauf
an **exchange** un échange *nm*
to **exchange** échanger *v*
**excuse me!** excusez-moi!
an **exercise book** un cahier *nm*
an **exit** une sortie *nf*
to **explain** expliquer *v*
to **express** exprimer *v*

## F

to **face, face up to** faire face à *v*
a **factory** une usine *nf*
to **fail** échouer *v*, rater *v*
**fair** juste* *adj*
to **fall asleep** s'endormir *v*
to **fall (to the floor)** tomber *v* (par terre)
a **fan** un(e) fan
a **farm** une ferme *nf*
a **farmer** un/une cultivateur/cultivatrice *nm*/*nf*
**fashion** la mode *nf*
**fashionable** à la mode
a **fast-food restaurant** un fast-food *nm*
**fat** gros/grosse *adj*
**fatty** gras/grasse *adj*
**favourite** préféré(e) *adj*
**February** février *nm*
I'm **fed up with** ... j'en ai marre de ...
to **fetch** aller chercher
**fifty** cinquante
a **file** un dossier *nm*
to do the **filing** s'occuper du classement
**finger** le doigt *nm*
to **finish** finir *v*, terminer *v*
a **firm** (business) une entreprise *nf*
the **first** le premier *nm*/la première *nf*
at **first** d'abord
on the **first floor** au premier étage
(to go) **fishing** aller à la pêche *nf*
**floor** (e.g. of a room) le plancher *nm*; (level) un étage *nm*
**fluently** couramment
to **fly** voler *v*
to **follow** suivre *v*
**food** la nourriture *nf*
on **foot** à pied
**football** le foot(ball) *nm*
**for** pour; (time past) pendant; (future time) pour; (ongoing) depuis
to **forbid** défendre *v*
**forbidden** interdit(e) *adj*
**foreign** étranger/étrangère *adj*
a **foreigner** un étranger *nm*/une étrangère *nf*
to **forget** oublier *v*
a **fork** une fourchette *nf*
**former** ancien/ancienne *adj* (placed before the noun)
**formerly** autrefois
a **fortnight** une quinzaine *nf*
**free** (without cost) gratuit/gratuite *adj*; (not busy) libre* *adj*
it's **freezing** il gèle
**French** français(e) *adj*
a **Frenchman** un Français *nm*
a **Frenchwoman** une Française *nf*
**fresh** frais/fraîche *adj*
a **friend** (male) un ami *nm*, un copain *nm*
a **friend** (female) une amie *nf*, une copine *nf*
**friendly** amical(e) *adj*
**friendship** l'amitié *nf*
**frizzy** frisé/frisée *adj*
**from** de; (time) à partir de
at the **front** à l'avant
**full (of)** plein/pleine *adj* (de)
**full-time** à plein temps
**fun(ny)** marrant(e) *adj*, amusant(e) *adj*
to have **fun** s'amuser *v*
**future** l'avenir *nm*
in **future** à l'avenir

## G

**garlic** l'ail *nm*
a **gate** une barrière *nf*
**generally** en général
**generous** généreux/généreuse *adj*
**gentle** doux/douce *adj*
to **get** (receive) recevoir *v*
to **get dressed** s'habiller *v*
to **get off** descendre *v*
to **get on to** monter *v* (*takes* **être**)
to **get on with ...** (a person) s'entendre avec *v*
to **get to know** faire la connaissance de
**ginger** (-haired) roux/rousse *adj*
a **girlfriend** une petite amie *nf*; une copine *nf*
to **give** donner *v*; (as a present) offrir *v*
to **give back** rendre *v*
a **glass** un verre *nm*
**glasses** les lunettes *nf pl*
**global** mondial/mondiale/mondiaux/mondiales *adj*
**global warming** le réchauffement climatique *nm*
to **go** aller *v*
to **go away** s'en aller *v*
to **go down** descendre *v* (*takes* **être**)
to **go for a walk** se promener *v*

**to go in** entrer *v* (*takes* **être**)
**to go out** sortir *v* (*takes* **être**)
**to go to bed** se coucher *v*
**to go to sleep** s'endormir *v*
**to go up** monter *v* (*takes* **être**)
**a goal** un but *nm*
**a goalkeeper** un gardien (de but) *nm*/une gardienne (de but) *nf*
**good** bon/bonne *adj*
**good at** fort/forte en *adj*
**no good at** faible* en *adj*
**grandchild** le petit-enfant *nm*
**grandfather** le grand-père *nm*
**grandmother** la grand-mère *nf*
**grandparents** les grands-parents *nm pl*
**grateful** reconnaissant(e) *adj*
**great** génial/géniale/géniaux/géniales *adj*; super!*
**green** vert(e) *adj*
**grey** gris(e) *adj*
**on the ground floor** au rez-de-chaussée
**to guess** deviner *v*

## H

**a habit** une habitude *nf*
**hair** cheveux *nm pl*
**a hairdresser** un coiffeur *nm*/une coiffeuse *nf*
**a half** une moitié *nf*
**half-brother** le demi-frère *nm*
**a half-hour** une demi-heure *nf*
**half-sister** la demi-sœur *nf*
**half-time** la mi-temps *nf*
**it's half past five** il est cinq heures et demie
**by hand** à la main
**on the other hand** par contre
**a handbag** un sac à main *nm*
**handsome** beau/bel/belle/beaux/belles *adj*
**to happen** se passer
**happiness** le bonheur *nm*
**happy** heureux/heureuse *adj*, content/contente *adj*
**happy birthday!** bon anniversaire!
**hard** dur(e) *adj*; difficile* *adj*
**hard-working** travailleur/travailleuse *adj*
**a hat** un chapeau (*pl* les chapeaux) *nm*
**to have to** devoir *v*
**a head** (e.g. of a school) un directeur *nm*/une directrice *nf*
**a headache** un mal à la tête *nm*
**healthy** sain(e) *adj*
**heat** la chaleur *nf*
**to heat** chauffer *v*
**heavy** lourd/lourde *adj*
**a helmet** un casque *nm*
**here is/here are** voici
**here it is!** voilà!
**to hide** cacher *v*
**a hike** une randonnée *nf*
**to hit** frapper *v*
**a hobby** un passe-temps *nm*
**a holiday** les vacances *nf pl*
**go on holiday** partir en vacances
**a holiday camp** une colonie de vacances *nf*
**at home** à la maison
**a home help** une aide-ménagère *nf*
**homework** les devoirs *nm pl*
**to hope** espérer *v*
**hope** l'espoir *nm*
**a horse** cheval (*pl* les chevaux) *nm*
**horse riding** l'équitation *nf*
**a hospital** l'hôpital *nf*
**it's hot** il fait chaud
**a househusband** un homme au foyer *nm*
**a housewife** une femme au foyer *nf*
**housework** les tâches ménagères *nf pl*
**to do the housework** faire le ménage
**a hundred** cent
**to be hungry** avoir faim
**in a hurry** pressé(e) *adj*

## I

**an idea** une idée *nf*
**an identity card** une carte d'identité *nf*
**illiteracy** l'analphabétisme *nm*
**impolite** impoli(e) *adj*
**to improve** améliorer *v*, perfectionner *v*
**including** y compris
**information** les renseignements *nm pl*
**an inhabitant** un/une habitant/habitante *nm/nf*
**inside** à l'intérieur, dedans
**instead of** au lieu de
**to be interested in** s'intéresser à *v*
**interesting** intéressant(e) *adj*
**an intern** un/une stagiaire *nm/nf*
**the Internet** l'Internet *nm*
**an internship** un stage *nm*
**an interview** un entretien *mn*, un/une interview *nm* or *f*
**to introduce oneself** se présenter *v*
**is there ...?** il y a ...?
**it doesn't matter!** ça ne fait rien!
**IT (= information technology)** l'informatique *nf*
**an IT expert** un informaticien *nm*/une informaticienne *nf*
**an island** une île *nf*

## J

**jam** la confiture *nf*
**January** janvier *nm*
**(a pair of) jeans** un jean *nm*
**a jewel** un bijou (*pl.* les bijoux) *nm*
**Jewish** juif/juive *adj*
**a job** un emploi *nm*, un poste *nm*; (less formal) un boulot *nm*
**a journey** un voyage *nm*; (short) un trajet *nm*

## K

**to keep an eye on** surveiller *v*
**kitchen** la cuisine *nf*
**a knee** un genou (*pl* les genoux) *nm*
**a knife** un couteau (*pl* les couteaux) *nm*
**to know** (a person, place) connaître *v*; (a fact) savoir *v*
**to get to know** faire la connaissance de

## L

**a lady** une dame *nf*
**a laptop** un ordinateur portable *nm*
**last** dernier/dernière *adj*
**last week** la semaine dernière
**last weekend** le week-end dernier
**late** tard* *adv*
**to be late** être en retard
**a leaf** une feuille *nf*
**a league** un championnat *nm*
**to learn** apprendre *v*
**at least** du moins; (with numbers) au moins
**to leave** partir *v* (*takes* **être**); to leave (e.g. a place, person, job) quitter *v*
**to leave** (behind) laisser *v*
**to/on the left** à gauche
**leisure activities** les loisirs *nm pl*
**a leisure park** un parc de loisirs *nm*
**a lemon** un citron *nm*
**to lend** prêter *v*
**a lesson** un cours *nm*, une leçon *nf*
**less than** moins que
**a library** une bibliothèque *nf*
**to lie down** s'allonger *v*
**life** la vie *nf*
**life expectancy** l'espérance de vie *nf*
**a lift** (elevator) un ascenseur *nm*
**light** la lumière *nf*
**light** (in weight) léger/légère *adj*
**to listen** écouter *v*
**to live** vivre *v*; (reside) habiter *v*
**live** en direct
**a living room** un salon *nm*; une salle de séjour *nf*
**local** du coin; local/locale/locaux/locales *adj*
**long** long/longue *adj*
**to look** regarder *v*
**to look ...** (e.g. tired) avoir l'air ...
**to look after** garder *v*
**to look forward to** attendre avec impatience
**to lose** perdre *v*
**to lose weight** perdre du poids
**to get lost** se perdre *v*
**lots of** beaucoup de
**love** l'amour *nm*
**to love** aimer *v*
**in love with** amoureux/amoureuse de
**loyal** fidèle* *adj*
**luggage** les bagages *nm pl*
**to have lunch** déjeuner *v*
**to be lying down** être couché(e)

## M

main principal/principale/principaux/principales *adj*
the **majority of** la plupart de
to **make** faire *v*
to **manage** (e.g. a company) gérer *v*
to **manage to** (do something) arriver à ... *v*, réussir à ... *v*
**March** mars *nm*
**maths** les maths *nf pl*
it doesn't **matter** cela ne fait rien
**May** mai *nm*
a **meal** un repas *nm*
that **means** ça veut dire
to **meet** rencontrer *v*; (by appointment) se retrouver *v*
**memory** (faculty) la mémoire *nf*
a **memory** (e.g. of an event) un souvenir *nm*
to **mend** réparer *v*
to **mention** mentionner *v*
at **midday** à midi
in the **middle of** au milieu de
at **midnight** à minuit
I don't **mind (either way)** cela m'est égal
to **miss** (e.g. a train) manquer v
I **miss you** tu me manques
to **mix** mélanger *v*
a **mobile (telephone)** un portable *nm*
**Monday** lundi *nm*
**money** l'argent *nm*
a **month** un mois *nm*
for **months** pendant quelques mois
**more (than)** plus que
in the **morning** le matin *nm*
a **mosque** une mosquée *nf*
**mother** la mère *nf*
a **motorbike** une moto(cyclette) *nf*
a **motorway** une autoroute *nf*
to **move house** déménager *v*
**moving** émouvant(e) *adj*
**MP3 player** un lecteur MP3 *nm*
as **much (as many)** autant de
a **musician** un musicien *nm*/une musicienne *nf*
**Muslim** musulman(e) *adj*
I **must** je dois
at **my house** chez moi

## N

**narrow** étroit(e) *adj*
it is **necessary to** ... il faut ...
to **need** avoir besoin de *v*
a **neighbour** un voisin *nm*/une voisine *nf*
**neighbourhood** les alentours *nm pl*
me **neither!** moi non plus!
**neither ... nor** ni ... ni
**nephew** le neveu *nm*
a **net surfer** un(e) internaute *nm/nf*
**never** ne ... jamais
**nevertheless** pourtant, néanmoins
**new** nouveau/nouvel/nouvelle/nouveaux/nouvelles *adj*
**news** les informations *nf pl*; les nouvelles *nf pl*
a **newspaper** un journal (*pl* les journaux) *nm*
**next** ensuite
**next** prochain(e) *adj*
**next to** à côté de
**nice** sympa* *adj*, gentil/gentille *adj*
**niece** la nièce *nf*
at **night** la nuit *nf*
a **night club** une boîte de nuit *nf*
a **nightmare** un cauchemar *nm*
**no** (not any) aucun/aucune *adj*
**no longer** ne ... plus
**no one** personne, ne ... personne
**noisy** bruyant(e) *adj*
a **note** (bank) un billet *nm*
to **notice** remarquer *v*
a **nuclear power station** une centrale nucléaire *nf*
a **number** (quantity) un nombre *nm*; (digit) un chiffre *nm*; (e.g. telephone, account) un numéro *nm*
a **nurse** un infirmier *nm*/une infirmière *nf*

## O

**October** octobre *nm*
**of** de
**of course** bien sûr, bien entendu
an **office** un bureau *nm*
**often** souvent
**OK** d'accord
**old** (after noun) ancien/ancienne *adj*; vieux/vieil/vieille/vieux/vieilles *adj*
**on** sur
**once (more)** une fois (de plus)
**only** seul/seule *adj*, unique* *adj*
to **open (up)** s'ouvrir *v*
**open** ouvert(e) *adj*
in the **open air** en plein air
**opening hours** les horaires (d'ouverture) *nm pl*
an **opinion** un avis *nm*; une opinion *nf*
in your **opinion** à votre (ton) avis
**opposite** en face (de)
**or** ou
an **orange** une orange *nf*
**orange** orange* *adj*
to **order** (e.g. in restaurant) commander *v*
in **order to** pour, afin de
**out loud** à haute voix
**(over) there** là(-bas)
**overseas voluntary work** le bénévolat à l'étranger *nm*
**overweight** en surpoids
to **own** posséder *v*

## P

a **painting** une peinture *nf*
a **paperback** un livre de poche *nm*
a **parcel** un colis *nm*
**parents** les parents *nm pl*
a **park** un parc *nm*, un jardin public *nm*
**part-time** à temps partiel
**party** une fête *nf*, une boum *nf*
a **path** un chemin *nm*
**patient** patient(e) *nm adj*
to **pay for** payer *v*
**PE** (= **physical education**) l'EPS (= éducation physique et sportive) *nf*
**peace** la paix *nf*
a **pen** un stylo *nm*
a **pencil** un crayon *nm*
a **pencil case** une trousse *nf*
**perfect** parfait(e) *adj*
a **person** une personne *nf*
a **pet** un amimal (les animaux) domestique(s) *nm*; un animal (les animaux) de compagnie *nm pl*
**petrol** l'essence *nf*
a **photo(graph)** une photo(graphie) *nf*
a **photographer** un photographe *nm*/ une photographe *nf*
**physics** la physique *nf*
a **pinch** une pincée *nf*
**pink** rose*
a **place** un endroit *nm*, un lieu *nm*
to **plan** planifier *v*
**platform** le quai *nm*
to **play** jouer *v*
a **play** une pièce de théâtre *nf*
**pleasant** agréable*
to **please** plaire *v*
**please** (to a friend or relative) s'il te plaît; (to more than one person, to someone you don't know well) s'il vous plaît
a **police station** un commissariat de police *nm*; un poste de police *nm*
**polite** poli(e) *adj*
**posh** snob* *adj*
**possibly** éventuellement
the **post** (letters) le courrier *nm*
the **post office** la Poste *nf*
a **poster** une affiche *nf*
a **present** un cadeau (*pl* les cadeaux) *nm*
at **present** actuellement
to **prevent** empêcher *v*
a **primary school** une école primaire *nf*
a **primary schoolteacher** un instituteur *nm*/une institutrice *nf*
**private** privé(e) *adj*
to be in the **process of** être en train de
a **product** un produit *nm*
a (TV) **programme** une émission *nf*
to **promise someone to ...** promettre à quelqu'un de ... *v*
**proud** fier/fière *adj*
to **pull** tirer *v*
a **pupil** un élève *nm*/une élève *nf*
to **push** pousser *v*

## Q

a **quarter of an hour** un quart d'heure *nm*
it's a **quarter past (three)** il est (trois) heures et quart
it's a **quarter to (three)** il est (trois) heures moins le quart
**quick** vite *adj*; rapide* *adj*
**quiet** calme* *adj*; tranquille* *adj*
**quite** assez

## R

a **(running) race** un course (à pied) *nf*
a **radio (set)** un poste de radio *nm*
**railway** le chemin de fer *nm*
it's **raining** il pleut
**rainy** pluvieux/pluvieuse *adj*
a **raspberry** une framboise *nf*
**rather** plutôt
**raw** cru(e) *adj*
to **read** lire *v*
**really** vraiment
to **receive** recevoir *v*
**recently** récemment
a **recipe** une recette *nf*
a **record** une fiche *nf*
to **record** enregistrer *v*
a **recycling centre** un centre de recyclage *nm*
**red** rouge* *adj*
to **refuse** refuser *v*
**relatives** les parents *nm pl*
to **relax** se détendre *v*
**religion** la religion *nf*
to **remember** se rappeler *v*; se souvenir de *v*
to **rent** louer
a **return ticket** un billet aller-retour *nm*
to **reply** répondre *v*
a **report** un reportage *nm*
to do **research (on)** faire des recherches (sur)
**responsible** responsable* *adj*
to **rest** se reposer *v*
**restful** reposant(e) *adj*
**rewarding** enrichissant(e) *adj*
to be **right** avoir raison
to/on the **right** à droite
a **river** une rivière *nf*, (large, tidal) un fleuve *nm*
to go **rock climbing** faire de l'escalade *nf*
a **room** une pièce *nf*
**rubbish** (household) les ordures *nf pl*; (of a factory) les déchets *nm pl*
it's **rubbish!** c'est nul!
to **run** courir *v*
**rural** campagnard(e) *adj*

## S

**sad** triste* *adj*
to go **sailing** faire de la voile
**salesman** un vendeur *nm*
**saleswoman** une vendeuse *nf*
**salt** le sel *nm*
a **sandwich** un sandwich *nm*
to **save** (money) économiser *v*
**school day** la journée scolaire *nf*
**scissors** les ciseaux *nm pl*
a **scooter** une patinette *nf*
to **score a goal** marquer un but
to **search for** chercher *v*
at the **seaside** au bord de la mer
a **seaside resort** une station balnéaire *nf*
a **secondary school** (11–15) un collège *nm*
a **secondary schoolboy** un collégien *nm*
a **secondary schoolgirl** une collégienne *nf*
to **see to** s'occuper de *v*
**see you later!** à tout à l'heure
**see you soon!** à bientôt!
to **seem** sembler *v*
it **seems that** il semble que, il paraît que
**selfish** égoïste* *adj*
to **sell** vendre *v*
a **sense of humour** un sens de l'humour *nm*
**sensible** sérieux/sérieuse *adj*
**September** septembre *nm*
to **set the table** mettre le couvert
to **settle** (a bill) régler *v*
**several** plusieurs* *adj*
that's a **shame!** (c'est) dommage!
to **share** partager *v*
a **sheet of paper** une feuille de papier *nf*
to **shine** briller *v*
a **shirt** une chemise *nf*
a **shop** un magasin *nm*, une boutique *nf*
to do the **shopping** faire les courses
a **shopping centre** un centre commercial *nm*
a **shopping list** une liste d'achats *nf*
**short** court(e) *adj*
**shorts** une culotte *nf*
**shoulder-length** (hair) mi-long/mi-longue *adj*
to **shout** crier *v*
to **show** montrer *v*
to have a **shower** se doucher *v*
**shy** timide* *adj*
**sick** malade* *adj*
**side** le côté *nm*
**since** depuis; (because) puisque
a **single bed** un lit d'une personne *nm*
**sister** une sœur *nf*
to **sit down** s'asseoir *v*
to be **sitting down** être assis(e)
**sitting room** le salon *nm*; la salle de séjour *nf*
to be **situated** se trouver *v*
a **sixth-form college** un lycée *nm*
**size** la taille *nf*, (shoe) la pointure *nf*
to **skate** patiner *v*
to go **skateboarding** faire du skate
a **slave** un esclave *nm*/une esclave *nf*
**slavery** l'esclavage *nm*
a **slice** une tranche *nf*
**slim** mince* *adj*
to **slip** glisser *v*
**slow** lent(e) *adj*
**small** petit(e) *adj*
a **smell** une odeur *nf*
a **snack** un casse-croûte (*pl.* les casse-croûte) *nm*
**snow** la neige *nf*
it's **snowing** il neige
**so** si, tellement
a **soap opera** un feuilleton *nm*
a **soldier** un soldat *nm* une soldate *nf*, un militaire *nm*
**so many** tant de
**so much the better!** tant mieux!
**someone** quelqu'un
**something** quelque chose
**sometime or other** tôt ou tard
**sometimes** quelquefois
**somewhere** quelque part
a **song** une chanson *nf*
**soon** bientôt
as **soon as** aussitôt que, dès que
**sorry** désolé(e) *adj*
**soup** la soupe *nf*
**south** le sud *nm*
a **space** une espace *nf*
a **spectator** un spectateur *nm*/une spectatrice *nf*
**speed** la vitesse *nf*
to **spend** (money) dépenser *v*, (time) passer *v*
**spoonful** une cuillerée *nf*
a **sports centre** un centre sportif *nm*
a **sportsman** un sportif *nm*
a **sportswoman** une sportive *nf*
on the **spot** sur place
**spring** (season) le printemps *nm*
a **square** (plaza) une place *nf*
a **stair** une marche *nf*
a **stall** un étal *nm*
to be **standing up** être debout
a **star sign** un signe astrologique *nm*
to **start** (a car) démarrer *v*
a **stay** un séjour *nm*
a (beef) **steak** le bifteck *nm*
a **stepfather** un beau-père *nm*
a **stepmother** une belle-mère *nf*
a **stone** une pierre *nf*
to **stop** (doing something) arrêter de *v*
**straight** (of hair) raide* *adj*
**straight on** (tout) droit
**strange** étranger/étrangère *adj*
**stranger** un étranger *nm*/une étrangère *nf*
a **strawberry** une fraise *nf*
**strength** la puissance *nf*
**stubborn** têtu(e)
a **student** un étudiant *nm*/une étudiante *nf*, (sixth-form) un lycéen *nm*/une lycéenne *nf*
to **study** étudier *v*
a **study** une étude *nf*
**stuff** (things) les affaires *nf pl*
a **subject** (e.g. at school) une matière *nf*
**suburbs** la banlieue *nf*
to **succeed** réussir à *v*
**suddenly** tout à coup
**suitcase** une valise *nf*
**summer** l'été *nm*
**summer holidays** les grandes vacances *nf pl*
the **sun** le soleil *nm*
to **sunbathe** se (faire) bronzer *v*
**super** super* *adj*
**sure (about/of)** sûr/sure (de) *adj*
to go **surfing** faire du surf
a **surgeon** un chirurgien *nm*/une chirurgienne *nf*
**surname** le nom de famille *nm*

to **surprise** surprendre *v*
**surroundings** les alentours *nm pl*
a **survey** un sondage *nm*
to **survive** survivre *v*
**sweet** doux/douce *adj*
to **swim** nager *v*
**swimming** la natation *nf*
a **swimming pool** une piscine *nf*

## T

to **take** prendre *v*
to **take a break** faire une pause
to **take an exam** passer un examen *v*
**take heart!** bon courage!
to **take part in** participer à *v*
to **take place** avoir lieu
**tall** grand(e) *adj*
a **taste** un goût *nm*
to **taste** goûter *v*
to **taste good/bad** avoir bon/mauvais goût
a **teacher** un professeur *nm*
a **teenager** un(e) ado (un adolescent/une adolescente) *nm/f*
to **telephone** téléphoner à *v*, appeler *v*
a **telephone call** un coup de téléphone *nm*; un appel de téléphone *nm*
a **television (set)** un poste de télévision *nm*
a **television programme** une émission *nf*
to **tell** dire *v*; (a story) raconter *v*
to **tend to** avoir tendance à
to **thank** remercier *v*
**that means** ... ça veut dire ...
**that's enough!** ça suffit!
**that's to say** c'est-à-dire
**there** y, là
**there aren't/isn't any ...** il n'y a pas de...
**there is/there are ...** il y a ...
**there would be...** il y aurait ...
**therefore** donc
**thick** épais/épaisse *adj*
**thin** (skinny) maigre* *adj*; (slender) mince* *adj*
a **thing** une chose *nf*
a **thingummy** un truc *nm*
to be **thirsty** avoir soif
**thirty** trente
a **throat** une gorge *nf*
**thousand** mille
**thousands of** des milliers de
**through** à travers
to **throw** jeter *v*
**thunder** le tonnerre *nm*
**Thursday** jeudi *nm*
to **tidy** ranger *v*
a **till** une caisse *nf*
**time** le temps *nm*; (clock) **time** l'heure *nf*
on **time** à l'heure
at the **time of** lors de
from **time to time** de temps en temps
**timetable** (school) l'emploi du temps *nm*; (transport) un horaire *nm*
**tiring** fatigant(e) *adj*
a **title** un titre *nm*
**tomorrow** demain
**too (much)** trop
**tools** les outils *nm pl*
**tourist office** l'office du tourisme *nm*
**towards** vers
a **town centre** un centre-ville *nm*
**traffic** la circulation *nf*
to **train** s'entraîner *v*
a **train station** une gare *nf*
**trainers** les baskets *nm pl*
to **translate** traduire *v*
to **travel** voyager *v*
a **travel agency** une agence de voyages *nf*
**trendy** branché(e) *adj*
**true** vrai(e)
to **trust** (someone) faire confiance à
to **try** essayer *v*
to **turn** tourner *v*
to **turn off** (e.g. a light) éteindre *v*
to **turn on** (e.g. a light) allumer *v*
**twenty** vingt
**twin** jumeau/jumelle/jumeaux/jumelles *adj*
**twin beds** les lits jumeaux *nm pl*
a **twin town** une ville jumelle *nf*
to **type** taper *v*

## U

**ugly** laid/laide *adj*, moche* *adj*; (nasty) vilain(e) *adj*
an **umbrella** un parapluie *nm*
**uncomfortable** inconfortable* *adj*
to **understand** comprendre *v*
**underwater diving** la plongée sous-marine *nf*
to **undress oneself** se déshabiller *v*
to be **unemployed** être au chômage
**unforgettable** inoubliable* *adj*
**unfortunately** malheureusement
**unknown** inconnu(e) *adj*
**unleaded petrol** l'essence sans plomb *nf*
**unmissable** immanquable* *adj*
to **unpack** défaire les valises
**untidy** désordonné(e) *adj*
**until** jusqu'à
**upstairs** en haut
to **use** utiliser *v*, se servir de *v*
to get **used to** s'habituer à *v*
**useless** inutile* *adj*
**usually** d'habitude

## V

a **van** une camionnette *nf*
**vegetables** les légumes *nm pl*
a **video game** un jeu d'ordinateur *nm*
a **village** un village *nm*
to **visit** visiter *v*; (a person) rendre visite à
**voice** la voix *nf*
a **voluntary worker** un(e) bénévole *nm/f*

## W

to **wake up** se réveiller *v*
to **want** vouloir *v*; avoir envie de
to go for a **walk** se promener *v*, marcher *v*; (to function) marcher *v*
**walking boots** les chausseures de marche *nf pl*
a **wardrobe** une armoire *nf*
to get **washed** se laver *v*
to do the **washing-up** faire la vaisselle
to **watch** regarder *v*
**water** l'eau *nf*
**water-skiing** le ski nautique *nm*
**way** une façon *nf*, une manière *nf*
**weak in** faible* en *adj*
**weather forecast** les prévisions météo *nf pl*
**week** une semaine *nf*
at the **weekend** ce week-end *nm*
at **weekends** le week-end
**weight training** la musculation *nf*
**well off** aisé(e) *adj*
**Welsh** gallois(e) *adj*
the **west** l'ouest *nm*
**what's the matter?** qu'est-ce qu'il y a?
**what rubbish!** quelle blague!
**when** quand
**whereas** alors que
**which?** quel/quelle
**wholefoods** les aliments complets *nm pl*
to **win** gagner *v*
a **window** une fenêtre *nf*, (shop) vitrine *nf*
**windsurfing** la planche à voile *nf*
**windy** venteux/venteuse *adj*
to **wish** souhaiter *v*
**with** avec
**without** sans
a **wood** un bois *nm*
a **worker** (labourer) un ouvrier *nm*/une ouvrière *nf*
to be **worried about** s'inquiéter de *v*
**worse** pire* *adj*
it is **worth ...** il vaut ... *v*
**wrong** faux/fausse *adj*
to be **wrong** avoir tort

## Y

a **year** un an *nm*; une année *nf*
**yellow** jaune*
**young** jeune* *adj*
**younger** cadet/cadette *adj*
**youth** la jeunesse *nf*